London:
Architecture, Building
and Social Change

London:
Architecture, Building
and Social Change

Paul L. Knox

Global Forum on Urban
and Regional Resilience

MERRELL
LONDON · NEW YORK

First published 2015 by Merrell Publishers Limited, London and New York

Merrell Publishers Limited
70 Cowcross Street
London EC1M 6EJ

merrellpublishers.com

Produced by Merrell Publishers Limited
Proofread by Rosanna Lewis
Indexed by Lynne Taylor

Printed and bound in China

AUTHOR'S ACKNOWLEDGEMENTS

The author is pleased to acknowledge the support of the Global
Forum on Urban and Regional Resilience at Virginia Tech in the
publication of this book.

My thanks are due to Bart Yavorosky for his painstaking
work in fact-checking. Thanks also to Kirsten Yavorosky for
her preliminary copyediting and to Anne-Lise Velez for her
enthusiastic support and assistance in undertaking field work.
Rosanna Lewis was a wonderfully effective proofreader. Any
remaining errors are of course my own responsibility.

Contents

A City of Districts

Behind everything in London is something else, and, behind that, is something else still; and so on through the centuries, so that London as we see her is only the latest manifestation of other Londons.

H. V. Morton, *In Search of London* (1951), p. 207

A singular metropolis not just in terms of its history and its landmark buildings, London is also, famously, a city of districts. Unlike most other great cities of the world, London did not grow from a single commercial, ecclesiastical or administrative centre, nor has it been laid out to an overarching plan or shaped by a single authority. Rather, it has grown piecemeal from an archipelago of villages and town centres to become a conglomerate metropolis of interdependent districts with twin cores. As such, it is more than anything else the product of changing social structure and a relatively free market in land and property. Moderated from time to time by policy and planning, market forces have converted unconnected villages and parishes into mini-towns and then integrated them as specialized districts with distinctive physical, economic and social characteristics into a single metropolitan fabric.

The legacies of history have left every district with a distinctive cityscape and instantly recognizable landmarks. Each chapter in every district's development has left its mark in the layout of its streets, the fabric of its buildings and the nature of its institutions. London's districts are thus both text and context: palimpsests of economic, social and architectural history.

London Shaped

London's early history unfolded around the site of a Roman settlement on the north bank of the Thames. It eventually became the city's commercial core: the territory of the present-day Corporation of the City of London. But from the eleventh century, a second nucleus developed on the north bank of the river 3 kilometres (nearly 2 miles) to the west: the centre of royal justice and administration around Westminster. The two were separated by farmland and marshland until the seventeenth century, and their very different character and functions have anchored the basic geography of the metropolis ever since. In the countryside surrounding these two cores were numerous villages: the tiny seeds of what would eventually become distinctive districts within the emergent metropolis. These included Bethnal Green, Chelsea, Hoxton, Islington and Kensington. Meanwhile, the patchwork of private estates just beyond Westminster and the City formed the basis of another set of distinctive districts as their owners developed them into discrete enclaves: Covent Garden, Bloomsbury, Fitzrovia, Belgravia and so on.

Nineteenth-century industrialization expanded the metropolis, added functionally specialized districts and new residential districts, and significantly altered the character of many older districts. The basic lines of London's economic geography had already been laid down in the eighteenth century, with river-based industries to the south and east of the City and specialized craft production to the north and west. The new industrial technology of the nineteenth century was absorbed into the existing framework of the metropolis in a way that tended to reinforce its polycentric, dispersed character. Industrialization and its accompanying changes in social structure and cultural sensibilities also served to intensify spatial segregation and establish sharper divisions between districts.

London's conglomerate geography, meanwhile, was reinforced by its fragmented administrative framework. Until the mid-nineteenth century there were several hangovers from the ecclesiastical sanctuaries of the Middle Ages: the Liberties of London, districts that were beyond the jurisdictions of both the City Corporation and the Court at Westminster. More generally, there was a mosaic of small parishes, whose vestries were deeply insular in outlook. Local government reform had come to the rest of the country in 1835, but London had to wait until the end of the century while the City and the vestries quarrelled and prevaricated. Meanwhile, an Act of 1855 did at least establish the Metropolitan Board of Works, charged with doing something to improve both the sewers and the streets of the capital as a whole.

London's growth phases. By 1700 the gap between the City and Westminster had been filled in. Outward growth was incremental until new transport systems unleashed the metropolis in the nineteenth century.

■	Before 1700
▦	1701-1750
▦	1751-1800
▦	1801-1850
▦	1851-1900

The vestries were eventually replaced, in 1899, by municipal boroughs and their coordinating governmental apparatus, the London County Council (LCC). The twenty-eight boroughs transcended the traditional parochialism of the vestries but established a new geopolitical framework for the metropolis that reinforced its polycentric geography. The London Government Act of 1963 replaced the LCC with the Greater London Council (GLC), a strategic authority with an extended territory covering thirty-two boroughs. The GLC was abolished in 1986, along with the country's other Metropolitan District Councils, by the government under Margaret Thatcher.

Tony Blair's New Labour administration returned a limited amount of strategic governance to London with the creation in 2000 of the Greater London Authority (GLA) with a directly elected mayor. Through all this the boroughs retained responsibility for most local services, including housing, education, social services, and land-use and transportation planning. But the City Corporation with its medieval system of government has resisted all attempts at incorporation into metropolitan governance. The City remains the most powerful, distinctive and clearly defined of all London's districts. The Corporation is a major landowner and property developer in its own right, and functions as its own planning authority.

Administrative boundaries notwithstanding, geographical uncertainties of one sort or another are grist for endless disputes on where London's district boundaries are to be drawn. More than 500 districts can be identified through the everyday informal designations used by Londoners, labels that are mostly adapted from historic parish, borough or ward boundaries. London has rich districts, poor districts, ethnic districts, residential districts, commercial districts, industrial districts, transitional districts and many other kinds. Each has its own distinct character and story, and each is constantly changing size, shape, built form and social character. Most reflect a long and chequered history of change.

As a result, it is often difficult to determine where one district ends and another begins. Few districts have clear boundaries, and only the City is unequivocally coincident with administrative boundaries of any kind. Most are loosely defined, the aggregate products of the perceptions and mental maps of their inhabitants and the everyday usage of

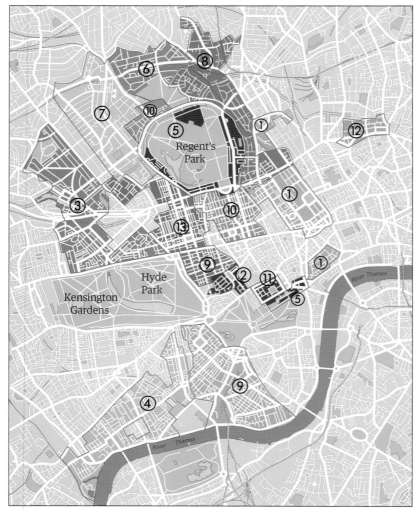

The Great Estates at the time of their first development. After Jenkins (1975). ① Bedford, ② Berkeley, ③ Bishop of London, ④ Cadogan, ⑤ Crown, ⑥ Eton, ⑦ Eyre, ⑧ Fitzroy, ⑨ Grosvenor, ⑩ Harley/Portland, ⑪ Jermyn, ⑫ Penton, ⑬ Portman.

do not help at all, as one district simply runs into another via unremarkable tracts of building.

London's Evolutionary Resilience

London has been remarkably resilient in its polycentric spatial organization. The city's institutional and constitutional framework has been severely ruptured and serially reinvented, while significant elements of the city have been burned, bombed or flooded. Political unrest and racial conflict have resulted in riots, while successive rounds of investment and disinvestment have replaced parts of the built environment many times over. Yet the basic spatial framework of the metropolis has persisted, along with the broad character of its districts.

In part this is the result of general processes of urbanization that are by no means unique to London. The social geography of the city, for example, is fixed around districts at the top of the social scale that are self-regenerating. The wealth and social cachet of the likes of Belgravia, Kensington and Mayfair ensure their continuation as élite districts, with persistently high land values, steady flows of investment, high-quality infrastructure and proximity to the city's most prestigious institutions. As elsewhere, middle-class districts cluster around these élite districts, while working-class districts are relegated to less desirable locations. Specialized office, retail and entertainment districts, meanwhile, are anchored to more accessible locations within the metropolis.

Dissolution and the Great Estates

The City's evolutionary resilience in the aftermath of major upheaval and disaster is especially remarkable. The first notable example came in the aftermath of the Dissolution of the Monasteries in the 1530s. Its impact on the built environment was arguably the most important event in London's history - more important even than the Great Fire or the Blitz - for it redistributed the ownership of property over large tracts of the City and its environs. Before the Reformation, there had been twenty-three religious

journalists and residents. Some, such as Belgravia, are clearly recognizable by the streets laid out by developers. Some, such as Bankside, have been defined and branded by business associations. All the districts described in this book have a widely recognized and generally accepted core area, but most have no conclusive consensus on their exact extent. While some boundaries are clear enough - the river, a park, railway sidings - others can be ambiguous. Oxford Street, for example, is generally accepted as a boundary between Mayfair and Marylebone, but at the same time the shops along the street itself arguably belong to both. In other cases, physical features houses in the City itself, while beyond the walls was a ring of hospitals, abbeys, priories, convents and ecclesiastical palaces that effectively constituted a medieval green belt. Their confiscation by the Crown gave London room to grow. The allocation of most of the undeveloped monastic land to a select group of Tudor and Stuart courtiers was a windfall privatization that established the Great Estates, which were later to be developed as the distinctive residential districts of the West End.

The Great Fire and Building Codes

Another important episode of evolutionary resilience followed the Great Fire of 1666. When London recovered, it did so with a system of building codes that shaped its cityscapes for centuries. The Fire raged for days. It destroyed more than 13,000 houses and most of the City's civic and ecclesiastical buildings, displacing almost ninety per cent of the population. But within five years the City had bounced back. With more than 8000 new houses and numerous public buildings, London returned to business as usual. Meanwhile, Clerkenwell and the East End were transformed as both the displaced poor and the moderately prosperous moved in, prompting the departure of better-off families to the West End.

At first glance it might seem like an opportunity missed: a rare chance to plan the City and lay it out in the Grand Manner, commensurate with the great Continental cities of the

time. Christopher Wren devised such a plan, as did John Evelyn and Robert Hooke. All three plans featured broad, straight streets with vistas of landmarks in public squares. Nothing came of them. The idea of comprehensive city planning was associated with the exercise of absolute and autocratic power and the 'popery' of France – anathema to English cultural sensibilities as well as to the City's unbridled commercialism. There were more practical reasons, too: a shortage of labour, lost records of property ownership, and concern that an extended process of reconstruction would cause the City to lose its commercial advantage over Continental rivals.

The rebuilt City is often described in terms of Wren's city of domes and spires. He introduced elements of Renaissance style to the City and is credited

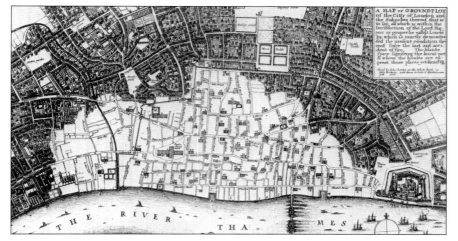

London after the Fire, 1666. Extract from a map by Wenceslaus Hollar, showing the extent of the devastation. *Credit*: Heritage Image Partnership Ltd/Alamy

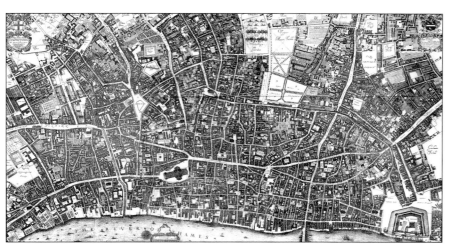

London rebuilt, 1677. This extract from Ogilby and Morgan's map of 1677 shows how quickly the City was rebuilt, mainly around the old street pattern. *Credit*: The British Library Board

with fifty-one churches, along with his masterpiece, St Paul's Cathedral. But of broader significance is the evolution of the City's building codes in the aftermath of the Fire. The Rebuilding Act of 1667 laid the basis for a regularized street hierarchy and produced a degree of architectural conformity in London that was without parallel in Europe. The Act required houses to be built in one of four standard elevations, each with its own regulations. This framework became the basis for a system of building control that regulated the great expansions of the eighteenth and nineteenth centuries, ensuring that streetscapes throughout the metropolis were developed as visual compositions of simple repetitive harmony.

The Railways: Disruptive Technology

The railway companies disrupted some of that harmony when they tore up London's suburbs in the 1830s and 1840s. But the prospect of the wholesale demolition of property and of the severance of crowded thoroughfares resulting from the many companies bringing tracks into the city prompted Parliament to introduce what was effectively the first element of strategic planning for London.

Following the recommendation of a Royal Commission in 1846, termini north of the Thames were allowed no closer to the centre of the metropolis

than the New Road (the present-day Euston Road and Marylebone Road). As a result, the Great Estates were spared the disruption of the railways, but the inner suburbs to the north of the New Road and south of the Thames were not. Here, the railways sought routes through slum areas, where the land was cheapest. The companies were given unprecedented powers of compulsory purchase, and slumlords - including the Ecclesiastical Commissioners - were only too happy to rid themselves of embarrassing slum properties while securing healthy compensation in return. The railway companies rehoused few of the displaced tenants, most of whom had no alternative but to crowd into neighbouring slum properties, at higher rents. The clusters of bars, hotels and shops drawn to the railway termini, meanwhile, gave character and definition to the surrounding districts. Further afield, the railways opened large areas of the suburbs for new housing, a process that accelerated the social polarization of the metropolis and the creation of new, socially homogeneous districts.

The Blitz and Repair

London's response to the Second World War illustrated the multiple dimensions of urban resilience - physical and social, short-term and long-term. The Blitz lasted just a few months in the winter of 1940 and the spring of 1941, but it brought the wholesale devastation of large areas of London, particularly in the City, the West End and the Docklands. Altogether the Blitz killed more than 20,000 civilians and destroyed or damaged more than 3.5 million homes in London. The immediate response, in the wartime spirit of 'make do and mend', was portrayed in newsreel images of matter-of-fact first responders and of citizens - especially East Enders - resolute and cheerful in the face of adversity. The total reconstruction required was greater than after the Fire. Just as in the aftermath of the Fire, the exigencies of commerce and the sanctity of private property precluded any grand modernization schemes. But again there was an evolutionary quality to London's resilience,

Railway viaducts. Nineteenth-century railway companies had to engineer their way through the dense fabric of the metropolis, as here above Great Suffolk Street, in Lambeth.

Bomb damage, 1940. Part of the LCC's bomb damage map of London, 1939–45. Courtesy of London Metropolitan Archive.
Key: **Black**: Total destruction; **Purple**: Damaged beyond repair; **Dark Red**: Seriously damaged, doubtful if repairable; **Light Red**: Seriously damaged but repairable at cost; **Orange**: General blast damage – not structural.

this time translating the logistics and manufacturing techniques of wartime aircraft and shipbuilding industries to housing and reconstruction. Prefabs were soon followed by system-built tower blocks and deck-access apartment buildings as the fabric of the metropolis was patched and repaired.

London's Cast of Characters

Shaping and reshaping London and its districts, repairing, repopulating, rebuilding and regenerating them, has generally been the product of a relatively free market in land and property. Nevertheless, free-market processes are always mediated and influenced by the entrepreneurialism, creativity and policy decisions of particular individuals as well as the needs and wants of different social groups. In London as elsewhere, some have been more influential than others, their legacy part of the palimpsest of building in many districts, their influence echoing across several generations.

Landowners and Developers

Landowners stand at the beginning of the chain of events involved in urban development and re-development. The landlords of the Great Estates - the Cadogans, the Crown, the Ecclesiastical Commissioners, the Fitzroys, the Grosvenors and so on - had a significant influence on the pattern and shape of development through the size and spatial pattern of the parcels of land they leased or sold to developers, along with the conditions they imposed on the nature of subsequent development. They remain influential today, along with modern conglomerate property companies like Development Securities, Land Securities, British Land, Capital and Counties, and estate agents Knight Frank International.

Developers play an influential role, often deciding on the type of project to be undertaken on a particular site and thereby inscribing their judgement on to the cityscape. One of London's earliest speculative developers was the notorious Nicholas Barbon (1640-1698; full name: Nicholas If-Jesus-Christ-Had-Not-Died-For-Thee-Thou-Hadst-Been-Damned Barbon). He acquired large tracts of land north of the Strand and in Bloomsbury after the Great Fire and built numerous houses and commercial properties, finally urbanizing the countryside that had separated the City from Westminster.

In the eighteenth and nineteenth centuries, the surveyors to the Great Estates effectively operated as developers. Samuel Pepys Cockerell, for example, surveyor to the Bishop of London, was responsible for developing the Bayswater Estate. London's most ambitious and influential speculative developer was Thomas Cubitt, who began building around 1810. He was one of the first to have his own construction company, complete with foremen, bricklayers and plasterers, operating out of workshops in Grays Inn Road. Cubitt built much of north Bloomsbury, Belgravia and Pimlico. In north London another successful builder-developer, William Willett, moved in on the undeveloped sections of the Eton and Eyre estates, building substantial houses for wealthy tenants. A Willett-built house had the high regard in the 1890s of a Cubitt-built one in the 1840s. In the twentieth century the most influential developers were the likes of Charles Clore, Felix Fenston, Harry Hyams, Harold Samuel and Joe Levy, who had picked up the pieces of the war-torn city and capitalized on its commercial redevelopment.

Architects and Engineers

Much better known are the architects associated with London's distinctive cityscapes. The pantheon includes Christopher Wren, Inigo Jones, Robert and James Adam, Nicholas Hawksmoor, Robert Smirke, Henry Holland, John Nash, John Soane, James Pennethorne, Charles Barry, George Gilbert Scott, Richard Norman Shaw, Berthold Lubetkin, Richard Seifert, Edwin Lutyens, Denys Lasdun, Norman Foster and Richard Rogers.

Less well-known are the engineers of the city's infrastructure, although one name stands unmatched: Joseph Bazalgette, Chief Engineer to the Metropolitan Board of Works from 1856 to 1889. Bazalgette was responsible for the modernization of the city's infrastructure, including the implementation of a sewerage system and the construction of new roads through demolished slums - the first set of new thoroughfares in London (with the exception of Nash's Regent Street, completed in 1825) since the Middle Ages. Bazalgette's greatest achievement was

arguably the embankment of the Thames, a brilliant piece of engineering that not only gave definition to the river's edge - and to the city itself - but also reclaimed land for new buildings, public gardens and a riverside boulevard, with massive sewer, gas and water pipes, electricity conduits and a tunnel for the new Metropolitan District Railway beneath.

Reformers and Philanthropists

Reformers and philanthropists have also been important mediators of the free-market forces shaping the city. Prominent in Victorian London were Octavia Hill, J. Passmore Edwards, Angela Burdett-Coutts and Samuel and Henrietta Barnett, along with Sydney Waterlow, George Peabody and others involved in limited-interest housing companies. Their impact on the lives they each touched directly was significant. But collectively they had an important longer-term influence on social awareness and the beginnings of public acceptance of the need to temper free-market forces. The novels of Charles Dickens, the graphic descriptions of slum districts by Andrew Mearns in *The Bitter Cry of Outcast London: An Inquiry into*

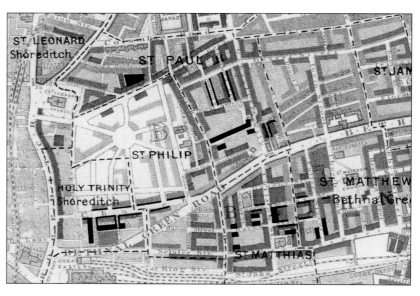

Localized poverty. Extract from Sheet 5, East Central District, of Charles Booth's 'Map Descriptive of Poverty 1898–99', showing part of Bethnal Green. Courtesy of LSE Library, Booth Collection.
Key: **Black**: 'Lowest class. Vicious, semi-criminal'; **Dark Blue**: 'Very Poor, casual. Chronic want'; **Light Blue**: 'Poor'; **Red**: 'Mixed'.

the Condition of the Abject Poor (1883) and the careful statistical compilations and maps published by Charles Booth in *The Life and Labour of the People in London* (1889) had a similar, cumulative effect. Shifting public opinion was reflected in the London Programme produced in 1891 by Sidney Webb by way of a manifesto for the emerging Progressive group of 'gas and water socialists' on the LCC. Much more radical reform was to come, of course, with the shift from laissez-faire capitalism to Keynesian capitalism and egalitarian liberalism after the Second World War. London's cityscapes were incrementally overlaid in the image of the Welfare State - especially visible in the built form of schools, clinics and social housing - until the advent of neoliberalism in the late 1970s.

Mayors

The introduction of a mayoral system of governance in 2000 has added a new role in the cast of characters shaping and reshaping the metropolis. Ken Livingstone, the first mayor of the GLA, had an agenda with a strong commitment to sustainability and the quality of public spaces. His administration included a small but influential Architecture and Urbanism Unit and aspired to create or upgrade 100 public spaces in just five years. Few were realized, largely because of the complexities of land ownership, funding and planning and the lack of any relevant statutory powers on the part of the GLA.

Meanwhile, Livingstone was to have a much more visible impact on the built environment as a result of his endorsement of tall buildings. For someone branded 'Red Ken' by the Tory press, the role of developers' friend was unlikely and unexpected. It was in fact a pragmatic response to the opportunity to assert and consolidate London's status as a 'global city' and to secure significant levels of planning gain from developers: they could build as tall as they wanted in return for statutory contributions to affordable housing and urban design.

London Assembled

This cast of characters, with their contemporaries and, not least, successive generations of Londoners and their political representatives, has produced the distinctive built environment of London and its districts. Such iconic structures as Westminster Palace, Tower Bridge and, now, the 'Gherkin' and the Shard are often taken to be symbolic not only of the metropolis itself but also of the United Kingdom. Other elements of the built environment, though, are more intimately characteristic of London, such as its patchwork layout of squares and terraces and its Georgian and Victorian architecture in stock brick, stucco and Portland stone. Others still, more generic in nature and more recent in construction, have been layered on this cumulative legacy, leaving each district with its own distinctive mix of settings.

Squares and Terraces

London's basic and most distinctive cityscapes derive from its squares and terraces. The template was set by the Great Estates in the seventeenth and eighteenth centuries. The enormous size of their holdings gave the owners of these estates the opportunity to exercise an exceptional degree of architectural and urban design control. The fourth Duke of Bedford had led the way in the 1630s with the development of land that was formerly the kitchen garden of Westminster Abbey, the Convent (later 'Covent') Garden. The sensibilities of the duke and the other aristocratic landowners of the Great Estates were derived from Renaissance rationality. The result was a series of layouts with simple rectilinear plans in which blocks of buildings surrounded open spaces configured in various primary geometric shapes: crescents, circles and, predominantly, squares. Squares, along with the linear terraces that ran from them, also had an economic rationale. Builders were able to maximize the density of large homes by setting tall houses next to each other in long runs.

A succession of Building Acts (1707, 1709 and, especially, 1774) had updated the post-Fire Rebuilding

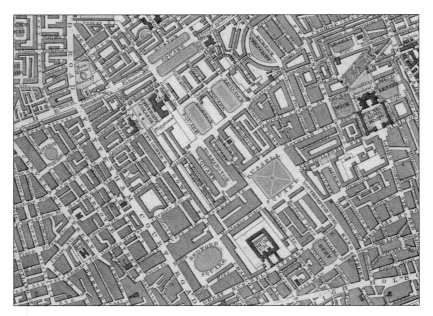

Terraces, squares and crescents. Extract from a map of 1843 by the Society for the Diffusion of Useful Knowledge, showing Bloomsbury and Fitzrovia. Courtesy of the David Rumsey Map Collection.

the development of Leicester Square, Soho Square and Golden Square. The next bout of building mania began shortly before the Treaties of Utrecht (1713) and lasted until around 1730; Hanover, Cavendish and Grosvenor squares appeared during this period. The fields north of Oxford Street were developed towards the close of the Seven Years' War (1756–63), while London's boom during the French Revolution saw the beginnings of even greater expansion, particularly in Bloomsbury. By 1800 there were more than thirty squares in the West End, and the Great Estates had formed an archipelago of inwardly orientated residential enclaves, each with discreetly located streets of shops and little side streets and mews for the staff and tradespeople necessary to keep the big households going.

They were London's newest districts: insulated, class-segregated communities that were to prove impermeable, for a long time, to the normal urban processes of penetration and succession by progressively less wealthy generations of households as housing becomes worn, obsolescent and relatively less expensive. The reason for this resilience, which has lent such distinctive character to West End districts, lies in the unified ownership and management of the estates. Instead of selling their freehold interest or building on their land themselves, the

Act of 1667, reinforcing the uniformity of architecture on London's streets. The sizes of rooms and their layouts were standardized, and four types or 'rates' of house were specified: First Rate Houses had more than 84 square metres (900 square feet) of floor space and were to face principal streets. Second Rate houses had 46–84 square metres (500–900 square feet) of floor space and faced principal streets, lanes of note and the Thames. Third Rate houses had 33–46 square metres (350–500 square feet) of floor space and faced mid-ranking streets. Fourth Rate houses occupied less than 33 square metres (350 square feet). Articulated in the extended geometric layouts of the Great Estates, the legislation resulted in the extensive compositions and uniform groupings that have become emblematic of London's built environment.

The Great Estates were developed one after another in response to the building booms of the seventeenth and eighteenth centuries. The first boom came in the 1670s, stimulated by the exodus from the City caused by the Fire. This saw

(Right) **Gordon Square** on the Bedford Estate. Begun in the 1820s, this square has remained almost impermeable to social change.

landlords to the Great Estates disposed of it to speculative developers on long building leases. The leaseholders constructed the houses and kept them in repair, according to the terms of their agreements and leases. When the leases expired, the land and the houses on it reverted to the ground landlord.

> By requiring sound building construction, disciplined exercise of architectural aesthetics, stylistic continuity (particularly in such understated English classical styles as the Georgian), and an orderly arrangement of building fronts around streets and gardens, they achieved a special sense of place in each estate.[1]

Meanwhile, London was denied the expansive Renaissance urban design typical of the great Continental cities of the time. It was not until the early nineteenth century that the architectural ambitions of the Prince Regent saw the imposition of a grand triumphal way (from Portland Place to Pall Mall via Regent Street) on London's patchwork street pattern. But by then London was beginning to be transformed in the image of industry and empire.

Segregation and Specialization

The Industrial Revolution transformed the country's class structure and introduced professionalization and specialization to every aspect of nineteenth-century thought and activity. As a result, London was systematically sorted out into largely single-purpose, homogeneous, specialized districts. For the new and rapidly expanding middle classes, privacy was paramount, and this was expressed in a new form of development: suburbs of detached or semi-detached villas. But a great deal of middle-class development followed the template of the Great Estates, with terraced housing relieved here and there by crescents, circles and squares. Geographical segregation of the middle classes from the even larger numbers of the greatly expanded proletariat was facilitated by the development of the omnibus and, before long, the railways and the Underground. For the proletariat, speculative developers put up street after street of terraced housing south of the Thames and in the East End. Terraced housing, in all its forms, became a major characteristic of the metropolis. The historian Donald J. Olsen noted the contrast with the apartment buildings that characterized other great cities of the time, attributing the popularity of terraced houses to the English preference for privacy, human scale and ownership.

> London's greatest flaw in the eyes of the aesthete – her interminable stretches of mass-produced houses, each with its walled garden in the rear, each displaying the lowest common denominator of contemporary taste in its street facade – was in fact its greatest glory. No continental city ... gave as large a proportion of its families the blessing of a house of its own.[2]

The more central districts that had been socially mixed became less so as improvement schemes swept away slums and developers rebuilt back-streets for commercial use. Wedged into this framework of increasingly specialized and distinctive districts were the imposing monuments, great museums, libraries, churches, theatres and other institutional and

(Left) **Derbyshire Street**, Bethnal Green. This speculative terrace of working-class dwellings was built in 1888 to replace a notorious slum.

Italianate stucco. Pembridge Square, Notting Hill. These grand monumental villas are in the stuccoed Italianate style that dominated building in west London in the mid-nineteenth century.

commercial structures that were to become the districts' landmarks.

Building Materials and Architectural Styles

London's surface geology is London Clay, and the traditional and characteristic building material is stock brick made from it. Its colour varies widely, from red through purple, brown and various shades of yellow to off-white, while well-fired, higher-quality London stock brick acquires a uniformly grey colour. No stone of any kind is quarried locally, and the expense of using high-quality stone meant that it was rarely used in construction before the nineteenth century. The districts that were built up during the eighteenth century were uniformly of Georgian style, with strict symmetry in their plain brick frontages, tall windows and pedimented doors. Georgian streets were the original and purest expression of the London terrace.

Yet fashions change and taste evolves. There were several strands of Georgian architecture with different emphasis on various neoclassical sources. As the century wore on, brick structures were increasingly embellished in response to a perceived need for social and architectural distinction. Given the expense of building stone, the solution was stucco. From about 1760 it was deployed by Robert Adam and other leading architects, and by 1800 it had become the dominant feature of fashionable residences, mostly in loosely Italianate neoclassical style. Coade stone,

a more durable synthetic product (see page 169), was also used, like stucco, to add street-level rustication as well as pillared porticoes, figurative sculpture, festooned friezes and other small-scale classical details to houses large and small.

Reactionary Impulses: Gothic Revival

Victorian aesthetics were not sympathetic to the artificiality of stucco and Coade stone, but the dislocation and new experiences introduced by the industrial era resulted in new ways of seeing, new ways of representing things, and a good deal of confusion and conflict over the appropriate physical expression of the new era. All this played out with great intensity in London. Contending styles were advanced as symbolic or representational of all sorts of ideals, including upper-class values, English tradition, national culture, the Empire, religious probity and moral rectitude.

The initial overall response to the radical changes of the Industrial Revolution was reactionary. In the face of turbulence and change, architects, builders and their clients opted for the reassurance of the traditional. The Gothic Revival style, with its national, religious, romantic and picturesque connotations, appealed to many. It was boosted by a succession of church-building Acts that sought to secure London's burgeoning suburbs for the established Church. The Acts specified Gothic style for new churches because it was symbolically charged

Gothic Revival. St James, Sussex Gardens, built in the early 1840s on the Paddington Estate in Bayswater.

with traditional, high-church values. Speculative developers, who built or paid for Anglican 'estate churches' as presumed beacons of respectability and order amid new residential developments, also opted for Gothic church architecture.

By the middle of the nineteenth century, architects and their clients were still struggling to find an appropriate response to industrialization and to the challenges and opportunities presented by new technology. Gothic Revival was by no means restricted to churches, vicarages and public institutions, but it did not have the widespread dominance of the Italianate neoclassical that had preceded it. Many businesses, in particular, still drew on classical architecture for legitimacy and status. Hence department stores masqueraded as museums of art, banks were fitted out as ducal palaces, and warehouses were built to imitate castles.

The Pre-Raphaelite Brotherhood of painters, poets and critics, along with the art critic John Ruskin, set out to challenge such reactionary classicism. The proper response for art and architecture, they argued, was a celebration of nature and its therapeutic and uplifting properties. Ruskin's *Seven Lamps of Architecture* (1849) and *The Stones of Venice* (1851) strongly rejected both classical architecture and the mechanization and standardization of the industrial era. Instead, he emphasized the importance of medieval Gothic style for what he saw as its reverence for nature and natural forms.

But it was not until the last quarter of the nineteenth century that the Arts and Crafts movement, based in large measure on Ruskin's romantic idealization of pre-industrial crafts, emerged as an alternative to eclectic revivals and mutations of sundry historic styles. Although it became an influential intellectual movement, it had relatively little impact on London's built environment. It was overshadowed by the popularity of Domestic Revival styles for the middle-class mansion apartment blocks that began to spring up (after much soul-searching as to their compatibility with Victorian ideas of propriety and family life).

Domestic Revival mansion flats. Montagu Mansions, on the Portman Estate in Marylebone, is typical of the intensification of the urban fabric in west London in the latter part of the nineteenth century.

Domestic Revival designs were especially popular among the city's expanded class of *nouveau riche* during the great phase of building from the 1870s to the 1920s, when large fortunes were being made in the City. The style was really just another reactionary impulse, based on English and Flemish houses of the seventeenth and eighteenth centuries and featuring steeply pitched roofs, shaped gables, bay and oriel windows, massive brick chimney-stacks and stone dressings. The use of harder and brighter red bricks from the Midlands and Northwest helped to signal both distinctiveness and a break from past aesthetics.

The Legacies of Reform

Intellectuals' responses to the shocking outcome of nineteenth-century urbanization, meanwhile, were also dominated by reactionary impulses. Industrial economic development was associated by the élite with corruption, exploitation and moral degeneration. At the same time, there was an abiding fear of the social and physical consequences of this exploitation and degeneration: the alienated 'mob' and its squalid and unhealthy neighbourhoods were seen as a threat to physical well-being and social order.

Parks became an increasingly important aspect of urban design. A Parliamentary Select Committee on Public Walks reported in 1833 that in the entire

Public open space. Part of the Diana Memorial Fountain in Hyde Park. The Royal Parks have been important elements in framing the social geography of the metropolis.

Meanwhile, the productivity of industrial workers, drawn in unprecedented numbers into the crowded slums of Soho, the East End and south London, was threatened by poor nutrition and such life-threatening diseases as influenza, tuberculosis, whooping cough and scarlet fever, as well as by occasional epidemics of smallpox, cholera, typhoid and even bubonic plague. Employers and the government were fearful of mob protest turning into mob rule, especially after the revolutionary events across Continental Europe in the 1840s. The respectable middle classes, for their part, were worried about the breakdown of moral order and, mindful of the cholera epidemic of 1832, the terror of contagious disease. These fears, coupled with a slowly emerging sense of shame engendered by exposés of the lives of the poor, gained expression in various charitable associations and philanthropic trusts.

metropolis the only open spaces available to 'all classes' of society were Hyde Park and Green Park. Three other royal parks, also on the western side of town - St James's Park, Kensington Gardens and Regent's Park - were open only to 'persons well-behaved and properly dressed'. The Committee felt that by bringing the working classes into contact not only with the spiritual energy of nature but also with the manners and comportment of other classes, parks could become a kind of universal moral force, a source of democratic and fraternal feeling. By 1840 Regent's Park was fully open to the public, and a few years later Victoria Park was created in the East End to provide open space for that part of the metropolis.

One of the first examples was the Association for Promoting Cleanliness Amongst the Poor, dedicated to establishing bath and laundry houses in London. The first 'model' baths opened in 1847 in Goulston Street, Whitechapel. Also founded in the 1840s were the Society for Improving the Condition of the Labouring Classes and the Metropolitan Association for Improving the Dwellings of the Industrious Classes. They began by constructing demonstration projects that sought to show how decent, affordable housing could be built for working-class households and still yield a (modest) profit.

By the early 1860s the scale of charitable activity in London was extensive. Sampson Low Jr's survey of the charities of London listed 640 charitable agencies of all kinds in the city in 1862.[3] By then, philanthropic housing efforts were dominated by wealthy individuals such as Sydney Waterlow, the Guinness family, and the American banker and diplomat George Peabody, who were willing and able to build workers' housing that yielded profits that were, for the period,

Philanthropic housing. The Peabody Estate just off Southwark Street opened in 1876 with twelve blocks of twenty-two flats.

strikingly low: typically between five and seven per cent. On this basis, the Peabody Trust alone built more than 20,000 dwellings in London from 1864 to 1890, pioneering model dwellings with such unheard-of amenities as separate laundry rooms and space for children to play.

But Victorian philanthropists avoided the poorest parts of London because they knew from experience that the population was too poor to allow even a modest return on investment. Their model dwellings were intended to protect a deserving working class with well-made, strictly managed accommodation, enabling the respectable working poor to remain just that, rather than slide into what the Victorian poet James Thomson called the 'City of Dreadful Night'.

Towards the latter part of the century, the government felt obliged to step in, accepting that local and charitable endeavours were insufficient foils to the growth of slum districts. Its first major piece of legislation was the Artisans' and Labourers' Dwellings Act (1875), which allowed local authorities to buy and demolish unfit housing and required that they then rehouse the former residents. The Housing for the Working Classes Act (1890) empowered the new LCC to demolish the worst slums and build new tenements and blocks of flats. The Boundary Street Estate, Bethnal Green, was one of the earliest council estates built under the terms of the Act (see page 48).

By the start of twentieth century, the role of government was firmly established. The Town Planning Act of 1909 was introduced by a Bill as follows:

The object of the Bill is to provide a domestic condition for the people in which their physical health, their morals, their character and their whole social condition can be improved by what we hope to secure in this Bill. The Bill aims in broad outline at, and hopes to secure, the home healthy, the house beautiful, the town pleasant, the city dignified, and the suburb salubrious. It seeks, and hopes to secure, more homes, better houses, prettier streets, so that the character of a great people, in towns and cities

and in villages, can be still further improved and strengthened by the conditions under which they live.

After the First World War, the Tudor Walters Report on the provision of dwellings for the working classes led to David Lloyd George's general-election pledge of 'Homes Fit For Heroes' and the subsequent expansion of public housing policy ('an insurance against Bolshevism and Revolution').

New Kinds of Building

Meanwhile, industrialization brought new kinds of building. The propagation of consumer culture and new lifestyles saw the introduction of arcades, department stores, cafés, restaurants, tea rooms, dance halls, theatres, hotels, public gardens, sports stadiums and amusement parks. These new spaces used new materials and technology - plate glass, cast iron and steel construction, and coloured electric lights - to display their goods dramatically, especially at night. Other new structures included libraries, schools, hospitals, bath houses and the tenement buildings of philanthropic organizations. Across much of the metropolis they stood out in high relief, together with churches and chapels, against a general background of cramped Victorian stock-brick terraced housing.

London's Board Schools were particularly distinctive. They were a product of the Education Act of 1870, which established local education boards that were empowered to raise revenues through property rates for the education of children between the ages of five and twelve (extended to thirteen in a bye-law of 1871). About two-thirds of London's 447 Board Schools were designed by the London School Board's architect, Edward Robert Robson. His schools became a common denominator among London's districts: distinctive three-storey edifices with separate playgrounds and entrances for boys and girls, invariably built in pared-down Domestic Revival style, with colourful brick, terracotta detailing and ornate gables.

Late Victorian London, meanwhile, was the capital of a worldwide empire: more than a quarter of the earth's surface and about a fifth of its population were governed from Westminster and Whitehall. This left a very visible imprint in the form of purpose-built offices for new and expanded government departments. The preferred styling (often just for facades) was stripped-down neoclassical in Portland stone. This style also became the default for many of the big commercial and financial firms of the City. Beginning around 1900, the other dominant style for municipal flats, office blocks, hotels and large public buildings was neo-Georgian, often in rather clunky and inflated form.

Modernization and Conservation

Few new features were added to London's built environment between the start of the First World War and the end of the Second, apart from ribbon development of semi-detached villas at the fringes of the metropolis. This was a product of cheap labour and materials and increasing car ownership in the interwar years. In inner London, the LCC and the metropolitan boroughs between them bulldozed their way through slum after slum, flattening the houses of some 180,000 Londoners in the 1920s and building new accommodation for them, prompting what was to become a

long-running debate about the desirability of high-density and high-rise formats for social housing.

After 1945 the most striking new features of the metropolitan landscape were point blocks and mid-rise buildings of social housing: the product of the Golden Era of Modernism in planning and architecture that had been foreshadowed by Abercrombie and Forshaw's *County of London Plan* (1943) and the radical Town and Country Planning Act (1947). Apartment buildings in the private sector tended to be timid and unexceptional versions of neo-Georgian and Moderne styles. Commercial buildings were mostly unremarkable versions of what the architectural historian Anthony Sutcliffe called Modern Free Style, using 'steel and concrete frames, simple, repetitive elevations, flat roofs, curtain walls and metal windows.'[4]

The postwar economic boom saw the replacement of much of London's older stock of buildings as well as the redevelopment of bomb sites. By the 1960s the pace of change had prompted a strong conservation movement, underpinned by the Civic Amenities Act of 1967. This introduced Conservation Areas, one of the most important policy instruments in sustaining the distinctive character of many districts. By the

Early LCC housing. The Millbank Estate, Westminster, a pioneering exercise in social housing. The fifteen blocks of flats on the estate, each named after an eminent artist, were built between 1897 and 1902.

Modern social housing. John Scurr House, in Limehouse, an early example – built in the mid-1930s – of what was to become a ubiquitous format. It was refurbished in 1997 by Architype with funding from the London Docklands Development Corporation.

early 1970s the focus was more on public opposition to the ambitious plans of some developers and to the evangelistic Modernism of London's planners and architects. One key target of dissent was a proposed Ringway system that would have torn through many districts and displaced about 100,000 people. Another was the GLC's proposal for the comprehensive redevelopment of Covent Garden, with a new road system and futuristic pedestrian walkways connecting office blocks, hotels, an international conference centre, schools and apartment blocks. Meanwhile, the Ronan Point disaster of 1968 – the partial collapse of a new tower block of system-built social housing in Newham – gave pause to the rash of high-rise council housing. By the late 1970s, after the international economic system-shock of OPEC-induced oil price rises, the postwar building boom was well and truly over, along with the credibility of Modernist planning. Tower blocks had become the tombstones of the Welfare State.

The Social Reconquest of Inner London

What happened instead of planned modernization was the social reconquest of inner London's districts through gentrification, a process involving the influx of more affluent households seeking the character and convenience of less-expensive housing in centrally located districts. The gentrification of central London was initially fostered by the Rent Act of 1957, which made it much easier for landlords to evict long-term tenants and make older properties available for sale. It was also boosted by the creation of Conservation Areas and by the expanded availability of mortgage credit.

Typically, the colonizing households are dominated by young professionals such as teachers, lawyers, designers, artists, architects, writers and creative staff in advertising firms. These incomers use sweat equity – their own, do-it-yourself labour, rather than contracted labour – for renovations and improvements. Their arrival pushes up rents and house prices and generates increased property tax

revenues. But it also displaces poorer households and prompts the closure of shops specializing in inexpensive goods and produce. Incoming gentrifiers, meanwhile, contribute to the physical renovation or rehabilitation of the older and usually rather deteriorated housing stock while supporting new businesses such as upscale restaurants, coffee shops, delicatessens, wine bars, galleries, clothing boutiques and bookshops.

Beginning in a few pockets in Camden and Kensington, gentrification spread north across Camden and Islington and west into North Kensington and Notting Hill. It has now affected every district except the outermost suburbs of the metropolis. In some districts, early gentrifiers have themselves been priced out and displaced by London's new global rich: a process of super-gentrification.

Neoliberalism and the Big Bang

Gentrification, and especially super-gentrification, has been greatly intensified by the shift to the free-market neoliberal policies that have dominated British politics since the late 1970s. Neoliberalism has meant a diminished role for the state, the nation-wide privatization of utilities, the sell-off of council housing to tenants and the handing-over

Gentrification. Converted mews dwellings, like these in Conduit Mews, Bayswater, were precursors of a more general trend of neighbourhood social change that has affected enormous tracts of the metropolis.

of remaining social housing estates to housing associations that have effectively acted as stalking horses for further rounds of privatization and gentrification. Particularly significant for London was the abolition of the GLC in 1986. Its buoyant municipal socialism had been a thorn in the side of Conservative governments, and its abolition left the metropolis effectively defenceless against the free-for-all commercial exploitation fostered by neoliberalism. It soon led to social distress and inequality of the kind that Keynesian economists and Welfare State planners had previously thought possible to eradicate.

Equally significant was the deregulation of financial markets that same year. 'Light-touch' regulation of the financial sector was seen by the Thatcher government as essential to London's status as a world banking capital. Long-standing rules that barred foreign companies from operating in the City were scrapped, and face-to-face dealing on the floor of the Stock Exchange was replaced with screen-based trading. The result was the so-called Big Bang: a restructuring and realignment of firms in stock and bond markets and an overall recasting of the City's office employment profile. It also led, of course, to the shameful and irresponsible role of many City financial firms in the international financial meltdown of 2008 and the subsequent multi-year recession.

Meanwhile, London's role as the pre-eminent financial hub of the global economy was indeed confirmed and consolidated, with enormous consequences for architecture, building and social change. The two districts whose physical fabric was most affected by the Big Bang were the City and the Docklands. The boom in banking and financial services created a seemingly insatiable demand for high-tech, large-floor-plate offices that the existing building stock could not satisfy. This encouraged both the government and private investors in the development of a major new office district, Canary Wharf, 5 kilometres (3 miles) to the east of the City, on the site of the derelict quays of the Isle of Dogs. The Thatcher government had established the London Docklands Development Corporation, an urban development corporation with extensive powers, and charged it with the regeneration of the docklands. While this initially resulted in an oversupply of office space, Canary Wharf began to prosper after several business cycles and is now effectively an adjunct of the City rather than a rival office cluster.

The Big Bang also created a great deal of wealth among a new, young class fraction that, in turn, was promptly reflected in the built environment in various ways, including a spate of new-build gentrification projects in the form of loft apartments and riverside condominium complexes. London's amped-up role in the global economy, together with its infrastructure of high-end consumption, also brought global investment, including 'flight capital' from the super-rich in less stable economies.

Three-quarters of all the new homes sold in London in 2013 were purchased by non-UK buyers, and almost fifty per cent of London's house sales of £1 million or more were accounted for by foreigners. Following the financial crisis of 2008, Swiss banks were less willing to fulfil their traditional role of no-questions-asked banking. Central London's property market filled the gap: somewhere for the global super-rich to park their money. Property in high-end residential districts like Belgravia, Kensington and Mayfair became a form of reserve currency for the 'one per cent' as rich foreigners paid large sums for properties in which they had no intention of living - except, perhaps, during one or two shopping binges each year. The consequent bubble overheated the housing market across the entire metropolis.

Architecture and Urban Design for a Global City

The boom associated with London's central role in the globalization of the financial and business services sector has added significant new architectural dimensions to the city. After a few very visible and, mostly, unfortunate excursions into postmodernism, the predominant genre of new architecture in London has been what the critic Owen Hatherley calls 'pseudomodern' because of the way it 'reverses the old function-over-form morality of Modernist architecture while rejecting the direct traditionalism of "vernacular", neo-Tudor, neo-Georgian or neo-Victorian styles'.[5] Thus buildings with basically regular, Modernist proportions are embellished with various 'interesting' shapes in a variety of materials.

Meanwhile, the collapse of London's manufacturing economy has left the metropolis with a wide variety of settings that have lent themselves to conversions to chic loft apartments, restaurants and studio spaces. At the same time, the combination of Millennium projects, Jubilee projects and the 2012 Summer Olympics has cleaned up much of central London and repackaged and redeveloped its museums and 'heritage' settings. The result has been a shift from a city that did not seem to care about its looks to one that, in parts at least, is well suited to the drama of exhibition and spectacle that is integral to the new political economy of cultural boosterism.

New Labour's ambitious Commission for Architecture and the Built Environment was established in the hope of influencing the people making decisions about the built environment and charged with championing well-designed buildings, spaces and places. Unfortunately, it was no match for the aggressive neoliberal political economy of the 1990s, and was eventually quietly merged with the Design Council. New Labour also established an Urban Task Force, chaired by London's leading architect, Richard Rogers, who also became Chief Advisor on Architecture and Urbanism to the first GLA mayor, Ken Livingstone. The Task Force was charged with identifying the causes of urban decline and establishing a vision for urban regeneration based on principles of design excellence, social well-being and environmental responsibility.

In spite of these laudable goals and Rogers's apparent social-democratic intentions, the result in London was to encourage a feverish spate of regeneration and mixed-use projects: 'The Urban Task Force that he led, and the planning advice he gave to Ken Livingstone, [merely] entailed making neoliberalism look nicer.'[6] Subsequently, Rogers himself has gone on to design two of the most outrageously extravagant projects in the entire city: One Hyde Park (see page 166) and Neo Bankside (see page 244): effectively vertical gated communities for the super-rich.

The profitability of property development, combined with the business-friendly policies of central and local governments, has led to public–private partnerships formulating big regeneration schemes with mixed-use complexes of offices, residences, retailing and hotels. In addition to Canary Wharf, the most ambitious of these include regeneration schemes at Paddington Basin, King's Cross and the Greenwich Peninsula. Developers and borough planners have also worked together with Business Improvement Districts to exploit London's traditional image as a metropolis of villages. Seven Dials, for example, is now promoted as 'Covent Garden's Hidden Village'.

The most dramatic visible change to the fabric of the metropolis, though, has been the appearance of the extravagantly high buildings that were seen by Mayor Livingstone and his successor, Boris Johnson, as key to boosting London's global brand image (see pages 96–97). For better or worse, they have permanently and irrevocably altered the character of the metropolis. There is much more to come: a survey in 2014 of local authority plans by the independent think tank New London Architecture found that at least 236 buildings of more than twenty storeys were either under construction, approved or awaiting approval. Thirty-three of them will be between forty and forty-nine storeys high; twenty-two will have fifty or more storeys.[7]

Bayswater + Paddington

Bayswater and Paddington have shared roots, both as part of the ancient parish of Paddington and as part of the initial development of the Paddington Estate, the major landholding in the district at the onset of urbanization at the beginning of the nineteenth century. Their mutual story is a sequence of speculative development, industrialization, deindustrialization, regeneration and social polarization. Until the 1790s the district had few inhabitants: parish records of the time list fewer than 1000 people. Within seventy years it was almost entirely built up, with fashionable terraces facing Hyde Park and Kensington Gardens, middle-class avenues around Westbourne Grove, and some of London's worst slums along the canal and railway lines that had bisected the district.

Two acts of Parliament in 1795 were crucial to these changes. The first authorized the Grand Junction Canal Company to cut a branch canal through Paddington. The canal opened in 1801, an important extension of the Grand Union Canal, which linked Midlands industry with the Thames at Brentford. The extension terminated at Paddington Basin and promptly attracted factories, warehouses and the yards of the builders and their suppliers who were giving shape to London's westward expansion. The canal system became even more important when the Regent's Canal joined the Paddington extension at Little Venice, thus connecting the Grand Union system to east London and the Docklands. The canalside industry in Paddington attracted labourers, many of them Irish immigrants, who crowded near by in shacks and cheap lodgings.

The second important Act of 1795 opened the Paddington Estate - owned mostly by the Church of England, in the form of the Bishop of London and his lessees - to speculative development. Land ownership was much more fragmented than in Great Estates like Bloomsbury, Grosvenor and Mayfair, however, so no overall plan was ever drawn up. The first area to be developed was what came to be known as Tyburnia, around the old hamlet of Tyburn, to the northwest of Marble Arch, close to Hyde Park and the nearest part of the district to central London. Here, the Church had a policy of sub-leasing relatively small amounts of land to local builders, seeking to foster the development of small, fashionable squares and streets. The success of Tyburnia encouraged the development of the land further west, in the Bayswater area just north of Kensington Gardens.

Both the Bayswater and Tyburnia developments shared in the building boom of the mid-1830s to the mid-1850s, when affluent merchants and professional men followed the aristocracy in moving west. The new developments attracted both the wealthy and the merely well-to-do, while artistic and literary figures were attracted to the fringes of the district, which were still semi-rural. The northward expansion of fashionable residences was limited by the arrival of the Great Western Railway and the construction of a new Brunel-designed terminus - Paddington station - in the 1850s. The opening of the terminus gave rise to many small hotels and boarding houses as well as the Great Western Hotel (now the Hilton London Paddington) at the station itself. The railway yards were adjacent to the canal basin, and the combination led to a rapid expansion of the area's industrial and population base. Here, Church land on the Paddington Estate was hastily developed for high-density working-class housing.

The growth of the entire district slackened from the late 1860s as Victorian London's ever-expanding upper-middle classes began to move further away from central areas. By the late nineteenth century, the social and functional character of Bayswater and Paddington had become mixed. The fashionable

Portsea Place. Part of Tyburnia, built in the 1820s by the Bishop of London's Trustees.

Little Venice.
Browning's Pool,
formerly a busy canal
port, is now a tranquil
spot with picturesque
canal-boat homes.

neighbourhoods near the parks became more cosmopolitan, attracting many wealthy foreign-born citizens. Their presence was marked by the consecration of a synagogue in St Petersburgh Place in 1879 and of a Greek Orthodox cathedral in Moscow Road in 1882. Meanwhile, in the distinctly unfashionable neighbourhoods around the railway and canal, Victorian entrepreneurs had opened hundreds of small factories, workshops and laundries that together employed more than 7000 people. Housing conditions in these neighbourhoods were extremely poor, with acute overcrowding and a high incidence of infant mortality. The Ecclesiastical Commissioners of the Church - by far the biggest of the slum landlords - attracted widespread criticism for deriving so much of their profits from impoverished tenants, but they did little in response. Between the World Wars this social polarization intensified, while shops, hotels, boarding houses and apartment buildings were inserted into the fabric of the district. There was relatively little direct damage during the Second World War, but by the 1950s there was widespread urban decay, and the economic base of the district was in sharp decline.

Conversion and Conservation

As leases of the district's Victorian properties fell in, postwar development brought Paddington its share of ugly and undistinguished office blocks, while conversions increased the number of flats. Some older properties were cleared to make way for another hallmark of the 1960s, an elevated urban motorway: the Westway, running parallel to the railway tracks and reinforcing the boundary between Bayswater and Paddington to the south and the rest of the Paddington Estate in Maida Vale to the north. The 1960s were also the Golden Era for British town planning, and Westminster and LCC and GLC planners set about Bayswater and Paddington with evangelistic zeal, charting comprehensive redevelopment strategies and building social housing estates with Modernist tower blocks. A good deal of conversion and some new building was also carried out by housing associations. The Ecclesiastical Commissioners sold off many of their slum properties, thereby removing at least some of the grounds for shame. At the same time it raised capital that the Commissioners needed in order to enter into partnerships with property companies and begin the renovation and rebuilding of Tyburnia.

The Westway. The Westway was built to form a link from Paddington to the Ringway system, a comprehensive network intended by the GLC to manage the flow of traffic into and out of the city. The scheme was cancelled in 1973 after a campaign by Homes Before Roads, at which point only three small sections of the Ringway had been built.

The dominant planning theme of the following decade was conservation. Several Conservation Areas were created under the Civic Amenities Act of 1967, effectively protecting the Victorian fabric of most of Bloomsbury and Tyburnia, from the comparatively plain villas and cottages of the 1820s and 1830s to the extravagant mid-century Italianate terraces and the ornate mansions of the turn of the century. Conservation also succeeded, of course, in hastening the gentrification of the district. Initially led by young professionals investing sweat equity, gentrification soon came to be dominated by wealthy foreigners: a reprise of the infiltrations of the late nineteenth century. Tyburnia and the southern part of Bayswater have become genuinely cosmopolitan. The latest phase of gentrification has been developer-led, aimed at the global super-rich. An example is the Lancasters, on Bayswater Road (see page 29).

Also in the 1970s, the movement of industry away from London began to be counterbalanced by an increase in tourism. Paddington, with good rail and Tube links, acquired many new hotels. Some were in hollowed-out and reconditioned sections of Victorian terraces; others were brand new. The latter included the London Metropole, designed by Richard Seifert & Partners, one of the most influential of London's postwar architectural practices.

Regeneration

Westminster City Council created a 30-hectare (75-acre) development framework known as the Paddington Special Policy Area (PSPA) in 1988. The objective was to facilitate the long-desired regeneration of Paddington Basin and the old goods yard adjacent to Paddington Station. The site was especially attractive to local politicians and planners because it afforded an opportunity to draw development pressure away from the borough's historical townscape and its affluent and influential residents. Several early proposals collapsed, but eventually a combination of factors led to the creation of one of London's flagship regeneration schemes, centred on the twin developments of Paddington Basin and Paddington Central.

The scheme's strategic importance was enhanced by the completion in 1998 of the Heathrow Express Rail Link, which made Paddington the London terminus for Heathrow passengers. This coincided with a rising demand for office space in London after the 'Big Bang' of financial-sector deregulation and the spectacular growth of London's global-city functions. It also coincided with the neoliberal trend for public-private partnerships and with government pressure for public-sector bodies to capitalize on their land assets.

Regeneration of the PSPA site has been co-ordinated since 1998 by the Paddington Waterside Partnership, an alliance of twenty public- and private-sector developers, landowners and tenant organizations. By 2014 over 186,000 square metres (2 million square feet) of commercial space had been built, accommodating more than 17,000 employees, together with about 1100 residential units.

With the opening of the new Crossrail station at Paddington in 2018, the site will be even more attractive to developers as a result of better links to Heathrow and new links to the City and Docklands. The Crossrail route will involve a six-way interchange at Paddington with regional and suburban rail services and London Underground's Circle, District, Metropolitan & City and Bakerloo lines. Because the station is in the Bayswater Conservation Area and its buildings are all listed either Grade I or Grade II, the Crossrail station is set in a huge cut-and-cover excavation underneath Eastbourne Terrace, with a glazed spine to let light into the concourse beneath.[1] By the time Crossrail is operational, it is expected that an additional 130,000 square metres (1.4 million square feet) of office space will have been built in Paddington Basin and Paddington Central, creating a node of more than 30,000 office workers. Property values in the immediate area have already begun to rise sharply in anticipation. Nevertheless, Bayswater and Paddington remain among the most socially polarized districts in London. The bedsits and social housing of northern Bayswater show up in government reports as some of the most deprived in the country. They are just a few hundred metres from the new condos of Paddington Central and no more than 550 metres (600 yards) from the super-luxury of the Lancasters.

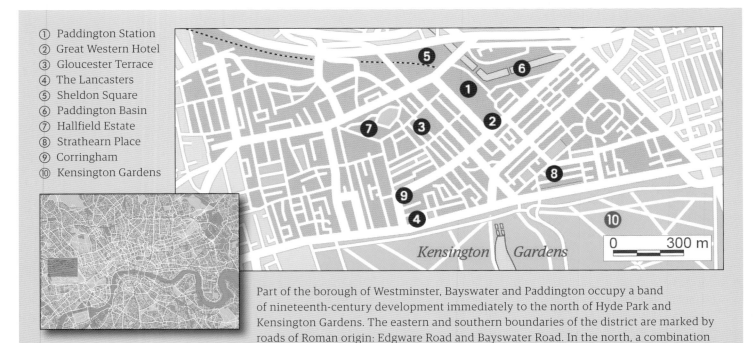

1. Paddington Station
2. Great Western Hotel
3. Gloucester Terrace
4. The Lancasters
5. Sheldon Square
6. Paddington Basin
7. Hallfield Estate
8. Strathearn Place
9. Corringham
10. Kensington Gardens

Part of the borough of Westminster, Bayswater and Paddington occupy a band of nineteenth-century development immediately to the north of Hyde Park and Kensington Gardens. The eastern and southern boundaries of the district are marked by roads of Roman origin: Edgware Road and Bayswater Road. In the north, a combination of modern infrastructure - the Paddington Branch Canal, the Great Western Railway line and the Westway - represent an important social as well as physical divide. Bayswater merges with Notting Hill to the west, the two districts separated only by the administrative boundary between Westminster and Kensington and Chelsea. Bayswater occupies the western half of this overall area, with Paddington to the east of Westbourne Terrace. The larger landholdings in the district were developed without an overall plan, resulting in a mix of relatively short, straight streets, a few long and imposing terraces, and a dozen or so enclosed squares in many different configurations, allowing for a variety of housing and open space arrangements.

❶ Paddington Station
Praed Street

The station was built in the early 1850s to the designs of Isambard Kingdom Brunel, chief engineer of the Great Western Railway and one the greatest of all Victorian engineers. The glazed roof is supported by wrought-iron arches in three spans. The original supporting columns, also in wrought iron, were replaced by steel columns in the 1920s. Most of the architectural detailing in the station was by Brunel's associate Matthew Wyatt, though much of this has been lost as a result of damage during the Second World War and several subsequent modernizations.

❷ Great Western Hotel (Hilton London Paddington)
Praed Street

The hotel, with its grandiose facade, was built for the Great Western Railway and opened in 1854. The Great Western was the first of the large purpose-built railway hotels in London. Designed in French Second Empire style by Philip Hardwick, it forms the main facade of the terminal, closing off the end of Brunel's trainshed at the head of the platforms. As a result, the station itself has no grand entrance. Hardwick made up for this by extensive and ostentatious ornamentation of the hotel, both inside and out. The pediment was designed by John Thomas and features sculpted figures of Peace, Plenty, Science and Industry. After the nationalization of the railways in 1948, the hotel gradually deteriorated. It was sold to the private sector in 1983 in accordance with government policy on privatization, and it was refurbished and reopened in 2001 as part of the Hilton chain.

❸ Gloucester Terrace
Gloucester Terrace was built on the Bishop of London's estate during the building boom of the 1840s and 1850s by William Kingdom, who also built most of parallel Westbourne Terrace. Both provided impressively long vistas with elaborate stuccoed facades, designed to attract the affluent merchants and professionals who were following London's gentry in moving west. By the 1930s most of the houses had been converted into flats and bedsits. The Church Commissioners' decision in 1954 to reorganize the Paddington Estate resulted in most of the properties being sold off, and for some time Gloucester Terrace continued to be run-down, with a reputation for being part of what became known as the Sin Triangle, the area between Paddington Station and Lancaster Gate with a high incidence of prostitution. Today it is largely gentrified, with a sprinkling of small guest houses and commercial offices.

❹ The Lancasters
Bayswater Road

Originally a terrace of fifteen mid-nineteenth-century houses facing Hyde Park on the northern side of the Bayswater Road, the houses were gutted in the 1970s and converted into a hotel. They were converted again in 2011, this time into seventy-five super-luxurious apartments and two houses with separate entrances. With twenty-four-hour concierge service for valet parking, housekeeping, personal shopping and catering, the project is a reflection of London's role as a global city, with many overseas purchasers and absentee owners. Service charges for a 465-square-metre (5000-square-foot) apartment cost owners about £40,000 a year. Reception rooms are 5 metres (16 feet) high, and double-height entrance halls have marble floors. Bedroom suites have embroidered silk walls, marble-lined bathrooms and bespoke walk-in closets; below ground are two levels of parking and a luxury spa.

❺ Sheldon Square

Sheldon Square is the focus of Paddington Central, a brownfield regeneration project on the site of the old railway goods yard. It is a flagship project for Westminster City Council, whose Special Policy Area created market confidence for private-sector developers. Paddington Central is a mixed-use development, intended as a node of office employment with a significant residential component, along with healthcare services, leisure facilities and a limited amount of retailing. The buildings and layout of Sheldon Square were designed by architects Sidell Gibson, Sheppard Robson and Kohn Pedersen Fox. Hemmed in by the railway, the canal and the Westway, the site has had to be virtually vehicle-free at street level: only taxis have access. The designers have made a virtue of this, with pedestrians gaining access from the cleaned-up canal towpath, which has a direct link into Paddington Station, just a few metres away. The terraced amphitheatre in the centre of Sheldon Square, although not strictly public space, provides an attractive setting for informal social activities in good weather.

A second phase has added two large office buildings and a 206-room hotel, but the development has been criticized for its lack of affordable housing and failure to obtain significant social benefits through developer contributions. The commercial success of Paddington Central, meanwhile, has increased the desirability of the Edwardian stucco houses of Little Venice, the area around the junction of the Paddington branch canal, the Grand Union Canal and the Regent's Canal that lies immediately to the north of the development.

❻ Paddington Basin (below and opposite)
North Wharf Road

The Paddington Basin project, combined with Paddington Central, is one of the largest and highest-profile urban regeneration projects in Europe. Together, they have prompted the re-branding of a formerly run-down area as Paddington Waterside. A critical element has been improved accessibility throughout the site. More than 1 kilometre (¾ mile) of new canal towpath has been laid, and five new pedestrian bridges across the canal have been constructed. Eventually, the Paddington Basin component will consist of more than 186,000 square metres (2 million square feet) of mixed-use development. Further along the canal, towards Paddington Central, a forty-four-storey loofah-shaped tower will finally provide Paddington Waterside with an area-defining building. But not a very elegant one.

❼ Hallfield Estate
Cleveland Terrace

Built on a site that was badly damaged during the Second World War and subsequently acquired from the Church Commissioners by the borough council, the Hallfield Estate is a seminal postwar social housing project that was the work of some of the twentieth century's most significant architects and, as a result, widely exhibited and published. The initial design was by Berthold Lubetkin and the Tecton Group, and it was completed in 1955 under the supervision of Lindsay Drake and Denys Lasdun. It was an attempt to realize Le Corbusier's scheme for a city in a park, based on his utopian vision of a 'Radiant City', an urban landscape comprising high-density housing blocks set in public open space. The estate consists of six residential blocks of ten storeys and eight blocks of six storeys,

grouped around a large open space. They were named after towns with stations on the Great Western Railway line from Paddington. At the time, they were thought to be a sophisticated and distinctive aesthetic approach to social housing, whereby the facades are treated like works of abstract art. They were listed Grade II by English Heritage in 2011. The scheme housed 2362 people, making it one of the largest and most ambitious housing schemes built in London in the immediate postwar years. Trees around the estate have matured, softening the small parkscape, but the buildings themselves have not been well maintained.

❽ Strathearn Place

Part of Tyburnia, Strathearn Place was the first phase of the Bishop of London's estate to be developed after Parliament granted permission in 1827 for building in the area immediately to the north of Hyde Park. Initially planned by S. P. Cockerell and subsequently modified and supervised by the bishop's surveyor, George Gutch, it was completed by 1850. At that time, Tyburnia had a social standing comparable with Belgravia. Strathearn Place was among the later streets to be built, a terrace of single-family homes whose uniformity was emphasized by a continuous cornice over the second floor, a cast-iron balustraded balcony carried across first-floor level, and spearhead iron railings at street level. The terrace is neatly terminated by the Victoria public house, which has a remarkably complete interior from the 1890s.

9 Corringham
Craven Hill Gardens

This minimalist apartment block is the only substantial architectural work of Kenneth Frampton, who went on to become an influential critic and writer on Modern architecture. Frampton was working for Douglas Stephen & Partners when he was project architect for this block in 1961. The building is notable for its use of an interior layout based on a 'scissor' arrangement, in which each apartment interlocks with its neighbouring apartments above and below. Strict planning restrictions meant that the height and depth of the block had to match the outline of the Edwardian buildings that once stood on the same site. The scissor solution allowed Frampton to meet these restrictions and still fit sufficient flats into the block for the developer to get an acceptable return on investment. The idea had been explored by the LCC in the mid-1950s and first tried out in its Tidey Street scheme in Poplar. Frampton's Corringham design allows all apartments to have west-facing living rooms with sunset views, while all bedrooms overlook the quiet communal gardens to the rear.

10 Kensington Gardens

Now part of London's Royal Parks, Kensington Gardens were once the private domain of Kensington Palace, established when William III purchased Nottingham House in 1689. Queen Anne enlarged the palace gardens by appropriating 12 hectares (30 acres) from Hyde Park, and commissioned the Orangery (probably designed by Wren but executed by Nicholas Hawksmoor) in the 1700s. Queen Caroline, the wife of George II, shaped the gardens to their present form in 1728 by creating the Serpentine and the Long Water from the Westbourne stream and adding the Round Pond and the Broad Walk. The landscape architects were Stephen Switzer, Charles Bridgeman and, later, William Kent. For most of the eighteenth century the gardens were closed to the public. They were opened gradually, but only to the respectably dressed. At the same time the formal layout was progressively softened, leaving largely open areas of grass, which were crossed by paths linking entrances and features within the park.

This amenity, together with its royal associations and the proximity of Kensington Palace, had a lot to do with the success of Bayswater's developers in attracting upper-middle-class households. A series of enhancements to the Gardens were carried out in the nineteenth century, including the Italian Garden with its fountains and sculpture (1860), the Albert Memorial (1863-72) and general improvements to mark the Diamond Jubilee and eightieth birthday celebrations of Queen Victoria (1897). The park now has numerous mature trees, including plane, chestnut, lime, sycamore, beech and ash. Like the other Royal Parks in London, it is popular for sunbathing and picnics in fine weather. It is also much-used as a pleasant walking route to work for commuters.

Belgravia + Pimlico

Belgravia, along with much of Pimlico, came into the possession of the Grosvenor family in 1656, when the daughter and sole heiress of Alexander Davies, of Ebury Farm, married Thomas Grosvenor. For a long time the boggy 7-hectare (17-acre) farm, located on the site of an old lagoon of the Thames, had seemed an unlikely asset. But as London grew during the boom years of the Regency after victory at Waterloo (1815), the land suddenly took on real potential for development. The conversion of the old Buckingham House, which stood just to the east of the farm, into Buckingham Palace made the land quite valuable. Robert Grosvenor (who had inherited the family fortune) saw the potential and secured an Act of Parliament to permit the site to be drained and its level raised in order to allow development.

Thomas Cubitt, one of London's great entrepreneurial developers, also saw the potential and took on the project. Cubitt was a new sort of master builder whose company was vertically integrated, with its own supply lines of building materials and an army of 1000 workers on permanent employment. He spent considerable sums of money draining and preparing the ground and installing sewers, road surfaces and pavements. His workers dug out the district's clay (turning it into bricks) and replaced it with enough soil and gravel from excavations at St Katharine Dock (see page 263) to raise the site above flood level. Development began in the 1820s in the classic Regency style of squares, streets and crescents aligned to overlook private gardens.

Unified Urban Design

The intention from the start was to create an exclusive district, which would be called Belgravia. The Grosvenor Estate insisted on covenants in every lease to prohibit trade or manufacture in its streets. The centrepiece of the entire development, designed by the young architect George Basevi, was Belgrave Square. Cubitt realized that the square had to succeed as a unified element, with no risk of individual parcels being let out just as and when the speculative market permitted. He therefore financed the building of the square with a group of City bankers whose credit would guarantee that the entire project was completed as planned. As a result, the unity of the whole scheme was maintained over the ten years of its development.

This was in sharp contrast to other speculative landed-estate developments of the period, where building styles typically changed considerably in a desperate effort to maintain sales during the cyclical downturns of the property market. The other key element in the overall design of Belgravia was Eaton Square (named after Eaton Hall in Cheshire, the principal residence of the Grosvenor family). The Grosvenor Estate took advantage of the New Churches Act of 1824 (meant to ensure religious adherence to the established Church in newly built-up areas), securing financing for Henry Hakewill's church of St Peter at the eastern end of the square.

Between and around these principal squares were grand terraces of white stucco houses of uniform mass, height (mainly four- and five-storey) and architectural treatment. Cubitt deployed the Palladian style on a grander scale than had previously been seen, drawing heavily on Greek and Roman motifs. Following the example of London's most fashionable architects, Robert Adam and John Nash, Cubitt coated his houses in stucco and arranged them in long, symmetrical compositions. The houses themselves ranged from large to enormous. There was typically a large basement for the use of servants, with access directly from the street down steps to a tiny front courtyard. Above this, access to an

Belgrave Square.
Statue of Robert Grosvenor, first Marquess of Westminster.

imposing front door was via a bridge of steps, often covered by a classical porch with columns and a pediment. To the rear of the terraces, accessed by narrow paved lanes and often screened by giant arches (copied from Nash's Regent's Park terraces), were mews - rows of stables and carriage houses, with living quarters above, each associated with one of the grand residences on the principal streets.

Eccleston Mews. Behind Eaton Place, in the heart of Belgravia.

Cubitt began to develop the southern reaches of the Grosvenor Estate, in Pimlico, a couple of decades later. By that time Greek and Roman styling had given way to the new Italianate fashion, but the general appearance of the streets in Pimlico was similar to that of those in Belgravia. It was, though, a less select development in social terms, aimed at the well-to-do genteel classes rather than rich nobility, so Cubitt included parades of small shops in his general plan, as well as pubs, typically placed on street corners. The overall scale of its layout was less grandiose than Belgravia, at least outside the three main squares - Eccleston, Warwick and St George's - and their connecting streets. The latest of Cubitt's houses in Pimlico, completed in the 1870s, are among the last of the stucco era in London.

Social Stability, Social Mix

Belgravia, in particular, was a great success, instantly rivalling Mayfair as a fashionable address. After the Second World War some of the larger houses ceased to be used as residences and were taken over as embassies, charity headquarters and professional institutes, while most of the mews cottages and carriage houses were profitably converted into apartments. But further change was precluded by the Grosvenor Estate's strict leases and by the district's designation as a Conservation Area in 1968. Belgravia's terraces were thus saved from the decay that overtook so much of Kensington and Paddington in the postwar period.

Pimlico's squares and terraces were also designated a Conservation Area in 1968, thus ensuring its subsequent gentrification. But Pimlico as a whole, less comprehensively controlled by the Grosvenor Estate, and with its initial development lacking the élite status of Belgravia, has always been more mixed in character, less sterile and conceited. This was inevitable after the construction of Victoria railway station (originally referred to as the 'Grosvenor Terminus') and the consequent agglomeration of hotels, bars and retailing in the 1860s. Pimlico also has a significant amount of social housing. Several Peabody estates were constructed in the nineteenth century, while council estates were added in the twentieth century. The most significant of these is Churchill Gardens Estate near the river, built after the Second World War on a slum clearance site. Its ambitious combination of parallel Corbusian slabs separated by landscaped open spaces, together with four-storey maisonettes, three-storey terraced houses, three new schools, shops and a community centre, was widely influential in postwar Britain.

A District for the Global Elite

From the mid-1980s London's prominence as a hub of the global economy began to draw increasing numbers of the international super-rich to Belgravia and nearby Chelsea and Mayfair to park (and, in some cases, launder) their money. The embassies remained and were joined by five-star hotels - the Berkeley, the Halkin and the Sheraton Belgravia - but the offices of many of the charities and institutes that had moved into Belgravia in the 1950s and 1960s moved away to the newly gentrifying districts of inner London, leaving their premises to be reconverted to residential space.

Belgravia has thus stood as a super-élite residential district over an unbroken span of more than 180 years. It has remained unchanged in physical appearance and broadly stable in terms of the socio-economic status of its residents. Its proximity to Westminster has seen some of its residences converted into consulates and embassies, while its proximity to the exclusive retailers, restaurants and clubs of Knightsbridge has precluded any significant invasion of commercial activity.

Today Belgravia is one of the world's quintessential élite residential districts, accessible only to the very affluent who are able to afford its remodelled contemporary studio apartments, its elegantly proportioned flats with high ceilings and its mews cottages, and to the seriously wealthy who are able to afford its larger town houses. Just as the landed classes of the eighteenth century flocked to London each year to spend 'the season' in proximity to the court, so many of today's global super-rich keep an address in Belgravia and spend part of the year catching up on conspicuous consumption at the specialized shops, art dealers and tailors of Knightsbridge and St James's.

Eaton Place. A Grade II*-listed terrace. Thomas Cubitt had his office in number 93.

There is little activity on the streets and few visitors to the district's private gardens except for maids exercising residents' pet dogs. The restrained neo-classical facades of the buildings mask extravagance and luxury that is only hinted at by the expensive automobiles that occupy the limited on-street parking. Number 11 Eaton Square, for example, with a relatively modest frontage like all its neighbours, has 1140 square metres (12,270 square feet) of living space, including six bedrooms, six bathrooms, three kitchens, a colonnaded indoor swimming pool, three staircases and an orangery. At the rear the mews house has three bedrooms and two bathrooms, plus a two-bedroom staff flat and separate chauffeur's bedroom and bathroom.

Within Belgravia there is very little commercial activity, except for the discreet collection of designer shops, hair and beauty salons, dry-cleaners, estate agents and a patisserie in Motcomb Street (referred to by local residents and property professionals as 'Belgravia Village'). But just to the south of the district are Elizabeth Street and Pimlico Road (now branded 'Lower Belgravia'), with their Michelin-starred restaurants, pubs, bars and small, exclusive boutiques. Harrods department store, meanwhile, is located just beyond the northwest corner of the district, with the upscale shops and galleries of Knightsbridge and Brompton Road just a few hundred metres to the west.

Motcomb Street. Early nineteenth-century houses with shops below, now Belgravia's mini-High Street.

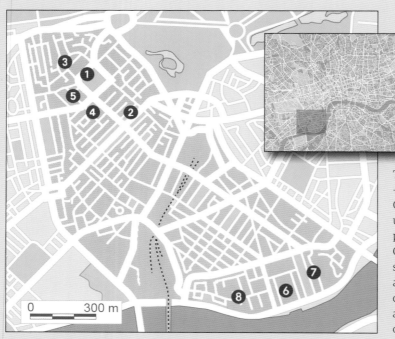

① Belgrave Square
② Eaton Square
③ Wilton Crescent
④ Roberts Mews
⑤ Belgrave Mews
⑥ Dolphin Square
⑦ St George's Square
⑧ Churchill Gardens

0   300 m

This part of the Grosvenor Estate - one of the largest of the city's Great Estates - was developed under a special Act of Parliament, passed in 1826, empowering Lord Grosvenor to drain the marshy site, raise its level and develop it as a residential district, thereby closing the gap between Mayfair and Chelsea. Belgravia represents one of the clearest imprints of the effect of large landholdings on London's morphology. The extraordinary architectural unity of Belgravia was ensured by the capacity of its principal developer, Thomas Cubitt, to lay out the entire district in just ten years. Pimlico, another part of the Grosvenor Estate developed by Cubitt, echoes the squares and terraces of the Belgravia development, but its character is relieved by a greater variety of building types. The western limit of the district corresponds with the administrative boundary between the City of Westminster and the Royal Borough of Kensington and Chelsea; Knightsbridge is to the north and Buckingham Palace Garden to the northeast.

❶ Belgrave Square

The Earl of Essex was the first to buy one of the houses in Belgrave Square, after which other wealthy and aristocratic families moved in. Belgravia quickly became a synonym for snooty respectability, so much so that endless small-time developers around the world have subsequently named avenues, drives, suburban estates and condominium towers after it. From the start, Belgravia attracted the rich, famous and powerful, and it has been home - or town home - to a succession of aristocratic families, prime ministers, cabinet members, wealthy industrialists and celebrities.

❷ Eaton Square

Named after Eaton Hall, the principal residence of the Grosvenor family in Cheshire, Eaton Square is an elongated rectangle with a busy road running through the middle. The road was originally the beginning of the royal route (the King's Road) from St James's Palace to Hampton Court. The Grosvenor Estate buffered itself from the road by laying out strips of private gardens on either side of it, with access roads to the residences on the far side of the gardens. The north side of the square (shown here) was developed by Thomas Cubitt and the south side by William Seth-Smith. Construction began in 1827 and was not completed until 1853. Like Belgrave Square, it immediately attracted wealthy residents and has maintained its fashionability ever since. A few embassies and other organizations moved in during the 1960s and 1970s (the Bolivian Embassy remains on this stretch), but the square is now very much in demand among London's new super-rich.

❸ Wilton Crescent

Distinctive within Belgravia's overwhelmingly rectilinear layout, Wilton Crescent was intended by the Grosvenor surveyors to form the grand entrance to the estate from Knightsbridge. Developed for the Grosvenor Estate by William Seth-Smith and Thomas Cubitt in the late 1820s, it was named after the first Earl of Wilton, Robert Grosvenor's father-in-law. The curvilinear north side of the crescent, shown here, was originally faced in brick and stucco, like most of the rest of the district. It was refaced in Portland stone in 1908-12 - a time when Portland stone was the preferred material for much new construction throughout central London.

Mews

Mews houses have no serious architectural merit, but they are a unique and distinctive element of London's cityscape. They are the legacy of an ingeniously practical solution to the problem facing the architects of London's first upscale terraced town houses: how to accommodate the horses, carriages and associated servant class without detracting from the distinction of the neighbourhood. With no gaps between the houses where stables might otherwise have been placed, the solution was to place a lane between the streets, giving access to the rear of the homes on both sides. The lane – or mews, as such lanes came to be called – was lined on both sides with a row of stables with living accommodation above for the grooms.

The word 'mews' originally referred to the cages of royal hawks in moult. When a fire destroyed Henry VIII's stables in Bloomsbury in 1537, he transformed the mews into stables with staff accommodation, and the term has been associated with rows of stables ever since. The first purpose-built mews were introduced in the 1630s as part of Inigo Jones's Covent

④ Roberts Mews. The distinctive archway entrance is itself designated as a Grade II-listed building.

⑤ Belgrave Mews North. Built to service the grand terraces of Belgrave Square and Wilton Crescent.

Garden scheme for the fourth Earl of Bedford. Jones laid out Hart Street (now Floral Street) and Maiden Lane at the back of the terraces facing the piazza. The surveyors and architects of the Great Estates that were subsequently developed in the West End adopted the same solution. It was a form of development that was possible only because the Great Estates controlled extensive tracts of land, and the resulting urban morphology was a clear reflection of the social structures and forms of transport of the era.

By the time Belgravia was developed, in the 1820s, the format had been refined to include, in some cases, mews courtyards entered through arches or gateways set into the facade of terracing. The front and rear elevations of the mews buildings had come to be highly differentiated, with a plain elevation when viewed from the mews lane, reflecting the humble station of its occupants, and an elaborate rear facade, often in classical design, in order to ensure a pleasant view from the main houses and their gardens.

The eclipse of horse-drawn transportation by motor cars resulted in the transformation of London's mews. Stables, obsolescent, were converted into garages and homes. The first recorded conversion of a stable into a dwelling house was in 1908. For several decades, mews houses were distinctly unfashionable, but after the Second World War they began to be early targets of gentrification. Artists and writers were drawn to them, partly for their bohemian chic, but mainly because they were cheap.

The cachet of mews living was cemented in the 1960s when they were depicted as the residence of lead characters of such cult television programmes as *The Avengers* and *The Saint*. Their image as fashionable and edgy residences increased dramatically during the Profumo crisis of 1963, which centred on the various liaisons of a government minister, a high-class prostitute and a Soviet naval attaché at Wimpole Mews in Mayfair. Mews living became emblematic of Swinging London.

An estimated 3000 mews residences still exist in the West End. They are quiet, safe and secure, and often have parking (estate agents value parking space in central London at the same price per square metre as they do residential accommodation). Mews' simple construction lends itself to interior modernization and occasionally even expansion. Many are in culs-de-sac, which helps to foster a sense of neighbourly community, yet they are sequestered and private. All this has made them very popular. Most have seven-figure price tags, although they rarely come on the open market. In 2012 a two-bedroom, three-bathroom property in Grosvenor Crescent Mews in Belgravia was sold for £4.2 million.

❻ Dolphin Square
Chichester Street

When it was completed in 1937, Dolphin Square was the largest block of flats in Europe. It occupies the former site of Thomas Cubitt's riverside dock and Pimlico works complex. Planned as a self-contained luxury development, it includes an indoor swimming pool, a gymnasium, squash courts, restaurants, bars, a winter garden, underground parking, an enclosed mini-mall of shops and more than 1200 flats. During the Second World War one of the blocks, Grenville House, was the headquarters of the Free French under General de Gaulle. The garage became an ambulance depot, and the gymnasium was adapted to hospital use. Dolphin Square's proximity to Westminster has made it popular with MPs, lawyers and senior civil servants. Other notable residents have included Oswald Mosley, Harold Wilson, Christine Keeler, Mandy Rice-Davies, C. P. Snow and Princess Anne.

❼ St George's Square

In 1839 Thomas Cubitt laid out two parallel streets next to his riverside works where bricks were brought in by barge, and joinery, glass and plasterwork were assembled for his building operations in Belgravia and Pimlico. Later, when the land between the two streets was landscaped and planted, it created a long, narrow square open to the Thames - a rarity in itself, but even more so in that it is a green space in Belgravia and Pimlico that is not behind locked gates.

❽ Churchill Gardens
Churchill Gardens Road

This social housing estate (now more than half of it in private hands) replaced Victorian terraced houses that had been badly damaged during the Blitz. It was promoted not only as a model for postwar rebuilding in response to the *County of London Plan* prepared in 1943 by Abercrombie and Forshaw, but also as a symbolic commitment to a modern and more egalitarian future. It consisted of 1661 dwellings, a covered shopping centre, pubs, a primary school, play areas and a community hall, and was originally heated with waste hot water pumped under the Thames from Battersea Power Station. Its combination of parallel nine- and eleven-storey slab blocks and three- and four-storey maisonettes in a vaguely Corbusian setting was widely influential on municipal housing in the 1950s and 1960s, but it was the only project to be completed under Abercrombie's *Plan*.

Bethnal Green

Vestiges of the original green, a medieval common, survive as Bethnal Green Gardens, close to the present-day Underground station. In the seventeenth century, merchants and noblemen had built large houses around the common. Samuel Pepys stayed there in the aftermath of the Great Fire, in a large mansion called Kirby's Castle that had been built a century before. The survival of part of the green can be attributed to affluent residents of the village who purchased and enclosed the common in 1678 to prevent its development. In addition to the remnant of the Green itself, eventually acquired as a public open space by the LCC, a few of the early buildings that fronted the common also survive. But the district as a whole is almost entirely a product of the industrial era. It had remained a pleasant country retreat on the outskirts of London for a few decades, but early in the eighteenth century the fields to the west of the village were developed as cheap housing in response to the expansion of the silk-weaving industry in neighbouring Spitalfields.

Bethnal Green soon developed as a manufacturing district, becoming a separate parish in 1743. It was known for its furniture industry and silk-weaving but also for its overcrowded, narrow streets and courts and the poverty of its residents. When the weaving industry collapsed under pressure from cheaper Continental imports in the latter half of the eighteenth century, the district's tenements were sub-divided and intermixed with back-room workshops and 'manufactories', where residents scraped a living making such odds and ends as matchboxes and clothes pegs. The eastern part of the district remained rural in character, with fields, market gardens and tree-lined lanes, until 1808, when 'Globe Town' was established just east of the green. Its tenements, too, promptly became a slum as displaced workers from Spitalfields and Whitechapel crowded in.

An ambitious plan to create a middle-class district around the edges of the newly created Victoria Park, at the eastern extremity of the district, was drafted by James Pennethorne, one of London's leading architects. He devised a grid of streets for the area that broadly traced the old field boundaries, adding three radial avenues that began at the gates of the park. The streets were to be lined with superior villas, as at Regent's Park, where Pennethorne had worked with John Nash a few years previously. But in the absence of a Prince Regent or similar sponsor, development devolved to local builders, who erected modest Italianate terraces aimed at a middle-class market of teachers, merchants and shopkeepers.

A Terrifying District

This small area of modest prosperity was an exception, however. Throughout the nineteenth century, Bethnal Green became notorious as one of London's most terrifyingly impoverished districts. Most of its workers - many of them children - were occupied in sweated industries, a system in which the production process was divided into stages, each subcontracted by different individuals operating in back rooms, garrets and cellars, far away from factory inspectors. Dominated by clothing, footwear and furniture, such industries were characterized by long hours and miserably low pay as well as poor working conditions, and were the lot of successive waves of migrants and immigrants to Bethnal Green in the nineteenth century: English, Huguenot, Irish and Jewish.

Bethnal Green and the rest of the East End was seen by outsiders as a dangerous place, in desperate need of pacification and sanitation. Its residents were portrayed as feckless, at best, and criminal,

Boundary Street Estate was built by the LCC in the 1890s to replace a notorious slum, the Old Nichol.

Bethnal Green Gardens. This remnant of the village green that gave its name to the district was transformed into a public park by the LCC in 1895.

degenerate and diseased at worst. Not surprisingly, the district became a focus of philanthropic intervention and legislative initiatives. By the early twentieth century, the district was still among London's poorest (in 1889 Charles Booth had found that almost forty-five per cent of the population lived below subsistence level), but thanks to urban philanthropic reformers, the Labour Party, the church, state education and slum clearance, it was in much better physical shape. Its residents, meanwhile, had been reconceived in the popular imagination as cheerful, salt-of-the-earth Cockneys, resilient in their hardship.

Liberal Interventions

The opening of Victoria Park in 1845 had marked the first significant attempt to bring amenity to the impoverished district. Philanthropic City merchants and bankers opened the London Chest Hospital in an old manor house in 1848, and various voluntary organizations introduced dispensaries and soup kitchens to the district in the 1850s. In the spirit of social and educational reform of the 1860s, Prince Albert directed the removal of the original buildings of the Museum of Ornamental Art in South Kensington (the institution that later became the Victoria and Albert Museum) to Cambridge Heath Road in Bethnal Green, using proceeds from the Great Exhibition. Its prefabricated iron structure was re-erected and encased in red brick. The building now houses the V&A Museum of Childhood and draws

Globe Road. This terrace of artisan housing was built in 1906 to replace weavers' cottages of the 1850s.

more than a quarter of a million visitors annually. Another beacon of Victorian cultural improvement arrived in 1884 in the form of Oxford House, which, like Toynbee Hall in Whitechapel (see page 291), was part of the settlement movement that sought to give future leaders direct experience of working-class conditions while they undertook voluntary work and engaged socially with local residents. The net effect, it was hoped, would be uplifting for all. In contrast to the progressive secular atmosphere of Toynbee Hall, Oxford House promoted a distinctly evangelical approach, with close links to the High Anglican Church.

It was housing reform, of course, that had the greatest impact on both the built environment and social conditions in Bethnal Green. Beginning in the 1860s, 'Five Per Cent' philanthropists built solid but rather grim-looking tenement housing for the deserving poor. Foremost among these philanthropists was Angela Burdett-Coutts, who had been encouraged by Charles Dickens to clear the refuse heap that had accumulated in Nova Scotia Gardens and build model tenements there. Burdett-Coutts employed Henry Darbishire as architect for Columbia Square, a scheme of four five-storey blocks. Built in Gothic Revival style in 1862, the scheme was unique in having stables for the horses and carts of costermonger tenants. Burdett-Coutts also funded a huge

Cheshire Street Baths. The first facility to be built in Bethnal Green under the 1897 Public Baths and Washhouses Act, the Cheshire Street baths and washhouse opened in 1900. They were converted into flats in 1999.

market hall, Columbia Market, intended as a place of honest and regulated commerce for the local community. Opened in 1868, it was described by Nikolaus Pevsner as 'easily the most spectacular piece of design in Bethnal Green and one of the great follies of the Victorian age'.[1] It was never a success as a marketplace and was eventually demolished in 1958. It did, however, spin off a street market that has survived to become London's most popular flower market.

Other notable philanthropic interventions included a project of four-storey tenements around Wilmot Street, opened in 1880 by Sydney Waterlow's Improved Industrial Dwellings Company, and a scheme of colossal red-brick tenements with three storeys of 'associated' flats (i.e. with shared toilets) above shops in the Globe Road area by Samuel Barnett's East End Dwellings Company. The turn of the century saw the initiative in housing reform shift to public authorities. Bethnal Green became a metropolitan borough in 1900, its civic identity signalled in 1909 with the erection of a new Town Hall. In addition to slum clearance, the council built libraries and washhouses. Meanwhile, the LCC had completed the landmark development of the Boundary Street Estate (see page 48) on the site of one of the most notorious of the district's rookeries.

Resilient East Enders

During the twentieth century, the district's built environment and population were thinned out, mainly as a result of slum-clearance schemes and the loss of most of the area's industries. The population declined from a peak of 130,000 in 1901 to less than 50,000 by the last decades of the century. The Blitz also had a significant impact on Bethnal Green: a population of around 70,000 in 1939 was reduced to only 47,000 two years later as a result of bombing and evacuation. The combination of slum clearance and bomb sites broke up long-established communities, and, pursuing the misguided optimism of radical, avant-garde architects associated with the MARS and Tecton groups, the council turned in the 1950s and 1960s

to building clusters of high-rise blocks where, it was posited, old neighbourhoods could be re-established vertically. Bethnal Green is now a chequerboard of council and housing-association projects dating from every decade since the late nineteenth century.

The social dimension of this transition was famously highlighted by Young and Wilmott in their book *Family and Kinship in East London* (1957). They portrayed Bethnal Green as having been full of close-knit family ties, mutual self-help, Cockney cheerfulness and social solidarity that was unravelling as people moved away to suburban LCC estates and exurban New Towns. It was an influential perspective among the design professions, but it was somewhat romantic and sentimental – somehow overlooking the parochialism, xeno-phobia and racism that were always to be found in the East End, along with stoicism and mutuality.

Approach Road. An exception to the residential fabric of most of the district, the 1860s terraces leading to Victoria Park were built for a middle-class market.

Meanwhile, the socio-cultural composition of the district continues to change. The most recent immigrants to Bethnal Green are Bangladeshi. It is still predominantly working class and still an area with its share of street crime and nuisance behaviour. But some of the few surviving Victorian terraces have undergone gentrification, and there is an increasing degree of cosmopolitanism to the demographic profile of the district. In the evenings the restaurants and bars in the western part of the district are increasingly frequented by the designer-clad media set who live and work in the City fringes of Hoxton, Shoreditch and Spitalfields near by. In short, the district is becoming emblematic of the diversity and socio-economic polarization that is characteristic of contemporary global cities.

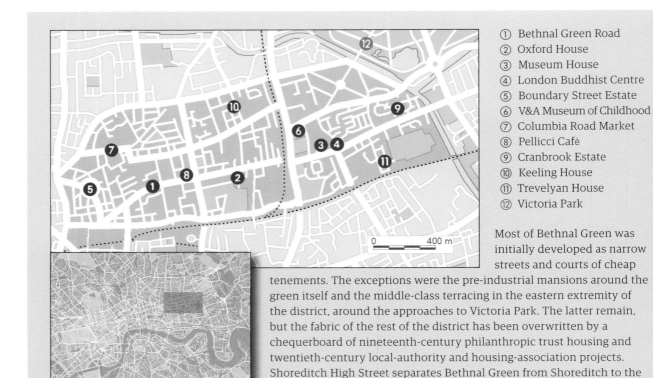

① Bethnal Green Road
② Oxford House
③ Museum House
④ London Buddhist Centre
⑤ Boundary Street Estate
⑥ V&A Museum of Childhood
⑦ Columbia Road Market
⑧ Pellicci Café
⑨ Cranbrook Estate
⑩ Keeling House
⑪ Trevelyan House
⑫ Victoria Park

Most of Bethnal Green was initially developed as narrow streets and courts of cheap tenements. The exceptions were the pre-industrial mansions around the green itself and the middle-class terracing in the eastern extremity of the district, around the approaches to Victoria Park. The latter remain, but the fabric of the rest of the district has been overwritten by a chequerboard of nineteenth-century philanthropic trust housing and twentieth-century local-authority and housing-association projects. Shoreditch High Street separates Bethnal Green from Shoreditch to the west, while it is effectively separated from Spitalfields to the south by railway lines. Hackney Road approximates to the northern boundary, while the Regent's Canal separates Bethnal Green from Bow to the east.

❶ Bethnal Green Road

Bethnal Green Road is one of the principal approach roads to London, linking the village of Bethnal Green with the eastern margin of the City. It was not built up until the early nineteenth century, when it was lined with a mixture of commercial buildings, pubs and small independent shops with accommodation above. By the late nineteenth century the surrounding residential streets had deteriorated into slums, and it was not until the second half of the twentieth century that even modest reinvestment took place.

❷ Oxford House
Derbyshire Street

Like Toynbee Hall in Whitechapel (see page 291), Oxford House was part of the settlement movement that sought to allow upper-middle-class volunteers to learn first hand about the problems of the poor while providing community service. Unlike Toynbee Hall, Oxford House was a bastion of high-minded Anglicanism, where spiritual nourishment was the principal objective. It was built in the early 1890s to a design by Arthur William Blomfield that vaguely echoed seventeenth-century manor houses. Refurbished in 2002, it is now more secular, emphasizing the arts, youth work and the needs of the local Somali community.

❸ Museum House
Burnham Street

Built in 1888 with three storeys of 'associated' flats (i.e. with shared lavatories) above shops on its Roman Road frontage, Museum House is the earliest surviving tenement building by architect Davis & Emmanuel for the East End Dwellings Company. It was built on the site of an early slum-clearance project by the Metropolitan Board of Works. Now part of the private market, two-bedroom flats in the tenement building sell for around £500,000 at the time of writing.

❹ London Buddhist Centre
Roman Road

Originally a fire station - one of many in London designed by Robert Pearsall, architect to the Metropolitan Fire Brigade - it opened in 1889 and operated as Bethnal Green's fire station until 1969. Ironically, the building was subsequently damaged by fire before being converted to its current use in 1978.

Boundary Street Estate

The Boundary Street Estate was a landmark in terms of both urban policy and urban design. It was one of the first ever local-authority housing projects, revolutionary in its provision of facilities for residents. Uncontrolled building in the eighteenth and nineteenth centuries turned what had been a rural hamlet on the fringe of London into the Old Nichol Rookery: a byword for poverty, crime and disease. The slum took its nickname from land leased from John Nichol in 1680 - originally for brickmaking but steadily developed in piecemeal fashion to accommodate workers in the silk-weaving trade early in the eighteenth century.

After a great deal of campaigning by such reformers as Edwin Chadwick, Henry Mayhew and the district's vicar, Osborne Jay, the Old Nichol was officially declared a slum under the Housing of the Working Classes Act of 1890. This allowed the LCC to announce a clearance scheme for the district on grounds of public health. It prompted fierce opposition from the district's major landlords, including Baroness Kinloss and the Ecclesiastical Commission, who claimed to support the scheme in principle but wanted their own property exempted. Another obstacle was that the LCC could not find developers who would pay the market price for the land and take on redevelopment of the cleared site. Reluctantly, the LCC decided to accept responsibility for redevelopment. Under the terms of the 1890 Act, slum landlords were paid handsomely for their property and relieved of any responsibility for rehousing tenants.

The master plan by Owen Fleming, the architect in charge, was a significant departure from the barrack-like dwellings on grid layouts that were typical of the philanthropic housing of the period. Fleming was influenced by Richard Norman Shaw's expensive mansion flats in South Kensington, and his plan envisaged a picturesque urban village, featuring a central open space laid out as an ornamental garden with seven tree-lined streets radiating from it. The central garden - allegedly the site of an old plague pit - was raised on a mound of rubble from the cleared slums, landscaped with terraced flower-beds and walks, with a playground and bandstand at the top. The fashionable Arts and Crafts style was adopted for the buildings, with decorative brick-and-tile-work and a variety of roof styles, including dormer, pitched, mansard and 'Dutch' gabling.

The estate also accommodated a live/work community, with small workshops included in the design to promote local business and employment. A new school was located in the heart of the estate, on Rochelle Street. Altogether, the Boundary Street Improvement Scheme consisted of 1069 tenements housing 4566 residents. They had the use of a central laundry with twelve baths, and most of the tenements had their own toilet facilities. The cost of improvement, combined with the LCC's constraints on subsidizing rents, meant that the new tenants were the 'quiet poor', as Charles Booth called them: cigar-makers, clerks, cabinetmakers, tailors, shoemakers, nurses and post-office sorters who could afford the rents the LCC was obliged to charge.

In the 1970s the tenements were restored and consolidated to create contemporary bedsit apartments and one-, two- and three-bedroom flats, with a reduced overall capacity of 1500 tenants. The entire estate was designated a Conservation Area under the Planning (Listed Buildings and Conservation Areas) Act of 1990, and the buildings themselves designated Grade II.

⑤ Boundary Street Estate. Sandford House, built in 1895–96 to a design by R. Minton Taylor. It is representative of the best of the LCC's redevelopment projects.

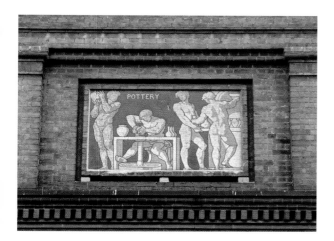

❻ V&A Museum of Childhood
Cambridge Heath Road

Originally an innovative structure using a prefabricated iron framework with corrugated-iron cladding, the museum was built in South Kensington under the supervision of William Cubitt in 1856-57 and used as temporary housing for the V&A collection of Ornamental Art. It became known as the Iron Museum (and, less respectfully, as the Brompton Boilers because of its cladding). As the V&A collection expanded, the structure was disassembled, a decade after its construction, and the iron framework moved to Bethnal Green and reclad with polished red-brick facades designed by the architect James W. Wild. The side elevations feature mosaic panels representing the arts, sciences, industry and agriculture, designed by F. W. Moody and executed by his students at the National Art Training School (now the Royal College of Art). The museum was relaunched as the Museum of Childhood in 1974.

❼ Columbia Road Market
Columbia Road

Columbia Road and the surrounding area were once the setting for all kinds of street trader. The Victorian philanthropist Angela Burdett-Coutts financed an enormous indoor market hall in an unsuccessful attempt to organize and regulate the costermongers and street traders; it was soon turned into workshops and was eventually demolished in 1958. The weekly flower market is the legacy of the area's street trading. It has been a catalyst for the gentrification of the area's surviving nineteenth-century terraces.

❽ Pellicci Café
Bethnal Green Road

Listed Grade II by English Heritage, the original café opened on this site in 1900. Its listed status is mainly a consequence of its remodelling in 1946, just as London was experiencing a fad for new cafés and espresso bars. English Heritage saw this as a continuation of a long London tradition that started with late seventeenth-century coffee houses and continued through late nineteenth-century tea rooms and 1930s milk bars. It was also a time when new materials and a new Modern sensibility began to take root among smaller commercial concerns, a reaction to the drab years of the Depression and the war. The exterior features bright yellow Vitrolite and bold steel lettering, while the interior features plastics, Formica and marquetry panelling in Art Deco styling.

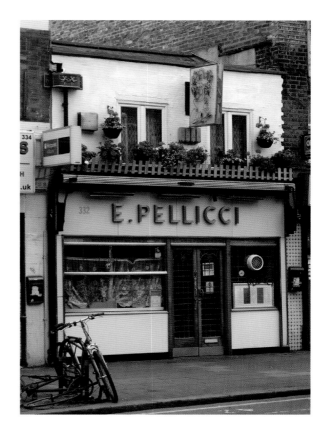

9 Cranbrook Estate
Mace Street

Cranbrook Estate is the largest of three developments by former Tecton architects Skinner, Bailey & Lubetkin for Bethnal Green Metropolitan Borough after the Second World War. Completed in 1968, the estate combines tall point blocks, paired in order of height, with four-storey slabs and, on the periphery, bungalows for seniors. One of the largest housing redevelopments of its time, the estate replaced several streets of old terraces, workshops and a factory. It was an essay in geometry, massing and perspective, set around a figure-of-eight street. The buildings are distinctive for their brick exteriors and green-and-white panelling. The estate was also an exercise in social reform, consistent with Berthold Lubetkin's belief in the redemptive attributes of rational Modernism. Now somewhat run-down, the buildings are drab, and the surrounding spaces sterile and unwelcoming.

10 Keeling House
Claredale Street

Keeling House was designed by Denys Lasdun and built in a slum clearance area in 1957–59 as social housing for the Metropolitan Borough of Bethnal Green. Lasdun's design avoided dingy corridors or long access balconies by grouping four blocks of slim towers around a central service tower. Each dwelling was a maisonette rather than a flat, intended to be similar inside to an East End terraced house. The four blocks are angled so that each flat has one side that is not overlooked, giving residents some privacy. The opposite side faces obliquely towards another block, which Lasdun hoped would engender a sense of community. Between the central lift tower and the front doors of the maisonettes were small communal areas, substitutes for the back yards of the East End terraces where the residents had lived before. In spite of these good intentions, the development suffered from social problems and was closed by the council in 1992. A few years later it was sold to a developer and converted into luxury flats with an additional penthouse storey and concierge service.

11 Trevelyan House
Morpeth Street

Also designed by Denys Lasdun, Trevelyan House was an early example of a 'cluster block' that could be slotted into a small site without disturbing the existing street pattern. The concept was well suited to postwar Bethnal Green, where the metropolitan borough had a collection of small sites on which to fit as much social housing as possible. By arranging flats in separate elements around a detached service core, Lasdun gave residents privacy, while the grouping of flats attempted to preserve the traditional neighbourliness of the district.

Victoria Park

The creation of public parks in impoverished urban areas was seen by Victorians as a means of providing a civilizing, spiritually uplifting and socially instructive setting for people. Access to a naturalistic landscape, a secluded escape from the dirt and noise of the city and a place for leisure and recreation, it was believed, would foster restraint and decorum and cultivate feelings of honesty, beauty, wholesomeness, cleanliness and natural order among the labouring classes. It was the same reactionary intellectual and aesthetic response to the industrial era that later found expression in Domestic Revival and Arts and Crafts architecture.

Victoria Park was the first and largest of London's nineteenth-century parks. It was created after an Act of Parliament in 1841, designed by James Pennethorne of the Office of Works, and opened in 1845. Pennethorne found the 117-hectare (290-acre) site, previously used for market gardens, flat and uninteresting, so he planted 40,000 trees and shrubs, created a series of lakes with waterfall islands, and installed much-admired bedding displays and several ornamental buildings, including a pagoda (acquired in 1847 from a Chinese exhibition in Knightsbridge) on an island in the main lake. Other features were added in the following decades, including a bandstand, a greenhouse, a Tudor Lodge and a Moorish arcaded shelter designed by Pennethorne. Angela Burdett-Coutts donated an extravagant drinking fountain designed by Henry Darbishire, the architect of her philanthropic housing scheme in Bethnal Green, Columbia Square (see page 44).

Victoria Park did indeed become an essential amenity for the working classes of the East End, but ironically, given the ideological roots of the park movement, it promptly became a setting for radical political speeches and rallies, gaining a reputation as the 'People's Park'. *Harper's Magazine* in February 1888 carried this description:

> On the big central lawn are scattered numerous groups, some of which are very closely packed. Almost all the religious sects of England and all the political and social parties are preaching their ideas and disputing ... On this lawn the listener, as his fancy prompts him, may assist on Malthusianism, atheism, agnosticism, secularism, Calvinism, socialism, anarchism, Salvationism, Darwinism, and even, in exceptional cases, Swedenborgianism and Mormonism.[1]

The park fell into disrepair in the twentieth century as responsibility for its maintenance was passed from one public authority to another. Much of it was dug up for allotments during the Second World War, and its structures suffered bomb damage. In the 1980s it was one of the first public parks to benefit from government funding to encourage the revival of interest in public open spaces. New railings, lamp standards and entrance gates were provided, along with a new café by the main lake. In recent years the park has become a major element in strategic planning for a more extensive green landscape. A new park, Mile End Park, finally opened to the south in 2002; the Olympic Park is just under 1 kilometre (½ mile) to the east; beyond it to the north are Hackney Marsh and the Lea Valley Regional Park.

⑫ **Victoria Park**. Pavilion café on the lake.

Bloomsbury + Fitzrovia

On the threshold of urban development in the late seventeenth century, Bloomsbury and Fitzrovia had two principal landowners: the Bedford Estate and the Southampton Estate. By far the largest of all the landholdings were those of the Duke of Bedford, who also owned two other estates in the city: Covent Garden and Figs Mead (see page 73). Irregular clusters of houses had begun to appear on the estate early in the seventeenth century, but it was not until the 1660s that a formal building plan was developed for the property. The central feature of the plan was an imposing mansion, Southampton House (later renamed Bedford House), on the north side of what came to be called Bloomsbury Square.

A century later, Francis Russell, the fifth Duke of Bedford, who had done very well with speculative developments in Covent Garden, joined forces with one of the most successful developers of the eighteenth century, James Burton. The centrepiece of their project was Bedford Square and the adjacent Montagu House (which later came to house the British Museum). The surrounding neighbourhood of big town houses was designed to appeal to the self-consciously respectable upper-middle classes. To defend the neighbourhood's snooty exclusivity, the dukes of Bedford maintained six bar gates with uniformed gatekeepers at the entrances to the estate.

This lasted until the LCC sponsored the London Streets (Removal of Gates) Act of 1890, whereupon the district began to slide down the social scale. Nevertheless, property values (and the social status of residents) remained relatively high, thanks to the dukes' insistence on keeping almost all of their estate free from shops and pubs, and their refusal to sell off land to the railway companies. The latter were consequently able to penetrate only as far into the city as Euston Road, the northern boundary of the Bedford Estate.

Meanwhile, other landowners had been busy. On the northern part of present-day Fitzrovia, the Southampton Estate had been developed by Charles Fitzroy (the first Baron Southampton), with Fitzroy Square as its centrepiece. Four of the fields to the east of the Bedford Estate owned by the Thomas Coram Foundation had been developed as the Foundling Estate. The property had originally been purchased as a site for the Foundling Hospital in 1741 (see page 54), but was large enough to allow ground rent from property development to provide a regular income for the hospital. The central portion of the estate was given over to two imposing squares - Brunswick and Mecklenburgh - in order to attract upper-middle-class households, while the northern and southern parts of the estate were set aside for cheaper houses, to be erected piecemeal by small builders. The Skinners' Company Estate (to the northeast of the Bedford Estate, around the present Cartwright Gardens) was not developed until the early nineteenth century, and was built out in fragmented pieces, like much of southern and northeastern Bloomsbury and southern Fitzrovia.

Speculative master builders were central to the plans of these major landowners. The two principal figures were Burton and Thomas Cubitt. Burton began his career as a speculative builder in Southwark and went on to build Georgian-style residences for middle- and upper-middle-class households not only for the Bedford Estate but also on the Foundling Estate, the Skinners' Company Estate and the Southampton Estate. Cubitt, who built Tavistock Square, Gordon Square and the surrounding streets into a fashionable residential area for the dukes of Bedford, was the first contractor to employ all his builders and craftsmen directly and to have a central builders' yard. The work of the two men established

Bedford Square. Laid out in the 1770s and completed in the 1780s, it is the best-preserved of all London's squares.

Senate House. The administrative centre of the University of London, designed in Art Deco style by Charles Holden and built in the 1930s.

the initial social geography of the district. Restrictive covenants were designed to sustain the pattern, but the removal of the bar gates around the Bedford Estate, coupled with the steady westward march of fashion, meant that many of the best families moved away, while houses in less expensive streets increasingly became divided and sublet to the likes of chandlers, boot repairers, signwriters, shopkeepers and clerks.

Worthy and Enlightened Institutions

By the mid-nineteenth century Bloomsbury and Fitzrovia were the addresses no longer of the élite but of a mixture of other classes, reflecting the transitions of an industrializing society and an imperial capital. The area also became the preferred location for progressive institutions that have shaped its character ever since. In Fitzrovia, the Middlesex Infirmary (later to become the Middlesex Hospital) opened in 1745 on Windmill Street to meet the needs of the sick and the lame of Soho and St Giles. The same mission was taken up by the Bloomsbury Dispensary for the Relief of the Sick Poor, which opened in 1801

University College Hospital. The original buildings were built between 1897 and 1906. The new £422 million, 75,822-square-metre (816,140-square-foot) hospital building, behind, was opened in 2005.

on Great Russell Street. Edward Jenner, the pioneer of smallpox vaccine, served on the Dispensary's medical committee and administered free vaccinations there. Meanwhile, the Foundling Hospital had been established (in 1741) by Thomas Coram's charitable foundation, to cater for the 'Maintenance and Education of Exposed and Deserted Children'.

The two most influential institutions in the district, however, have been the British Museum and University College London (UCL). The museum had been housed in Montagu House and open to the public from 1759. By the mid-nineteenth century the collection, swollen by Britain's imperial reach, was accommodated in a huge new neoclassical building on the site of Montagu House and its grounds. Serial expansion and renovation have allowed the museum to become a globally ranked tourist destination and have forced Bloomsbury to become a popular hotel district.

The idea behind UCL, founded in 1826, was that, unlike at Oxford or Cambridge, neither teachers nor students were to be required to declare Anglican faith. The university, located just south of Euston Road, grew steadily southwards towards the Museum, gradually replacing the Georgian fabric with world-class educational institutions, including Birkbeck College, the Royal Academy of Dramatic Art, the School of Oriental and African Studies, and the School of Hygiene and Tropical Medicine.

Bloomsbury and Fitzrovia also attracted more than their share of the philanthropic hospitals and dispensaries that sprang up in Victorian London. These included the Royal Free Hospital (1837), the Royal London Homeopathic Hospital (1849), the Hospital for Sick Children (1852), the National Hospital for the Paralysed and Epileptic (1860, now the National Hospital for Neurology and Neurosurgery), the Alexandra Hospital for Children with Hip Disease (1867) and the Italian Hospital (1884), the last founded for Italian immigrants. In 1896 UCL established England's first legitimate medical school and teaching hospital.

Together, these medical institutions and their successors have had a strong and lasting impact on the district. Along with the progressive atmosphere fostered by UCL, the British Museum and the Foundling Hospital, they attracted other worthy and reformist institutions, including the Ladies College (now part of Royal Holloway College), the Society for the Diffusion of Useful Knowledge, the Marie Stopes 'Mothers' Clinic for Constructive Birth Control' and the Passmore Edwards Settlement (now Mary Ward House), which provided facilities and activities for the 'deserving poor'.

Radical Intellectualism

In addition to all this enlightenment and worthiness, Bloomsbury and Fitzrovia acquired a neo-bohemian and anti-establishment character. Radicals, intellectuals and immigrant anarchist dissidents roomed in the ageing and subdivided housing stock in the south of the district and kept warm in winter in the Reading Room of the British Museum. At the other end of the social spectrum were the members of the so-called Bloomsbury Group, a mixture of writers, artists and thinkers formed around a group of Cambridge University friends in the early years of the twentieth century.

At the core of the group were the novelists Virginia Woolf and E. M. Forster, the biographer Lytton Strachey, the economist John Maynard Keynes, the art critics Roger Fry and Clive Bell, the civil servant Saxon Sydney-Turner, and Walter Lamb, long-serving Secretary of the Royal Academy. Their Thursday and Friday evening 'at homes' developed into outspoken opposition to the religious and moral standards of orthodox society. Their deliberate upper-middle-class rebelliousness, their progressive attitudes towards pacifism and feminism, and their predilection for transgressing sexual boundaries earned them a great deal of notoriety. In retrospect, they have been credited by some with fostering a modern sensibility that was symptomatic of or even catalytic to the transition from high Victorianism to Modernism. They might equally be portrayed, though, as a bunch of smug idealists whose private incomes and social status insulated them from the reality of life in London.

Contemporary with the Bloomsbury Group was the city's first artists' collective, the Fitzroy Street Group (which included Walter Sickert, Spencer Gore, William Coldstream and Augustus John), formed to explore contemporary styles and methods and to challenge the mainstream traditions of Victorian art. After the First World War, many more artists and writers were drawn to the district, not only for its progressive atmosphere but also for the relatively low rents for large, sublet rooms. The Fitzroy Tavern, on Charlotte Street, became famous as a favourite of the neo-bohemian set from the 1920s until the 1950s.

Two Tiers

Bloomsbury and Fitzrovia still have a reputation for literary and intellectual life. They also continue to possess some of London's finest Georgian architecture. The legacy of the Great Estates and the speculative developers of the eighteenth and nineteenth centuries is still an important part of their character, and the most attractive streets and squares have been conserved, preserved and gentrified. However, about fifteen per cent of the housing was destroyed during the Second World War, and the subsequent redevelopment of the bomb sites was uneven in quality and function. Many of the second-rate Georgian terraces have been replaced by uninspiring multi-storey office blocks or student residence halls, while the northern edge of Bloomsbury, close to the busy Euston Road and the railway termini on its northern side, has lapsed into a scruffy mix of launderettes, burger bars, mini-markets, computer-repair shops and pubs.

The net result is a two-tier, two-speed district. The middle-class – and, still, some upper-middle-class – residents in the remaining terraces and squares convey an affect of permanence and regularity. In contrast, there is a strong overlay of transience as a result not only of the daily influx of tourists to the British Museum but also of the ebb and flow of guests in the district's hotels, hospital patients and their visitors, the seasonal hospitality-industry workers, and the temporary student population.

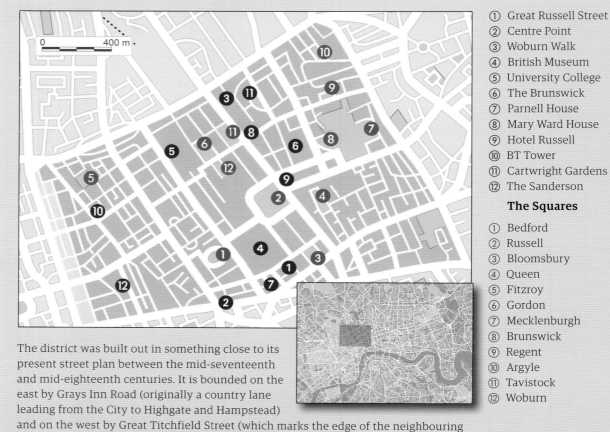

① Great Russell Street
② Centre Point
③ Woburn Walk
④ British Museum
⑤ University College
⑥ The Brunswick
⑦ Parnell House
⑧ Mary Ward House
⑨ Hotel Russell
⑩ BT Tower
⑪ Cartwright Gardens
⑫ The Sanderson

The Squares

① Bedford
② Russell
③ Bloomsbury
④ Queen
⑤ Fitzroy
⑥ Gordon
⑦ Mecklenburgh
⑧ Brunswick
⑨ Regent
⑩ Argyle
⑪ Tavistock
⑫ Woburn

The district was built out in something close to its present street plan between the mid-seventeenth and mid-eighteenth centuries. It is bounded on the east by Grays Inn Road (originally a country lane leading from the City to Highgate and Hampstead) and on the west by Great Titchfield Street (which marks the edge of the neighbouring Portland Estate). At the southern edge of the district is New Oxford Street, which was carved through the slums of the St Giles Rookeries in the 1840s to connect Oxford Street and High Holborn. The northern edge of the district is much more pronounced: Euston Road, a broad and extremely busy thoroughfare that separates the Great Estates from the mainline railway stations and working-class districts to the north. It was built in the 1750s as a link between Paddington and the City and was known as the New Road until 1857. Tottenham Court Road, running northwest-southeast between Euston Road and New Oxford Street, marks the conventional division between Bloomsbury and Fitzrovia.

❶ Great Russell Street

Part of a terrace dating from the late 1770s, this was the first work of the architect John Nash and one of the earliest examples of stuccoed houses in London. When Francis Russell, the fifth Duke of Bedford, embarked on the development of his estate to the north of the street, it was quickly transformed from one of London's old country lanes. In the 1840s the corner house of this terrace accommodated the founding London office of the Thomas Cook travel company.

❷ Centre Point
New Oxford Street

When it was completed in 1966, the thirty-five-storey Centre Point was the tallest building in London. Located at the major traffic intersection of New Oxford Street and Tottenham Court Road, and with its striking facade created by hundreds of pre-cast concrete units, the tower had immediate symbolic importance. It had been designed for the property tycoon Harry Hyams by Richard Seifert & Partners in collaboration with LCC planners, who endorsed the speculative development as part of their urban-design strategy for the West End. But Hyams kept the building deliberately unlet for years: with the rapid escalation of rents in 1960s London, its value quadrupled in just ten years. Not surprisingly, Centre Point became a symbol of both greedy capitalism and the ineptitude of planners. The ground level of the building itself became a haunt of vagrants and drug users. This prompted the launch of a charity, called Centrepoint, for homeless young people. Because the charity was widely believed to occupy part of the tower, homeless children were drawn to it, and from there were assisted by the charity. Meanwhile the building itself was eventually leased. Having been refurbished under new ownership, it is now somewhat redeemed in terms of its architectural reputation. It was listed Grade II ('nationally important and of special interest') by English Heritage in 1995. The terrace in the middle ground of the photograph - eighteenth-century houses on Museum Street, refaced in 1855–64 by William Finch Hill - is also listed Grade II.

❸ Woburn Walk

Woburn Walk is a relic of the social segregation imposed by the Bedford Estate in the early nineteenth century. The upper-middle-class residents of the area needed shops, but in order to preserve the exclusivity of the development, shopkeepers were relegated to the fringe of the estate. The result was an early example of a planned shopping precinct, built by Thomas Cubitt in 1822. By the late nineteenth century, the street had become popular with the Anglo-Irish literary set - W. B. Yeats lived there from 1895 until 1919. By the 1950s the street was badly in need of renovation, which was eventually undertaken by St Pancras Borough Council. The bow-fronted shops are original, but they are now mainly occupied by cafés and galleries.

The Squares

The geometric street plans of Bloomsbury and Fitzrovia's Great Estates are organized around squares with central gardens of trees, lawns and bedding. The district's surviving squares are Argyle, Bedford, Bloomsbury, Brunswick, Fitzroy, Gordon, Mecklenburgh, Queen, Regent, Russell, Tavistock and Woburn squares. This distinctive form of urban design brought nature into the city and softened the harshness of Georgian brick, cobblestone, slate, cast iron and masonry. The layout of the squares was exclusionary: most were, until the late eighteenth century, gated enclaves designed to convey an inner order, sequestered from noise, dirt and - most importantly - the social inferiors of the residents. The gardens of Bedford, Mecklenburgh and Fitzroy squares remain closed to the public (only householders around these squares have access to them), but the rest are now accessible, beautifully maintained by Camden Council.

Most of the district's squares are more or less intact, although they have inevitably changed somewhat in both appearance and function. The speculative nineteenth-century housing around Argyle Square, for example, was badly damaged in the Second World War, leaving big gaps that were filled in with council housing and chain hotels. A combination of gentrification and historic preservation, however, has safeguarded the best of the district's squares.

Bloomsbury Square was the first to be laid out. Thomas Wriothesley, the fourth Earl of Southampton, established the square in the 1660s, with his mansion, Southampton House, occupying the north side. He pioneered the idea that development should be like a 'little towne', with a market and cheaper houses in side streets. His market was in a street just south of the square, now known as Barter Street. Southampton House was replaced by late Georgian terraces in the 1880s, and the rest of the square has also been completely redeveloped, although there are survivors from the 1660s hidden behind 1860s stucco on the western side of the square.

Easily the best preserved of all the squares is Bedford Square, built in 1775–86 for Francis

2 **Russell Square.** In 2002, almost 200 years after its construction, Russell Square gardens were given a facelift, restoring the original landscaping by Humphry Repton.

1 **Bedford Square** (west side). London's most important and complete example of eighteenth-century town planning.

Russell, the fifth Duke of Bedford, on a site known as 'St Giles ruins', where a slum known as the Rookery had stood. Each side of the square was designed to be a coherent and dignified whole, with a grand five-bay stuccoed house in the centre of each terrace to suggest a great country house. Strict conditions were imposed on the builders: facings, balustrades and windowsills had to be of Portland stone, roofs of slate, gutters and pipes of lead, and the pavements of York stone. Door cases had to be of Coade stone.

It was intended to attract the aristocracy, but in the end many of the square's first inhabitants were lawyers, drawn by its proximity to the Inns of Court. During the nineteenth century the homes were favoured by doctors and architects as well as lawyers. Today the square is occupied almost entirely by the offices of publishers, accountants, literary agencies and the like, with a big chunk of the west side occupied by the Architectural Association.

In 1800 the Russells built the biggest square in London and named it after themselves. The northern end of the Bedford Estate was laid out soon afterwards around Gordon Square and Tavistock Square, with much of the housing put up by the great commercial builder Thomas Cubitt. Over to the west, Fitzroy Square, which was begun in the 1790s to designs by Robert Adam, was completed in 1835.

❸ Bloomsbury Square (west side). The square now stands above a seven-storey underground car park, and the surrounding buildings are occupied by offices and university departments.

❹ Queen Square. Laid out in 1716–29, it is now dwarfed by the hospitals on its eastern side.

❺ Fitzroy Square (west side). Now a pedestrian precinct, the square is regarded by some as London's finest.

❹ British Museum
Great Russell Street

An Act of Parliament in 1753 brought together several significant collections that were henceforth to be housed in Montagu House on the Bedford Estate. Beginning in 1757 the antiquities were at first shown grudgingly, by appointment only, to exclusive parties of not more than ten people. Over the next century the museum acquired the libraries of George II and George III, a collection of Greek vases, the Rosetta Stone, the Elgin marbles and Egyptian mummies. Montagu House, having been outgrown, was replaced in the 1820s by a new building designed by Robert Smirke in Greek Revival style. The Great Court of the museum was remodelled in 2000 to a design by Norman Foster after the museum's library had been moved to a new site on Euston Road.

❺ University College London
Gower Street

The UCL Main Building was designed by William Wilkins, who also designed the National Gallery. The site had been intended for development as a residential square, but was purchased for the university in 1824. The building, in loose Greek Revival style (the capitals of the ten columns fronting the portico are Corinthian, while the simple triangular pediment is entirely Greek), was completed in 1829. Along with subsequent additions and extensions, it was restored in 1954 after heavy war damage. UCL was initially derided as a 'Cockney College', 'the Godless Place in Gower Street', but it is now acknowledged as having been a formative institution in the modernization of the United Kingdom's educational system and its intellectual heritage.

❻ The Brunswick
Marchmont Street

The Brunswick is a pioneering example of low-rise, high-density housing, an unlikely megastructure amid Bloomsbury's terraces and squares. A combination of neglect and bomb damage on the western side of Brunswick Square created the opportunity for something new at a time – the mid-1960s – when Modern architecture and planning were at the peak of their redemptive ambitions. The outworn and war-damaged Georgian terraces were in such poor shape that they had been condemned by Camden Council as unfit for human habitation. Camden's planners saw the proposal by the architect Patrick Hodgkinson as a chance to create a new experiment in urban living. By deliberately flouting the prevailing zoning regulations, the scheme was able to achieve a housing density of 500 people per hectare within Bloomsbury's 24-metre (79-foot) height limit while also including retailing and public open space. But the developers ran out of money (partly because they had not budgeted to pay compensation to the tenants of the houses that had to be demolished), and the project was taken over by Camden Council. Adjusted to meet the council's budget and priorities, the scheme was finally completed in 1972, consisting of two five-storey A-frame blocks of flats and maisonettes linked by an internal precinct with rows of shops at raised ground level, all set above two levels of underground car parking.

In spite of Camden's corner-cutting on Hodgkinson's design, the Brunswick was widely acclaimed as well as reasonably popular with residents. It initially provided an edgy, futuristic backdrop for urban television dramas and films, but failure to carry out maintenance for thirty-five years left the Brunswick with a neglected, decayed and desolate appearance. It was not until 2006 that the site's new owner, Allied London Properties, undertook a £25 million makeover, repaving the precinct and terraces with white Chinese granite, painting all the exterior facades and replacing the old shops and supermarket with boutiques, coffee shops, restaurants and an up-market supermarket.

❼ Parnell House
Streatham Street

A plaque embossed on the facade states 'Model Homes for Families'. Built in 1849 by the Society for Improving the Condition of the Labouring Classes, Parnell House provided accommodation for the 'deserving poor' in regular employment. It was subsequently taken over by the Peabody Trust, one of London's largest providers of charitable housing. It is the earliest surviving block of philanthropic flats in London. But it has become gentrified, ironically as a result of government legislation aimed at ensuring a minimum standard for social housing (the 'Decent Homes Standard', administered by the Department for Communities and Local Government). The Peabody Trust was obliged to put Parnell House properties on the market, along with hundreds of others, in order to raise the funds needed to renovate other properties to standard. Peabody and its tenants could only watch as estate agents pounced and then 'flipped' the flats to private buyers.

❽ Mary Ward House
Tavistock Place

Mary Ward House is an example of the Settlement Movement that was popular among upper-middle-class reformers between 1880 and 1920. The idea was to get the poor to learn from their social superiors by locating 'settlement houses' in low-income neighbourhoods, in which middle-class volunteers would live. Working at their usual occupations by day, their spare time would be spent among local residents, who were encouraged to join the settlement and use its facilities as a sort of social club. In short, middle-class individuals would be able to demonstrate their comportment and spread their values by way of daily interaction with local residents.

The Mary Ward Settlement was founded by Mrs Humphrey Ward, who had secured funding for the project from the newspaper owner and philanthropist J. Passmore Edwards. Built in 1898, it was designed by Arnold Smith and Cecil Brewer and is now considered to be one of the better Arts and Crafts buildings in London. It currently houses a conference and exhibition centre for the National Institute for Social Work.

❾ Hotel Russell
Russell Square

The eastern side of Russell Square was developed between 1800 and 1817 by James Burton for the fifth Duke of Bedford. Among the buildings to be demolished to make way for the set piece of the emergent Russell Square was Baltimore House, built in 1759 for the seventh Lord Baltimore. Burton's residential buildings on the square were occupied by, among others, the suffragette Emmeline Pankhurst, a youthful Edgar Allan Poe and F. D. Maurice, the founder of Christian Socialism. These homes were in turn demolished around the end of the nineteenth century to build two extravagant *fin-de-siècle* hotels. The Hotel Russell was one of these, designed by Charles Fitzroy Doll, surveyor of the Bedford Estate, in a style that seems to evade consistent description by architectural historians. Variously described as Franco-Flemish Gothic, French chateau and Arts and Crafts Italianate, it is an outrageous seven-storey confection in red brick and terracotta.

⑩ BT Tower
Cleveland Street

At the time of its completion in 1965, the tower - then known as the Post Office Tower - was the tallest building in London, at 189 m (620 ft). It had been designed by Eric Bedford, Chief Architect of the Ministry of Works. The main function of the tower was to support the ultra-high-frequency microwave aerials then used to carry telecommunications traffic from London to the rest of the country, but there were also viewing galleries, a souvenir shop and a rotating restaurant. The tower instantly became an iconic landmark of 'swinging London' of the 1960s. Incredibly, despite being the most conspicuous building in London, Cold War protocol meant that it was classed as an 'official secret' and omitted from all Ordnance Survey maps until the mid-1990s. Until then, taking or possessing photos of the tower had technically been an offence under the Official Secrets Act.

The tower was closed to the public in 1980, but it still serves as an important telecommunications centre, relaying broadcast, internet and telephone communications around the world. The rotating restaurant is now used only for private functions. Obsolescent antennae have been removed from the top of the tower, and a 360-degree full-colour LED-based display system has been installed, which has helped to give the tower a more contemporary aspect. Berners Mews, in the foreground of this photograph, along with much of the area to the south of the tower, was badly damaged in the Second World War, and much of the commercial and residential stock was replaced with mediocre buildings. More recently, an influx of media, advertising and architectural firms has prompted a new wave of reinvestment and redevelopment.

⑪ Cartwright Gardens

Underscoring Bloomsbury's reputation for progressivism, this Georgian crescent is named after Major John Cartwright, an important figure in the history of English radicalism. He lived here in the 1820s for a few years, having spent the previous fifty years campaigning for universal suffrage, annual parliaments, secret ballots and uniform electoral districts. He was widely referred to as the Father of Reform, and his statue stands in the gardens that front the crescent. Until 1831 the crescent was known as Burton Crescent, after the architect James Burton, one of the key developers of Georgian Bloomsbury. Burton's critics accused him of being little more than a pattern-book builder, turning out uniform brick-and-stucco terraces one after another. He built this crescent in 1809-20 as the centrepiece of the Skinners' Company Estate.

⑫ The Sanderson
Berners Street

One of London's better examples of the International Style, this building was completed in 1960 as a headquarters and showroom for the Sanderson wallpaper company. In a part of Fitzrovia that was badly damaged in the Second World War, it is one of the few postwar structures in the area that did not suffer at the hands of developers. Designed by the architectural firm of Slater and Uren, the building was advanced for its time, allowing reconfiguration of the floor plan. In 2000 Sanderson moved its headquarters to Denham, Buckinghamshire, and the building was purchased by the Morgans Hotel Group. Renovated to designs by Philippe Starck, it is now a five-star fashion hotel. Its presence has contributed to the commercial gentrification of the area, which has seen an influx of media, advertising and architectural businesses.

Borough + Southwark

One of London's less glamorous districts, Borough and Southwark has nevertheless been central to the overall development of the metropolis. As the immediate hinterland of the Bankside area, it has served mainly as an industrial and working-class residential district, with alternating periods of expansion and contraction, prosperity and impoverishment that have followed the overall trajectory of the British economy.

Crime and Punishment

Between the twelfth and seventeenth centuries, the northern part of the district was part of the Liberties of the Clink and the Mint - hangovers from ecclesiastical sanctuaries established in the Middle Ages and, therefore, beyond the authority of both the Crown and the Sheriff of the City of London. In 1161 the Bishop of Winchester, who maintained a palace in Bankside, was granted the power to licence brothels in the Liberty of the Clink. As a result, both the Clink and the Mint became notorious for bawdiness and petty crime as well as prostitution.

In his *Survey of London* (1598), the historian John Stow referred to a burial ground for 'single women' - a euphemism for the prostitutes who worked in the district's brothels or 'stews'. On rusty railings fronting a small parcel of wasteland on Redcross Way is a bronze plaque bearing the epitaph 'R.I.P. The Outcast Dead.' The land has been used by Transport for London as a storage yard; beneath it are the bodies of more than 15,000 prostitutes and paupers. The railings have become a people's shrine, a communal project of ribbons, flowers, notes and cheap jewellery that is constantly renewed.

The historic heart of the district was Borough High Street, which led directly to London Bridge and the City. For centuries it was lined with inns and alehouses for the use of travellers between London and the coast. Talbot Yard, just off the High Street, was the home until the mid-1870s of the Tabard Inn, where Chaucer's fourteenth-century pilgrims gathered and entertained one another with stories on the road to Canterbury. Most of the inns and alehouses, though, developed a reputation as convenient settings not only for drinking but also for gambling, prostitution and the fencing of stolen goods. Early tenements were built around the inn yards, and Borough High Street gradually became surrounded by a fringe of narrow courts and alleys. To the east of the High Street, just beyond the Liberty of the Mint, were two notorious prisons, the King's Bench and the Marshalsea, both dating back to the fourteenth century. Both had become debtors' prisons by the eighteenth century, by which time the immediate area had also acquired a local gaol and a 'house of correction' for penitent prostitutes.

Industrial Suburb

It was not all crime and punishment, however. The introduction of hop-growing in Kent in the fifteenth century stimulated the brewing industry in Southwark, while an influx of migrants from the Low Countries and Germany brought not only accomplished brewmasters but also skilled manufacturers of tin-glazed blue-and-white imitations of Delft and Ming porcelain. The district also housed significant numbers of tailors, seamstresses, leatherworkers and cobblers, and by the seventeenth century had gained a reputation for glassmaking, printing and the manufacture of such precision items as spectacles and watches.

Until the second half of the eighteenth century the ground beyond the vicinity of the High Street and the Liberties - St George's Fields - lay open and too swampy for development. The opening of Blackfriars

The Shard, with the Tower Wing of Guy's Hospital to the left and part of the Tyers Estate in the foreground.

West Square. Built on the newly drained St George's Fields in 1791.

Bridge in 1769 and the development of its main approach road, now Blackfriars Road, stimulated the construction of several coaching roads across the southern part of the district, linking the City and Westminster with the south and southeast of England. At the junction of roads coming from Westminster Bridge, Blackfriars Bridge and London Bridge (and, later, Lambeth Bridge) was an inn, the Elephant and Castle, on the site of a former smithy. The awkward junction quickly became a dysfunctional bottleneck that has persisted through several iterations of transport technology and transportation planning.

The construction of the new bridges and coach roads gave a tremendous boost to the expansion of London's southern suburbs. St George's Fields were soon drained and developed, much of it laid out by the architect Robert Mylne, who had designed Blackfriars Bridge. St George's Circus and its surrounding streets were laid out in 1769-71; Union Street was laid out in 1774-81 in connection with the erection of a new workhouse there; West Square and its adjacent streets from 1791; and Nelson Square in 1807-14. In spite of Mylne's layout, which was clearly influenced by contemporary Parisian neoclassicism, the quality of the houses was generally so poor that only households of very modest means could be persuaded to live in them.

Hardship

By the mid-nineteenth century the poverty, crowding, crime and disease of the Clink, the Mint and Borough High Street had spread to the rest of Southwark. The district's own Medical Officer of Health, William Rendle, characterized the area in 1856 as 'low level and low in circumstances', a social sump of the metropolis:

The lowest and poorest of the human race drop from higher and richer parishes into our courts and alleys and the liquid filth of higher places necessarily finds its way down to us. We receive the refuse as well as the outcomings of more happily situated places.[1]

This was the squalid world with which Charles Dickens had terrified his Victorian readers. For a few months, Dickens had lodged a couple of streets away from the Marshalsea while his father was imprisoned there. His memories of the experience were echoed in *David Copperfield* (1850), and he described the alehouses and inns of the High Street in *Pickwick Papers* (1836-37). Dickens, in turn, has been recognized in the built environment of the district. A London Board School dating from 1877 has been named after him, along with several streets bearing the names of his characters: Copperfield Street, Pickwick Street, Weller Street and Little Dorrit Court.

Not surprisingly, little else of the built fabric of the previous century was to last. The arrival of the railway saw the demise of the old coaching inns. Old slums were demolished but replaced only by newer tenements for the poor and near-poor who found work in the district's leather trades, brewing, printing, broom-making and tin-can manufacturing.

This part of south London played an important part in the awakening of the Victorian conscience to the problem of poor housing and the desirability of council and philanthropic housing to replace

Peabody Square, Blackfriars Road. Built in the early 1870s and designed for the Peabody Estate by Henry Darbishire.

demolished slums. One especially influential pamphlet, *The Bitter Cry of Outcast London: An Enquiry into the Condition of the Abject Poor* (1883) by Andrew Mearns, was based on fieldwork in the neighbourhood of the Marshalsea. Southwark itself already had the Magdalen Hospital, England's first reformatory for penitent prostitutes (moved there from Whitechapel in 1772), along with the Philanthropic Society for child criminals and the 'offspring of convicted felons' and a School for the Indigent Blind. In the 1880s the social reformer Octavia Hill was employed by the Church Commissioners to manage their extensive property portfolio in Southwark. She established a community hall and two rows of picturesque half-timbered terraces, Redcross Cottages and Whitecross Cottages, together with Redcross Gardens as an 'open air sitting room for the tired inhabitants of Southwark'. Near by are the Cromwell Buildings, a surviving five-storey tenement block built by the Improved Industrial Dwellings Corporation.

Other philanthropic housing organizations also targeted Southwark, and the Metropolitan Board of Works initiated a programme of slum clearance around the site of the Marshalsea Prison. Nevertheless, the district remained desperately impoverished: *terra incognita* for Victorian middle- and upper-classes. Charles Booth's survey in the 1890s recorded just how bad things were. Between Borough High Street and Blackfriars Road were 'a number of courts and small streets which for vice, poverty and crowding, are unrivalled in London as an aggregate area of low life form perhaps the most serious blot to be reformed on the whole of our map'.[2]

Resilient Communities

The worst of the slums were gradually replaced by local-authority housing during the twentieth century. Much of that is now managed by housing associations and trusts. Further inroads to the older fabric of Borough and Southwark were made by the Luftwaffe during the Second World War. After the war a feature of planning and rebuilding was the reconstruction of the Elephant and Castle junction in an attempt to address the increasing congestion of automotive traffic. In terms of transportation engineering, it was only moderately successful; in terms of

aesthetics, it was drab and uninspiring. A great deal of social housing was added, a mixture of walk-up deck-access blocks and 1960s tower blocks, also unexceptional in terms of design.

The social fabric of the district was more resilient. The closely defined neighbourhoods were settings for highly localized communities organized around local shops and markets and the interlocking support networks of families. The district's surviving pubs were crucial as 'third places' (outside home and the workplace) for socializing. They also functioned as a basis for sports teams, outings, whip-rounds and illegal betting, as well as being places where casual workers could be hired.

The regeneration of the adjacent Bankside area and the office development around the Shard and London Bridge station have introduced a certain amount of speculative development to the district. The forty-three-storey Strata tower, opened in 2010 just south of the Elephant and Castle junction, is a landmark that is especially striking as a result of the three wind turbines at the top of the building – an ungainly element that was intended to signal its sustainability credentials but that in practice produces very little power. Inevitably, regeneration and speculative development have also prompted the first sproutings of gentrification. Between the district's industrial buildings and its social housing stock there are in fact relatively few opportunities for 'pioneer' gentrifiers. Rather, it is new-build gentrification and speculative housing for students that have begun to shift the socio-demographic profile of the district.

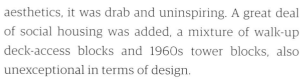

The Morocco Store, a converted Victorian spice warehouse with an adjoining new building, now contains twelve flats.

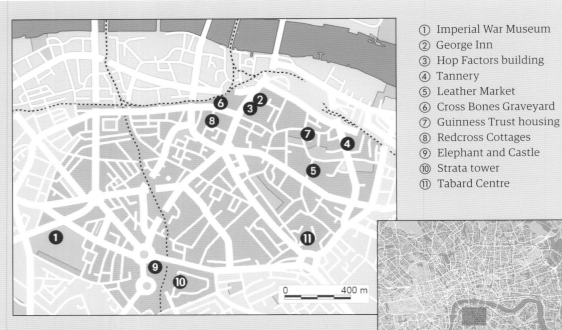

① Imperial War Museum
② George Inn
③ Hop Factors building
④ Tannery
⑤ Leather Market
⑥ Cross Bones Graveyard
⑦ Guinness Trust housing
⑧ Redcross Cottages
⑨ Elephant and Castle
⑩ Strata tower
⑪ Tabard Centre

Two major landmarks - the Shard and the Elephant and Castle - anchor the northeastern and southwestern corners respectively of the district, but it is roads and railways that dominate its morphology. It is bounded to the north by the tracks and viaducts that run parallel to the Thames, while to the south the New Kent Road and the Bricklayers Arms flyover effectively separate it from Walworth. The western boundary follows Southwark's municipal boundary, while to the east Tower Bridge Road marks the approximate division between Borough and Bermondsey.

❶ Imperial War Museum
Lambeth Road

The Imperial War Museum building, formerly the Bethlem Hospital for the Insane (known colloquially as 'Bedlam'), opened in 1815 and was enlarged to designs by Sydney Smirke in 1835. The hospital moved to Beckenham in 1930, and the buildings were occupied by the museum in 1936.

❷ George Inn
Borough High Street

This image shows the surviving gallery of the seventeenth-century inn, one of a string of coaching inns along Borough High Street. Each inn was the starting point for a different destination: services from the George went to Canterbury, Dover, Brighton and Hastings.

③ Hop Factors building

Borough High Street

The hop trade was a significant part of Southwark's economy until the early 1970s. The district's two great breweries were both called the Anchor Brewery. Their hops came from Kent and were traded by hop factors, who acted on behalf of the growers. The LeMay hop factor building was one of several where samples from growers were inspected by merchants acting on behalf of the breweries. The grand Hop Exchange on Southwark Street (inset) was built speculatively as a unified trading floor. But the hop factors and hop merchants all had their own premises, and did not need an exchange. Consequently, the building was divided up for general office use.

④ Tannery

55 Bermondsey Street

With noxious industries banned by the City authorities, Southwark became the logical location for them: just across from the City and with the Thames a convenient means of disposing of unpleasant byproducts. By 1700 Southwark had become the centre of the leather tanning trade and also had a concentration of brewing, pottery, glassmaking and hat-making activities. The building shown here was part of a complex built for the Tempo leather company in the nineteenth century - a group of industrial buildings with internal courtyards, now converted into luxury flats and offices for Bermondsey Street's growing cluster of creative and lifestyle industries.

⑤ Leather Market

Weston Street

By the beginning of the nineteenth century, a third of all the processed leather in the country came from Borough and Southwark. The London Leather, Hide and Wool Exchange was established in the 1830s to facilitate these trades. Within a few decades the Exchange had outgrown its original buildings, and these new ones were opened on the old site in 1879. The complex included slaughterhouses and animal pens as well as processing facilities and the market exchange. All leather work generated foul smells: key ingredients for the alum used in tanning included urine and dogs' faeces. The trade began to decline in the twentieth century, undercut by cheap imports. The Leather Market itself is now reconditioned as commercial space in the form of studios and offices.

❻ Cross Bones Graveyard
Redcross Way

Beneath a Transport for London storage yard are the bodies of more than 15,000 people in unconsecrated ground. On the yard's railings is a bronze plaque bearing the epitaph 'R.I.P. The Outcast Dead.' The burial ground dates from the twelfth century. The bishops of Winchester, who licensed prostitutes and brothels in the Liberty of the Clink, nevertheless would not allow prostitutes to be buried in hallowed ground. They ended up here, along with paupers and other sinners, in what was euphemistically referred to as a burial ground for 'single women'. Early in the nineteenth century it became the haunt of body-snatchers seeking specimens for the anatomy classes at nearby Guy's Hospital. The burial ground was finally closed in 1853 because it was 'completely overcharged with dead' and a danger to public health. The railings have become an impromptu memorial, adorned with messages and mementoes, ribbons, flowers and other totems.

❼ Guinness Trust housing
Snowsfields

The Guinness Trust, founded in 1889 by Edward Guinness, great-grandson of the founder of the Guinness Brewery in Dublin, was the first new philanthropic body since the foundation of the Peabody Trust in 1862. The architect for the Guinness Trust was Joseph & Smithem. Conscious of critiques of existing tenements erected by philanthropic organizations, the firm took real care to avoid an uncompromising, barrack-like appearance, using red brick instead of grey or yellow London stock brick, and deploying various architectural devices designed to reduce the scale and the effect of sheer physical bulk.

❽ Redcross Cottages
Ayres Street

The great housing reformer and philanthropist Octavia Hill was given responsibility in the 1880s for managing the properties and real estate of the Ecclesiastical Commissioners in Southwark. She built a community hall and two rows of picturesque half-timbered terraces, Redcross and Whitecross cottages, on Ayres Street, just a few metres from the Cross Bones burial ground on Redcross Way. All were designed by Elijah Hoole. Redcross Cottages face Redcross Gardens, established as an 'open air sitting room for the tired inhabitants of Southwark'.

❾ Elephant and Castle
London Road

Badly damaged in the Second World War, the notoriously congested junction at the Elephant and Castle had the misfortune to be redeveloped in the early 1960s in the idiom of the time: unlovely and poorly built. A market area, a covered shopping centre, government office buildings, a cinema and college buildings were arranged around two big roundabouts, with pedestrian access from surrounding neighbourhoods via labyrinthine concrete underpasses. Successive refits and renovations have failed to mitigate the unpleasantness and unpopularity of the site, and the area is now undergoing a fifteen-year, £3 billion regeneration project that will build nearly 5000 new and replacement homes, fifty new shops and restaurants, a new park and improved pedestrian, bicycle and automobile circulation.

❿ Strata tower
Walworth Road

Intended as the first of three towers constituting the centre-piece of a community-orientated regeneration of the Elephant and Castle, the Strata promptly won *Building Design* magazine's Carbuncle Cup as the worst new building in the United Kingdom when it opened in 2010. Its owlish presence looms over the south London landscape as another symbol of corporate opportunism and the weakness of the public side of public–private initiatives. The 'green' credentials signalled by the wind turbines at the top of the tower are capable of generating only eight per cent of the building's energy needs. Although twenty-five per cent of the 408 apartments in the tower were reserved for 'affordable' homes (that is, at up to eighty per cent of the local market rent: not affordable to most residents of the area's housing estates scheduled for demolition), most of the rest were bought off-plan before construction began, mainly by investors.

⓫ Tabard Centre
Hunter Close

In its time this building, the former Great Hunter Street School, later known as the Tabard Street School, also stood out both physically and symbolically within its neighbourhood. Built for the London School Board soon after the passage of the Elementary Education Act (1870), which compelled the attendance of young children at school, it was one of the Board Schools described by Arthur Conan Doyle as 'beacons of the future'. It was converted to residential use in the 1990s and is now known as the Tabard Centre.

Camden

St Pancras Old Church stands on a small rise immediately to the north of St Pancras railway station. For hundreds of years it stood isolated in a thinly populated parish, rarely visited by anyone from London. Its situation changed suddenly when Parliament sanctioned the construction of the New Road (now Euston Road) from Paddington to Islington in 1756. The road ran just 550 metres (600 yards) to the south of the church, and soon drew urban development towards it. Today the Old Church stands squeezed between the approach road to St Pancras station and the tracks leading into the terminus.

Although the New Road was intended to provide a route for sheep and cattle to be driven to Smithfield Market, the enabling Act of Parliament stipulated that nothing should be built within 15 metres (49 feet) of the road: a provision designed to serve the interests of the Great Estates to the south and, in particular, the ostentatious exclusivity of the Duke of Bedford's Bloomsbury Estate. The result was that the road became wholly residential, with long gardens fronting the houses. It was not exactly a Parisian-style boulevard, but its breadth and location made it fashionable. To the north of the New Road, towards the Old Church, piecemeal development soon began to appear, but any prospect of fashionability was quickly dispelled by the construction of the Regent's Canal (1812-20). The canal and its two basins - Cumberland Basin and St Pancras Basin - attracted wharfside yards, factories and workshops, and nearby landowners quickly moved to develop housing for the new industrial workforce.

Somers Town, just to the north of present-day Euston and St Pancras stations, was developed as a working-class neighbourhood on land formerly belonging to the Charterhouse Estate. It was laid out in rectilinear form, mostly with two-storey terraces in London stock brick. Among its first inhabitants were refugees from the French Revolution. To the north of Somers Town was Figs Mead, an outlier of the Bedford Estate. It was developed in the 1830s as Bedford New Town in a conscious effort to create an affordable model suburb for the lower-middle classes. Just to the north again, towards the Regent's Canal, Camden Town had already begun to emerge as a working-class neighbourhood. Writing in 1952, the authors of the *Survey of London* observed pompously that 'For the most part the streets of Camden Town retain their original houses, but they are not distinguished by sufficient architectural character to merit description.'[1]

Railway Infrastructure

The railway boom of the 1840s introduced dramatic new architectural elements to the city: bridges, viaducts, grand stations and enormous railway hotels. The railways also rewrote the city's geography, and no district felt greater impact than Camden. In 1846 a Royal Commission decided that no new surface railways should be permitted within the central area of London south of the New Road. Not surprisingly, the termini of railway companies with routes entering London from the north ended up being aligned along this boundary. All were in Camden: Euston (for the London and Birmingham Railway), St Pancras (for the Midland Railway) and King's Cross (for the Great Northern Railway). Their location represented a compromise between the property interests of the Great Estates and the desire of the new railway companies to arrive in and depart from the heart of the city.

By the 1850s London was at the heart of a flourishing national rail network, and Camden was bustling with railway workers, coalmen, factory operatives and warehouse hands. Commuters, business visitors and transients enlivened the southern part

Camden High Street. The stretch near Camden Lock has come to specialize in shops selling alternative gear: everything from clubwear and ethnic styles to hippy, punk, goth, burlesque and fetish.

St Pancras Old Church.
Originally an eleventh-
century chapel, it was
extensively altered and
enlarged in 1848, when
Camden began to grow in
population.

Lock Keeper's cottage
on the Grand Union
Canal, directly across
from the King's Cross
Central regeneration
site. It was designed as a
pumping house in 1898
by John Wolfe Barry, and
converted into a cottage
in 1926.

of the district around the railway termini on Euston Road (renamed from New Road in 1857). The very first of these termini was Euston, planned by the pioneer railway engineer Robert Stephenson, who by then was employed by the London and Birmingham Railway Company. The station opened in 1837 with a gigantic architectural frontispiece, a 21-metre-tall (69 foot) Doric portico known as Euston Arch, designed by Philip Hardwick. Euston was gradually enlarged throughout the nineteenth century as passenger traffic increased, railway companies merged and the symbolic power of the railways intensified.

King's Cross station was built a few hundred metres to the east, on the site of an old smallpox hospital. It took its name from a memorial to King George IV that had been erected on the site in 1830. It was designed by Lewis Cubitt, the brother of Thomas, and opened in 1852, connecting London with York. St Pancras, next door, opened in 1868. Like King's Cross, it had direct access to the canal docks and extensive goods yards, as well as impressive passenger facilities. While the great iron structure of the station represented the latest in building technology with an aesthetic to match the progressive engineering of the age, the station hotel, which forms the station's street frontage, embodied the reactionary aesthetic espoused by

John Ruskin. His *Seven Lamps of Architecture* (1849) and *The Stones of Venice* (1851–53) strongly rejected both classical architecture (too bourgeois) and the muscular functionality of the industrial era (too philistine). Instead, Ruskin emphasized the importance of medieval Gothic style for what he saw as its reverence for nature and natural forms. The design by George Gilbert Scott, who won the architectural competition for the hotel, is massive and overbearing. The urban historian Anthony Sutcliffe acknowledges that Londoners love St Pancras but skewers Scott's flashy eclecticism:

The Venetian arches belie Scott's claim that Italian influence was excluded, and the North German stepped gables are out of place on a French Gothic building. So is the Purbeck marble on the main frontage.[2]

Building the railways had devastated much of Camden, and the disruption triggered the decline of some older neighbourhoods. Yet the location of the termini turned out to have an important indirect effect in stimulating the development of other parts of Camden and, indeed, the rest of outer London. The fact that the railway companies' termini were strung out in a circle around the city centre with no direct connections among them stimulated the development of the city's underground railway system. The Metropolitan Railway opened its first line in 1863, connecting Paddington station with Euston and King's Cross. It was so successful that the District Railway Company promptly opened a parallel line to the south, linking Hammersmith to the City by way of Victoria and Charing Cross mainline stations. Twenty years later the two companies combined into the Circle Line, dramatically improving the circulation of the increasingly complex metropolis. Meanwhile, Camden itself had become something of an artists' quarter as writers and painters found cheap lodgings and inspiration in the bustling environment. Notable examples included Ford Madox Brown, Spencer Gore, Charles Lucy and Walter Sickert.

Social Change, Planned and Unplanned

After the Second World War, London's planners sought to make good on the backlog of working-class housing. A combination of dereliction and bomb damage in Camden meant that there were many sites available. In the radical spirit of the Welfare State established by the postwar Labour government, LCC architects were able to put London on the map as one of the world's leading centres of progressive public housing. In Camden, Somers Town in particular became associated with council housing estates.

Much of the surviving fabric of the district consisted of ageing, unmodernized Victorian housing, mostly two- and three-storey terraced houses. It may not have been of 'sufficient architectural character to merit description', but it was ideal for colonization by young, educated households who wanted to avoid suburbia. It was particularly attractive in property terms because of its proximity to the established middle-class districts of Hampstead, Bloomsbury and Primrose Hill. In the 1970s and 1980s British architectural magazines were full of features of gentrification and upgrading projects in Camden.

Gradually, a large fraction of the district's working-class households was displaced by this process. But the residual working-class population (in both Victorian housing and new local-authority projects), together with the district's remnant industrial architecture and its street markets, has left Camden with a distinctive identity. It has attracted a population that has fostered a series of alternative subcultures, including punk, goth and emo. It has also become a hotbed for creative music and fashion design, and these in turn have attracted media and design-led businesses.

The street buzz of Camden Lock and Camden High Street, with their alternative clothing shops and market stalls selling cheap T-shirts, scarves, bags, books, antiques and organic fast food, is slightly anarchic. The gritty authenticity, with a whiff of danger and the unexpected, attracts thousands of tourists and visitors from across the city. Their influence, in turn, has added upgraded bars and restaurants as well as cheap London souvenir shops to the mix.

Regeneration

In stark contrast to Camden High Street, the regeneration of the King's Cross area is very much in the image of 'global' London: all about high-profile architecture and international business. The heart of the scheme is a triangular 27-hectare (66-acre) brownfield site that fans out northwards between the railway lines leaving King's Cross and St Pancras stations. St Pancras station has already been extended and refurbished as the terminal for the Eurostar service. The station hotel, having been clumsily retrofitted as office space in the 1960s and subsequently threatened with demolition in the 1980s, has been restored and modernized by the Marriott group and is now a five-star luxury hotel.

King's Cross station has also been extended and refurbished, and work has commenced on the redevelopment of the brownfield site, where close to 93,000 square metres (1 million square feet) of mixed-use space is to be derived from historic industrial buildings and structures. The latter will include a housing development designed by Wilkinson Eyre that sits within the cast-iron framework of a trio of Victorian gasometers. Multiple architects have been engaged elsewhere on the site in the hope of creating an impression of organic growth that will complement the legacy structures. The King's Cross scheme is projected to comprise about 2000 homes plus 316,000 square metres (3.4 million square feet) of commercial office space and 46,500 square metres (500,520 square feet) of retail space, making it the largest regeneration project in Europe.

Royal College Street. Part of Camden Town, built in the mid-nineteenth century: 'not distinguished by sufficient architectural character to merit description' (see text, page 73).

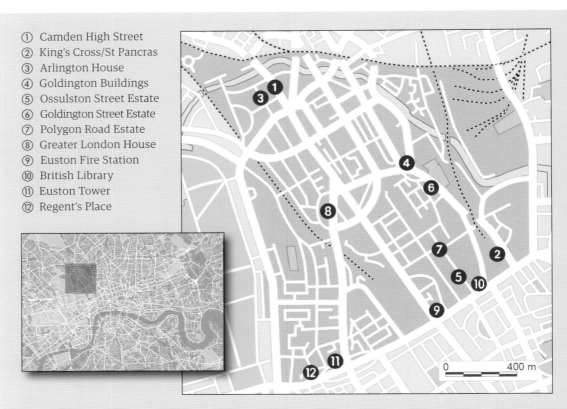

① Camden High Street
② King's Cross/St Pancras
③ Arlington House
④ Goldington Buildings
⑤ Ossulston Street Estate
⑥ Goldington Street Estate
⑦ Polygon Road Estate
⑧ Greater London House
⑨ Euston Fire Station
⑩ British Library
⑪ Euston Tower
⑫ Regent's Place

Camden has a very varied morphology that has been both disrupted and constrained by canal, road and railway infrastructure. The district was clearly separated from the Great Estates of Bloomsbury and Fitzrovia by the droving route that is now the busy commercial corridor and traffic artery of Euston Road. To the east, the eastern margin of the King's Cross/St Pancras railway complex coincides neatly with the administrative boundary between the boroughs of Camden and Islington. To the west there is an abrupt change from Camden's social housing estates to the neoclassical terraces facing Regent's Park. The Regent's Canal provides a cognitive boundary to the north, separating Camden Town from Kentish Town.

❶ Camden High Street

Since the 1970s Camden High Street has been transformed from an unexceptional local shopping street into a colourful strip of retailing for 'alternative' apparel and accessories. The transition has been accompanied by the proliferation of markets and food stalls in Camden Town's side streets. Together, they draw more than ten million visitors each year from across the city and beyond, making the locality one of London's most popular attractions.

❷ King's Cross/St Pancras
Euston Road

The British government's Urban Task Force, set up in 1997 under the leadership of the architect Richard Rogers, sought to establish a vision for urban regeneration founded on principles of design excellence, social well-being and environmental responsibility within a viable economic and legislative framework. The physical and economic regeneration of the King's Cross area - branded as King's Cross Central - has the potential to meet these aspirations. With no population to displace and no more local jobs to be lost, the potential social and economic gain may for once match the potential profits for developers. The scheme will provide fifty new buildings, 2000 new homes, twenty new streets and ten new public squares on a site that has long stood as a void in the fabric of the district. Character and place identity is provided by several legacy structures from the railway era. The Great Northern Hotel (1854), one of the earliest purpose-built railway hotels in the country, has been restored as a luxury boutique hotel. The brick arches of the restored Coal Drop buildings provide the framework for a new retail quarter. The old goods yard has been redeveloped for Central Saint Martins College of Art and Design, and one of the landmark gasometer frames will be refurbished and re-erected next to Regent's Canal. Regeneration around the formerly derelict King's Cross Central site has already transformed the area from a seedy quarter to a busy and prosperous one. The two passenger stations have been extended and refurbished, and the St Pancras railway hotel has been extensively renovated. Just to the west of St Pancras is the enormous British Library, built in the 1990s, and immediately to the north of that is a new biomedical research centre, the Francis Crick Institute. The streets to the east of King's Cross, in Islington, have been extensively redeveloped and gentrified.

Fish and Coal Offices. The first block was built in 1851 as part of Lewis Cubitt's design for the Goods Yard. The buildings, which follow the curve of the Regent's Canal, are being restored for use as offices and studios with restaurants on the ground floor.

St Pancras Renaissance Hotel (formerly the Midland Grand Hotel), designed by George Gilbert Scott and built 1868–76 in bold High Victorian Gothic: a big building that sought to express the power of the railway and the clamour of the great metropolis. It is now a Grade I-listed building.

Granary Square, part of the old Goods Yard complex. The building shown here was used to store wheat arriving from Great Northern routes. It was designed by Lewis Cubitt, who was also the architect for King's Cross passenger station. Restored and transformed by Stanton Williams architects, the building now forms the entrance to Central Saint Martins College of Art and Design, part of the University of the Arts London.

Social Housing

Before the LCC was established in 1889, housing poor and low-income families had been left entirely to philanthropists and philanthropic institutions. The Housing of the Working Classes Act (1890) provided for slum clearance and redevelopment, but the returns on cheap housing were not attractive to investors, so the LCC began building housing itself. The first major step towards large-scale public housing provision came in 1919, when an acute shortage prompted Prime Minister David Lloyd George's highly publicized election promise of 'Homes Fit For Heroes'. Local authorities were given responsibility and funding to provide working-class houses to let.

After the Second World War there was again a shortage of housing, this time intensified by war damage. In addition, the incoming Labour government was heavily committed to the public sector and in 1949 passed a Housing Act that removed the caveat restricting local authorities to the provision of housing for the 'working classes'. In London, the exurban New Town strategy incorporated in Patrick Abercrombie's *Greater London Plan* (1944) siphoned off a great deal of demand for working-class housing, but there was still a great need for slum clearance and rehousing in many of the boroughs. The LCC and local councils became heirs to the tradition of Great Estates, laying out, building and managing large public housing estates.

The first social housing to be built in Camden was Goldington Buildings, opened in 1902 with fifty flats accommodating 300 people in a horseshoe-shaped structure around a courtyard. The most notable social housing development in Camden is the Ossulston Street Estate,

3 **Arlington House**, opened in 1905, the last of a chain of hostels built in London by the great Victorian philanthropist Lord Rowton. The hostel was taken over by Camden Council in the mid-1980s and extensively refurbished, tenant numbers being halved and room size doubled.

between Euston and St Pancras stations – a part of Somers Town that had, by the early twentieth century, deteriorated into a slum notorious for its overcrowding, squalor and vice. The estate is one of the most distinguished products of the LCC Architect's Department. Built in 1927–37, it is strikingly different from the 'Municipal neo-Georgian' generally favoured by the LCC for its apartment blocks during that period. The overall scale of its blocks – the longest of which runs continuously for more than 200 metres (656 feet) – has been compared to the Karl Marx Hof (1927–30), the most famous accomplishment of Viennese civic socialism.

After the Second World War, the boom in public housing construction created scores of examples of functional but austere housing in London, much of it in an abrasive Corbusian style of prefabricated point blocks and slabs. Many of these projects came to be associated fairly quickly with problems of alienation,

4 **Goldington Buildings**. The first social housing scheme to be built in Camden, it has been extensively renovated and modernized, reopening in 2011 under the ownership and management of a housing association.

physical deterioration and social disorder. Camden had its share of these, but from the mid-1960s to the mid-1970s, under the tenure of the borough architect Sydney Cook, the preferred solution was for high-density, low-rise schemes like the Polygon Road Estate (1976), a block to the north of the Ossulston Estate.

Another example, the Tolmers Square scheme, just off Euston Road, occupies the site of the notorious 'Battle for Tolmers Square', seventeen years of conflict between, on one hand, property developers (who wanted to demolish the 1860s terraces and build 46,000 square metres (495,140 square feet) of office space) and, on the other, tenants' groups, trade unionists, students and squatters. The activists failed to prevent the destruction of the original housing but succeeded in persuading Camden Council to purchase the site compulsorily from the property company.

With the Thatcher governments of the 1980s and the implementation of neoliberal policies, the stock of public housing began to be dissolved by the Conservatives' policy of encouraging the sale of local-authority housing to sitting tenants at a discount of up to sixty per cent of the assessed value of the property. Much of the residual social housing originally built and managed by Camden Council is now owned and managed by housing associations and trusts.

5 **Ossulston Street Estate**, designed by George Topham Forrest, Superintending Architect to Camden Council. This final scheme replaced two earlier proposals that were among the first attempts by a British local authority to develop high-rise housing incorporating social facilities, local shopping and commercial premises.

6 **Goldington Street Estate** (1950). Now a mix of private and council accommodation, with one block of sheltered housing.

7 **Oakshott Court, Polygon Road Estate.** Low-rise, high-density flats in striking red brick, designed for the London Borough of Camden by Peter Tábori under the leadership of Sydney Cook.

8 Greater London House
Hampstead Road

Built in the 1920s as the Carreras Cigarette Factory, this was the first industrial building in Britain to make use of pre-stressed concrete technology. It was designed by M. E. and O. H. Collins and A. G. Porri in Egyptian Revival Art Deco style. They clearly did not hold back, adding huge statues and mouldings of the company's black cat logo (associated with its Craven A brand of cigarettes) to multiple references from ancient Egyptian architecture. The site was formerly an open space used by residents of Mornington Crescent, and the construction of the factory became a cause célèbre for social reform organizations that were campaigning to prevent the disappearance of London's open spaces. The loss of Mornington Crescent's gardens was an important factor in the establishment of the Royal Commission on London Squares in 1927 and the London Squares Preservation Act of 1931. The factory building has recently been restored and converted to office and studio space.

9 Euston Fire Station
Euston Road

Designed by the Canadian architect Percy Nobbs in a Free Style interpretation of Arts and Crafts principles, Euston Fire Station was one of a series of distinctive fire stations that appeared throughout London during the building boom of the 1890s and 1900s. Until the late nineteenth century, insurance companies each maintained their own fire brigade. The Metropolitan Fire Brigade was established in 1866 as part of the Metropolitan Board of Works by an Act of Parliament that made firefighting in London a public responsibility. Robert Pearsall, architect for the Metropolitan Fire Brigade, sought to give character to his new fire stations but defaulted in most cases to the Gothic Revival style that was generally expected for Victorian public buildings. The newly formed LCC took over the Metropolitan Fire Brigade in 1889, and from 1896 new stations were designed by a group of architects seconded from the LCC Housing Department. They brought with them the innovative approaches that had evolved for designing new social housing, and drew on a huge variety of influences to create unique and imposing stations, each built to a bespoke design. Euston Fire Station was one of these, completed in 1902.

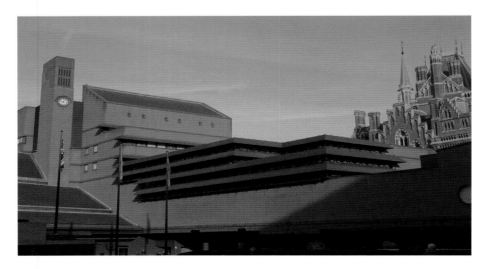

10 British Library
Euston Road

A massive complex with nearly 650 kilometres (400 miles) of shelving, the library houses a copy of every new British publication. Designed by Colin St John Wilson in the 1970s, the library was not completed until 1998 as a result of delays caused by budget problems, political wrangling and press criticism. By then, the complex seemed to the architectural cognoscenti to be dated, while to traditionalists it was uninspiring. The Prince of Wales likened it to 'an academy for secret policemen'. Library users, though, have found it functional and accommodating, and it brings an element of calm and civility to an otherwise frenetic commercial corridor.

⑪ Euston Tower
286 Euston Road

It became clear in the 1950s that Euston Road would become one of the most important traffic arteries and commercial corridors in north-central London. Road improvements in the early 1960s resulted in the destruction of the entrance to Euston station and the construction of an underpass at the junction with Tottenham Court Road. Among the office developments drawn to the location, branded as Euston Centre, was Euston Tower, a thirty-four-storey International Style building with glass curtain walls, designed by Sidney Kaye and opened in 1970. It was originally planned by the developer to be one of three identical buildings, which would have lent an unfortunate Corbusian affect to Euston Road. Thankfully, the LCC insisted that they should step down in height along the site, and the other two towers were never built. The base of Euston Tower was constructed as a raised platform with a series of walkways at the first-floor level connecting the tower with the other office buildings on the Euston Centre site. After adjoining property to the west was acquired in 2005 by the owners of the tower, the base was opened up, with cafés and shops designed to integrate it with the development of the new property. The entire package is now branded as Regent's Place (see below).

⑫ Regent's Place
Triton Square

Together with the Euston Tower site, Regent's Place amounts to 5 hectares (12 acres) of high-end, mixed-use development that fronts the north side of Euston Road at its busiest point. With an aggregate total of 140,000 square metres (1.5 million square feet) of office, retail and residential space, it accommodates some 12,000 workers and residents. In broad context it is very much a result of the impact of London's role as a global city. The explosive growth of the financial sector and advanced business services since the 1980s, and the consequent increase in an affluent class fraction seeking upscale accommodation, has not only affected the City and driven the regeneration of the Docklands but also shaped Regent's Place and similar mixed-use developments such as Paddington Central and More London Riverside (see page 239).

Chelsea

The core of the medieval village of Chelsea lay at the foot of present-day Old Church Street, where settlement had clustered from Neolithic times, protected by marshland to the east and west and with the river itself as a route for local commerce. The first real change to the district can be traced to 1524, when Thomas More, Henry VIII's chancellor, moved into a mansion just upriver and slightly inland from the village. More's presence made Chelsea fashionable among courtiers and royal officials who could not find room in the limited spaces of Tudor Westminster. After More's execution in 1535, Henry VIII himself acquired the entire manor of Chelsea and subsequently gave it to his sixth wife, Catherine Parr, as part of her dowry. The route from Westminster to Chelsea was private to the king, and officially remained so until 1830, when it became a public thoroughfare, the King's Road.

A 'Village of Palaces'

Chelsea's royal associations and its pleasant situation - south-facing, with a gentle, well-drained slope to the river - attracted a cluster of country estates and mansions along the banks of the river: a 'village of palaces'. The Worshipful Company of Apothecaries also took advantage of the south-facing riverbank, leasing land in 1673 to establish a Physic Garden for their *materia medica*. In 1722 the garden was endowed in perpetuity by Hans Sloane (whose vast scientific and literary collection later provided the basis for both the British Museum and the Natural History Museum), and it remains open to the public.

Just downstream from the Physic Garden is the Royal Hospital, founded in 1682 by Charles II as a home for soldiers unfit for further duty. Built to a design by Christopher Wren, it is widely held to be one of London's finest secular buildings.

In the late seventeenth century an accretion of small-scale development occurred inland from the river and around a hamlet known as Little Chelsea, along the Fulham Road. The first systematic development came after the purchase of Chelsea manor by Hans Sloane in 1713, when he released formerly unbuilt land around Cheyne Walk for speculative building. For the most part, though, eighteenth-century Chelsea functioned as a riverside pleasure resort, where people could come for the day or perhaps take lodgings for the summer. The main focus of the resort was Ranelagh Gardens, opened in 1742 next to the Royal Hospital. For about forty years it was a very fashionable site for open-air concerts and other respectable entertainments.

Until the building boom of the 1760s, the northern part of the district remained undeveloped, an area of walled nursery gardens and scattered cottages. The boom prompted the Fulham architect Henry Holland to acquire building rights for a large parcel of land straddling northern Chelsea and Knightsbridge. Hans Town, as it was originally known, became the model for the many new 'towns' that sprang up around central London. Holland built moderately sized houses for sale, together with a mansion for himself, with grounds landscaped by Lancelot 'Capability' Brown.

A Metropolitan Suburb

With the next building boom, in the 1820s, speculative development became denser, and Chelsea began to acquire coherence and individuality as a metropolitan suburb. After the King's Road was made public, in 1830, houses and grand squares began to be built along its length. Later in the nineteenth century the embankment of the river raised property values, encouraging redevelopment and modernization throughout the district. The first phase of redevelopment, in the 1870s, took place along the

Chelsea Embankment. The houses here were almost all built in the late 1870s, a collection of grand red-brick town houses in Domestic Revival style, and some of the first to break with the stucco of Belgravia and Kensington.

Old Church Street. This stretch near the river is one of the oldest streets in Chelsea. It is now lined with buildings of many different ages and styles.

newly embanked river: a collection of eighteen grand, individualistic red-brick town houses in Domestic Revival style. Designed by some of the leading proponents of the style, including Richard Norman Shaw and Charles Voysey, the steeply pitched roofs, shaped gables, oriel windows, carved red brickwork and moulded terracotta of these town houses introduced a dramatic change to a townscape that hitherto had been small-scale and picturesque.

Redevelopment and Displacement

Domestic Revival and its variations rapidly became the preferred style for another new fashion: apartment-style buildings. For thirty years or so, beginning in the late 1870s, most new buildings in Chelsea featured the red brick and terracotta that were the signature of the style. The Cadogan Estate seized the opportunity to redevelop much of its Chelsea property, including all of Hans Town. Old cottages were razed to make way for block after block of speculative apartment buildings in the fashionable new style. In an early example of spin, the estate claimed its redevelopments were philanthropic: clearing obsolescent working-class properties for rehousing. It did build new model artisans' dwellings, but they accommodated only 400 people, while the demolition displaced more than 4000.

The new apartment buildings, meanwhile, united northern Chelsea and Knightsbridge with the social geography of the upper-middle-class district of Belgravia to the east. Much of the rest of Chelsea remained an unexceptional backwater of lower-middle- and working-class housing. Local industry included Thomas Crapper's porcelain sanitaryware factory. Housing conditions in parts of the district were bad enough in the 1870s and 1880s to draw the efforts of limited-interest industrial dwellings companies. 'Philanthropy at Five Per Cent' saw blocks of flats put up by the Peabody Trust in Lawrence Street and by the Chelsea Park Dwellings Company on the corner of King's Road and Park Walk.

An Artists' Quarter

Chelsea's picturesque old buildings, stately mansions and gardens by the river had long been favoured subjects for paintings and engravings. Towards the end of the nineteenth century, as older properties became more affordable, the area became popular among artists and writers. By the early decades of the twentieth century it had become established as a centre of artistic and literary life, with a socially mixed and quasi-bohemian society. Tite Street, sometimes known as Artists' Row, was home at one time or another to Julian Barrow, Simon Elwes, Augustus John, John Singer Sargent and James Abbott McNeill Whistler. Other Chelsea notables included Thomas Carlyle, George Eliot, Dante Gabriel Rossetti, Bram Stoker, J.M.W. Turner and Oscar Wilde.

The processes of change established in the last quarter of the nineteenth century carried over to the first half of the twentieth. Philanthropic housing trusts nibbled away at the dearth of decent, affordable housing for working-class families. They were assisted by the borough council, one of the few in London to have built noticeable amounts of social housing before the First World War. But the Cadogan Estate continued to redevelop tracts of artisan housing into more profitable streets of upper-middle-class apartment buildings. More than 20,000 people were evicted during the first two decades of the century as leases fell in and their homes were demolished. The consequent negative publicity and widespread disapproval of the actions of one of the wealthiest families in the country did not slow the process, but it did give impetus to a nascent conservation movement.

Conservation and Infill

The threat to parts of old Chelsea led to the formation in 1927 of the Chelsea Society, one of London's first conservation groups. The society was concerned not only by the replacement of small terraced houses by massive blocks of flats, but also by the changing social geography of the district, and supported the council's efforts to provide better housing for working-class households. The district's need for modernized infrastructure after 1945 put even more pressure on affordable accommodation. New and expanded educational and healthcare facilities, new institutional and office buildings, and the conversion of houses to hotels all put pressure on space in the 1950s and 1960s. The borough council and housing trusts were again able to increase the pool of accommodation for low-income households, but rapidly rising rents and property values began to displace middle-class households from Chelsea. The district was beginning to become polarized, with working-class and upper-middle-class households but a disappearing middle class.

The high cost of living and the scarcity of cheap studio accommodation also began to diminish the quasi-bohemian atmosphere that had been associated with Chelsea's artistic and literary set. But the district immediately acquired a distinctive new cultural dimension as the commercial and creative core of the liberated youth culture of the 1960s. Mary Quant had opened a boutique in 1955 called Bazaar at the corner of Markham Square and King's Road, designing and selling Mod clothes that expressed rebellion against both the adult establishment and the social élite and allowed girls to stop dressing like their mothers. Within a few years, other independent, youth-orientated boutiques had colonized King's Road, which became synonymous with the Swinging Sixties. Mick Jagger and Keith Richards, among other youth-culture celebrities, both bought homes in Chelsea (although in the more sequestered and rarefied environs of Cheyne Walk, rather than the hectic King's Road area).

The shift in Chelsea's image accelerated gentrification. Houseboats moored along the Thames, as well as most remaining small town houses, were bought up by journalists, architects, editors and other young professionals. Larger and better properties, meanwhile, were being converted into embassies and headquarters for big international companies. Alarmed, the new borough council established Conservation Areas under the Civic Amenities Act of 1967. From 1969 to 1971 eight neighbourhoods were designated, together amounting to about half of Chelsea's cityscape. This only intensified pressure on the rest of the district, especially during the property booms of the 1980s and 1990s. There was constant pressure to redevelop as leases fell in. Older properties were gutted and modernized with high-quality finishes and fittings (and commensurately high rents), while commercial yards and other spaces were filled in, mostly with underwhelming architecture.

Royal Avenue. The avenue itself was laid out as early as the 1690s; the terrace is from the early nineteenth century.

Meanwhile, Chelsea's Mod moment had ended. The King's Road briefly hosted a commodified version of 1970s East End punk culture, spearheaded by Vivienne Westwood and Malcolm McLaren's boutique Sex, before succumbing to the cloned stores of national clothing, footwear and cosmetics chains. At the same time, the eastern fringe of Chelsea, between Knightsbridge and Sloane Square, solidified into a bastion of conservative wealth, associated particularly with the affluent and self-indulgent young women ('Sloane Rangers') who shop in the high-end fashion and jewellery boutiques of Sloane Street and drive around Chelsea in big sports utility vehicles ('Chelsea Tractors').

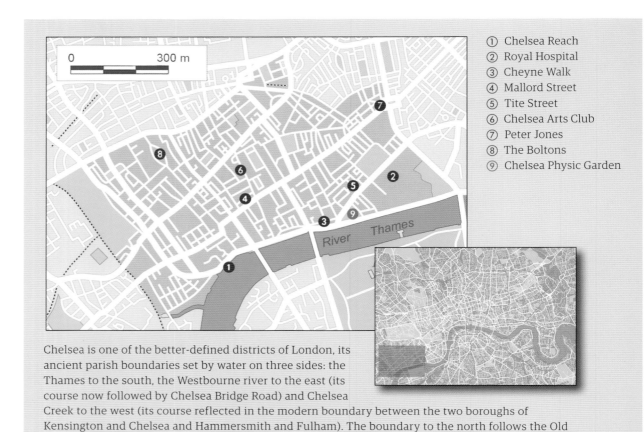

1. Chelsea Reach
2. Royal Hospital
3. Cheyne Walk
4. Mallord Street
5. Tite Street
6. Chelsea Arts Club
7. Peter Jones
8. The Boltons
9. Chelsea Physic Garden

Chelsea is one of the better-defined districts of London, its ancient parish boundaries set by water on three sides: the Thames to the south, the Westbourne river to the east (its course now followed by Chelsea Bridge Road) and Chelsea Creek to the west (its course reflected in the modern boundary between the two boroughs of Kensington and Chelsea and Hammersmith and Fulham). The boundary to the north follows the Old Brompton Road before shading seamlessly into Knightsbridge through the Hans Town development. Chelsea has an unusually dense network of short streets, with the massing of mansion apartment buildings relieved only by small and irregular squares. The squares off King's Road are distinctive because they are mostly three-sided, with the fourth side being the King's Road frontage.

❶ Chelsea Reach

Cremorne Road

A community of fifty or so boats had become established along Chelsea Reach after the Second World War, using converted Motor Torpedo Boat and Landing Craft Assault vessels. They attracted a neo-bohemian community of artists, theatre people, journalists, architects, editors and students. After the Chelsea Yacht & Boat Club added extra pontoons with new mains services and a new vacuum system for sewage in the late 1970s, the houseboats attracted a much wealthier group of occupants.

❷ Royal Hospital

Royal Hospital Road

Founded as a home for army veterans by Charles II, the Royal Hospital was built in 1682-92 around three courtyards with an open face to the river. The principal architect was Christopher Wren, assisted by Nicholas Hawksmoor, and the overall concept was evidently inspired by Louis XIV's Hôtel des Invalides in Paris. The Hospital is still home to more than 300 ex-servicemen, the Chelsea Pensioners. The buildings are largely unchanged. Since 1913 the lawns to the south of the Royal Hospital have been used as the site for the Royal Horticultural Society's Chelsea Flower Show, held annually in May.

❸ Cheyne Walk

This stretch of the embankment boasts some of London's highest property values. It has become famous for the succession of talented celebrities who have lived here, including Hilaire Belloc, George Eliot, Elizabeth Gaskell, Dante Gabriel Rossetti, J.M.W. Turner, Sylvia Pankhurst, Ian Fleming, Mick Jagger, Keith Richards, Bob Geldof and Ken Follett. Already a fashionable riverside walk in the seventeenth century, with a few mansions along with inns and coffee houses, Cheyne Walk was completely filled in by the early eighteenth century. The photograph on the left shows surviving houses of one of the earliest terraces, built around 1686 by Thomas Lawrence. The photograph on the right shows late nineteenth-century infill in the Domestic Revival styles popular at the time. In between is a mix of mansion apartment buildings and several surviving terraced houses from the 1890s, when the Chelsea riverside was a thriving artistic community.

❹ Mallord Street

Developed early in the twentieth century on one of the last remaining plots of open land in the district, Mallord Street was designed to appeal to artistic types (Mallord was one of J.M.W. Turner's given names), with street frontages deliberately varied within a broadly Arts and Crafts idiom. The author A. A. Milne lived at number 13 (shown here with the blue plaque), while the painter Augustus John lived further along in a small, detached yellow-brick house of similar vintage but distinctively different styling.

❺ Tite Street

Laid out in 1877 as an access road to the newly completed Chelsea Embankment, the street was named after William Tite, president of the Royal Institute of British Architects and member of the Metropolitan Board of Works responsible for the construction of the embankment. Most new buildings in Chelsea at this time were built in the red brick and terracotta that were the preferred materials of the new Domestic Revival styles and for which the eastern part of Chelsea became famous. The architect most associated with Tite Street was E. W. Godwin. The street quickly became known as Artists' Row. John Singer Sargent, Simon Elwes, Augustus John, James Abbott McNeill Whistler and Oscar Wilde are among those who lived there at one time or another.

❻ Chelsea Arts Club
Old Church Street

The district's popularity with neo-bohemian artistic and literary types resulted in the creation in 1891 of the Chelsea Arts Club, a breakaway rival to the establishment-orientated Arts Club in Mayfair. These premises, which include club bedrooms, meeting spaces and a large and pleasant garden, were acquired in 1902. The club now has a membership of over 2400, including artists, poets, architects, writers, dancers, actors, musicians, photographers and filmmakers.

❼ Peter Jones
Sloane Square

Widely regarded as one of the best examples of twentieth-century commercial architecture in west London, and recognized by English Heritage as a Grade II* building, the store was one of the first examples in London of a curtain wall (a non-structural wall spanning multiple floors). It opened in 1939, having been designed for John Lewis by William Crabtree of the firm of Slater, Crabtree and Moberly. Erich Mendelsohn's Schocken store in Stuttgart (1926–28) evidently had a significant influence on the design. The Peter Jones building was extensively renovated between 1999 and 2004 at a cost of around £100 million.

❽ The Boltons

The Boltons are a product of increased material prosperity in the mid-nineteenth century and the resulting tendency towards ostentation among the growing upper-middle classes. The large semi-detached Italianate villas arranged around the curved sides of the central garden are a unique feature in London. They were built in the 1850s by Robert Gunter, a wealthy Breconshire landowner who donated the oval piece of land between the double crescents of the Boltons for his estate church, St Mary, the Boltons. The combination of substantial villas set in attractive parkland so near to the heart of London has made the Boltons one of the most expensive streets in London. Unlike many other buildings of similar size elsewhere in London, many of the houses have retained their original function as single-family homes.

❾ Chelsea Physic Garden
Royal Hospital Road

Known originally as the Apothecaries' Garden, the Physic Garden was founded in 1673 by the Worshipful Company of Apothecaries as a training ground for apprentices. By 1679 more than 1200 different plants were recorded on the land they had leased - about 1 hectare (2½ acres) altogether, with 100 metres (109 yards) of river frontage. In 1772 the grounds were leased to them for £5 a year in perpetuity by Hans Sloane, who had purchased the entire manor of Chelsea. The apothecaries' botanical experiments were influential in developing the American cotton industry and the tea trade in India. In 1899 the company relinquished its trust, after which the gardens were somewhat neglected until they fell under the administration of the Chelsea Physic Garden Company in 1983. The garden was then opened to the public, and it now has almost 5000 plant species from all over the world.

The City

In the heart of London, on the site of the capital of Roman Britain, the City has become the specialized office district that anchors London's status as a truly global city. Its buildings reflect its long history as the commercial heart of the British Empire as well as its current role as a hub of international business, and its dense fabric and narrow streets contain an eclectic mixture of architecture. Most of what we see today is a mixture of Victorian construction, post-Second World War redevelopment and the post-1980s office boom resulting from the globalization of finance.

There is, nevertheless, plenty of residual evidence of the City's earlier development. There are fragments of the defensive wall built by the Romans after Boudicca sacked the settlement in 60 AD: admittedly mostly core rubble, since most of the facing and cut stone was carted off for other building after the Romans left Britain. Echoes of the medieval city gates (from west to east: Ludgate, Newgate, Aldersgate, Cripplegate, Moorgate, Bishopsgate and Aldgate) persist in the City's place names. More substantively, the winding cobbled lanes and courtyards of the Blackfriars area are a legacy of the medieval era, as are the alleys and courtyards in the area around Mansion House and the Guildhall, completed in 1440 as the new home for the City's government, the City of London Corporation. In Merchant Taylors' Hall, the chefs still work in a great kitchen built in 1425-33. But a great deal of the City's older fabric was lost in the Great Fire of 1666, including eighty-five of the City's 107 parish churches. Lost records of property ownership and the need to get businesses going precluded planning and rebuilding the City in ways that would have improved circulation, increased the general coherence of the district's layout and created dramatic central public spaces typical of many of Europe's capitals.

Post-Fire Reconstruction

Charles II's Act for the Rebuilding of the City of London (1667) established controls that dramatically upgraded the standards for building and regularized the street hierarchy, a system of building control that was later extended to regulate the expansions of Georgian and Victorian London. Although the pre-Fire property and street lines were retained, there were some new streets and many widenings. St Paul's Cathedral was rebuilt to the design of Christopher Wren, along with fifty-one churches whose design and construction were overseen by him. There had been nearly 100 Company halls in the City - the headquarters of livery companies, specialized trade associations derived from medieval guilds: Armourers and Brasiers, Brewers, Drapers, Goldsmiths, Grocers, Mercers, Saddlers, Skinners, Vintners and so on. Nearly all were rebuilt, most on their pre-Fire sites, typically standing back from the street and approached through an alley or with subsidiary buildings forming a courtyard.

The Fire permanently altered the relationship between the City and the rest of London. At least a quarter of the residents never returned. The nobility and gentry went west, and manufacturers went north and east. The result was that the mercantile character of the City was reinforced. After the Fire, City businesses made almost nothing but traded in almost everything. The financial markets of the City developed hand-in-hand with London's sea trade. The insurance industry was established in the seventeenth century as ship-owners, merchants and financial backers gathered in coffee houses to exchange information and spread their risks. Commodities and futures markets, meanwhile, were a by-product of warehousing. With the expansion

Bishopsgate. The City Corporation's Griffin boundary marker. Similar markers are located all along the boundary of the City.

Monument.
Erected in 1677 to commemorate the Great Fire and located near the Fire's source on Pudding Lane. To the left is Wren's rebuilt St Magnus the Martyr.

of the British Empire, trade boomed, as did the associated finance and advanced business services. Eighty per cent of the City's buildings were replaced during the second half of the nineteenth century, mostly with Italianate office blocks. City banks and finance houses provided capital for the development of manufacturing around the world, together with credit to finance the import of primary products from the colonial world.

Postwar Reconstruction

A second major phase of rebuilding took place after almost one-third of the City's buildings were destroyed by enemy action in the Second World War. Although St Paul's Cathedral famously survived, large swathes of the City did not. The conservatism of the City of London Corporation and its business élite meant that the new buildings and bomb-site replacements were generally dreary neoclassical edifices clad in Portland stone. A notable exception was the (then) futuristic redevelopment of the bomb-damaged Barbican area on the City's northern edge. It incorporated all the latest thinking about Modernist urban design: pedestrian walkways, underground car parks and Brutalist-style concrete buildings.

Elsewhere, redevelopment was constrained not only by the conservatism of the business community but also by historic preservation orders that had been imposed on the surviving pre-Fire fabric and Wren's city of spires and domes: a total of over 500 buildings and twenty-three streets. Building height limits designed to protect views of St Paul's Cathedral imposed a further constraint on postwar redevelopment, resulting in the construction of 'groundscrapers'. Since 1937 the City of London Corporation has operated a unique policy known as

the 'St Paul's Heights' to protect and enhance important local views of the cathedral from the South Bank, from the Thames bridges and from certain points to the north, west and east. In addition, local views of St Paul's Cathedral along Fleet Street, Ludgate Hill, Watling Street and Cannon Street are protected by 'setback' limitations applicable to building frontages. Upon redevelopment, the upper storeys are required to be set back from the building frontage in order to respect pedestrians' views of the cathedral.

Global Finance

The globalization of the economy that began in the mid-1970s provided the impetus to overcome these challenges and constraints. Britain's first skyscraper – the 183-metre (600-foot), forty-three-storey NatWest Tower (now rebranded as Tower 42) – was opened in 1980. Competition from the two other global financial centres – New York and Tokyo – was met with legislation in 1986 that lifted restrictions on entry to the London Stock Market and replaced face-to-face dealing on the floor of the Stock Exchange with an electronic share-price display system, allowing screen-based trading. The result was the 'Big Bang': a restructuring, realignment and resurgence of firms in stock and bond markets and the overall recasting of the City's office employment profile. London's emergence as a dominant world city meant that office development gradually displaced other activities. By 2014 the resident population of the City had decreased to less than 10,000. The daytime working population of the City, however, is now more than 300,000, the great majority of whom are financial-sector office workers.

The cornerstones of the City economy today are the London Stock Exchange, Lloyd's of London and the Bank of England. In general, the City specializes in 'dealing in deals': that is, services to other financial business or corporate customers, international lending, bond trading, foreign exchange trading and investment management. There are around 500 foreign banks with offices in the City, many of them specializing in areas such as foreign exchange markets, Eurobonds and energy futures. City firms are dominant players in the marine and aviation insurance markets. Additionally, the City has emerged as an important alternative investment market, providing equity for smaller firms from around the world.

Since the Big Bang more than half of the City's office space has been rebuilt. The immediate response to the need to accommodate international banks and other financial businesses attracted to London by the financial deregulation was the Broadgate development, on the site of the old Broad Street station on the northern fringe of the City. It was not enough, however, even with the mega-development of Canary Wharf on the Isle of Dogs (see page 207) as a competing overspill office setting.

The historic dominance of the City means that a credible address there is highly desirable for banks, legal firms and management consulting businesses. The right address turns a law firm into a 'City law firm', a form of branding that supposedly projects image, trust and reputation and so helps to gain market share. For many advanced business services and specialized financial services, the tightly bound

Cheapside. St Mary-le-Bow, rebuilt in 1670–83 by Wren, now separated from St Paul's by Jean Nouvel's One New Change, a shopping centre catering to the City's affluent workforce.

geographical setting of the City is essential in fostering the localized networks, both formal and informal, that are an important channel for the accumulation and transfer of knowledge. Proximity allows meetings to be called at short notice and takes advantage of clients, suppliers, customers and others being able to walk to the meeting place. As a result, the City has an unusually strong pedestrian character for an office district, with people walking to one another's offices, to lunches and to after-hours bars, private members' clubs and fitness centres.

A New Skyline for a Fortified City

All this, together with the banking and financial derivatives boom of 1995–2008, prompted a rash of proposals for high-rise office towers in the City. It coincided with Greater London Mayor Ken Livingstone's strategy of boosting London's global brand image through contemporary urban design and an enhanced skyline. Planning restrictions were lifted, and a series of high-rise office towers has duly sprouted. The first of these, the forty-one-storey 30 St Mary Axe, opened in 2004. Unlike Tower 42, it was well received by the public and the media and was promptly nicknamed the 'Gherkin'. This helped pave the way for successful planning applications for other towers: Broadgate Tower (thirty-three storeys, completed 2009), Heron Tower (forty-six storeys, 2011), the Leadenhall Building (the 'Cheesegrater', fifty storeys, 2014), 20 Fenchurch Street (the 'Walkie-Talkie', thirty-four storeys, 2014), the Bishopsgate Tower (the 'Pinnacle', sixty-four storeys) and 52–54 Lime Street (the 'Scalpel', thirty-eight storeys).

Meanwhile, heightened concern for security following the suicide bombings in London on 7 July 2005 has resulted in a significant fortification of the monuments, public buildings and financial nerve centres of the City. The 'Ring of Steel' installed in the 1990s to deter the Provisional IRA and other threats has been not only reinforced but also rendered more sophisticated and better integrated into the design of public spaces.

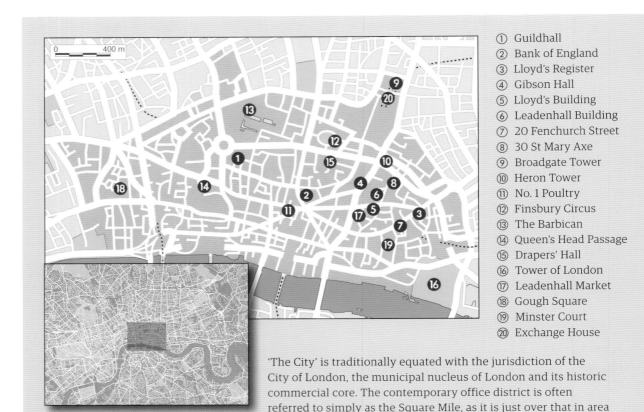

① Guildhall
② Bank of England
③ Lloyd's Register
④ Gibson Hall
⑤ Lloyd's Building
⑥ Leadenhall Building
⑦ 20 Fenchurch Street
⑧ 30 St Mary Axe
⑨ Broadgate Tower
⑩ Heron Tower
⑪ No. 1 Poultry
⑫ Finsbury Circus
⑬ The Barbican
⑭ Queen's Head Passage
⑮ Drapers' Hall
⑯ Tower of London
⑰ Leadenhall Market
⑱ Gough Square
⑲ Minster Court
⑳ Exchange House

'The City' is traditionally equated with the jurisdiction of the City of London, the municipal nucleus of London and its historic commercial core. The contemporary office district is often referred to simply as the Square Mile, as it is just over that in area (nearly 3 square kilometres). The City's location in the heart of the metropolis is at once one of its biggest advantages and one of its greatest challenges. Its centrality gives it both access and accessibility within the broader context of the metropolis. But it is hemmed in by the commercial districts of the West End and by the residential and workshop communities of the East End, and has a legacy of outdated infrastructure.

❶ Guildhall
Gresham Street

Situated in the heart of the City, the Guildhall is the seat of the City of London Corporation's political authority. Fiercely protected by the City's moneyed interests, the Corporation's power derived originally from medieval guilds, and their fifteenth-century Guildhall - the third such structure on the site - has survived substantially intact. The late eighteenth century saw the addition of a four-storey Gothic porch, designed by George Dance the Younger, while the roof was rebuilt to a new design by Giles Gilbert Scott after air-raid damage in 1940. A Roman amphitheatre, dating from the first century AD, was discovered in 1988, during exploratory excavations prior to construction of the Guildhall Art Gallery next door.

❷ Bank of England
Lothbury

The bank was founded in 1694 to provide William III with money to finance his war against France. It was established as a private bank that would lend its share capital to the government, but it operated as a direct agent for the government from 1706. The bank moved to its present location in 1734 and was extended through several major stages of construction, extension and reconstruction to cover the present 2-hectare (5-acre) site. When John Soane was appointed architect to the Bank in 1788, he encircled the island complex with a high, blank screen wall relieved only by 'Tivoli Corner' (shown here) with an open screen of close-set Corinthian columns, apparently inspired by the circular Roman temple of Vesta at Tivoli, Italy.

❸ Lloyd's Register
Fenchurch Street

Lloyd's Register of Shipping was at the heart of London's pre-eminence as a global centre of insurance in the days when the city was one of the world's leading ports and the capital of a major maritime trading nation. It is quite separate from Lloyd's of London, although with similar seventeenth-century origins in Edward Lloyd's coffee house. It is located in a late Victorian building by T. E. Colcutt in the specialist insurance sub-district east of Gracechurch Street and Bishopsgate that also contains Richard Rogers's Lloyd's Building and 30 St Mary Axe (the 'Gherkin'), built by the reinsurance company Swiss Re, which still has offices there.

❹ Gibson Hall
Bishopsgate

Built as the head office for the National Provincial Bank, Gibson Hall was threatened with demolition when the bank merged with the Westminster Bank in 1968 to become the National Westminster Bank (later rebranded as NatWest). The new bank redeveloped its extended property, featuring Tower 42, behind Gibson Hall. But the old banking hall itself was spared after a heated conservation battle. Designed by John Gibson in 1864 with an extension in 1878, it is widely regarded as having set new standards of architectural magnificence in the City as it strove to compete with the Bank of England complex just down the street. It now functions rather prosaically as a venue for upscale corporate entertainment, wedding receptions and the like.

Skyscrapers and Starchitecture

The City's role as a hub of global finance has changed its skyline dramatically. With limited space in a booming local property market, there was a great deal of pressure from the 1990s onwards to build skyscrapers. In a visual *coup d'état* against established conservation-orientated planning policy, Ken Livingstone, Greater London's first democratically elected mayor, strongly supported the development of tall buildings in the City. Livingstone apparently saw the skyline as an important means of asserting and consolidating London's status as a global city. Fostering the development of tall buildings was also a way of helping to secure planning gain from developers: they would be allowed to build tall as long as they contributed to public infrastructure, improved urban design and affordable housing.

⑤ Lloyd's Building, Richard Rogers + Partners (1978–86), is the building that established Rogers's stardom, and set a crucial precedent for projects in the City.

⑥ Leadenhall Building (the 'Cheesegrater'), Rogers Stirk Harbour + Partners (2010–14).

Livingstone argued that this would help to make London a more sustainable city in the face of growing pressure for new offices and housing.

The Commission for Architecture and the Built Environment and the Urban Task Force created by the 1997–2010 Labour government, meanwhile, had placed a strong emphasis on urban design and the desirability of office towers of the sort crafted by 'starchitects' (blue-chip international architects) elsewhere in the world: more innovative than the austere and aggressive towers of earlier eras (such as the City's Tower 42). Just as starchitects derive some of their standing through the visible presence of their built work in major cities, so the potency of the symbolic capital of world cities is derived in part from their association with starchitecture. Stardom and city branding become mutually reinforcing. Developers were quick to see the prestige associated with starchitects as key not only to securing public consent for big projects but also to assembling the necessary amounts of risk capital, ensuring

⑦ 20 Fenchurch Street (the 'Walkie Talkie'), Rafael Viñoly Architects (2010–14).

the market value of their products, and leasing the interior space of the building to commercial tenants.

The ability of a high-profile building of radical design to put a city on the global map had first been demonstrated strategy began to take form. Since then, the City has acquired a distinctive cluster of novel and sculptural architecture that almost automatically became instantly 'iconic': the Broadgate Tower (Skidmore, Owings and Merrill), Heron Tower (Kohn Pedersen Fox), the 'Cheesegrater' (Rogers Stirk Harbour + Partners), the 'Walkie-Talkie' (Rafael Viñoly), the 'Pinnacle' and the 'Scalpel' (both Kohn Pedersen Fox).

⑧ 30 St Mary Axe (the 'Gherkin'), Foster + Partners (1997–2003); Lloyd's building in the foreground. The popular response to the Gherkin's unusual and distinctive shape encouraged policymakers to assemble a skyline of 'starchitecture'.

by Sydney Opera House, designed by Danish architect Jørn Utzon in the late 1950s and completed in 1973. The Centre Georges Pompidou, designed by Richard Rogers and Renzo Piano and opened in 1977 in the run-down Beaubourg area of Paris, provided a second example, and it became a trend after the success of Frank Gehry's Guggenheim Museum in Bilbao, opened in 1997, prompted many other cities to seek to replicate the 'Bilbao effect' of elevating their perceived status within the global economy. The City's first example of starchitecture was the Lloyd's Building, designed by Richard Rogers and opened in 1986. For a long time it was widely regarded as a singular phenomenon. It was not until the appearance in 2004 of Norman Foster's 'Gherkin' at 30 St Mary Axe that Livingstone's

⑩ Heron Tower, Kohn Pedersen Fox (2008–11).

⑨ Broadgate Tower, Skidmore, Owings & Merrill (2005–2009).

London's skyline in 2014, from Waterloo Bridge.

⑪ No. 1 Poultry

Sited at the confluence of ancient routes into the City, No. 1 Poultry replaced a listed 1870s Gothic office building by John Belcher that had been acquired by the developer Peter Palumbo. Ludwig Mies van der Rohe had been commissioned to design a tower for the site, prompting a protracted fight between Modernists and pro-growth business interests on the one hand and, on the other, conservationists and conservatives (including the Prince of Wales). The compromise, presided over by the government, coincided with London's unfortunate fad for postmodern architecture, and No. 1 Poultry is the result. Designed by James Stirling in 1986–88, it was finally completed a decade later. The Prince of Wales, in another of his public interventions, described it as looking like 'an old 1930s wireless'. More recently, the architecture critic Owen Hatherley has described it as 'a screamingly City-Boy building, aggressive and bumptious'.[1]

⑫ Finsbury Circus

The only significant Georgian square in the City, Finsbury Circus was developed on a large piece of land, Moor Fields, that was not drained until the sixteenth century. The space remained as gravelled walks across open fields until Bethlem Royal Hospital ('Bedlam') moved into buildings designed by Robert Hooke in 1676. In 1815, after the buildings had been demolished (and the hospital relocated to Southwark), the City developed the Circus to a plan by George Dance the Younger. Early in the twentieth century, the original houses began to be demolished for commercial development, the proximity to Liverpool Street station and Moorgate Underground station being especially attractive to developers of large office buildings. The first was Salisbury House, shown here, an early mixed-use development of offices, banks, shops and flats designed by Davis & Emmanuel and completed in 1901.

⑬ The Barbican
Silk Street

The area now occupied by the Barbican was reduced to rubble during the Blitz. After the war, the City developed the project as an ideal Modernist planned development of both private and social housing, schools, shops and pubs, along with what was to be the largest arts complex in Europe. It was, more than anything, an attempt to bring people back to a City whose resident population had dwindled alarmingly, leaving the entire district lifeless after hours and at weekends. It has been, by most criteria, a great success - an exception to most of London's other Modern redevelopment projects of the period. The inspiration for the design and layout of the project was Le Corbusier's conceptual Ville Radieuse, and in particular its principle of insulating pedestrian movement from automotive traffic by means of elevated walkways ('ped-ways' in the planning jargon of the time). The first of the flats were completed in the early 1960s, but the arts centre took another two decades to build. By that time there were 2113 flats housing 6500 people in a mixture of tall towers and long terrace blocks of up to eleven storeys. At the heart of the complex are gardens and an ornamental lake with a terrace that connects to the arts centre. Financed by the City Corporation, the Barbican was built with good-quality materials, and well maintained. It was justifiably held to be one of the best projects of its type in Europe, although its critics point to the Brutalist concrete styling specified by the Barbican's architects, Chamberlin, Powell and Bon. The concrete is now stained and has unfortunate echoes of the likes of the notorious Robin Hood Gardens in Poplar. The other caveat to the success of the Barbican is that it has failed to develop into the socially mixed community that was envisaged in the 1950s, a result of the combination of the 1980s property boom and the Thatcher government's encouragement of the sale of social housing to private owners. It is a shame, in every sense, that the Barbican is now occupied by bonus-day millionaires. Not only has their ascendance displaced working- and middle-class households, but also their consumer behaviour and lack of community involvement has led to the closure of the local shops and pubs that had been built into the Barbican.

⓮ Queen's Head Passage

Once a narrow alley amid a specialized sub-district of printers and publishers, this approach to St Paul's Cathedral took its name from the Queen's Head Tavern, which dated from the early eighteenth century. The entire sub-district was flattened during the Blitz, leaving the precincts around St Paul's, now known as Paternoster Square, available for redevelopment. Inevitably, perhaps, such an important symbolic setting became the arena for an architectural style war. In the immediate postwar period, Modernists were unchallenged, and the first redevelopment of the area featured gaunt concrete slabs rising above plazas and decks. In practice it was not loved, and it had become obsolescent by the mid-1980s. A new owner, Stuart Lipton of Mountleigh Estates, responded to the emerging commercial sensibilities of the time – a preference for high-concept architecture by starchitects – by inviting seven architects and firms, including Richard Rogers, James Stirling, Norman Foster and Arata Isozaki, to submit proposals for a second redevelopment of Paternoster Square. The preferred design, by Rogers, was famously denounced by the Prince of Wales at the Corporation of London Planning and Communication Committee's annual dinner at Mansion House. 'You have to give this much to the Luftwaffe,' he told them, 'when it knocked down our buildings, it didn't replace them with anything more offensive than rubble.' The eventual compromise was a layout that sought to echo the City's medieval street plan, with narrow passages between mixed-use buildings leading to a Mediterranean-style piazza with an unfortunate postmodern flavour in the neo-traditional, New Urbanism style that was briefly popular in the 1990s.

⓯ Drapers' Hall
Throgmorton Avenue

Founded to regulate the City's cloth trade, the Drapers were issued with a royal charter in 1364, making them third in precedence among City livery companies after the Mercers and the Grocers. The halls of the City's livery companies were typically converted from early mansions, as here with Drapers' Hall, which sits on the site of the town mansion of Thomas Cromwell, Henry VIII's chief minister. After Cromwell's execution in 1540, his house was forfeit to the king, who sold it three years later to the Drapers, then based in St Swithin's Lane. The building was destroyed in the Great Fire and rebuilt in 1668-71, only to be replaced again in 1772 as a result of another fire. The neoclassical design by the Company's surveyor, John Gorham, was subsequently remodelled in the late nineteenth century.

16 Tower of London
Tower Hill

Now one of London's principal tourist attractions, the Tower stands just beyond the formal eastern boundary of the City. Sited strategically at a bend in the Thames and commanding the City on its seaward and most vulnerable side, it was a crucial element in balancing the commercial and political power of the City with the authority of the monarchy. Founded by William the Conqueror in 1066, it had the role not only of providing protection for the City but also of controlling the citizens of the City by means of the Tower garrison.

The Tower palace-fortress complex extends over 7 hectares (18 acres), a result of a continually developing ensemble of royal buildings from the eleventh to the sixteenth century. The whole complex has come to be known as the Tower of London, the name that originally applied only to the keep of 1076. From the late thirteenth century, the Tower served as home to the Royal Mint and as a major repository for official records and precious goods owned by the Crown. It has been the setting for some of the most momentous events in British and European history, including the execution on Tower Green of prisoners for whom public execution was considered dangerous. According to legend, the kingdom and the Tower will fall if the six resident ravens should ever leave the complex.

🄗 Leadenhall Market
Gracechurch Street

One of three Victorian market buildings in the City (the others Billingsgate and Smithfield), Leadenhall Market has been commodified as a setting for fashion outlets, food shops, wine bars, brasseries and a chocolatier, all aimed at affluent City workers. The market was refurbished in the early 1990s by the City Corporation with a vibrant Victorian colour scheme and the restoration of rows of wrought-iron hooks on shopfronts where game used to hang. Leadenhall was a poultry and game market dating from the fourteenth century, when the traders gathered in the courtyard of a mansion known as La Ledene Hall. In the fifteenth century the market was enlarged to provide a permanent site for the sale of poultry, grain, eggs, butter, cheese, herbs and other foodstuffs. The Victorian structure was designed in 1881 by Horace Jones, City Corporation Architect, the big central glass-and-iron dome almost certainly inspired by the great Galleria Vittorio Emanuele II in Milan (1865-77).

🄘 Gough Square

Unremarkable in broader context, this courtyard is one of the few fragments of Georgian architecture to have survived within the City. Built in 1700 and originally home to the Gough family of wool merchants, it was both home and workplace from 1748 to 1759 for Samuel Johnson, the conversationalist, wit, writer, journalist and, most famously, author of the *Dictionary of the English Language*. After Johnson's departure in 1759, his house was run as a lodging house, then a hotel and, in the late nineteenth century, a print shop. By the early twentieth century, it was in a derelict condition, but in 1911 it was bought by MP Cecil Harmsworth, who restored it and opened it to the public as a museum.

⑲ Minster Court
Mincing Lane

At the southern edge of the City's specialized insurance sub-district, Minster Court consists of a glazed courtyard surrounded by three linked buildings, the largest of which houses the London Underwriting Centre. The complex handles 2000–2500 brokers every day, occasionally rising to a peak of 4000. Designed by GMW Partnership in gruesome Gothic postmodern style and clad in pink granite, it opened in 1990, just as London's fling with kitschy postmodernism was coming to an end.

⑳ Exchange House
Primrose Street

Built in 1990 to a signature Skidmore, Owings & Merrill design (with expressed cross-bracing that recalls SOM's iconic John Hancock Center in Chicago), this ten-storey office building is effectively an inhabited bridge, located directly above the railway tracks of Liverpool Street station. The building's four parallel structural arches direct the load of the building to foundation piers on either side of the tracks. The solution allows for an open interior with two atria running through the building, and has the convenient effect of referencing the cast-iron arches of Victorian railway sheds.

Clerkenwell

The townscape of Clerkenwell contrasts with the districts to the south and west in that first-rank buildings, squares and terraces are few in number. Nevertheless, its variety and its multiplicity of layers make it one of inner London's most interesting districts. As the Survey of London's comprehensive two-volume tome on Clerkenwell notes,

Masterpieces of urban ensemble naturally do not abound in an inner London suburb that has been so often raked over and redeveloped. Yet much excellent second-order architecture is on offer, while the chance juxtaposition of disparate scales and styles adds spice to main roads, side streets and set-pieces alike.[1]

Medieval Clerkenwell was London's first real suburb. It was seeded by the presence of three religious foundations in the southern part of the district, adjacent to the City. The priory of St John of Jerusalem and the convent of St Mary were founded in the twelfth century. The priory became the home of the Knights of the Order of St John of Jerusalem in England, the vanguard (along with the Knights Templar) of imperialist Catholic crusades. Fragments of the priory itself have survived, while the order has morphed into the St John Ambulance service. The third of the district's monastic foundations, the Carthusian priory of Charterhouse, was established in 1371. After the Dissolution it was initially used to store hunting gear before being sold as a rambling private mansion. It was eventually purchased (in 1611) by Thomas Sutton, a philanthropist, who endowed a school for forty poor boys and an almshouse for eighty male pensioners. Royal officials and courtiers were drawn to the environs of the three religious foundations, creating a small suburb that remained high in social standing until the Great Fire of 1666, when the arrival of evacuees prompted the departure of the nobility.

On the higher ground north of this medieval suburb were natural springs, the principal source of the City's water supply. One of them, the Clerk's Well, gave its name to Clerkenwell. Another, Sadler's Wells, later gave its name to a music hall, then a theatre and, now, a dance theatre. Clerkenwell became a recreational district in the two centuries before it was built over. The springs were promoted for their medicinal value and increasingly used as venues for organized amusements, tea-gardens, grottoes and the like. Clerkenwell has a claim as the earliest known specific location in London for the performance of plays (including religious dramatizations advertised as 'miracles' by the prioress of St Mary's). Moorfields, to the northeast of the monasteries, had ponds for duck-hunting and was also used for archery, bear- and bull-baiting, cock-fighting and wrestling. Like other districts just outside the limits of the City, Clerkenwell was also used as a dumping ground and wound up with the City's unwanted activities.

Early Development

The first continuous urban development naturally took place nearest to the City, along three main roads that ran northwards from the entry points into the City at Smithfield and Aldersgate, and along the valley of the River Fleet that flowed towards the Thames along the western edge of the district. But much of Clerkenwell remained undeveloped even after building had leapfrogged north to Islington. The reason was that the heart of the district was covered with a dense network of water pipes that the New River Company had installed to supply the City from its springs and reservoirs. Only when the company installed buried cast-iron pipes, beginning in 1810, was the land freed for building. The company's surveyor, William Mylne, promptly prepared plans for

Farringdon Road. The former printing warehouse of William Dickes, chromolithographer, built in the mid-1860s. It is currently used as offices.

St John's Gate. Built in 1504 as the south gateway to the Priory of Clerkenwell, which became the headquarters of the Knights of St John of Jerusalem.

development, and the surveyors of the neighbouring Northampton, Lloyd Baker, Skinners' and Brewers' estates were able to address remaining gaps in the district's urbanization.

A widespread building boom that lasted through the decade up to 1825 got things off to a good start. There was an exceptional degree of liaison and co-ordination among the surveyors of the major estates, and they managed to maintain design control over numerous small builders and developers: 'Even judged against West End standards there are terraces, squares and other set pieces with dignity, grace and even grandeur.'[2] By 1850 Clerkenwell had been completely built over. But, meanwhile, some of the courts and closes hidden behind the more respectable streets had become terribly overcrowded. In the second half of the nineteenth century the problem was intensified as houses were divided as lodging for students, immigrants (French, Swiss and Italian) and single workers. Very rapidly, large sections of Clerkenwell degenerated into slums.

Watchmakers, Printers and Dissidents

Nineteenth-century Clerkenwell was by no means simply a residential district, however. A proto-industrial district had arisen in the valley of the Fleet, where the priory and the convent had established water-powered mills (on Turnmill Street). In the

eighteenth century, metal-based trades began to spill northwards from the City's northern fringe, where skilled metalworking in gold and brass had long thrived along with furniture- and instrument-making. Clerkenwell developed a distinctive industrial cluster of barometer- and chronometer-makers, engravers, jewellers, locksmiths, penmakers, print artists, silversmiths, surgical instrument-makers and watchmakers, most of whom worked independently out of their houses or in lean-to workshops behind them.

The articulate artisan class that developed around these industries established Clerkenwell as the heart of the radical political scene in Victorian London. The district already had a reputation for rebellion and nonconformity. Clerkenwell had been where the London Mob gathered at the start of the Gordon Riots in 1780, sparked by Parliament's intention to relax discriminatory laws limiting the rights of Catholics but fuelled by feelings of economic disadvantage and exploitation. In 1816 public disorder erupted in Spa Fields after one of the first ever cases of mass public meetings.

In the mid-nineteenth century Clerkenwell Green became a central venue for public meetings, demonstrations and frequent clashes between Chartists (campaigners for radical political reform) and the recently formed Metropolitan Police Force. Clerkenwell's radical-left tradition continued until the mid-twentieth century, closely associated with journalism and the printing trades. Lenin edited *Iskra*, the political newspaper of Russian émigrés, from a former schoolhouse on Clerkenwell Green (now the Marx Memorial Library). The Socialist League was based on Farringdon Road, and the *Daily Worker*, the newspaper of the Communist Party of Great Britain, was published from offices on Cayton Street in the 1930s before being taken over by the People's Press Printing Society and later relaunched as Britain's socialist tabloid, the *Morning Star*, in 1966.

Slum Clearance and Industrial Building

As in every other inner-London district, the Victorians undertook a variety of reforms and metropolitan improvements. Slums were cleared, sewers, roads, railways and model housing constructed, and institutions - churches, schools and dispensaries - added to the townscape. One of the most expedient ways of dealing with the rookeries and slums of the city was to drive roads through them. In Clerkenwell, this led to one of the greatest urban engineering achievements of the nineteenth century. The valley of the River Fleet had become a desperate slum, the river itself a virtual sewer. It was the obvious route from the new Metropolitan Cattle Market (1855, later the Caledonian Market) at King's Cross down to the newly modernized (1868) Smithfield meat market on the northern fringe of the City. The solution was to purge, widen and deepen the valley, creating underground tunnels both for the river and for a branch of the Metropolitan Railway. It all ran beneath a wide new road - Farringdon Road - that connected the King's Cross area with the rebuilt (1869) Blackfriars road bridge across the Thames. Clerkenwell Road and Rosebery Avenue were also driven through the district's slums, while charitable trusts, including the Improved Industrial Dwellings Company, the Metropolitan Association for Improving the Dwellings of the Industrious Classes and the Peabody Trust, did their best to accommodate the households displaced from the old slums.

Most of the sites freed up by Clerkenwell's slum clearances, though, were taken up by industry for purpose-built workshops, factories and warehouses. Rebuilding by ebullient Victorian entrepreneurs along Farringdon Road and Rosebery Avenue in the 1880s featured facades intended to demonstrate to the world their owners' taste and prosperity. Functional interiors were belied by showy Italian or French Gothic fronts with terracotta mouldings: lion- or Neptune-head keystones above the windows; panels of scrollwork, garlands, fruits, swags; and so on. Towards the turn of the century, the introduction of refrigeration led to the displacement of many of the small meat and poultry dealers in the streets near Smithfield market by large cold-storage facilities. In side streets and backstreets, meanwhile, speculative developers built smaller, plain-looking factory and warehouse space for the multitude of small industrial enterprises that were heirs to Clerkenwell's metal and printing trades: electroplating and the manufacture of cathode-ray tubes, gas and electrical meters, printing inks, photographic paper, surveying equipment, weighing machines and specialized tools.

Sadler's Wells. The sixth theatre on the site since 1683, when Edward Sadler opened a 'Musick House', one of the first public theatres to open in London after the Restoration.

Progressive Local Government

Clerkenwell found itself in the new Metropolitan Borough of Finsbury as a result of the London Government Act of 1899. The new local authority was to face more than five decades of economic decline and social deprivation before being amalgamated with the London Borough of Islington in 1965. The new transport systems of the early twentieth century resulted in the decentralization of both industry and population, leaving behind small and uncompetitive firms and a residual and impoverished population. Clerkenwell's housing stock, most of it about a century old by the end of the First World War, was in a very bad state. The LCC had undertaken a couple of social housing projects, the Bourne Estate on Clerkenwell Road (1901-1907) and Mallory Buildings on St John Street (1904-1906). But it was not until the 1930s that Clerkenwell's social needs were seriously addressed. Finsbury acquired a progressive reputation for public welfare and housing provision that was highlighted through a series of high-profile Modernist projects designed for the borough by the socially committed architectural practice the Tecton Group, led by Berthold Lubetkin. Three of the four projects by Tecton and Lubetkin were in Clerkenwell: the Finsbury Health Centre and the Spa Green and Bevin Court housing estates. Other projects reflected the sequential fashions of council-house design, from the prefabricated concrete Brutalism of the early 1960s to the mid-rise, deck-access and contextual brick developments of the mid-1970s. By that time, much of Clerkenwell's industry had moved out of the area, along with its workforce. For all Finsbury's social progressivism, the district had become a classic case of inner-city decay and dereliction.

Creative Industries and Loft Living

Since the mid-1980s Clerkenwell has been rejuvenated. Its Victorian industrial fabric proved to be well suited to conversion into small new-economy offices, studios and loft apartments. Design, media and advertising firms found their way into renovated spaces around Sekforde Street and along St John Street and Cowcross Street. New land-use policies introduced by Islington borough council in 1989 required every major site to be mixed-use, enabling bars and restaurants to coexist more easily with offices, workshops or flats. This shift was crucial to the subsequent trend of loft living that started with the conversion of a warehouse in Summer Street in 1992, followed by Warner House, a former printing works, in 1993-96 and the Metropolitan Water Board offices and laboratory at New River Head in 1995-98. Other conversions followed, along with new buildings marketed by

Warner House. One of the first large-scale loft conversions in the district, the apartment building was formerly a printing works.

large national commercial housebuilders as loft-style apartments. The demand for all this new residential space came not only from the design, fashion and media types whose firms had moved in to the district, but also from City business service and financial workers whose numbers - and salaries - had been boosted by the deregulation of the financial sector in 1986 and the consequent influx of a large number of international financial institutions to the City.

Thus, in the space of a decade or so, Clerkenwell went from a dingy backwater to a booming, revalorized district with a distinctive new form of gentrification. The transformation was accompanied by the appearance of numerous gastropubs and minimalist restaurants catering to the new loft-living community of 'design-aware' young professionals. The change is reflected most vividly by the transformation of Exmouth Market, a once-thriving market street with grocers and cheap household goods stalls, which had become squalid and depressed. In the late 1990s it was recast by a public-private partnership as a pedestrianized and commodified re-creation of 'village London', with organic food stalls, bars, restaurants and shops linked to nearby Sadler's Wells Theatre.

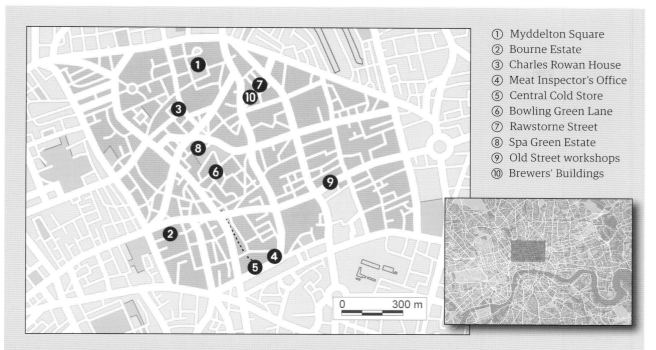

① Myddelton Square
② Bourne Estate
③ Charles Rowan House
④ Meat Inspector's Office
⑤ Central Cold Store
⑥ Bowling Green Lane
⑦ Rawstorne Street
⑧ Spa Green Estate
⑨ Old Street workshops
⑩ Brewers' Buildings

0   300 m

Clerkenwell has a dense, irregular network of small streets, some of which are medieval in origin. Most of the district was laid out between the 1760s and the 1850s, including several small set pieces of urban design – Northampton Square, Myddelton Square, Percy Circus, Lloyd Square and Wilmington Square – conceived by the surveyors of the small estates of the district and resulting in an unselfconscious townscape with broad appeal. The varied character of the surviving fabric reflects the piecemeal land-ownership of the area and its development in the nineteenth century by numerous small building firms. The dense street pattern was overlaid by several broad thoroughfares that were driven through the district by engineers in the late Victorian period. More recently, parts of the original street pattern have been obliterated by precincts of council housing. Pentonville Road and City Road provide a commercial seam between Clerkenwell and Islington to the north, while Charterhouse Street effects an equivalent seam between Clerkenwell and the City to the south. Clerkenwell merges to the east with Hoxton and Shoreditch, and to the west with Bloomsbury and Fitzrovia.

❶ Myddelton Square

The development of Myddelton Square and the surrounding streets in the mid-1820s prompted a famous political cartoon of 1829, *The March of Bricks and Mortar*, by the illustrator George Cruikshank. The square was the centrepiece of the New River Estate, developed by William Mylne, the company surveyor. The north side of the square, shown here, was badly damaged during the Second World War and rebuilt in replica by the New River Company in 1947–48.

❷ Bourne Estate
Portpool Lane

One of the LCC's earliest and largest inner-London slum-clearance estates, the Bourne was built in the early 1900s before the LCC's subsequent strategy of building 'cottage estates' further afield. The layout and design of the five- and six-storey blocks of balcony-access flats, with large arches leading through them to a sheltered central area, was a significant precursor in form and style of interwar housing estates throughout Britain. It also influenced tenement housing in continental Europe, beginning with critically acclaimed social housing in Vienna immediately after the First World War. The Viennese model was subsequently brought back to London – in the Ossulston Estate, Camden, for example (see page 79) – and in some private mansion blocks in central London in the 1930s. The Bourne Estate was designed by the LCC Architect's Department under W. E. Riley and used first to house families displaced by the LCC's Kingsway project (see page 124).

❸ Charles Rowan House
Margery Street

Charles Rowan House was built in the late 1920s as quarters for married policemen. It was generally acknowledged that housing policemen in large barracks away from the rest of the population was undesirable, but by the early twentieth century decent, affordable housing in central districts was scarce, making it difficult to call on men at short notice. The building was designed by Gilbert Mackenzie Trench, architect and surveyor for the Metropolitan Police (who also designed the original Police Box, made famous as the Tardis in the television series *Doctor Who*). Strikingly different, austere and forbidding, it provided ninety-six flats, each with its own scullery, integral bathroom and WC, along with a designated uniform cupboard. There were also twenty-four pram shelters and a basement playground. It was turned into council flats in the 1970s and is now in owner-occupation.

4 Meat Inspector's Office
Charterhouse Street

Clerkenwell's southern boundary faces Smithfield wholesale meat market, which has influenced the pattern of land use for several blocks around. There had been a cattle market at Smithfield for centuries, but it was moved to the Metropolitan Cattle Market next to King's Cross in 1855. The wholesale meat market was built just over a decade later, serving the entire metropolis. The Meat Inspector's Office dates from 1930, a product of an intensified awareness of the importance of sanitation and a more highly regulated trade. The architecture is also very much a product of its time, in Portland stone with strong Art Deco influences and an impressive frieze featuring a parade of livestock walking straight ahead, as if being led to market.

5 Central Cold Store
Charterhouse Street

Just to the west of the Meat Inspector's Office is the old Central Cold Store, built for the City in 1899. It marked an important transitional phase in the district: the transport revolution and the coming of refrigeration, both of which displaced many of the district's small, independent meat and poultry dealers. Cold-storage facilities opened along Charterhouse, Cowcross and St John streets, but subsequent improvements in freezer technology and the logistics of distribution made the cold stores themselves obsolescent. The Central Cold Store building now disguises a city-centre cogeneration power station.

6 Bowling Green Lane

The former Bowling Green Lane Board School was built for the School Board for London soon after it had been established in 1870. The ragged schools and church- and chapel-affiliated schools of the early nineteenth century were not sufficient to meet the needs of an industrializing and modernizing society, and the School Board sought to combat the ignorance and illiteracy of the slums by building impressive new facilities. The Bowling Green Lane school was one of the best, designed for 800 pupils by the School Board's first architect, Edward Robert Robson. The name of the street derives from Clerkenwell's early history as a recreational suburb; bowling greens are shown on Ogilby and Morgan's map of 1676. Improbably, the former school now houses the offices of Zaha Hadid, a prima-donna starchitect whose design sensibilities are totally at odds with Robson's Domestic Revival-style Board Schools.

❽ Spa Green Estate
Rosebery Avenue

In the 1930s the borough council developed the Finsbury Plan, an ambitious scheme for borough-wide rebuilding. The progressive architectural firm the Tecton Group, led by Berthold Lubetkin, designed the proposed social housing, but the project was halted by the war. Instead, the flats built after 1945 were on scattered sites: Spa Green, Bevin Court in Holford Square and Priory Green in Pentonville, all under the supervision of the new firm of Lubetkin and Skinner. The Spa Green Estate consists of two eight-storey blocks and one four-storey one. As with Lubetkin's other work, it was critically acclaimed for its innovative features as well as decorative elements in what were basically slab blocks. Spa Green has aerofoil elements designed to channel breezes for the fast drying of laundry, scientifically designed kitchens, soundproofing between flats, a refuse-disposal system to eliminate dustbins and bedrooms facing on to landscaped gardens.

❾ Old Street workshops

When Old Street was widened in the 1870s, it attracted investment in new, purpose-built workshops to accommodate the district's many instrument-making and light manufacturing firms. This example was designed by Herbert Ford and Robert Hesketh in 1880 for Samuel Haskins, manufacturer of window blinds and roller shutters. Ford was a specialist in warehouse design, and at his death in 1903 was said to have designed 400 warehouses in London. Like many of the other workshop buildings and warehouses along Old Street, this one is now occupied by offices and showrooms.

❿ Brewers' Buildings
Rawstorne Street

The Brewers' Company is a City livery company whose charter was granted by Henry VI in 1438. The company inherited an estate in Clerkenwell, which it began to develop in the late eighteenth century. This block of flats was built as philanthropic housing by the company between 1871 and 1882.

❼ (opposite) Rawstorne Street

This austere Georgian terrace on the Brewers' Company Estate was built in the late 1780s by Thomas Rawstorne, brickmaker.

Greenwich

Situated on the most dramatic outer curve of the Thames, where the river's current has scoured a deep channel, Greenwich is London's most famous maritime district. Historically, anyone attacking London from Europe via Dover - the shortest sea crossing - was forced either over Blackheath by land or past Greenwich by river. Either way, Greenwich represented a prime defensive site with excellent river access. Archaeological digs have found remains of prehistoric, Roman, Saxon and Danish settlements. The making of the district, though, was royal patronage, and the result was a collection of buildings in a distinctive setting that have been added to UNESCO's World Heritage List, keeping company with Stonehenge, the Tower of London, Venice and the historic centre of Paris. As noted in UNESCO's summary of the significance of Greenwich,

> the ensemble of the 17th century Queen's House, part of the last Royal Palace at Greenwich, the palatial Baroque complex of the Royal Hospital for seamen, and the Royal Observatory founded in 1675 and surrounded by the Royal Park laid out in the 1660s by André Le Nôtre, reflects two centuries of Royal patronage and represents a high point of the work of the architects Inigo Jones and Christopher Wren, and more widely European architecture at an important stage in its evolution. It also symbolises English artistic and scientific endeavour in the 17th and 18th centuries.[1]

Much of the land in the district had become Crown property by the mid-fifteenth century. It was first developed as a royal residence when Henry VI gave a Palace, Placentia, to his wife, Margaret of Anjou. The Tudor monarchs Henry VIII, Mary I and Elizabeth I were all born there. It was Henry VIII who intensified the naval presence along this stretch of the Thames, founding two new shipyards as his navy grew: one upriver from Placentia, at Deptford, and the other downriver at Woolwich. Meanwhile, the riverfront town that grew up at the gates of the palace naturally acquired a strong maritime character. The monarchy, for its part, gradually developed and improved its estate. In 1616 James I of England (and VI of Scotland) commissioned the building of the Queen's House from Inigo Jones, Surveyor of the King's Works. The project was suspended when the queen's health failed the following year (she died in 1618), but Jones later resumed work for Henrietta Maria, wife of Charles I, completing the building in 1637. It was the first strictly classical Renaissance building in Britain and the direct inspiration for Palladian houses and villas all over the country well into the nineteenth century.

A Baroque Complex

The hillside behind the Queen's House was landscaped into Greenwich Park at the instigation of Charles II. André Le Nôtre, who had designed the park at the Palace of Versailles, was given the commission in 1662. On the brow of the hill, the king sited his Royal Observatory, designed by Christopher Wren with the assistance of the scientist Robert Hooke, and opened in 1675. The observatory quickly became pre-eminent in the study of the role of astronomy in transoceanic navigation, and its reputation eventually resulted in the adoption of the Greenwich Meridian and Greenwich Mean Time as the global reference points for measuring space and time.

Meanwhile, the king had decided to demolish Placentia and build a new palace by the river. A small wing of the planned palace was completed before Charles died, but his successors did not want to live in Greenwich, preferring Kensington. Eventually Queen Mary, wife of William III, decided to incorporate the partially built palace into a naval almshouse,

Maritime Greenwich and Greenwich Park. The classic view from the Royal Observatory, with the Isle of Dogs on the far side of the Thames.

Cutty Sark. The clipper ship built in 1869 for the tea trade with China.

King Charles Court. Completed in 1705 as part of what was intended to be Greenwich Palace and now home to the Trinity Laban Conservatoire of Music and Dance.

the Royal Hospital for Seamen. The hospital was laid out to a master plan in the grand manner by Christopher Wren with the assistance of other leading architects, including Nicholas Hawksmoor and John Vanbrugh. Building began in 1696 and continued throughout much of the eighteenth century. The result was Britain's most outstanding group of Baroque buildings. The hospital complex became a symbol not only of intellectual and artistic refinement but also of Britain's growing naval power. At the height of British sea power, in 1873, the complex was converted to house the Royal Naval College. This brought the navy's officer class, its families and its suppliers to Greenwich, shaping the character of the district for more than a century before the hospital complex was converted again, this time for use by the University of Greenwich and the Trinity Laban Conservatoire of Music and Dance.

Building Greenwich

Although the departure of the royal court and the rise of dockyard-related industries deprived the town

of its fashionable cachet, it remained prosperous, favoured in particular by sea captains and merchants as well as naval officers. They had money to spend and status to maintain, and they built lavishly in order to make their mark. The result was a collection of handsome private villas and formal stuccoed terraces set around Hawksmoor's St Alfege's church in the centre of the town. Croom's Hill, which runs along the western edge of Greenwich Park, is 'a textbook of quietly wealthy individuality, ... a street which is not just a statement of wealth and taste, but a living architectural history lesson'.[2] At the top of the hill is the Ranger's House, built for Admiral Francis Hosier at the beginning of the eighteenth century. On the other side of the park is Vanbrugh Castle, the home of Vanbrugh, who is perhaps best known as the architect of Blenheim Palace.

Further down the social scale, Nelson Road became a centre of bankers and brokers, while mid-ranking officers gravitated towards houses in the streets around the park. Streets nearer the river tended to house skilled hands in trim cottage terraces, while slightly grander double-fronted houses in side streets would be for petty officers, shipwrights and shipping clerks. Greenwich Park became one of London's chief centres of genteel leisure, especially after the new Greenwich Pier, built in 1836, improved accessibility for leisure steamers from central London.

However, Greenwich was not all gentility and aspiration. The district had its share of low-grade terracing, back alleys, dosshouses, brothels and pawnbrokers. It also had a fine collection of alehouses and inns, several of which specialized in whitebait suppers that drew customers from upriver. By the early decades of the nineteenth century, parts of the town centre had become sufficiently degraded to warrant what today would be called a regeneration scheme. A master plan was devised by Joseph Kay, former architect and surveyor to the Foundling Hospital in Bloomsbury. The scheme was implemented in 1829, with Nelson Road the first section to be completed. Greenwich Market was rebuilt and opened in 1831.

Small-town Character

For a century or so the physical character of the district hardly changed. Speculative building ceased altogether, and there were few new industrial or commercial activities. As a result, Greenwich is distinctive for its lack of Victorian urban fabric. There was considerable damage during the Second World War as a result of the district's proximity to the docklands. This included the loss of one of the famous whitebait taverns, the Ship Tavern, which was destroyed by a bomb in 1941, leaving a convenient space in which to put a dry dock for the Cutty Sark, a twice-restored nineteenth-century tea clipper with Greenwich connections.

The core of Greenwich today has a combination of impressive historical buildings and neglected minor buildings that reflect their original purpose and that add an important dimension of the district's small-town character as well as providing an appropriate setting and approach for the main ensemble of Grade I-listed buildings. Inevitably, the attractions of the latter have brought an assortment of cheap cafés, souvenir shops, second-hand and specialist bookshops specializing in nautical and maritime texts, and the odd nautical memorabilia shop. The village atmosphere of the town centre, along with the proximity of the attractions of Maritime Greenwich, would make it an excellent candidate for pedestrianization. Contemporary urban designers would have a field day. But the town centre is also a significant traffic junction, permanently busy, especially during the summer. The market area retains Kay's comfortable proportions and its neat cobbles, and is somewhat sequestered from the worst of the traffic. It no longer operates as a general market, however: like many of London's street markets, it now sells little by way of essentials and much by way of food treats, craft jewellery, cheap watches, candles, scarves and framed prints.

Greenwich Peninsula

For centuries Greenwich Peninsula remained an undeveloped, marshy area – just like its physical counterpart across the river, the Isle of Dogs. In the past decade or so it has begun to be integrated with the rest of Greenwich. It was first developed at the end of the nineteenth century, when the Metropolitan Gas Company opened the largest gasworks in Europe – big enough to have its own internal railway system. After the Blackwall Tunnel had been built under the Thames to link the peninsula with the north bank, light industry moved in, along with a chemical works and wharves. In the second half of the twentieth century, though, industry gradually dwindled.

By the mid-1980s the peninsula was left largely derelict, one of the most isolated locations in the metropolis. In 1997 the GLA purchased a large tract of land at the tip of the peninsula that became the site for the Millennium Dome (now named the O2). Controversially built as an isolated flagship project, divorced from any strategic planning context, it has nevertheless become an iconic structure. The regeneration of the rest of the peninsula has been led by a government agency, English Partnerships. A key development was the opening in 1999 of North Greenwich Tube station, paving the way for the development of Greenwich Millennium Village, a mixed-tenure housing estate of 1800 dwellings with its own village shopping centre and community facilities.

Greenwich Town Centre. A traditional town centre that has been absorbed into the polycentric fabric of the metropolis.

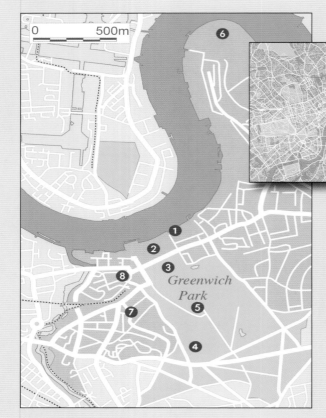

① Trafalgar Tavern
② Old Royal Naval
   College
③ The Queen's House
④ The Ranger's House
⑤ Royal Observatory
⑥ The O2
⑦ Royal Hill
⑧ St Alfege's Church

The historic centre of the district, with a mixture of medieval, Georgian and Regency streets, is situated close to the junction of the River Ravensbourne and the River Thames. To the east, fronting the Thames, is the ensemble of Grade I-listed buildings that constitute Maritime Greenwich. Behind them is Greenwich Park, which retains some of its geometric Renaissance layout. Residential development around the other three sides of the park dates mainly from the nineteenth century and is dominated by detached and semi-detached homes. Terraced housing predominates towards the peninsula, where much of the nineteenth-century layout has been overwritten by recent regeneration projects.

❶ Trafalgar Tavern

Park Row

Greenwich riverfront taverns were popular among Victorian London's intelligentsia. The Trafalgar Tavern was built on the site of the Old George Inn in 1837, its Regency-style bay windows giving splendid views along the river. By the 1860s it had become famous as a political meeting place, with Prime Minister William Gladstone, among others, travelling by ferryboat from Westminster for a whitebait supper. Shoals of tiny fish were caught locally, deep-fried, dressed with lemon juice and cayenne pepper, served with brown bread and washed down with iced champagne. Charles Dickens and William Thackeray were also among the notables who came to the Trafalgar for its whitebait suppers. It closed as a tavern before the First World War and was used in turn as an institute for merchant seamen, a working men's club and flats before being redeveloped as a pub in 1968.

❷ Old Royal Naval College
King William Walk

King Charles Court, the only part of the planned royal palace to be built, was already falling into disrepair when Queen Mary made it her purpose in life to convert and extend it into a hospital for veteran sailors. It was to be like the one being built for veteran soldiers in Chelsea, but grander in scale. Christopher Wren and his assistant Nicholas Hawksmoor, the architects of the Royal Hospital in Chelsea (see page 87), were employed to devise the master plan for Greenwich, and both contributed to the design of its buildings. But the complex took decades to complete and involved the services of several other leading architects, including John Vanbrugh, Thomas Ripley and James 'Athenian' Stuart. The first veteran seamen were admitted in 1705, and the hospital was home to as many as 3000 at a time before it finally closed in 1869. The Royal Naval College moved there from Portsmouth a few years later and remained until 1998. Now that the complex is shared by the University of Greenwich and the Trinity Laban Conservatoire of Music and Dance, the buildings are much more accessible to the general public. The four main components, King Charles, King William, Queen Mary and Queen Anne courts, are arranged symmetrically alongside the Thames and aligned with the Queen's House, just across the street in Greenwich Royal Park.

Top: Interior courtyard, Queen Mary Court
Middle: The twin domes and colonnades of King William Court and Queen Mary Court
Bottom: The classic view of the complex from across the Thames. The Queen's House can be seen in the distance.

❸ The Queen's House
Romney Road

The Queen's House, commissioned by James I for his wife, Anne, and designed by Inigo Jones, was the model, directly or indirectly, for classical houses and villas across London and throughout the country for 200 years after its completion in 1637. The industrial era introduced new aesthetic sensibilities, new building technology and a new class structure with different ideas about how best to express taste and social standing, but until then the Italianate villa was the standard for aristocratic sophistication. In 1807 the Queen's House became a school for young seamen, with the addition of long colonnades and wings, and in the 1930s it became part of the National Maritime Museum.

❹ The Ranger's House
Chesterfield Walk

Greenwich was a popular area for senior naval figures to build their homes, and the ridge running east to west across Greenwich Park provided an elevated position, enabling scrutiny of the river from their roofs, which in the days before electronic communications was an important consideration. The Ranger's House was built around 1690 for Admiral Francis Hosier. In 1813 it was bought by the Crown, and it became the official residence of the Rangers of Greenwich Park. It is now in the care of English Heritage and open to the public, with a collection of works of art amassed by the diamond magnate Julius Wernher (1850-1912).

❺ Royal Observatory
Blackheath Avenue

With the increasing importance of maritime trade and naval power in the seventeenth century, the role of astronomy in navigation became critically important. Charles II founded the Royal Observatory in 1675 to solve the problem of finding longitude at sea. The observatory, located on a bluff overlooking the river, was designed by Christopher Wren and the scientist Robert Hooke. The first Astronomer Royal was John Flamsteed. As a result of the observatory's pre-eminence in the field, together with British imperial hegemony, the Greenwich Meridian and Greenwich Mean Time were adopted as global standards for the measurement of space and time in 1884.

➏ The O2
Peninsula Square

A distinctive landmark at the tip of the Greenwich peninsula, the O2 was commissioned by the government as one of London's millennium projects, along with the Millennium Bridge, Tate Modern, the London Eye and stations on the Jubilee line extension. The structure was designed by Richard Rogers in collaboration with Buro Happold. Called the Millennium Dome, it was intended as a home to a latter-day Great Exhibition, but the exhibition itself was a flop and barely lasted a year. Subsequently, the whole complex, apart from the dome itself, was demolished. It is now an entertainment complex including a multipurpose indoor arena with a capacity of up to 20,000, a music club, a cinema and bars and restaurants. It takes its name from its main sponsor, the telecommunications company O2.

➐ Royal Hill

In the early nineteenth century the rapidly expanding maritime community prompted the development of streets and terraces to the west of the royal park. Royal Hill was one of these. The modest doorcases, railings and stuccoed basements of its terraces signalled social respectability and a degree of affluence, echoing the design of grander West End terraces.

➑ St Alfege's Church
Greenwich Church Street

A medieval church stood on a site where Viking raiders were reputed to have killed Alfege, Archbishop of Canterbury, in 1012. It collapsed during a storm in 1710, just in time for the parishioners to petition for funding for a new church from the provisions of the Fifty Churches Act of 1711. St Alfege was designed by Nicholas Hawksmoor, completed in 1714 and consecrated in 1718.

Holborn

Holborn, immediately to the west of the City, owes its development to Henry III's declaration in 1234 that no institutes of legal education should be located in the City. As a result, the district attracted hostels and schools for lawyers that eventually became the Inns of Court. The Inns flourished under Elizabeth I, setting the tone of the district as a centre for legal and professional services. Today the Inns dominate the area. Their sequestered buildings and grounds are self-contained precincts that provide libraries, dining facilities and professional accommodation for barristers in training and practice.

In addition to the early Inns of Court, a few aristocratic and clerical élite households also settled in Holborn. But Queen Elizabeth's proclamation in 1580 that no new buildings should be erected within 3 miles (nearly 5 kilometres) of the City gates meant that for a long time Holborn was known mostly for its productive market gardens. Early in the seventeenth century the Inns of Court petitioned James I to allow several nearby fields to be landscaped into public walks – a task that was eventually undertaken by Inigo Jones. The landscaping inevitably attracted the prospect of residential development, and the Society of Lincoln's Inn moved quickly to secure the open space, arranging a 900-year lease that effectively turned Lincoln's Inn Fields into a large public park.

Post-Fire Development

The protection of Lincoln's Inn Fields as public open space was just in time. Shortly afterwards, the Great Fire changed everything. Holborn survived virtually intact, but post-Fire reconstruction, together with the building boom that followed the Restoration, meant that it was quickly redeveloped. The district's proximity to the City meant that some of the new construction was for people of means. The bulk of post-Fire construction in Holborn, though, was for somewhat less affluent households, speculatively built by developers who would take the ground-lease on a plot and build the shell of a house for sale on the open market to a final client.

Most began as master builders, but in Holborn one of the most active developers of the period was a medical doctor, Nicholas Barbon, who turned out to be one of London's most rapacious and unscrupulous developers. His book *The Discourse of Trade* (1690) is credited with identifying building construction as a stimulant of economic growth. He is also credited with inventing commercial fire insurance. His most important project in Holborn was Red Lion Square, laid out in the 1680s. Nothing remains today of Barbon's work in that square, but in another of his projects, New Square (which he completed after the death of the original developer, Henry Searle), three sides of matching four-storey houses still stand as part of the Lincoln's Inn complex.

Meanwhile, the district as a whole became increasingly overcrowded, the older courtyards and alleys colonized by the city's growing and impoverished underclass. By the 1730s Lincoln's Inn Fields had become 'a Receptacle for Rubbish, Dirt and Nastiness of all Sorts', such that

many wicked and disorderly Persons have frequented and met together therein, using unlawful Sports and Games, and drawing in and enticing young Persons into Gaming, Idleness and other vicious Courses; and Vagabonds, common Beggars, and other disorderly Persons resort therein, where many Robberies, Assaults, Outrages and Enormities have been and continually are committed.[1]

Eventually, Parliament established a board of trustees for the Fields, and the board enclosed the space with an iron palisade and relandscaped the interior.

Warwick Court.
A cul-de-sac adjacent to Gray's Inn, occupied mostly by lawyers' chambers.

Lincoln's Inn Fields, London's largest square, is surrounded by a mix of buildings of different ages and styles.

Nevertheless, the extension and development of the Inns of Court continued to attract wealthy and professional classes to the district throughout the eighteenth century. After the arrival in London of the Adam brothers in the 1760s and the passage of the Building Act in 1774 (which systematized the size and layouts of four types or 'rates' of house), the post-Fire simplicity of street facades was displaced by more elaborate neoclassical designs. One notable personage in this context is the architect John Soane, who bought number 12 Lincoln's Inn Fields in 1792 and later acquired numbers 13 and 14. He demolished and rebuilt all three houses, converting them into a residence and a museum for his vast and eclectic collection of paintings, architectural drawings and sculptures. He established the house as a public museum by Act of Parliament in 1833, requiring that the interiors be kept as they were at the time of his death, with admission free to the public.

New Cityscapes

By the Victorian era, Holborn was virtually devoid of fashionable private residences. On the other hand, the worst of the slums were eradicated as the upper reaches of the stinking River Fleet were covered and transportation infrastructure projects were carved through the city. It was the Edwardian development of the eastern and southern fringes of the district, though, that framed Holborn as a distinctive physical as well as functional district. The LCC laid out Aldwych at the beginning of the twentieth century, demolishing a web of old streets and carving out a wide avenue - Kingsway - that divided the legal quarter to the east from Covent Garden and the Bedford Estate to the west. Kingsway was built with an underpass to take electric trams, with the Holborn to Aldwych branch of the new Piccadilly line beneath it.

In line with the spirit of the times, the new streets were lined with impressive offices and public buildings. By this time steel-frame construction had made it possible to build tall, but the London Building Act of 1894 had set a limit of 24 metres (80 feet) on buildings on the widest streets. As a result Kingsway, mercifully, did not become too far out of scale, even though many of the buildings had something of the quality of American downtown architecture of the period. Nevertheless, Kingsway grew canyonlike and inhospitable, out of character with both Covent Garden and Soho to the west and Holborn to the east. The massing of the buildings on the curve of Aldwych was more successful, with the grouping of Bush House and the High Commissions of India and Australia built at a monumental scale in stripped classical style. The new Kingsway/Aldwych scheme made smart shopping developments profitable in the area, prompting the Bedford Estate to create Sicilian Avenue, London's first open-air pedestrian shopping street. Robert Worley's design included a pompous classical screen at each end to establish the Bedford Estate's right of way.

Beyond the Strand, Kingsway and Aldwych, land use in Holborn has remained dominated by institutions. The district has no major retail settings, and its principal streets function mainly as traffic arteries. As a result it has a relatively low profile: so much so that for several years hopeful estate agents and hotels looking to attract American tourists have referred to it as 'Midtown' rather than Holborn. The district's strategic situation will in fact be greatly enhanced with the arrival in 2018 of Crossrail stations at Farringdon and Tottenham Court Road, prompting a coalition of business interests - the InMidtown Business Improvement District - to commission the architectural practice Farrells to develop a master plan to revamp Holborn along with Bloomsbury and St Giles.

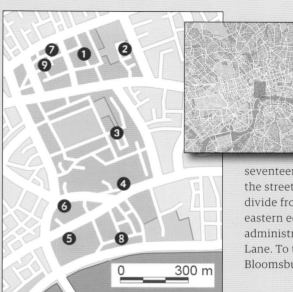

Most of Holborn is dominated by large institutional complexes - including Somerset House, the Royal Courts of Justice, the Inns of Court, King's College and the London School of Economics - and their associated open spaces. Only in the northwestern corner of the district, an area first built over by the speculative developer Nicholas Barbon in the seventeenth century, are big institutional buildings absent from the streets. The broad avenue of Kingsway makes for a sharp divide from Covent Garden and Soho to the west, while the eastern edge of the district is marked by Grays Inn Road and the administrative boundary of the City of London along Chancery Lane. To the north, Theobalds Road separates Holborn from Bloomsbury and Clerkenwell.

① Bedford Row
② Gray's Inn
③ Lincoln's Inn
④ Royal Courts of Justice
⑤ Somerset House
⑥ Bush House
⑦ Conway Hall
⑧ Cabmen's shelter
⑨ Red Lion Square

❶ Bedford Row

Even though twenty of the houses were burned out during the Blitz, this street is reckoned to be among the best in London for surviving buildings of the late seventeenth and early eighteenth centuries. The street takes its name from the Bedford Estate, owner of the ground on the west side of the street, which was developed around 1690 by Nicholas Barbon, who was arguably the most important of the building speculators in London during the last quarter of the seventeenth century. The houses on the west side of Bedford Row had an open view across to Gray's Inn for some twenty-five years after their erection, when the east side, shown here, was developed by Robert Burford, a carpenter, and George Devall, plumber. The street is now occupied almost exclusively by solicitors and barristers.

❷ Gray's Inn

South Square

Gray's Inn has been home to lawyers since the fourteenth century and is today one of the four Inns of Court responsible for the education and training of barristers before and after their Call to the Bar. The Inn originally formed part of the Manor of Purpoole belonging to the de Grey family, and law students used the Hall of the Manor as an 'Inn' in which to dine and hold the legal debates that formed part of their training. The Hall (centre left) was rebuilt in the 1550s, when Elizabeth I herself was the Inn's Patron and the Inn was renowned for its 'shows', including the staging of Shakespeare's *Comedy of Errors*. Most of the lawyers' chambers (top left and above) date from between 1680 and 1750 and conform to post-Fire building regulations. Their pristine appearance reflects extensive repair after the Second World War. Early nineteenth-century expansion saw the addition of new chambers in the Verulam Buildings (bottom left).

❸ Lincoln's Inn

New Square

At one time there were at least twenty Inns associated with lawyers. In late medieval times, 'inns' were large town houses that not only had accommodation for a whole retinue of guests but also typically included a large hall. Many of them were situated in the Holborn area, exurban but convenient for both Westminster and the City. With legal education proscribed from the City, some of the Inns gradually became places where it was offered. The Society of Lincoln's Inn moved to this site in the 1420s, taking over the town house of the bishops of Chichester. The Society acquired the freehold of the whole site in 1580. At that time the buildings comprised the Old Hall, a chapel and a cluster of chambers, all surrounded by a brick wall separating it from the street.

The Inn is still walled off from the rest of the city, although the medieval buildings were gradually replaced; the earliest now surviving is the Old Hall (1489-92). The Inn complex now consists of three squares. Old Square was built in early seventeenth-century Gothic style, with later extensions in Tudor style (left) by George Gilbert Scott in 1874 and his son John Oldrid Scott in 1878-86. New Square (above, right), which had formerly been an open space contiguous with Lincoln's Inn Fields, was begun in 1680 as a private venture by Henry Searle, but two years later the lawyers secured his agreement that it should be used by Lincoln's Inn. The square was finished after Searle's death in 1690 by the prolific Nicholas Barbon. The third square is formed by the neoclassical Stone Buildings, partly built in 1780 and finished in 1845.

❹ Royal Courts of Justice
Strand

Victorian modernization extended to many of the country's institutions. The Royal Courts of Justice were built in 1874–82 to accommodate in one place all the superior courts concerned with civil (i.e. non-criminal) cases: the Court of Appeal, the Crown Court and the High Court, and their subsidiaries. One-third of the cost of construction was provided by unclaimed funds in Chancery. Faced in Portland stone, the complex has more than 5 kilometres (3 miles) of corridors and more than 1000 rooms, including thirty-five courts. The Gothic design was the outcome of a competition held in 1866, a continuation of the 'Battle of the Styles' between adherents of Gothic Revival and classical architecture that had erupted a decade earlier over the design for the modernized Foreign Office on Whitehall (see page 274).

❺ Somerset House
Strand

Somerset House stands on the site of a riverside mansion of the same name that had passed into the hands of the Crown before being demolished in 1775. The new Somerset House was designed to accommodate learned societies as well as various government offices. The architect, William Chambers, solved this problem by treating the offices as a series of town houses arranged in a quadrangular layout. Over time, the building has seen a succession of occupants, including the Registry of Births, Marriages and Deaths and the Inland Revenue. No longer suited to modern government offices, Somerset House is now run by a trust charged with conserving the complex and developing it as a cultural centre. The Embankment Terrace has been reopened, and the Courtyard has been transformed from a hidden car park into a much-used public space.

❻ Bush House
Aldwych

The construction of Aldwych in 1902 created a prime new site that attracted several important buildings, including Australia House and the Indian High Commission. Bush House was planned as a major new trade centre and designed by the American architect Helmle & Corbett. Notorious for its lavish construction and fittings, it never took off as a trade centre, and in 1940 the BBC took over much of its space for offices and studios. Bush House became synonymous with the BBC's World Service until it moved out in 2012, leaving the building in need of a major refit in order to attract new clients.

❼ Conway Hall
Red Lion Square

Secular ethical societies flourished in the intellectual radicalism of the late nineteenth and early twentieth centuries. The South Place Ethical Society was founded in 1787 as a congregation of nonconformists, and in 1824 they built a chapel on South Place, Finsbury. They built Conway Hall in 1929 on the site of an old music hall. The hall was named in honour of Moncure Daniel Conway, an anti-slavery advocate, supporter of free thought and biographer of the revolutionary Thomas Paine. In its early days it was connected with a number of important figures including the secularist writer and lecturer Joseph McCabe, Herbert Burrows, a socialist reformer, and John Hobson, a social theorist and economist. The Society is still active, the oldest surviving institution of its kind in the country, renamed the Conway Hall Ethical Society.

❽ Cabmen's shelter
Temple Place

In the last quarter of the nineteenth century and the first decade or so of the twentieth, sixty-one cabmen's shelters were built at cab stands around London, funded by the Cabmen's Shelter Fund. Most of the shelters were staffed by an attendant who sold food and (non-alcoholic) drink, but only to cabbies. Thirteen of them are still in operation; this one dates from around 1900 and is a Grade II-listed structure.

❾ Red Lion Square
Red Lion Square was originally a Nicholas Barbon development, completed in the 1680s and incrementally redeveloped in subsequent years. Numbers 16 and 17 are unusual in having survived the Blitz as well as having been home to a succession of artistic talent: Dante Gabriel Rossetti, William Morris and Edward Burne-Jones. It was the problem of providing furniture for these rooms that first led Morris to abandon architecture and try his hand at furniture design.

Hoxton + Shoreditch

Situated just beyond London's city walls, Hoxton was seen by the London gentry in the late seventeenth century as being far enough away from the dirt and squalor of the City but close enough for a short journey to work. It was duly transformed into a superior sort of district, a phase that is marked by a few surviving Georgian residences and by its formal street pattern, featuring Charles Square and Hoxton Square. The Industrial Revolution brought another transformation. The completion of the Regent's Canal in 1820 meant that raw materials could be shipped into the area quickly and easily. By the middle of the nineteenth century Hoxton had become a working-class district, the centre of the London furniture industry, with workshops and warehouses surrounded by hastily erected housing for a rapidly increasing population of migrants and immigrants.

By the end of the nineteenth century Hoxton and Shoreditch had become run-down and notorious for poverty and degradation. For much of the twentieth century, despite incremental improvements to infrastructure, the elimination of the worst of the slum housing and the provision of social housing, it remained a classic inner-city problem area, its manufacturing base sharply diminished and its population trapped in a cycle of deprivation. It is still one of the most underprivileged and run-down areas of London, with poor schools, high levels of unemployment and a built environment dominated by obsolescent and semi-derelict structures. The streets of northern Hoxton and Shoreditch are largely filled with social housing, relieved only by the shops and pubs of Hoxton Street. Yet the southern part of the district has famously undergone a double transformation since the mid-1980s as the fickle processes of gentrification have unfolded across the landscape, while to the northwest the area near Regent's Canal is being transformed through new-build gentrification and warehouse conversions.

Brit Art and Avant-garde Design

The trigger for the gentrification of Hoxton and Shoreditch towards the end of the 1980s was that it had acquired a neo-bohemian aspect. Aspiring artists and young designers, musicians and unemployed or entry-level cultural-industry workers had found inexpensive live/work spaces in the district's industrial lofts and buildings. It helped that some of the incomers were key members of a much-heralded new generation of artists led by the likes of Damien Hirst, Rachel Whiteread, Sarah Lucas and Tracey Emin and known collectively as Young British Artists (YBA), exponents of 'Brit Art'.

The streets of Hoxton began to be used for experimental shows, and the buzz attracted galleries and dealers. Soon, the atmosphere generated around the social aspect of the neighbourhood, together with the existence of a reserve army of design-orientated workers, began to attract an avant-garde of graphic-design firms, independent music labels and studios, interior-design firms, photographic studios and galleries, architecture firms and new-media companies that colonized the old furniture workshops of the district. Disused and obsolescent workshops and warehouses were renovated as offices, galleries and bookshop-cafés. Loft spaces were renovated as flats, while as-yet unimproved housing provided cheap accommodation for aspiring creative types.

The district's neo-bohemian street atmosphere met important personal identity needs for many artists and design professionals as well as contributing to the image and branding of the firms for which they worked. By moving into a neo-bohemian scene, designers could signal their radical-progressive

Curtain Road. The hub of the furniture trade in the nineteenth century, now better known for its pubs and clubs.

White Cube art gallery. The opening of the prestigious gallery in a 1920s light industrial building cemented the district's reputation as a 'creative quarter'.

commitment both to themselves and to others, including clients. They had distinct ideas about what living like a designer should entail, and this in turn affected the atmosphere of the district. Hoxton's signature identity was fashion rebel: scruffy clothes and daft haircuts. For men, the 'uniform' was vintage Levi jeans paired with T-shirts bearing the names of obscure record labels. The 'look' was completed by a haircut that became known as the Hoxton Fin. The Hoxton-girl look was deliberately trashy, featuring Blondie T-shirts, plastic jewellery and pixie boots.

Several projects funded through government inner-city regeneration programmes helped to reinforce this production-orientated phase of gentrification, including basic refits of warehouses, the remodelling of an old electricity generating station into Circus Space (large warehouse spaces and studios housing, literally, a circus school), and a new cinema for the London Film and Video Workshop, the Lux.

Meanwhile, other government policies - fewer controls on development, a reduction in support services for working-class people and the privatization of the public housing stock - contributed to a gradual displacement of the existing multicultural working-class community. In their place came the

pioneer gentrifiers, attracted by the low rents, the neo-bohemian atmosphere of the district and the gritty authenticity of the built environment, with its warehouses and workshops with loading bays and wall cranes for furniture to be hoisted up. Abandoned warehouses began to be converted into lofts and pubs, and clubs, including a pioneering gay club, the London Apprentice, opened around Hoxton Square. The now-famous YBAs socialized a couple of blocks away in the Bricklayer's Arms on Charlotte Road. Media representations of the district, ignoring its less glamorous aspects and the displacement of disadvantaged households, helped to promote Hoxton as the exemplar of an edgy and innovative cultural quarter: *Time* magazine, for example, referred to Hoxton as one of the 'coolest places on the planet' in 1996.

By the late 1990s an incoming Labour government had put the propagation of creative industries and urban culture at the heart of urban policy, with Hoxton and Shoreditch often held up as an example of how inner-city districts could experience an 'urban renaissance'. In the district itself, gentrification was reinforced by the appearance of several key 'cultural incubators', including the prestigious White Cube art gallery, which opened in 2000 in a 1920s light-industrial building on Hoxton Square, and, nearby, the Prince's Drawing School, founded in 2000 by the Prince of Wales. Ultra-cool clubs and celebrity-chef restaurants also began to appear, notably the Shoreditch Electricity Showrooms, the Cantaloupe bar and restaurant, the Cargo club, and Fifteen and the Hoxton Apprentice (both training restaurants under the tutelage of celebrity chefs).

Cultural Consumption

These developments strengthened the reputation of Hoxton and Shoreditch as a 'cultural quarter' but made it unaffordable for the neo-bohemians at the heart of its initial transformation, since most of them never had the capital or the creditworthiness to purchase their property and protect themselves from rent increases. As property prices began to rise, many of these neo-bohemians and 'cultural proletariat' left for cheaper space further east, around Brick Lane and, further still, Dalston and Hackney Wick. In their place has come a more affluent cohort of gentrifiers with the capital and creditworthiness to purchase and renovate loft apartments and to patronize an increased number of galleries, upscale cafés, noodle bars, sushi restaurants and Italian delicatessens. Near enough (about 1 kilometre/½ mile) to the expanding fringe of London's banking and financial quarter, Hoxton and Shoreditch has also developed an embryonic night-time economy, its restaurants, clubs and bars catering increasingly to affluent office workers.

As a result, a second transformation has occurred, tipping Hoxton and Shoreditch from a district of cultural production to one of cultural consumption and from an avant-garde neo-bohemia to just another gentrifying district. In addition to the arrival of white-collar gentrifiers, the social mix of the district has been upgraded as local government agencies and not-for-profit institutions targeted a new 'worthy poor' of key workers (such as nurses, firemen and teachers) for their new and refurbished social housing. In the Peabody Trust's Nile Street project, for example, there are three kinds of affordable home: rented flats and studios for key workers; flats for

Peabody's own tenants; and shared-ownership flats where it is possible to take out a mortgage for some of the value of the flat and pay a subsidized rent on the remainder. Of the 175 homes in the project, 128 are 'affordable', the remainder having been sold privately to cross-subsidize the affordable units.

One way or another, Hoxton is no longer the real frontier of cool. The White Cube moved out of Hoxton Square in 2012. In the hands of local designers House of Jazz, the Hoxton-girl look had by then reached the catwalk and gone on to be reproduced for chain stores. The Hoxton Fin had been adopted by professional footballers and, through their influence on popular culture, by trend-conscious youth everywhere. Nevertheless, the district has retained a neo-bohemian atmosphere and, given its location within the metropolis, still has relatively cheap rents, especially for commercial space. Since the recession of 2008, this has attracted a distinctive cluster of internet start-up companies in the area around the Old Street junction – a cluster large enough to have earned the area the nickname of Silicon Roundabout.

Old Street Junction. Ugly new offices and apartment buildings at the hub of a cluster of internet start-ups and highly specialized small-to-medium-sized high-tech businesses that has become known as 'Silicon Roundabout' – and optimistically branded as 'Tech City' by the government.

Nile Street. The Peabody Trust building, completed in 2005, provides 175 homes with a communal courtyard, roof gardens and a youth centre.

The district is situated immediately to the north of the City of London and extends northwards to the Regent's Canal. It is bordered to the east by Bethnal Green and to the west by Clerkenwell and Islington. Like Bethnal Green, Hoxton and Shoreditch were initially developed at a high density, dominated by low-income housing and workshops. In the northern neighbourhoods of the district, the original layout and morphology of the area have largely been overwritten by social housing developments of various styles and vintages. The southern part of the district has retained more of its nineteenth-century fabric of residential terraces, shops and workshops. Closer to the City, there are remaining fragments of Georgian housing.

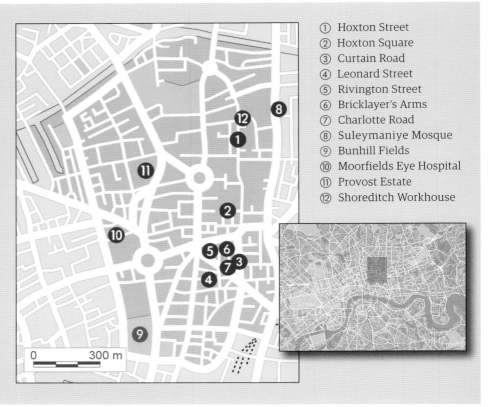

① Hoxton Street
② Hoxton Square
③ Curtain Road
④ Leonard Street
⑤ Rivington Street
⑥ Bricklayer's Arms
⑦ Charlotte Road
⑧ Suleymaniye Mosque
⑨ Bunhill Fields
⑩ Moorfields Eye Hospital
⑪ Provost Estate
⑫ Shoreditch Workhouse

0   300 m

❶ Hoxton Street

One of the principal routes for travellers into the City from the north in the seventeenth century, Hoxton Street was lined with places of enter-tainment and refreshment but surrounded by countryside. In the nineteenth century it was built up with terraces of working-class housing, and it is now surrounded by social housing. It has the feel of a close-knit London community, relatively untouched by gentrification. This is partly because of the no-nonsense Hoxton Market, with fruit & veg stands, flower stalls and fishmongers. The market moved here after it had outgrown its original site to the west of Hoxton Square, and the increased trade that it brought has sustained locally orientated shops along the length of the street.

❷ Hoxton Square

Soon after it was laid out in 1683, Hoxton Square became the heart of a fashionable residential area. One or two of the early town houses, such as number 32 (right) survive. For the most part, though, the square is now a mix of nineteenth- and twentieth-century light-industrial buildings. Following the property crash of the early 1990s, some of the landlords of properties in the square offered cheap rents for live/work spaces for artists. A few young graduates from the Royal College of Art and Goldsmiths College moved in and were soon joined by photographers, writers and designers.

This was, of course, the catalyst for gentrification. Hoxton became increasingly attractive to designers, new-media companies and large galleries seeking to identify with and market the shabby chic associated with the area. The square's neo-bohemian art community moved out at about the same time, along with the last of the light manufacturing activities. They were replaced by more affluent households in buildings that were suddenly more valuable. Their new owners rapidly converted them into remodelled apartments, with the ground floors of many being dedicated to bars and restaurants.

❸ Curtain Road

From the 1850s for almost a century, Hoxton was the hub of the international furniture trade. Curtain Road, laid out in the 1870s, was at the heart of a cluster of interrelated specialist workshops, warehouses and showrooms in purpose-built premises. The various stages of furniture-making and finishing were carried out by different firms in different premises. This photograph shows the showroom-warehouse built in the early 1880s for the wholesale furniture manufacturer C. and R. Light. Successive generations of the Light family had worked as cabinetmakers in the area since about 1750. By the late nineteenth century, the firm was one of the largest in the area, with a catalogue of nearly 2000 items that ran to 435 pages. The building now houses new-media workshops and offices, and a brasserie.

❹ Leonard Street

On the southern edge of the district's historic furniture manufacturing agglomeration, these workshop buildings were erected in the 1870s. A century later they were obsolescent and empty, but in the 1990s their industrial aesthetic, with spruced-up external furniture hoists and renovated interior spaces with high ceilings and large windows, was attractive to a new and very different cluster of interrelated enterprises: new-media firms, printers, photographers, commercial artists and graphic artists.

⑤ Rivington Street

Together with Curtain Road, Rivington Street stood at the heart of the district's agglomeration of furniture workshops that prospered in meeting the demands of the growing Victorian middle class and its focus on domesticity and the home. This terrace was erected in 1897. Space was rented by the floor to independent craftsmen - cabinetmakers, chair-makers, French polishers and the like - who operated as sub-contractors to nearby wholesalers. Note the broad workshop windows.

⑥ Bricklayer's Arms

Charlotte Road/Rivington Street

The pub enjoyed a brief spell as a district landmark during the 1990s when it was popular with the artists and impresarios associated with the Brit Art movement. The gentrification of the district saw the traditional pub stripped back and turned into a would-be hipster 'style zone', with a restaurant upstairs. As the frontier of gentrification moved on, the pub has returned to the role of an ordinary corner boozer.

⑦ Charlotte Road

This group of furniture workshops and warehouses was built in the 1870s and occupied by an umbrella-maker and a feather dealer as well as by specialists in the furniture trades. After the building was refurbished in the 1980s, one of its occupants was the art dealer and cultural impresario Joshua Compston, who opened the area's first permanent gallery and organized arty street fairs in an attempt to promote Hoxton as an up-and-coming cultural quarter.

⑧ Suleymaniye Mosque
Kingsland Road

The Turkish community in London is estimated to be between 150,000 and 200,000 strong. The majority are Turkish Cypriots, many of whom moved to the United Kingdom as a result of the conflict in Cyprus between Greek and Turkish Cypriots. The community tends to be tight-knit, spatially concentrated in Shoreditch and the northern districts of the metropolis, and Sunni Muslim in terms of cultural heritage. There are now half a dozen Turkish mosques in London, and this one in Shoreditch is one of the most recent, opened in 1999. Designed by the architect Osman Sahan with a towering minaret and an Ottoman-style dome tacked on to a rather bland and clunky yellow-brick building, it can hold 3000 people.

⑨ Bunhill Fields
City Road

Located beyond the jurisdiction of the City, Hoxton and Shoreditch was a popular district among non-conformists when it was first developed in the seventeenth century. Bunhill Fields was their burial ground until 1854, after which it was taken over and managed as a public open space by the City of London.

⑩ Moorfields Eye Hospital
Peerless Street

Established in 1805 and moved to its present site in 1899, Moorfields Eye Hospital is the single most important insti-tution in the district: the largest specialized eye hospital in the world, internationally renowned for its comprehen-sive clinical and research activities. The Richard Desmond Children's Eye Centre (shown here) was added to the site in 2007. Its southern facade features aluminium louvres in front of glass curtain walling, minimizing solar gain and creating a distinctive street presence.

⑪ **Provost Estate**
Allerton Street

Much of the northern part of the district consists of social housing - or former social housing - of various ages. The Provost Estate replaced a slum-clearance scheme of 1900 by the LCC and is typical of 1920s and 1930s social housing, with six five-storey blocks, each with between twenty and forty separate flats. It had become badly run-down by the 1980s, when the Thatcher administration's neoliberal policies promoted the sale of council housing to sitting tenants. Having been purchased, many were flipped to newcomers: the district's proximity to the City and the cool image of the Hoxton Square area made it attractive. Much of the estate is now in private ownership, with flats selling for between £175,000 and £250,000 in 2014.

⑫ **Shoreditch Workhouse**
Hoxton Street

St Leonard's parish workhouse in Shoreditch opened in 1777, but by mid-Victorian times the need was so great (and conditions in the old workhouse so bad) that a new workhouse and infirmary to accommodate 1200 was built in the 1860s. One of the Assistant Matrons was the First World War heroine Edith Cavell, who was executed in 1915 by the Germans for helping British prisoners to escape. The LCC took over the running of St Leonard's in 1930, closing the workhouse and incorporating the buildings into the infirmary. It operated as a general hospital until 1984. Since then it has been a coordinating centre for district community services and health centres.

Islington

Islington developed as a halting point for drovers on their way into the livestock market at Smithfield. The first significant village north of London, Islington was situated on the crest of a hill at the junction of several north-south roads that had been important Anglo-Saxon, Roman and medieval routes between London and East Anglia. By the early eighteenth century Islington High Street boasted three big coaching inns: the Angel, the Peacock and the White Lion. When the east-west bypass (New Road and City Road) around the northern fringe of London was built in the 1750s it intersected with the north-south highways and immediately created one of the most important junctions in London. Islington's inns and taverns became the motorway hotels of their time, and eventually the locality came to be known simply by the name of the biggest inn, the Angel.

The Rise and Fall of Pentonville

Henry Penton, who owned land along the north of the New Road, seized the opportunity and began to develop a grid of terraced housing for the middle classes. Building began in 1769, and by the 1790s Pentonville, as the area came to be called, was a fully fledged suburb. Even though it was too far east to be properly fashionable, Pentonville's elevated position, with views over the City and fresh, breezy air, attracted solid middle-class households. The first inhabitants of the new houses included an assortment of barristers, doctors, merchants, artists, printers, publishers, booksellers and watchmakers.

Their houses, some of them with big bow windows to take advantage of the views over the City, were mostly in the western section of Pentonville - the area now overwritten with twentieth-century social housing. In the eastern section, towards the Angel and the old High Street, the houses were more modest and the households less prosperous, mixed with industrial, commercial and institutional buildings and a busy street market. The Penton Estate was relatively lax in imposing or enforcing restrictive covenants against infill development, allowing leaseholders to squeeze courts of cheap two-room houses into small gaps and back lots. This prompted a steady social decline, and by the mid-nineteenth century the eastern end of Pentonville had begun to be dominated by unskilled labourers, many of whom were Irish immigrants who had been displaced by the potato famine of 1845-49.

Caledonian Road

Another major landowner, George Thornhill, had initially leased out family land to the north of Pentonville for brickmaking. In 1826 he invested in the construction of a road running north from the western end of Pentonville, past the wharves of the newly opened Regent's Canal towards open fields, where he began to build terraces of middle-class housing. The road itself - Caledonian Road - meanwhile, acquired a tremendous mix of working-class commerce: butchers, bakers, greengrocers, tobacconists, undertakers, hawkers, flower and fruit sellers, stewed-eel stalls, pie-and-mash shops, Turkish baths and public houses.

The Beer Act of 1830 was designed to ensure more competition among brewers, and as a result the comfort and style of their pubs became important. By mid-century pubs had become huge, most often in Italianate style with ornate interiors. The biggest and most luxurious were known as gin palaces, and among them were the Star and Garter and the Milford Haven Arms on Caledonian Road, along with the latest iterations of the Angel and the White Lion. In 1852 the Great Northern Railway opened its new King's Cross railway terminus and

Stonefield Street, part of the Cloudesley Estate in Barnsbury, built in 1828.

goods yard immediately to the west of Caledonian Road, and three years later the Metropolitan Cattle Market opened for business next door, with eight abattoirs and space for 7000 cattle and 42,000 sheep. Not surprisingly, the lower reaches of Caledonian Road near the station and the cattle market were soon vacated by all but the poorest.

More Rising and Falling

The Thornhill family, meanwhile, set about developing their fields and meadowland to the east of Caledonian Road into squares, terraces and crescents for the well-to-do professional classes. The centrepiece was the elliptical ensemble formed by Thornhill Square and Thornhill Crescent, laid out in the mid-nineteenth century with St Andrew's church in the centre of the crescent. Further east, land formerly held by the canons of St Paul's had already been split up into small parcels and developed into a variety of squares, crescents and terraces that together constitute the sub-district of Barnsbury.

For the most part, however, Islington was a thoroughly working-class district. Pentonville Road

Shepherdess Walk. A lonely mid-nineteenth-century terrace that escaped 1970s clearance schemes after a public inquiry.

(renamed from the local section of the New Road in 1857) was colonized increasingly by a wide range of warehousing and light manufacturing activities (including makers of weighing machines, electric lamps, amusement machines, rubber jointings, toilet brushes, band saws, tin boxes, typewriters, motor radiators, billiard tables, musical instruments, furniture and jewellery), together with cafés, pubs and dining rooms catering to factory workers. The area immediately around King's Cross became established as a zone of low-end prostitution and occasional violence, and throughout the late nineteenth century there was growing poverty and overcrowding in much of the district. The first decade of the twentieth century saw the tipping point in the social composition of the formerly middle-class developments in Barnsbury and the Thornhill Estate, both of which steadily declined into slums, the houses split into poorly maintained, multi-occupation apartments.

Modernist Social Housing

By the mid-twentieth century, the district's social deprivation was matched by its physical desolation and economic decline. Derelict housing sat amid slum clearance areas, wartime bomb sites and abandoned factories. A significant fraction of the population left in search of jobs or better housing, many of them ending up in one of the New Towns

Manze's stewed-eel and pie house. Opened in 1898 on Chapel Street (now Chapel Market), this is a rare surviving example of a type of shop that was once common in London.

beyond London's Green Belt. Those left behind were mainly entrenched working-class households.

Few remnants of the district's initial developments remained. In some cases not even the streets survived. The western half of Pentonville, for example, was almost entirely razed and replaced with council-housing developments. The most notable of these was Priory Green, built in 1948-57 and designed by Berthold Lubetkin, one of the star Modernist architects of the pre-war period. Social housing projects like Priory Green provided an opportunity to realize the progressive possibilities of Modernism. Industrialized production, modern materials and functional design, it was believed, would improve the physical, social, moral and aesthetic condition of cities. This, at least, was how evangelistic postwar planners and architects felt things should work. When Priory Green was completed in 1957, Finsbury Council actually interviewed would-be residents to make sure they were 'good enough' to live there. As with so many Modernist housing estates, it all went badly wrong in practice: Priory Green soon became a sinkhole of drug use, prostitution and violent crime.

Gentrified Islington

The conventional wisdom began to change in the 1960s, away from slum clearance and pre-cast concrete social housing in favour of the renovation and improvement of the older housing stock. The shift was codified by the Civic Amenities Act of 1967, which enabled local councils to create Conservation Areas and award grants for the repair of listed buildings, and the Housing Act of 1969, which enabled local councils to award matching restoration grants to homeowners. As elsewhere in London - notably Kensington and Notting Hill - this encouraged a first wave of 'pioneer' gentrifiers to buy old properties and fix them up. The value added to the housing stock through gentrification was welcomed by local authorities (as well as, of course, by the gentrifiers themselves) because it helped their property-tax base. The aesthetic improvements and social changes

Stonefield Street. The barrier is part of a local traffic-calming scheme introduced after campaigns by incoming gentrifiers.

associated with gentrification were generally hailed as positive: restoring character and vitality to slum districts. Only later was any attention given to the social displacement that inevitably accompanies gentrification.

Within Islington, it was Barnsbury that attracted the pioneers. Before long, a second wave of gentrifiers appeared, the product of a new middle-class appetite for amateur property speculation, encouraged by newspapers and weekend colour supplements and orchestrated by estate agents, some of whom were not above 'winkling out' working-class households in order to create opportunities for gentrifiers and property speculators. As gentrifiers became a significant fraction of Barnsbury residents, they began to exert a critical, sometimes disproportionate, influence on local affairs. The Barnsbury Association used journalists among its membership to promote the idea of the area as a self-contained 'urban village' with its own special character and needs, and used professional

Donegal Street. Rodney House (foreground) and Prospect House (rear) on the O. M. Richards Estate. Emberton, Franck & Tardrew, architects (1962–65).

planners to formulate manifestos and forge links with the local council. They got the council to pay for tree-planting, restoring cast-iron streetlamps and railings, and laying granite setts to give the roads a traditional aesthetic, and they successfully lobbied for a traffic-calming scheme that closed off middle-class streets to through traffic, funnelling traffic instead through working-class parts of the area. They also successfully backed the Islington Society and the Homes Before Roads lobby in a campaign against a government-approved scheme to modernize the notoriously busy Angel intersection.

Fragmented Islington

Gentrification brought a distinctive and radically different sense of place to the district. At first, the dominant affect was one of conspicuous thrift, associated with the cheap-but-stylish items preferred by young couples on a limited budget. Second-wave gentrification brought an element of radical chic, designer clothes and interiors, and a landscape of consumption characterized by settings for fashionable eating, drinking and shopping. Overlaid on this has been the conspicuous consumption of a third wave of gentrification as 'City types' moved into Barnsbury after the Big Bang of financial deregulation

(and rocketing salaries of financial-sector managers). Second-wave gentrifiers were displaced, priced out in their turn in a process of super-gentrification.

Contemporary Islington thus has a tripartite class division between super-wealthy professionals and managers, middle-class professionals and working-class households; a division that is clearly mirrored in its townscapes. A half-century of gentrification means that working-class households are largely confined to the social housing sector. This, too, has changed. The Housing Act of 1980 introduced tenants' 'right to buy' council housing, and local authorities were encouraged to divest themselves of their housing stock. In 1999 Pentonville's housing estates - including the notorious Priory Green - were transferred to the Peabody Housing Trust and extensively renovated as part of the regeneration strategy for King's Cross Central (see page 77). The rest of Islington's remaining social housing stock - 25,000 homes - is now managed by Homes for Islington, an Arms Length Management Organization company solely owned by Islington Council.

Richmond Avenue. Semi-detached villas built in 1841, at the height of Victorians' fascination with Egypt.

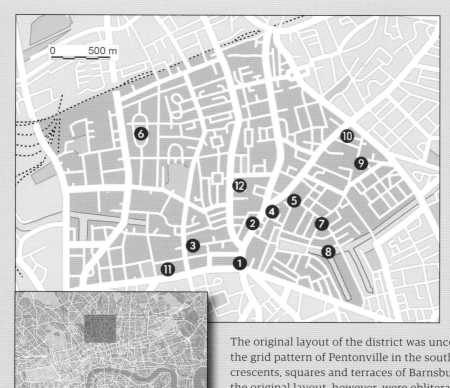

① Angel
② Upper Street
③ Chapel Market
④ Camden Passage
⑤ Charlton Place
⑥ Thornhill Square
⑦ Danbury Street
⑧ Regent's Canal
⑨ Bishop Street Almshouses
⑩ Peabody Square
⑪ Pentonville Road
⑫ Royal Free Place

The Angel has always been the focal point of Islington. It is where three ancient north-south routes converge (present-day Liverpool Road, Upper Street and Essex Road) and intersect with Pentonville Road/City Road. The original layout of the district was uncoordinated and fragmentary, the grid pattern of Pentonville in the southwest contrasting with the crescents, squares and terraces of Barnsbury to the north. Large chunks of the original layout, however, were obliterated by a combination of Second World War bomb damage and postwar slum clearance. Street patterns were rewritten as the sites were redeveloped into social housing estates. The district is bounded to the west by the King's Cross redevelopment and to the south by Pentonville Road and City Road. To the east it is separated from Hoxton and Shoreditch by the Regent's Canal and the New North Road, while to the north Islington merges quietly into the suburbs of Highbury.

❶ Angel
Upper Street

Named after the Angel, the largest of a row of coaching inns providing for overnight travellers approaching London, the road junction is notoriously busy. A 1970s GLC scheme that included a roundabout with shopping subways and a Tube station was defeated by strong opposition from the Islington Society and the Homes Before Roads group, culminating in the designation of the Angel Conservation Area in 1981. The Angel itself, rebuilt in 1903, stands on the corner, now converted to a bank. Near by stood the Angel Picture Theatre, one of the earliest cinemas in the country (1913). The cinema has also gone, the foyer occupied by a Starbucks, but its tower remains as an important landmark.

❷ Upper Street

As recently as the late 1980s, Upper Street was distinctly shabby and depressed. The residential gentrification of the district prompted Islington Borough Council to invest in the redevelopment of the area around Angel Tube station, and this in turn accelerated the commercial gentrification of the street. The southern end of the street, nearest the Angel, has attracted a mixture of small, specialized shops and more expensive shops and restaurants. Further north, near Barnsbury, there are trendy independent boutiques and furnishing shops that cater to the super-gentrifiers.

❸ Chapel Market

Amid the escalating gentrification of the entire district, Chapel Market has kept its shops and stalls and long-established working-class character. The street dates from the late eighteenth century and was at first almost entirely residential. Over the next hundred years, shops were gradually added to the ground floor of properties, many of which were rebuilt. Among them was the first branch of Sainsbury's Drury Lane grocery shop, opened in 1882. By that time the street market had become officially licensed, and by the turn of the century it was one of London's busiest and most popular, open every day except Monday. Together with Penton Street it is now a Conservation Area and part of a Heritage Economic Regeneration Scheme, jointly funded by English Heritage, the King's Cross Partnership and Islington Council.

❹ Camden Passage

Just off Upper Street near Islington Green, Camden Passage began to host a street market in 1960 featuring antiques, silver, glass, furniture, paintings and bric-a-brac. It has become popular, and there is now a book market on Thursdays and a farmers' market on Sundays as well as the antiques market on Wednesdays and Saturdays. Specialist antiques, retro clothing shops, delicatessens and cafés provide the backdrop for the market stalls. The houses in Camden Passage were built in the 1760s, when the area was first developed by Thomas Rosoman, the manager of Sadler's Wells theatre.

6 Thornhill Square

George Thornhill inherited his family's estate in Islington and in 1826 invested in the creation of Caledonian Road in order to open the area to speculative development. Thornhill Square was laid out by the family in 1848 as the centrepiece of their Barnsbury Estate. The square forms an oval with Thornhill Crescent, with gardens and St Andrew's church in the middle. The area soon became a favourite with well-to-do professional classes, but gradually slipped down the social scale during the first part of the twentieth century. In 1947 the gardens, previously accessible only to keyholders, were opened to the public, and in 1953 the park was redesigned to mark the Queen's coronation. It was an early catalyst for the gentrification of the square, and by the mid-1960s the gentrification of the surrounding streets was well under way.

5 Charlton Place

Charlton Place is a terrace of houses built speculatively by the architect James Taylor in the mid-1790s for respectable families of modest means. Coloured purple on Booth's map of 1899 ('Mixed. Some comfortable others poor'), it has risen back up the socio-economic ladder.

7 Danbury Street

This photograph shows the junction of Danbury Street and Noel Road, near the Regent's Canal. At the time of the canal's opening in 1820, the land here belonged to Thomas Cubitt. He leased it for development in the 1840s: classic Georgian terraces of London stock brick.

❽ Regent's Canal

The final stage of the canal, from Camden to Limehouse and the Thames, was opened in 1820. It had an immediate effect on property values, land use and social composition in Islington, but the impact was relatively short-lived as the railway boom of the 1840s drew industry and investment to Camden and its mainline stations and goods yards. There were even serious suggestions at various times during the nineteenth century to turn the canal into a railway. Nevertheless, the canal was an important element of the city's infrastructure. Connecting with the Grand Union system at Little Venice, the Regent's Canal linked the English Midlands to London's Docklands, allowing London's industrialists to take advantage of goods and raw materials flowing in both directions. Locally, George Thornhill used his Islington estate to dig clay and fire bricks in the 1820s and 1830s, sending the bricks east and west on the canal as other parts of the city were being built up. Thomas Cubitt acquired land near by and made his own bricks, again relying on the canal. In the southeastern corner of the district, the City Road and Wenlock canal basins drew a cluster of warehouses and workshops. Having gone through decades of obsolescence and eventual dereliction, the canal is now an important recreational amenity, the towpath a busy bicycle route for commuters and the warehouses converted into waterside flats.

❾ Bishop Street Almshouses

In the sixteenth century the Clothworkers Company was bequeathed land in Islington by Dame Ann Packington. The Company built several groups of almshouses on small parcels of their land, including these, built in 1855 in Jacobean style for widows of freemen of the Company. The widows were given an annual allowance of twenty pounds, a gown and twenty-four sacks of coal.

⑩ Peabody Square
Greenman Street

This estate was built by George Peabody's Trust in 1865, just a year after the first Peabody project, in Spitalfields. The architect for the estate, as in Spitalfields, was Henry Darbishire. The style was a sort of austere Italianate, with yellow stock bricks and slate tiles, and it became standard for other Peabody estates across the city. The blocks were separated from one another to allow good ventilation, with the central space providing a play area for the tenants' children. Each of the blocks was five storeys high, with shared laundries on the top floor. Railings separated the estate from the surrounding streets, and the gates were closed at 11pm each night. The flats were not self-contained: there were shared sinks and lavatories on the landings, in a style known as 'associated dwellings'. This enabled the facilities to be inspected regularly for cleanliness.

⑪ Pentonville Road

Little of Barnsbury's new wealth has made its way south towards Pentonville Road, although the latter is certainly picking up from its low point in the 1970s. Initially developed in the 1770s as a good-class residential address, it gradually filled with shops and lodging-houses. During the late nineteenth century more and more premises were given over to light manufactures of various sorts, but after the turn of the century the introduction of trams siphoned off many of the area's skilled workers, who left for the new suburbs. Now, situated between the regenerated King's Cross area and the busy Angel junction, it is poised for significant reinvestment.

⑫ Royal Free Place
Liverpool Road

Shown here is the former administration building of the London Fever (later Royal Free) Hospital. Built in the late 1840s, the hospital treated patients 'above the pauper class': servants of the upper classes and better-off people living alone. The hospital closed in 1975, and its buildings were subsequently converted into 178 flats and houses for the Circle housing trust and Hackney Housing Association, to the designs of Charles Fowler and David Mocatta.

Kensington

Cheek-by-jowl with a royal park and its palaces, Kensington was built for London's Victorian *haute bourgeoisie* and has never really gone out of fashion. Kensington Palace, in the western corner of Kensington Gardens, has been a royal residence since it was bought by King William and Queen Mary in 1689. The nearest street, Kensington Palace Gardens, 100 metres (109 yards) to the west, is often cited as the most exclusive (and, naturally, the most expensive) address in London. It is a broad, tree-lined avenue of mansions with crash barriers and armed police checkpoints at both ends. A number of its mansions are now national embassies or ambassadorial residences; private owners include the Saudi royal family and the Sultan of Brunei.

A few hundred metres to the west again is Holland Park, where a huge Jacobean mansion was built in the early seventeenth century for Walter Cope, chancellor to James I. Holland House became noted as a high-society literary and political centre in Kensington's formative years in the nineteenth century, reinforcing the social desirability of the district. The mansion itself has long been a ruin, having been hit by twenty-two incendiary bombs one night in 1940, but the grounds - Holland Park - were bought by the LCC in 1952 and now form one of London's most sequestered green spaces.

The district as a whole is overwhelmingly a Victorian creation. Before the nineteenth century it had been an area of meadowland, market gardens and nurseries, with a small village and a series of Jacobean mansions in spacious grounds. Early in the nineteenth century a few ribbon developments of terraced housing, mostly in the flat-fronted late Georgian style, began to spread westward into the area. By 1820 Kensington had become fully subject to the metropolitan building cycle, with speculative development gradually filling the meadowland and replacing the market gardens. The arcadian setting, combined with the proximity of Holland House and the royal park, encouraged the development of big detached homes for the rich. These included the grand Italianate mansions of Kensington Palace Gardens, built in the 1840s.

Albertopolis

With the transformation from rural parish into city suburb well under way, a powerful stimulus to further growth was provided by the purchase of a substantial parcel of land across from the site of the Great Exhibition of 1851 in Hyde Park by the Exhibition Commissioners. The estate was intended for institutions that would encourage the application of science and art to industry, as advocated by the Commissioners' president, Prince Albert. In due course it became the complex of museums, educational institutions and display buildings that has made South Kensington one of London's great visitor attractions. The patronage of Prince Albert, meanwhile, added further lustre to the social reputation of a Kensington address. The prince himself took an active interest in the quality of residential development in and around the Commissioners' estate. His influence was such, in fact, that the institutional core of South Kensington came to be known as 'Albertopolis'.

Gothic Churches, Palladian Homes

This was Kensington's formative period. Between 1841 and 1881 its population increased sixfold. Most of the new residents were upper-middle-class households from elsewhere in London moving away from the increasingly congested and industrialized centre. At its fashionable peak in the 1860s, Kensington was a mirror of the top end of the transitional Victorian

Holland Park. Part of the Holland Estate, developed in the 1860s for London's westward-moving upper-middle classes, this has remained a very fashionable address.

St Jude's, Courtfield Gardens (1867–70), an estate church promoted by a wealthy businessman with evangelical leanings. Its rough-hewn stone facing deteriorated significantly as a result of air pollution in the first half of the twentieth century.

class system. Its residents included a few titled families and a few landed families who owned a country seat as well as a town house in Kensington, but the bulk of its homeowners were industrialists and merchants, bankers, lawyers, doctors, engineers, military officers and retired administrators from the Indian civil service. They brought with them, of course, a very different class fraction: the servants who lived in the attic-level rooms of the big houses and the coachmen and grooms who lived in the mews cottages behind. The new community also prompted a burst of Anglican church-building: both 'estate churches', promoted by landowners and developers to make property in their district more attractive, and 'private churches', initiated by the clergy and their patrons to take advantage of the affluent new congregations (or in some cases to further a particular brand of churchmanship). St Paul's (Onslow Square) and St Jude's (above, in Courtfield Gardens) are examples of estate churches, while St Augustine's (Queen's Gate) and St Stephen's (Gloucester Road) are examples of private churches.

Most of Kensington's churches were built in Gothic style, in accordance with Anglican aesthetics of the period. They stand in stark contrast to the richly stuccoed neoclassicism that was the preferred aesthetic for residential Kensington until the 1880s. Typically, the ground-floor frontage of Kensington terraces was stuccoed, with balustraded balconies above, commonly extended over columned porches. Grey or brown brick and stucco were used in varying proportions, with a great variety of facade treatments that were designed to furnish the all-over richness that was so much sought-after at the time.

The style was the work of a large number of different builders and developers, only a few of whom ever built more than fifty houses. Many of the speculative developers were architects, a normal combination of activities before the profession redefined and codified its professional turf in order to protect contractual opportunities from the predations of construction companies, surveyors and civil engineers. In retrospect their work, all of it drawing on the same architectural vocabulary, gives much of Kensington a rather lifeless and monotonous feel. The consistently similar massing of the homes and the ubiquity of their pillared porticoes was intended to speak of sobriety and respectability; now, even the Italianate decorations seem routine and perfunctory, the fetishes of a defunct social class (but nevertheless valuable to the current caste of the *haute bourgeoisie* as heirloom tokens of social status).

Changing Tastes and Styles

The Metropolitan District Railway opened stations at Notting Hill Gate, Kensington High Street, Gloucester Road and South Kensington in 1868. This had the immediate effect of speeding up the conversion of remaining greenfield sites to bricks and mortar but also of diminishing the overall social cachet of a Kensington address. Kensington began to take on more of the characteristics of the urban core of the metropolis, with longer terraces of brick-and-stucco houses without associated mews accommodation. By the late 1870s the district's new accessibility began to be reflected in a proliferation of hotels, many of them formed by joining terraced houses together.

Meanwhile, society had changed, with new household structures and new metropolitan lifestyles and sensibilities. After much debate as to their compatibility with traditional notions of propriety and family life, there was a demand among the affluent classes for flats in Parisian-style apartment buildings.

The demand was met, from around 1882–83, by an abrupt and decisive change in building form. This was accompanied by an equally sudden and decisive shift in architectural style. Italianate neoclassical was superseded by Domestic Revival styles (often described as Queen Anne or, by architectural historians, Free Classic).

The appeal of these styles, in an increasingly industrialized society, lay in their deployment of small-town imagery, based mainly on English and Flemish houses of the seventeenth and eighteenth centuries. They featured gables, bay and oriel windows, massive brick chimney-stacks, stone dressings and cut-brick decoration. The use of smooth bright-red brick from the big Midlands brickfields helped to signal both distinctiveness and a break from past aesthetics. Among the first of the big apartment buildings in this vein were Albert Hall Mansions in South Kensington, adjacent to the concert hall that had been built on the Commissioners' estate in the 1860s. Soon, mansion blocks began to appear throughout west London. The grander examples offered every modern convenience: lifts, bathrooms and lavatories and electric lights. The impact and appeal of the package was such that high-pitched roofs, red brick and elaborate stone dressings became the dominant style for London apartment blocks until the outbreak of the First World War.

Good Bones

With the ascendance of motor vehicles after the war, the district's mews accommodation became redundant. As elsewhere in London, they were rapidly converted into bijou residences, and they have remained in great demand ever since. With the entire district built out by the 1920s, the fabric sound and the address still desirable, there was little scope for the emergence of new residential forms or architectural styles. Some of the bigger residences were converted to embassies or consulates, while many others were subdivided into apartments. As the stock aged, it did filter down the social scale a little, especially on

streets where owners and landlords had not been able to meet the high costs of maintaining stuccoed facades. For two or three decades after the Second World War, the social geography of the district was less homogeneous than it had been. But Kensington had 'good bones' as well as a desirable location, and it became an early target for gentrification.

Since the 1980s Kensington has been a preferred location for the beneficiaries of London's pre-eminence as a global financial centre. Its best streets are once again the domain of the *haute bourgeoisie*, including a fair number of its immigrant super-rich. Now, oligarch parents post private security personnel with not-so-discreet earpieces outside Kensington's private elementary schools. Their houses, along with those of the merely very rich, are fortified with gates, spikes, anti-climb paint and surveillance cameras. The scaffolding of jobbing builders and the smell of paint has become a feature of almost every street as, one by one, exteriors are restored and interiors updated with designer kitchens and bathrooms. Property prices throughout the district have become prohibitive, with some addresses, including Campden Hill Square, Drayton Gardens and Duchess of Bedford's Walk, now among the ten most expensive streets in the whole of London.

Kensington Court. Typical of the blocks of luxury mansion flats that began to go up all over west London in the 1880s, Kensington Court was developed by Jonathan Carr and designed by J. J. Stevenson.

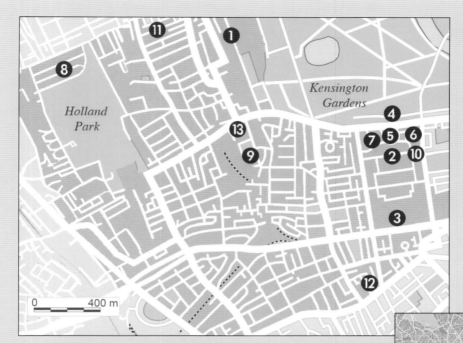

① Kensington Palace
   Gardens
② Royal College of Music
③ Natural History
   Museum
④ Albert Memorial
⑤ Royal Albert Hall
⑥ Albert Hall Mansions
⑦ Royal College of
   Organists
⑧ Holland Park
⑨ Kensington Square
⑩ Albert Court
⑪ Mall Chambers
⑫ Gloucester Grove East
   Board School
⑬ Barkers Department
   Store

Kensington wraps around the southern and western sides of the royal park of Kensington Gardens. The busy Warwick Road marks the district's effective limit to the west, separating it from Fulham and Shepherd's Bush. To the north of Kensington is Notting Hill, and to the south is Chelsea. The institutional quarter around the Albert Hall stands between Kensington and Knightsbridge, to the east. Much of the district is laid out in patchwork grids of streets, reflecting the piecemeal nature of Victorian speculative development. Within this layout, the traditional west London morphology of terraces and squares is the predominant arrangement.

❶ Kensington Palace Gardens

Laid out in 1843 by James Pennethorne, the street was developed with palatial mansions from 1845 onwards by society architects like Sydney Smirke, Owen Jones and James Thomas Knowles. The freehold still belongs to the Crown Estate, and its proximity to Kensington Palace (the official London residence of second-tier royalty) has helped to maintain the exclusivity of the address. The predominant style of the mansions is loosely Italianate. Some remain in private ownership, but many have become embassies or ambassadorial residences.

❷ Royal College of Music
Prince Consort Road

One of the world's great conservatoires, with 750 students from more than sixty countries, the Royal College of Music is also one of the significant legacies of Prince Albert. He had urged the creation of a National Training School for Music on the South Kensington estate that had been assembled by the Commissioners of the Great Exhibition of 1851. The school was eventually established in 1883, well after his death. It was housed, initially, in the building now known as the Royal College of Organists (see page 157). By 1887 the school had become a college and had outgrown the building. The Commissioners offered the college a new site directly across from the Royal Albert Hall on the south side of a new road, Prince Consort Road, with a lease for 999 years. The new building was designed by Arthur William Blomfield in French Baronial style and completed in 1894 in the red brick and stone that had become de rigueur in the previous decade. Blomfield had to make the building big in order to be in scale with its neighbours, but it had to contain many small rooms in storeys of modest height. The resultant facade, with its small-scale subdivisions, was criticized for its lack of monumentality and grandeur.

❸ Natural History Museum
Cromwell Road

By the 1850s the natural-history collections of the British Museum had outgrown their Bloomsbury site, and after much debate it was decided in 1860 - coincidentally, the year after the publication of Charles Darwin's *Origin of Species* - to build the collections a new home in South Kensington. The new Natural History Museum opened to the public in 1881. The architect was Alfred Waterhouse, who was just thirty-six years old when he won the commission. In contrast to the red brick and stone of other institutional buildings in the area, Waterhouse's museum is iron-framed and clad in pale terracotta. The style is German Romanesque, the Cromwell Road facade reminiscent, perhaps, of a cathedral front or a medieval market hall. It was the first building in Britain to be faced entirely in terracotta, but the most interesting feature was the decoration of the east and west wings: representations of extinct and living species, respectively, corresponding to the interior layout of the museum's geological and zoological collections.

❹ **Albert Memorial**
Kensington Gardens

When Prince Albert died suddenly of typhoid in 1861, Queen Victoria decided that a memorial should be built to honour him. Seven leading architects were invited to submit designs for a monument to be built in Kensington Gardens, and the winner was George Gilbert Scott, well known for his Gothic Revival churches. His design consisted of an Italianate canopy in the Gothic Revival style, containing a gilded statue of Albert. At the four corners below the statue of the prince are allegorical sculptures of Agriculture, Commerce, Engineering and Manufacturing in brilliant-white Campanella marble from Carrara. At the outermost corners are allegorical sculptures of Europe, Asia (right foreground in the photograph), Africa and the Americas, reflecting Albert's international concerns and his patronage of the Great Exhibition of 1851. The podium frieze depicts prominent Victorian poets, musicians, sculptors, painters and architects (including Scott).

⑥ Albert Hall Mansions
Kensington Gore

This group of three large apartment buildings (1879-86) was among the first to meet a new demand among the metropolitan upper-middle classes for apartment living. The massive buildings not only represented a striking shift in west London building form (from terraces of large homes) but also in architectural style to Domestic Revival (from Italianate neoclassical) and materials (to polished red brick from yellow or grey brick and stucco). The three buildings stand on a site immediately to the east of the Royal Albert Hall and were built after the Commissioners of the Great Exhibition of 1851 decided to take advantage of the buoyant property market of the 1870s by leasing out parts of their estate. The architect, Richard Norman Shaw, studied the apartment buildings lining the (then) new boulevards in Paris before completing his design for Albert Hall Mansions.

⑦ Royal College of Organists
Kensington Gore

This unusual building was built in the mid-1870s for the new National Training School for Music. The architect was H. H. Cole, the eldest son of Henry Cole (mastermind of the Great Exhibition, prime mover of the Victoria and Albert Museum and designer of the first postage stamp). Its combination of an Old English style with Italianate plaster ornament was in deliberate contrast with the neighbouring Royal Albert Hall. The building stood vacant from 1896 until 1903, when the Royal College of Organists took a lease for the site. The organists left the building in 1990, and it has now been converted and restored for use as a private residence.

⑤ (opposite) Royal Albert Hall
Kensington Road

Built in 1867-71, the hall was intended originally to be both a large concert hall and a conference centre for meetings of learned societies: a 'Central Hall of Arts and Science'. It was renamed the Royal Albert Hall by Queen Victoria. The design, by Henry Scott, was intended as a modern-day version of the Roman amphitheatre, apparently inspired by the examples in Nîmes and Arles, in the south of France. The exterior was built in dark-red brick with dark joints, contrasting with fawn-coloured terracotta mouldings. The women of the South Kensington Museum's mosaic class made the 800 slabs that make up the frieze, which depicts various countries involved in the Exhibition of 1851 as well as the themes that had been featured in the Exhibition and propagated by Prince Albert. Unfortunately, the concert hall soon became famous for its poor acoustics. The acoustics were finally improved in 1969 with a series of large diffusing discs. From 1996 to 2004 the hall underwent a £20 million programme of renovation and modernization.

8 Holland Park

Built for a decidedly upper-middle-class market at the height of Kensington's fashionability in the 1860s, Holland Park remains an exclusive address. The developers, William and Francis Radford, acquired the parcel of land between Holland House and the Uxbridge Road (now Holland Park Avenue) in 1859. The purchase agreement included restrictive covenants intended to ensure that only high-quality residential development could take place. The Radfords built two long streets, connected by a short street at each end. Maximizing the cachet of proximity to Holland House, they named them all Holland Park. They built four rows of identical detached Italianate villas and an intermediate row of mews coach houses and stables, all designed by Francis Radford himself. The villas, although detached, are generally set so close together that they have the appearance of a grand terrace.

9 Kensington Square

One of the oldest squares in London, Kensington Square was laid out in 1685 by Thomas Young, who hoped to profit from the proximity of the Royal Court at Kensington Palace and the continuing exodus from the City after the Great Fire. The area proved fashionable until the Court departed from Kensington (in the early 1750s), after which the square became something of a social backwater. In the late nineteenth century the success of nearby department stores began to impinge on the square. Barkers (see opposite) parked its trade vehicles in the square and began to buy up houses for use as staff hostels. By 1939 the company owned two-thirds of the houses in the square and wanted to demolish some of them to make room for a loading dock. Postwar planning authorities, however, reaffirmed the residential status of the square, and now most of the houses have been listed as of architectural and historical interest.

10 Albert Court
Prince Consort Road

Typical in form and style of west London *fin de siècle* speculative apartment buildings, Albert Court is also typical of many in having had a history of financial trouble and litigation. As with Albert Hall Mansions, the initial project stemmed from the decision of Commissioners of the Great Exhibition of 1851 to lease parts of their estate for private building. After a series of deals among various principals, building began in 1890 only for the financing to collapse two years later. The collapse also ruined the project's builder and developer, and it was not until 1900 that further deals, new ownership and new architects resulted in completion of the building. To present-day eyes, it has a certain postmodern quality, with an eclectic mix of neoclassical, Regency and French Empire touches (and more).

⑪ Mall Chambers

Kensington Mall

A stone's throw from the palatial mansions of Kensington Palace Gardens, Mall Chambers is one of the few developments in Kensington to have been targeted at a working-class market - albeit 'a class somewhat above ordinary mechanics and labourers', as the *Building News* put it in 1865. A classic case of unpredictable urban development, it was built on a piece of land that had belonged to Samuel Peto, who had used it for temporary stables while his mansion on Kensington Palace Gardens was being built. The expenses incurred in that project prompted him to sell off the land to Lucas Brothers, contractors who put up Mall Chambers in 1865 as a speculative venture. It is an extremely well-preserved example of Victorian 'industrial dwellings' that, thanks to gentrification, has risen a long way up the social scale.

⑫ Gloucester Grove East Board School

Clareville Street

Board Schools were created by the groundbreaking Elementary Education Act of 1870, the first legislation to establish secular provision for the education of children aged five to thirteen. The Act required elementary schools to be established in areas where existing provision was inadequate, to be managed by elected school boards and funded, in part, by the state. The School Board of London established a bye-law in 1871 compelling parents to send children to school - something that was not compulsory nationally until 1880. By the early twentieth century few neighbourhoods in London were without a Domestic Revival style, three-storey school designed by Edward Robert Robson, the Board's architect (as in this example), or his successor, T. J. Bailey. The Board's adoption of newly fashionable Domestic Revival styles created a distinctive and highly influential board-school aesthetic. There is a small irony here, given the secular provisions of the 1870 Act, as the school now operates as Our Lady of Victories Roman Catholic Primary School.

⑬ Barkers Department Store

Kensington High Street

At one time wealthy Kensington supported three large department stores on Kensington High Street. By the 1920s Barkers had bought out the other two but continued to run all three as separate entities. In the late 1930s it began to remodel its own store in Moderne style. The renovated building reflects the era's fascination with technological progress, with stone reliefs of streamlined cars and aircraft on the Portland stone facing. The incomplete result was sufficiently impressive to have supported the rumour, a few years later, that Adolf Hitler's chief architect, Albert Speer, had selected it for his London headquarters in anticipation of a Nazi victory. Renovation was completed in the late 1950s, just as the parent firm was bought out by the national department-store group House of Fraser. Changing preferences and consumer behaviour led to the closure of Barkers' companion department stores on the High Street in the 1970s. Barkers itself closed in 2006, and the building is now occupied by Whole Foods and the headquarters of Associated Newspapers.

Knightsbridge

Tucked in between Belgravia, Chelsea, South Kensington and Hyde Park, Knightsbridge is properly considered as a sort of town core to west London's élite suburbs. Its flagship department stores, Harrods and Harvey Nichols, stand on the nucleus of the original settlement, where coaching inns and hostelries clustered around the junction of roads leading into central London from the west and southwest. The most important of these roads was the Kensington Turnpike, the route of present-day Brompton Road. For decades it was lined merely with an intermittent ribbon of development, with most of the land on either side given over to market gardening. During the building boom of the 1760s the road was lined with speculative terraces, mostly set well back with long front gardens to shield the houses from the dirt and noise of the turnpike. A little further away to the south, the architect Henry Holland acquired building rights from the Cadogan Estate for a large parcel of land straddling the boundary with Chelsea. Holland laid out Sloane Street (named after Hans Sloane, Lord Cadogan's father-in-law) and developed Hans Town as an area of modest housing along its western fringes.

Initial Development

After several decades of infilling, another boom - in the 1820s - prompted the suburbanization proper of the district, the northern reaches of which came to be known for a while as 'New Brompton'. Anchored by its own church, Holy Trinity, planted by the Ecclesiastical Commissioners, it was framed around the terraces and squares that had by then become the conventional template for developers in west London. While the residential streets were prosperous and desirable, Brompton Road itself became increasingly busy and commercialized. This was largely a result of the growth of South Kensington after the Great Exhibition of 1851 and the construction of Cromwell Road, in 1855, to serve the westward expansion of Kensington. Among the retailers who established themselves in the area was Benjamin Harvey, who opened a linen shop in a terraced house on the corner of Knightsbridge and Sloane Street in 1831. His wife inherited the business and went into partnership with the store's silk buyer, Colonel Nichols, aiming to supply luxury items to the district's residents. Charles Harrod, who had established wholesale and retail businesses in Southwark, Clerkenwell and Stepney, opened a mixed-goods shop a few doors away, on Brompton Road itself, in 1849.

Make Way for Mansions

The last quarter of the nineteenth century and first decade of the twentieth brought the redevelopment of much of the district. Much of this was driven by the Cadogan Estate's determination to redevelop Hans Town - by now obsolescent and fallen significantly down the social scale - into the fashionable and profitable new format of mansion apartment buildings. In 1874–86 the estate razed the existing fabric of the area and reframed the layout of Hans Town around Pont Street, Hans Place, Lennox Gardens and Cadogan Square. The estate wanted to identify Hans Town socially with the upper-middle-class districts to the east, while making it distinctive in terms of built form. The result was high-density apartment buildings in Domestic Revival styles. Individual houses had already appeared in such styles on Chelsea Embankment, but in Hans Town the style was used extensively in speculative building for the first time. It was radically different from the existing stock brick and stucco in neoclassical style that existed in Hans Town and neighbouring Belgravia, and it was

Harrods. The largest store in Europe, with 55 hectares (136 acres) of floor and some 5000 staff serving as many as 30,000 customers a day.

Hans Place. The fashionable new format of mansion apartment buildings that replaced the Cadogan Estate's original development in the 1880s.

enthusiastically received by both the architectural cognoscenti and well-off households who believed themselves to be at the forefront of advanced taste. The general press and the broader public, seeing one of the wealthiest families in the country evicting thousands of working-class families from the old Hans Town in order to house London's élite in more profitable properties, were less impressed.

The architects employed by the estate included J. J. Stevenson, William Young and G. T. Robinson, and they all drew on the architectural language of seventeenth-century Flemish town houses. All were faced with dark-red brick, with detailing in moulded brick and terracotta. The overall result was famously dubbed 'Pont Street Dutch' by the social and architectural satirist Osbert Lancaster. In retrospect, one of the most innovative features of the development was the use of varied frontages with standardized interior layouts. While the appeal of Domestic Revival styles did not last beyond the First World War, the strategy of relieving standardized plans with minor variations of frontage has become a routine approach in speculative building.

Just as Hans Town was being redeveloped, so was much of the Brompton

Brompton Square. A classic London square with terraced housing, built speculatively by James Bonnin in 1821–39.

Road area. The social upgrading of Hans Town and the proximity of Belgravia and South Kensington provided a rich catchment area for retailers. Harvey Nichols expanded into a big new building in the 1890s, and Harrods commissioned C. Q. Stephens to design a new emporium, which opened in 1903 and has become the district's signature building. Small, specialized shops colonized nearby Beauchamp Place to cater for the same wealthy customers. Today, like Harrods and Harvey Nichols, they are known for luxury goods at silly prices, serving a mixture of affluent local residents and international visitors.

Densification

The character of the district changed relatively little throughout the first half of the twentieth century, as Knightsbridge became established as the town centre of west London's élite districts. Improvements to roads and infrastructure were accompanied by a densification of the residential fabric, mainly in the form of five- to nine-storey blocks of flats that appeared here and there as sites became available. After 1945 rebuilding took place on a more ambitious scale, with office blocks predominating over flats. In the spirit of postwar planning and development, a major property company acquired a strategic parcel of land around the increasingly busy junction of Knightsbridge and Brompton Road, proposing to create an island of office development, ringed by a traffic circulation pattern, all surrounded by more office blocks. Given the legacy of postwar architecture elsewhere in London, it is a mercy that the plans were scuppered by the incoming Labour government in 1964. The junction remains a traffic bottleneck, and luxury apartment towers have subsequently appeared at its head; but for the most part, the fabric of the district retains a good deal of its nineteenth-century appearance.

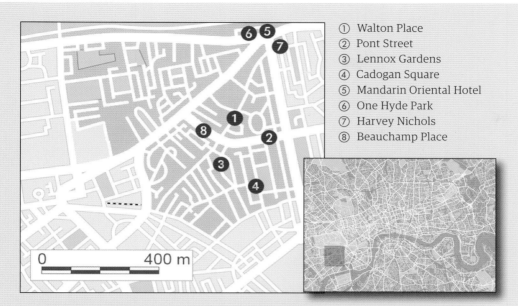

① Walton Place
② Pont Street
③ Lennox Gardens
④ Cadogan Square
⑤ Mandarin Oriental Hotel
⑥ One Hyde Park
⑦ Harvey Nichols
⑧ Beauchamp Place

0   400 m

The district is framed around three principal roads: Knightsbridge, which borders Hyde Park and which leads west to Kensington; Sloane Street, which leads south to Chelsea; and Brompton Road, which leads west towards Hammersmith and the M4 motorway. Around the convergence of these three roads is the heart of the district's upscale shopping. Between Knightsbridge and Brompton Road, the built environment is dominated by Italianate brick-and-stucco terraces and squares. Between Brompton Road and Sloane Street, it is dominated by the red brick and terracotta of the mansion apartment blocks of Hans Town that spill southwards into Chelsea. To the west the district is bounded by the museum precinct of South Kensington, and to the east it is bounded by the neoclassical grandeur of Belgravia.

❶ Walton Place

An exception to the district's predominant Domestic Revival mansion blocks, Walton Place survived the wholesale redevelopment of the district in the late nineteenth century, mainly because it lay just beyond the Cadogan Estate, in a relatively small parcel of land owned by the Henry Smith Charity Estate. The trustees of the estate appointed George Basevi as their architect in 1828, and he designed this terrace, with an identical terrace on the other side of the street, shortly afterwards. While it has the stucco facing characteristic of the period, it is distinctive for its relative lack of Italianate embellishment.

② Pont Street

In 1874 the Cadogan and Hans Place Improvements Act enabled the Cadogan Estate to extend Pont Street through the area west of Sloane Street. Although not well suited to London's squares and terraces, the Domestic Revival style adopted by the estate was very favourably received by the architectural press. The distinctive new mansion buildings in red brick and terracotta were also immediately popular with the city's wealthy upper-middle classes, and the landlords of adjacent estates quickly adopted the new style, resulting in a distinctive new morphology for the West End, labelled 'Pont Street Dutch' by the contemporary satirist Osbert Lancaster.

③ Lennox Gardens

The success of the Cadogan Estate's developments along Pont Street prompted the trustees of the neighbouring Henry Smith Charity Estate to develop a former cricket ground into mansion apartments. Laid out around a lozenge-shaped ornamental garden, the apartment buildings, together with attendant and soon-to-be-redundant mews streets, were completed by 1885.

④ (opposite) Cadogan Square

Cadogan Square has some of the most elaborate of the district's houses, all variations on the same Flemish-influenced Domestic Revival style. Like the generic 'Pont Street Dutch' architecture of the district, it is often loosely labelled Queen Anne. This example was built in 1878 to a design by Richard Norman Shaw, better known for his country houses and commercial buildings. It is listed Grade II* by English Heritage.

⑤ Mandarin Oriental Hotel
Knightsbridge

Originally built in 1889 as an exclusive 'Gentleman's Club' known as Hyde Park Court, the building overlooks Hyde Park on one side and Knightsbridge on the other. It was furnished extravagantly, with both family suites and bachelor's suites. Damaged by fire in 1899, it reopened in 1902 as the Hyde Park Hotel and had the reputation of being London's most luxurious. A century on, it was no longer able to offer the amenities expected by wealthy visitors to Knightsbridge. The Mandarin Oriental Hotel Group purchased the property in 1996 and reopened it as a five-star hotel in 2000 after a £57 million renovation. An underground tunnel connects the hotel to the neighbouring super-luxury apartment towers of One Hyde Park (see below), allowing the hotel's Heston Blumenthal-run restaurant to cater to the residents of the towers.

⑥ One Hyde Park
Knightsbridge

One Hyde Park (2010), a Qatari investment, is emblematic of the super-prime property market that has resulted from London's role in the contemporary world economy. It is also an example of the speculative luxury developments that have driven the soaring inflation of metropolitan-wide property prices, supercharging the gentrification of central London and intensifying housing shortages for the general population. Designed by Richard Rogers, erstwhile champion of progressive urban planning and design, it is fortified and insulated from the rest of the city, with internal services and amenities geared to the oligarch and sheik classes. Each of the four penthouses has its own panic room, and the complex has a golf simulator, swimming pool, saunas, squash courts, cinema and gentlemen's-club-style reading room.

❼ Harvey Nichols
Knightsbridge

Drapery was the predominant trade in nineteenth-century Knightsbridge. Among the hatters, tailors, dressmakers and jewellers were two small shops that grew to be great London emporia: Harrods and Harvey Nichols. The success of both in the nineteenth century is reflected in their buildings. The present Harvey Nichols store was designed by C. Q. Stephens and built in stages from 1889 to 1894. Always a shop for the upper-middle classes, Harvey Nichols, like Harrods, came into its own with the neoliberal climate of the 1980s. As an entire generation shifted its focus from radical idealism to self-orientated materialism, credit gave consumers access to such a wide array of high-end goods that traditional markers of status lost much of their meaning. In their place came an increasingly crude calculus of status: the newer, the more expensive, the flashier, the better. The affluent middle classes began acquiring luxury goods and symbols - designer clothes, shoes and bags, expensive luggage, and prestige watches and pens - and Harvey Nichols (like Harrods) was able not only to supply them but also to provide an appropriate setting and address for the performance of conspicuous consumption. Since the mid-1990s the appetite for luxury goods and the power of the firm's brand image has allowed Harvey Nichols to open branches in Leeds, Manchester, Edinburgh, Birmingham, Bristol, Dublin, Riyadh, Hong Kong, Istanbul, Ankara, Kuwait, Dubai and Baku.

❽ Beauchamp Place

Beauchamp Place is now an adjunct to the conspicuous consumption of Brompton Road's and Knightsbridge's emporia and upscale chain stores. Geared more to the district's affluent residents, it has become lined with self-consciously smart restaurants, jewellers, boutiques, beauty clinics and health shops. It is an unlikely outcome for a street that was something of an afterthought in the district's development. The houses on Grove Place, as it was called when it was first laid out in the 1820s, were to be at least of the Fourth Rate under the terms of the lease granted to John Henry Goodinge. Few of the properties included shops; most were modest middle-class homes, although by the 1860s two houses in the street had become common brothels. By the turn of the century more of the houses were functioning as shops, but the transformation of Beauchamp Place into a street almost exclusively of shops and restaurants is a postwar phenomenon. In the 1970s it was known for its antiques shops. Its fashionable status is more recent still, a product of the same aestheticization of consumption that transformed Harrods, Harvey Nichols and Brompton Road.

Lambeth

Apart from a thin strip along the riverfront, Lambeth has a relatively short history, its built environment largely a product of the industrial era and its role as a working-class industrial suburb. Until the mid-eighteenth century most of the district was marshland, traversed only by drainage ditches and one or two roads fringed with houses. The only place of any real significance was Lambeth Palace, the official London residence of the archbishops of Canterbury since the thirteenth century. While it was convenient enough for the archbishops to make occasional trips across the Thames to Westminster and the Royal Court by ferry, the lack of a bridge across the river rendered the rest of Lambeth relatively isolated. For centuries, any suggestion of a bridge remained contentious because of the opposition of Thames watermen and of City aldermen, who were keen to preserve the comparative advantage that London Bridge gave their business community.

London's geography and metropolitan structure began to be reshaped with the construction of Westminster Bridge, which opened in 1750. At first, Lambeth's exurban character lent itself to its development as a series of pleasure gardens, including the Flora Tea Gardens, Belvedere Gardens, Cumberland Gardens, Cuper's Gardens and Lambeth Wells. The most famous was the very fashionable Vauxhall Pleasure Gardens, where visiting nobility and upper-middle classes from north of the river could enjoy food, drink, music and plays. Like the other pleasure gardens of the period, it could be louche, especially in the evenings:

At night the Gardens twinkled with a thousand lanterns whose light served only to deepen the darkness round about. From the start it was impossible to keep tarts of both sexes and varying degrees of professionalism from descending upon such a vast outdoor business opportunity.[1]

A remnant of Vauxhall Pleasure Gardens survives today as a public park, Spring Gardens.

Coade's Works

Lambeth's early industry included several potteries making tin-glazed earthenware, gin and vinegar distilleries, timber yards, boat-builders' yards, glassworks, and candle and soap factories. One of Lambeth's most interesting industrial enterprises, especially in terms of its impact on London's evolving cityscapes, was Coade's Artificial Stoneworks Manufactory, which functioned from 1769 until about 1837 at King's Arms Stairs, on the site of what is now Jubilee Gardens. Robert Adam, John Soane, John Nash, Samuel and James Wyatt and every other notable architect of the period used Coade stone ornamentation. Timber ornament had been disallowed under a Building Act of 1774, and Coade stone was much cheaper than quarried stone. It was produced using a secret formula involving ground-up fired clay, raw clay and various minerals, all pressed into plaster moulds and then fired again at very high temperature. The Coade works turned out an extensive range of classical statuary and architectural detail that found its way all over late Georgian London. Whole streets were adorned with Coade stone columns and capitals, acanthus leaves, dentils, cornices and allegorical figures.

Integration and Industrialization

It was not until after the end of the Napoleonic Wars in 1815 that Lambeth itself was extensively developed. The growth of the metropolis meant that draining the district for building at last became financially worthwhile. The broad sweep of metropolitan change also saw the construction of two new bridges that brought south London fully into the

Vauxhall Tower (2014), a fifty-storey residential tower, part of the St George Wharf development on the Albert Embankment.

fabric of the metropolis: Vauxhall Bridge, opened in 1816, and Waterloo Bridge, opened a year later. Some of the houses in the southern part of the district, in the Kennington area, were fancy enough to warrant Coade stone; but Lambeth was quintessentially an industrial district with working-class housing.

Among the industries established in nineteenth-century Lambeth were printing and engineering. Maudslay Engineering Works was a major employer. The enterprise began as a specialist marine engineering works but expanded into railway locomotives and subsequently all kinds of heavy machinery that would power the British Empire. Located on Westminster Bridge Road, it exerted an agglomerative power that attracted other engineering companies and suppliers to Lambeth. One of these was the Vauxhall Iron Works, located a little to the south on Wandsworth Road. Throughout the nineteenth century the works produced engines for the Admiralty, as well as steam and, later, petrol engines for the merchant marine. Early in the twentieth century the firm began to produce automobiles under the Vauxhall brand. This expansion soon required more extensive space, and production moved to Luton before the firm was sold to General Motors in 1925.

A Sea of Housing

Lambeth's traditional pottery industry also expanded during the nineteenth century. The most notable firm, and one of Lambeth's largest employers, was Doulton & Company, which rode the wave of Victorian metropolitan expansion to become a major producer of both architectural terracotta and the high-quality drainage pipes that were crucial to Joseph Bazalgette's sanitary improvements for the Metropolitan Board of Works. The firm also rode the wave of metropolitan consumerism, drawing on design expertise at the Lambeth School of Art and expanding production to art pottery and bone china. The firm received a royal warrant from Edward VII in 1901 and became Royal Doulton. Like Vauxhall, it eventually found Lambeth both cramped and expensive, prompting a relocation from Lambeth High Street - in this case to Burslem, in the Staffordshire Potteries.

Meanwhile, metropolitan expansion brought widespread speculative building to Lambeth - most of it undertaken by small-scale builders and almost all of it architecturally undistinguished - aimed at low-income working-class households. The railways intensified property development, but were also disfiguring. Waterloo station opened in 1848, the approach tracks carving through some of the older streets adjacent to the river. Sixteen years later the South Eastern Railway opened its service to Charing Cross, across the Hungerford Bridge. Both stimulated inner-suburban development, but they also disrupted streets and created a series of dark, damp arches under the tracks that harboured some of the more disreputable elements of the population.

Lambeth also bore the imprint of another aspect of London's growth: the high mortality rate of a rapidly increasing population and the consequent shortage of burial space. A partial solution was implemented by the London Necropolis & National Mausoleum Company, which acquired 850 hectares (2100 acres) of sandy common land near Woking in Surrey, some 50 kilometres (31 miles) from central London. The company landscaped the area as Brookwood Cemetery and contracted with several London boroughs for the burial of their poor. The company had a special casket-loading platform at Waterloo station, and trains containing funeral parties ran daily to a Gothic station built within the cemetery itself.

As in much of south London, Lambeth's churches, chapels, schools and public buildings stand out in high relief against a general background of cramped Victorian and Edwardian stock-brick terraced housing. Among the more notable institutional

Walcot Square.
Speculative housing laid out in the 1830s by local bulders on land belonging to the Walcot Charity.

buildings to have survived from the Victorian era is St Thomas's Hospital. Another important landmark with Victorian origins is the Oval, playing fields that were used for rugby and cricket matches and for all but one of football's Cup Finals until 1893, and which is now a modern cricket stadium.

The people who occupied the speculators' new terraced houses were clerks, shopkeepers, skilled artisans and the rank and file of the commercial world. Those who occupied the older dwellings that had degenerated into grim slums were some of London's poorest. In 1899 Charles Booth wrote in his notebook:

> The story of Lambeth in the last 10 years is a story of worsement. The fairly comfortable have left & are leaving. The poor Remain & additional poor are coming in. The effect of cheap trams & cheap railway fares is most marked in this area. Brixton & Stockwell have claimed the mechanic & artisan, while the labourer remains here & his ranks are reinforced by displacements in Westminster across the river.[2]

Clearance and Rebuilding

By the end of the nineteenth century, Lambeth's dereliction and poverty, all too visible from across the Thames in Westminster, had become a matter of public concern. A first attempt at upgrading the cityscape of the Lambeth riverside and introducing white-collar employment to the district came in 1911, when the LCC decided to build a new headquarters building, London County Hall, opposite Whitehall. It was opened in 1922, but its presence failed to trigger investment in the area. Meanwhile, the LCC declared much of Lambeth's older housing 'unfit for habitation', and set about razing it. Lambeth Metropolitan Borough Council began to make up the deficit with walk-up apartment buildings. Abercrombie and Forshaw's *County of London Plan* (1943) proposed that north Lambeth should become a Comprehensive Development Area, a strategy that became almost inevitable after severe bomb damage in the Second World War increased the housing deficit.

Vauxhall Street. One of the famous gasometers behind Kennington Oval cricket ground.

One parcel of damaged and derelict land by the river was used for the postwar Festival of Britain (1951), but for most of the rest of the district, the recipe was wholesale clearance and rebuilding. By the census of 1981, almost half the households in the entire borough of Lambeth lived in council housing. Nikolaus Pevsner sneered at Lambeth's 'straggling amorphous estates of dreary four- and five-storey walk-up blocks', but as the Lambeth historian Hannah Renier observes, 'This is the view of someone who had never had to share a single room with a wife and four children, or a single lavatory with three other families.'[3]

Since the 1980s the imprint of neoliberalism has wrought Lambeth into a deeply polarized state: a division that is starkly reflected in its built environment. On the one hand there are the impoverished Victorian terraces and twentieth-century council estates; on the other are the riverside redevelopments. The wall of offices on the Albert Embankment has been converted into hotels and flats, and a lot of money has been spent on landscaping this south London frontier of gentrification. Lambeth's embankment is now part of a 'string of pearls' - the series of signature buildings along the Jubilee Walkway that extends eastwards along the South Bank and Bankside (see page 237). A giant Ferris wheel, the London Eye, opened in 1999 next to the old County Hall, which had been redundant since Margaret Thatcher's abolition of the GLC in 1986. A few years later County Hall itself was purchased by a Japanese developer and its spaces converted to the London Sea Life aquarium, hotels, a film museum, restaurants, flats and the London Dungeon exhibit.

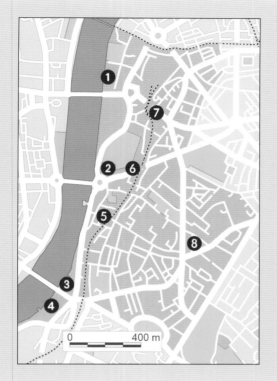

This northern tip of the borough of Lambeth is part of Victorian south London, an extensive tract of inner suburban working- and lower-middle-class housing and mixed industry. It has been subject to a great deal of rebuilding, for one reason or another, and consequently has a very mixed and uneven morphology. Close to the Embankment are large slab-like buildings, both public and private, of mixed vintage and mostly of little architectural merit. The base layer of the rest of the district was Victorian brick terraced housing, interspersed with local industrial premises. Much of this fabric has been overwritten by social housing of varying ages and styles, from the five-storey walk-up flats of the 1930s and 1940s to the concrete slab blocks and mid-rise point blocks of the 1960s and the small-scale infilling of the 1970s and 1980s.

① County Hall
② Lambeth Palace
③ Vauxhall Cross
④ St George Wharf
⑤ Southbank House
⑥ Lambeth Road
⑦ Westminster Bridge House/Waterloo station
⑧ Denny Street

❶ County Hall
Belvedere Road

Once a symbol of metropolitan civic pride, County Hall is now an unwelcome symbol of neoliberal policies, its parent institution – the GLC – abolished by the Thatcher government and the building sold off to a Japanese company. It now houses an aquarium, fast-food outlets, a 'funscape', a horror show, the ticket office for the London Eye and chain hotels. The LCC held a competition in 1908 for the design of its new headquarters, specifying an English Renaissance style for

the 2.5-hectare (6-acre) site across the river from the Palace of Westminster. Ralph Knott, a twenty-nine-year-old architect, won the competition, beating, among others, Edwin Lutyens. Construction began four years later but was interrupted by the First World War. When the building was finally completed, in 1933, it marked the start of Lambeth's slow evolution from an industrial district to a more mixed economy.

❷ Lambeth Palace
Lambeth Palace Road

Originally built as Lambeth House by Archbishop Hubert Walter in 1197, the palace complex has been the official residence of the Archbishop of Canterbury ever since; apart, that is, from the republican interlude in 1649–60, when the palace was used as a prison. Most of the medieval structures have been lost - most recently a thirteenth-century crypt that was irretrievably damaged by incendiary bombs during the Second World War. The gatehouse, shown here, was built by Cardinal John Morton in about 1495. Bread and broth were distributed from these gates to the district's desperate poor three times a week: the 'Lambeth Dole'. The practice continued until 1842, when cash grants from the archdiocese replaced the food handouts.

❸ Vauxhall Cross
Albert Embankment

The Vauxhall Cross headquarters of the Secret Intelligence Service - MI6, Britain's counter-intelligence agency - has become one of the most recognized landmarks of the capital, not least because of James Bond films. It stands on a portion of the eighteenth-century Vauxhall Pleasure Gardens, a riverside site that was subsequently occupied by a succession of factories. Developers acquired the site in the 1980s for a speculative project designed by Terry Farrell, first as an 'urban village' and then as an office block, prospectively for lease to the government. After it was decided to allocate the building to MI6, the government opted to purchase the building outright. It was completed in 1994 after extensive security additions: cameras inside and out, special bomb- and bulletproof walls, triple-glazed glass to block electronic eavesdropping and jamming, two moats and (rumour has it) a tunnel to Whitehall. The net result is memorable, but not loved by many.

❹ St George Wharf
Wandsworth Road

This mixed-use cluster of buildings on a former brownfield site - 93,000 square metres (1 million square feet) of space including more than 1100 luxury flats - has twice earned the architect, Broadway Malyan, the dubious distinction of being voted the 'worst building in the world' by readers of the *Architects' Journal*. On an important riverside site, it is a monument to the inflated property market of 'global' London. The architecture historian and design critic Tom Dyckhoff called it, memorably, 'Britain's finest exponent of bling brutalism'. The look-at-me roofline, in particular, has provoked ridicule in the architectural press.

⑤ Southbank House
Black Prince Road

Built in 1878 in a classic Victorian Gothic design by R. Stark Wilkinson as Royal Doulton's principal office, Southbank House is the surviving element of what was a huge pottery complex on Black Prince Road. The business had previously been located on Lambeth High Street, but success - built mainly on making the pipes for Victorian London's investment in sanitary infrastructure - made expansion necessary. The move to Black Prince Road coincided with the firm's shift towards the production of bone china, to take advantage of the late Victorian expansion of middle-class affluence. The firm's production gradually moved to Burslem in Staffordshire, while production at the Lambeth pottery declined. By the early 1950s most of the factory in Lambeth had been demolished. The surviving buildings have been reconditioned as offices, studios and event space.

⑥ Lambeth Road

Although nineteenth-century Lambeth was quintessentially industrial and working-class in character, it did have several streets and a few squares of finer homes built for the merchant class at the beginning of the century, before industrialization set in completely. This terrace was built in about 1800. By mid-century the homes were in multiple occupation, the original residents having moved out to newer suburbs.

7 Westminster Bridge House/Waterloo station
Westminster Bridge Road

The former office block of the London Necropolis Company (left), built in 1900, just as the passenger terminus was beginning to be expanded to designs of James Robb Scott. The Necropolis railway company had a special casket-loading platform at the station and ran special trains to its cemetery at Brookwood station, near Woking. The redeveloped station eventually incorporated a grand new entrance and Victory Arch (above) in typical post-First World War monumental baroque style.

8 Denny Street

The southern areas of the district were historically part of the Duke of Cornwall's Manor of Kennington. For a long time the Duchy did not exercise any real control over the standard of building on its land, but after the First World War it launched an ambitious project to redevelop a large tract of properties. Denny Street was part of this. Designed for the Duchy by J. D. Coleridge, it was a fine example of early twentieth-century urban planning, with a strong arcadian flavour.

Marylebone

The first settlements in this area developed along the banks of the Tyburn stream: a series of small medieval villages that were prosperous enough to support a small church. The church and the surrounding area later became known as St Mary-le-Bourne and, later still, as Marylebone. Marylebone High Street, which curves gently southwards towards the Thames, follows the old course of the Tyburn, which now runs beneath the street in a culvert. Similarly, the urban fabric of Marylebone – its eighteenth- and nineteenth-century residential estates – reflects the lineaments of the geometric field pattern of the farm holdings that surrounded the medieval villages of St Mary-le-Bourne.

Until the onset of urbanization in the eighteenth century, the district had a very marginal relationship to the City. Marylebone Gardens, to the east of the High Street, was a setting for raffish entertainments – gambling, bowling, bear-baiting and prizefights by members of both sexes – as well as concerts and firework displays, while Marylebone Fields was a popular setting for duelling. Tyburn Gallows, in the extreme southwestern corner of the district, near present-day Marble Arch, had been a place of public spectacle for hundreds of years (from 1196 to 1783, in fact). Tens of thousands of men and a good number of women and children were executed there, often for fairly trivial offences by today's standards. Several felons could be hanged at once on the 'Tyburn Tree', a spectacle that often drew thousands.

Estate Development

When John Holles, Duke of Newcastle, purchased the village and manor of Marylebone for £17,500 in 1710, the area was almost entirely rural. A few years later, the estate passed to the duke's daughter, who married Edward Harley, second Earl of Oxford. Subsequently, the estate passed by marriage to the dukes of Portland and, eventually, to Baron Howard de Walden, whose family estate company still owns, leases and manages a sizeable chunk (about 37 hectares/91 acres) of the district. Many of the streets and squares in Marylebone take their names from members of these families, their country residences, their titles or other estates in their possession.

The first component of the estate to be developed was Cavendish Square. It was the focal point of a master plan commissioned by the Oxford family for the area just to the north of Oxford Street, the southern boundary of the estate. The plan, by the architect John Prince, was based on a grid that roughly followed the ancient field system of the area. After a slow start – because of national financial instability caused by the South Sea Bubble of 1720 – development of the estate proceeded apace, succeeding in attracting the wealthy and fashionable to its tall Georgian town houses.

The dukes of Portland, who controlled the estate from the 1730s until 1879, were responsible for most of the original building programme. In the 1760s and 1770s the Adam brothers, London's leading architects of the period, were employed by the estate to design Chandos House, Mansfield Street and the overall layout and design of Portland Place. Portman Square was laid out in 1764, and the characteristic eighteenth-century grid of streets was then extended to the east with Manchester Square (1776) and Wimpole Street (1770s), to the west with Bryanston and Montagu squares (c. 1820) and to the north along Baker Street (c. 1800). First and Second Rate houses tended to be built around the principal squares, while in the northern and northwestern reaches of the district – in, for example, Knox Street,

The Prince Regent, a Grade II-listed Edwardian public house on the revitalized Marylebone High Street.

(Right) **First Rate houses** on New Cavendish Street, built by John Johnson for the Portland Estate in 1775–77. The unusual balconies and canopies were probably a response to the direct southern aspect of these houses.

(Far right) **Fourth Rate houses** built by the Portman Estate in 1810–20 on Knox Street. The ground floors were originally shops.

Shouldham Street and Wyndham Street – the estate built a few streets of Fourth Rate houses for middle-class households.

For the most part, Georgian Marylebone was very fashionable. 'The neighbourhood', wrote the topographer J. P. Malcolm in 1808, 'is distinguished beyond all London for its regularity, the breadth of its streets, and the respectability of the inhabitants, the majority of whom are titled persons, and those of the most ancient families.'[1] One of the district's most celebrated residents was Elizabeth Montagu, whose house on the northwest corner of Portman Square became the meeting place for some of London's most progressive thinkers. A power in the literary world, she was the founder of the Blue-Stocking Club, named after the informal blue hose worn by many of her group. Meanwhile, the cessation of public executions at Tyburn had removed the stigma associated with the western end of Oxford Street, which consequently blossomed as a shopping street. In the early nineteenth century it became fashionable to promenade along its whole length.

Economic and Social Transformation

By the early nineteenth century, Marylebone had been filled out, its built fabric dominated by late Georgian and Regency architecture. Much of it has survived intact, but an equal amount has been overwritten or replaced, while many of the surviving terraces and mansions have changed in function if not appearance. The economic and social

transformations of the nineteenth century left their mark on Marylebone in several ways. The district was favoured by London's expanding middle class, but the increasing polarization and changing class structure of Victorian London meant that pockets of poverty and vice appeared in the district. Octavia Hill began her career as a housing reformer in the northern part of Marylebone in the 1860s; and Ossington Buildings, model tenements for the working classes, were erected off Moxon Street in 1888, replacing a warren of slum houses.

The economic specialization that transformed Victorian London also left its mark on Marylebone. Doctors began to move into the Harley Street area in the 1860s, the beginning of what was to become a unique concentration of professionals and professional institutions. At about the same time, big hotels began to appear here and there in the district. Marylebone was no longer a residential suburb but part of central London and its numerous attractions and activities. Department stores and chain stores began to line the district's major shopping arteries – Wigmore Street, upper Regent Street and, especially, Oxford Street – early in the twentieth century. Some shopping streets, meanwhile, began to develop their own retail specializations, drawing customers from across the metropolis and beyond.

Changing property markets and obsolescence also played their part. Streets in the less prestigious northern part of the district were partly redeveloped in the late nineteenth century with mansion blocks, while the de Walden Estate carried out a great deal of rebuilding along Marylebone High Street at the turn of the century. Later in the twentieth century, a good deal of the residential fabric behind Oxford Street and Edgware Road and along Baker Street was converted to hotels and commercial premises, while the ever-increasing demand for flats in central London resulted in some of the original grand Georgian houses in Portman Square and the surrounding area being redeveloped as mansion blocks.

Marylebone High Street

The most distinctive element in Marylebone has always been its High Street. Until the 1950s it was a thriving community high street with independent greengrocers, butchers and other shops. But it lost its way in the 1960s and suffered a long and gradual decline throughout the 1970s and 1980s before finally collapsing during the recession of the early 1990s. By 1995 a third of the shops were either vacant or occupied by temporary charity shops; the rest were dominated by photocopying shops, travel agents and struggling retailers.[2]

Today, however, Marylebone High Street is widely regarded as one of Britain's finest: the result of the enlightened self-interest of the de Walden Estate. Recognizing the desperate commercial situation of the High Street's shops and its depressing effect on property values in the area, the estate undertook a major project to re-inject life into the area. Buying out struggling businesses enabled the estate to increase its ownership of properties along the street to about seventy per cent. With that much control, it was able to design a friendly 'urban village' atmosphere for the district's relatively affluent residents. This meant eschewing the cloned chain stores that dominate most of Britain's high streets. The tone was set by leasing a central site to Waitrose, a self-consciously upmarket supermarket, and by converting a derelict tyre depot into a 2300-square-metre (24,750-square-foot) Conran store selling modern furniture and furnishings. Careful selection of tenants for the remaining properties has resulted in an interesting and distinctive shopping street that has strong appeal for the gentrifiers who now dominate the area's population. Residential property in what has become one of central London's most desirable locations now commands premium rents.

Change and Diversity

Elsewhere within Marylebone, many fine Georgian and Regency buildings remain, rarely in single-family occupation, but in use and well-maintained as residential conversions, private hotels and commercial premises. Nevertheless, 200 years of change since the completion of the Georgian estates has resulted in a patchiness and fragmentation that is characteristic of the cityscapes of west-central London. Manchester Square remains largely intact and in character, and Montagu and Bryanston squares remain long, narrow, leafy and quiet. But Portman Square has been largely rebuilt since the 1920s and now has an uninspiring collection of buildings of different vintages. The honourable exception is Home House, a surviving (1773–76) Grade I-listed town mansion by Robert Adam. Cavendish Square has been spoiled by an underground car park and dull 1970s infill buildings. The terraces of Portland Place have been rudely interrupted by twentieth-century hotels, offices and flats and overwhelmed by the looming Victorian pile that is the Langham Hotel. Oxford Street's role as London's high street means that it has been under continuous redevelopment. On the eastern margin of the district, Edgware Road, an arterial highway that had become characterized by greasy-spoon cafés and run-down restaurants, has now become a centre of Arabic life with Middle Eastern restaurants, food shops, banks, pharmacies, estate agencies and hair salons.

Ossington Buildings. Model tenements for the working classes built in 1888; flats here are now marketed as part of 'Marylebone Village'.

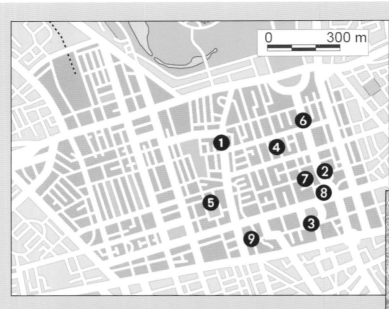

① Marylebone High Street
② Broadcasting House
③ Cavendish Square
④ Harley Street
⑤ Hertford House
⑥ Portland Place
⑦ Chandos House
⑧ Langham Hotel
⑨ Stratford House

Marylebone is framed to the south and west by two Roman roads: respectively, Oxford Street (which follows the line of the Via Trinobantina to Oxford) and Edgware Road (part of Watling Street, which stretched from Dover to the Midlands via London). Marylebone Road - formerly the New Road - effectively marks the northern boundary of present-day Marylebone, while Great Titchfield Street follows the boundary between the Marylebone estates and the Southampton Estate in Fitzrovia. Apart from the gently curving Marylebone High Street, which follows the course of the old Tyburn stream, Marylebone's townscape is based on a formal eighteenth-century planned hierarchy of squares, thoroughfares and side streets. The plan is mirrored by the hierarchy of surviving Georgian houses, with First and Second Rate houses on principal roads and squares and Third and Fourth Rate houses on side streets.

① Marylebone High Street

Until the middle decades of the eighteenth century, the manor of Marylebone was entirely rural. The village street followed the line of the Tyburn stream, with the Old Parish Church and the manor house, built in the time of Henry VIII, at the north end. Marylebone High Street developed along this axis. Much of the property along and around the street is owned, leased and managed by the Howard de Walden Estate, which has successfully revitalized the area with a smart and eclectic mix of shops.

❷ Broadcasting House
Portland Place

One of London's landmark buildings, Broadcasting House has always been appreciated much more by the public than by architectural critics. Designed by George Val Myer and F. J. Watson Hart in 1931 as the headquarters of the BBC, it soon became a symbol of national unity during the Second World War, its latticework masts becoming signifiers of the BBC's radio broadcasts and Winston Churchill's speeches. But its unfortunate mix of monumental streamlined Moderne form and Georgian fenestration could not be forgiven by design critics. Nikolaus Pevsner, in *The Buildings of England*, mentions Broadcasting House only to emphasize its ugliness: 'It cast a blight on the whole delightful Georgian neighbourhood ... A specially unfortunate feature is the windows of the Georgian shape. They make the grimness of the sheer stone walls twice as painful.'[3] It is, nevertheless, listed Grade II* by English Heritage. It is sited at the awkward junction of Portland Place and Langham Place, along John Nash's processional route between Regent's Park and Pall Mall and next door to All Souls, a Commissioners' church designed by John Nash and built in the early 1820s. The distinctive circular portico of the church provided a neat articulation of the junction as well as a terminating view from Regent Street to the south; but its subtle effect was undermined by the construction of Broadcasting House, much to the displeasure of Pevsner and others.

❸ Cavendish Square

This pair of grand Palladian stone-fronted town houses flank the north axis of the square. Although they have the appearance of aristocratic town residences, they were built in 1769–72 as a speculative venture by G. F. Tufnell. Their classical style and unusually elaborate facades stand in contrast to the rest of the square, which was developed piecemeal, mostly between 1720 and 1760, and mostly in Georgian style, following the master plan devised by John Prince, surveyor to the Portland Estate. The south side of the square was subsequently replaced by undistinguished mid-twentieth-century buildings: the backs of Oxford Street shops. Their proximity prompted the creation, in 1970, of an underground car park beneath the square itself.

Harley Street

Originally an upper-middle-class residential street, Harley Street has become synonymous with specialized medical services. An early development of large and stylish Georgian town houses by the Portland Estate, it housed several generations of London gentility before the economic and social upheavals of Victorian London transformed Harley Street and its immediate environs into an unprecedented urban phenomenon: a professional precinct.

During the early part of the nineteenth century, the dominant setting for medical care in British cities was the home. The bulk of the population provided their own care, with friends and relatives nursing the sick and relying on cheap medicinal cures. In more serious cases, where professionals were consulted, the home was also the setting: this time for 'heroic' therapeutics such as blistering, bleeding, leeching and dosing with mineral poisons designed to act as purgatives and emetics. The more affluent were also subjected to the dubious benefits of heroic medicine in their own homes, with charges based in proportion to the distance travelled by the physician, sometimes including a surcharge for travel at night or during bad weather. Until the early eighteenth century the doctors themselves tended to live close to the great hospitals in the city. Later, the custom was for doctors to receive private patients at regular hours in certain coffee houses or to enter by the back or side door of the houses of the great.

During the second half of the nineteenth century, advances in medical knowledge, together with the professionalization of medicine and the economic logic of specialization, changed the geography of medical care as well as its practice. Medicine became professionalized in response to the threat of unorthodox therapeutics, the 'overcrowding' of the orthodox profession (aggravated by the proliferation of commercial 'cramming' schools, which followed the loose licencing requirements of the Apothecaries Act of 1815) and the emergence of competing paramedical professions. The British Medical Association was established in 1832 and, together with the privileged institutions of the Royal Colleges of Physicians and Surgeons, ensured the dominance and respectability of 'scientific' medicine. Meanwhile, of course, the city itself was being realigned into a mosaic of distinctive districts sprawling over a much larger territory and providing a new logic for the locational decisions of every kind of enterprise.

Doctors began moving into Harley Street in the 1860s, attracted by Marylebone's affluent clientele and by the commodious town houses that could accommodate both consulting rooms and private apartments for the doctors themselves. The area was also within easy reach of the great new railway termini at Paddington and Euston. For a long time it had been customary to charge a guinea a mile for consultations outside London, so there was considerable incentive for a patient seeking specialized opinion to travel to London to avoid this extra fee. The area's reputation was given additional impetus when the Medical Society of London moved to Chandos Street in 1872 and the Royal Society of Medicine to Wimpole Street in 1912. From a total of about twenty in 1860, the number of doctors in Harley Street grew to eighty by 1900 and to almost 200 by 1914.

Gradually, it was only the most highly qualified and specialized of practices that could afford to move to the street. The agglomerative logic of specialization was reinforced as the telephone made it more logical for doctors to establish orderly appointment hours at the surgery. Improved urban transport also facilitated the local clustering of consultant physicians; and it was further reinforced as doctors' fees rose in relation to the incomes of the population at large, thus encouraging patients to substitute their own time for that of the doctor by travelling to the surgery. By the time the National Health Service was established in 1948, there were around 1500 doctors in and around Harley Street. Today Harley Street, along with nearby Wimpole, Welbeck, Queen Anne, New Cavendish, Weymouth and Devonshire streets, hosts a concentration of consultants, clinics, paramedical practices, medical organizations and hospitals that is of global significance.

❹ **Harley Street**. Terraced town houses (c.1822–25) probably by John White for the Portland Estate.

❺ Hertford House
Manchester Square

Hertford House (1776) was a town mansion built for the Duke of Manchester, who developed Manchester Square on the Portman Estate. The mansion occupies the north side of the square; the other three sides were developed as a speculative venture of brick terraces with stuccoed ground-floor facades. Overall, it is one of the better-preserved squares in Marylebone. Only the northwest corner of the original terracing has been lost, replaced by a brick office building in the 1950s. The duke's mansion was enlarged and rebuilt in the nineteenth century by Richard Wallace, the fourth Marquess of Hertford, to accommodate his vast art collection (which included the *Laughing Cavalier* by Frans Hals, and works by Rembrandt and Rubens). When he died in 1890, Wallace left the collection to his wife, who later bequeathed it to the nation. Since 1900 the collection has been open to the public free of charge.

❻ Portland Place
Prince Consort Road

Part of a terrace of large First Rate town houses, Portland Place was built in 1776-80 by Robert and James Adam on a Portland Estate lease. They had initially planned Portland Place as an enclave of detached private mansions, but a depressed economy during the American War of Independence led them to switch to grand terraces. The terraces formed the widest London street of their day, but Portland Place did not develop into a thoroughfare until 1826, when John Nash incorporated it into his grand route from Regent's Park to Pall Mall. Robert Adam evidently favoured street facades that could be split into sections, with emphasis on the central and end sections but with a plainer treatment of the houses in between - as here, where numbers 46 and 48 (in the left-hand photograph) are stuccoed and crowned with a pediment to give the illusion of a single mansion. This section, between Weymouth Street and New Cavendish Street, is the only stretch of the Adams' development that remains intact, the rest having been replaced with hotels, offices and flats during the twentieth century.

❼ Chandos House

Queen Anne Street

A Grade I-listed Georgian town house, Chandos House was designed by Robert Adam and built for the third Duke of Chandos in 1769-71. In the nineteenth century it was purchased by the Austro-Hungarian government for its London embassy. A century later it had become almost derelict. It is now owned by the Royal Society of Medicine, and since being extensively refurbished in 2004, it functions as a bed and breakfast and conference venue.

❽ Langham Hotel
Portland Place

The Langham, designed by Giles and Murray and opened in 1865, was Europe's first 'Grand Hotel'. It was built at a time when London was acquiring a slew of big Victorian hotels, including the Great Western, the Midland Grand, the Grosvenor and the Great Eastern. The Langham was exceptional in being located in the middle of an upper-class residential quarter rather than near one of the new railway stations, and it was notable for its luxury and grandeur. One hundred of its 600 rooms had their own toilet, and there were thirty-six suites with their own bathrooms. It was, for a long time, a favourite hotel of celebrities and minor royalty, but by the Depression it had begun to be obsolescent, and afterwards it was unable to recover its former glory. After the Second World War it was leased to the BBC, whose new headquarters were across the street. The BBC purchased it outright in 1965; the ballroom became the BBC record library and dining areas became recording studios. Having been listed Grade II in 1973, it survived the BBC's attempt to demolish it, and in 1986 it was sold, to be reopened as the Langham Hilton in 1991 after a £100 million refurbishment. Further renovation took place in 2004-2009 at an estimated cost of £80 million after the hotel was sold on again, this time to a Hong Kong property company.

❾ Stratford House
Stratford Place

Stratford Place is a short cul-de-sac just off busy Oxford Street. It was originally part of the City of London's Conduit Mead Estate, and the mayor had built a banqueting house there in the sixteenth century. The land was bought in the 1760s by Edward Stratford, second Earl of Aldborough, who built a street of terraced houses that widens at the end into a small square with his own mansion, Stratford House, facing south to Oxford Street. Designed by Richard Edwin in the fashionable style that had been advanced by the Adam brothers, the mansion was built in 1771-73. At the peak of the street's exclusivity, the entrance to Stratford Place was gated and guarded. The brick guard-box on the eastern side of the entrance to the street remains, with a Coade stone lion on its top. Apart from the mansion and its flanking three-storey wings, built in matching style in the early twentieth century for the Earl of Derby, only the eastern side of the Georgian terracing is still intact. After the Second World War the mansion was purchased by the publisher Hutchinson. It is currently owned by the Oriental Club, a traditional private members' club, which moved there from nearby Hanover Square in 1962.

Mayfair

The patch of farmland to the west of the built-up area of seventeenth-century London was the site of the extended and boisterous celebration of the City's annual May Fair. The land belonged to the estates of several noble families, including the Berkeleys, Burlingtons, Curzons, Grosvenors and Lumleys. They were all quick to take advantage of the feverish speculative housing boom that followed the Peace of Utrecht (1713–14) and the Hanoverian succession (1715), collectively building the district that today is known as Mayfair. The fair itself continued until 1764 in the fields near what is now Shepherd Market, by which time it had become so rowdy and disreputable – and the land so valuable – that it had to be suppressed.

The first development – Hanover Square and its surrounding streets – was undertaken by Richard Lumley, Earl of Scarborough, who owned the north-eastern corner of the district. The largest and most influential landowner was the Grosvenor Estate, where building began in the 1720s, centred on the massive Grosvenor Square. Berkeley Square followed in 1738, and small-scale speculative builders filled in the streets around the edges of the estates' developments. They all sought to capture the westward shift of the nobility that had been accelerated by the Great Fire and sustained by fear of disease in the more crowded parts of the capital. Mayfair was quickly established as one of the most fashionable parts of the city, and it has remained so ever since, largely because the Great Estates imposed very strict demands for improvements to their properties as tastes in residential architecture changed over time.

Socially, Mayfair has thus been a resilient and self-regenerating district, as one wealthy household has serially replaced another, each generation collectively investing in maintaining the quality of the built environment. As a result, the district has been subject to continual rewritings and refacings. In Mayfair, what looks like a Georgian terrace may be only a Georgian facade, and what appears to be Victorian or Edwardian infill or rebuilding may simply be refacing. Grosvenor Square itself has been so thoroughly rebuilt that almost no traces of the initial development survive. Meanwhile, nineteenth- and twentieth-century flats, shops and office blocks have been superimposed on the townscape, further diversifying the architectural personality of the district.

Early Development

The biggest influence on Mayfair's early development was the Grosvenor Estate. Richard Grosvenor and the estate's first surveyor, Thomas Barlow, created by far the largest single area of high-class domestic building in eighteenth-century London. The layout, a regular grid of broad streets and narrow mews with a grand square in the centre, was characteristic of early Georgian development. The preferred architectural style for the estate, at first, was a conservative Palladian. But there was little coordination of leasing in terms of the appearance of adjacent buildings, thus undermining the disciplined streetscape expected of the Palladian canon. The exception was the centrepiece of the estate, Grosvenor Square, a huge (3-hectare/7-acre) space around which the developer, John Simmons, arranged large town houses to form symmetrical blocks on three sides of the square, with taller elements at the centre and at each end. The architectural historian John Summerson suggested that this was probably the first occasion on which London terraced houses were grouped as though in a single, monumental building or palazzo – which he described as 'grandly monotonous'.[1] Barlow's layout took the Georgian square principle to its logical

Burlington Arcade, opened in 1819. The newfangled iron framing and glass provided a sheltered, top-lit setting for genteel shopping.

conclusion, with two streets at precise right angles to each other running into the corners of the square, thus making each side of the square a continuation of the grid of streets around it.

A number of big detached houses were built on the western part of the estate across from Hyde Park, precursors of later Park Lane mansions, but most of the rest of the estate's development, as in the rest of Mayfair, followed the common London terrace layout. The district was almost completely built over by the end of the eighteenth century. The last part to be developed was in the northwestern corner of the Grosvenor Estate, where builders were reluctant to take up leases because of the proximity of Tyburn gallows (which were in use until 1783). While the overall social character of the district was distinctly aristocratic, it took a large number of servants and tradespeople to service the rich. In terms of numbers, only ten to fifteen per cent of Mayfair's residents were well-to-do; the rest lived in attic rooms, servants' quarters and the courts, passages and mews leading off the principal streets. It was not until the second half of the nineteenth century that Mayfair's demographic profile became more consistently upper- and upper-middle-class, partly as a result of changes in social practices that resulted in fewer servants, and partly as a result of the policies of the Great Estates and their agents.

Charles Street. A palimpsest of well-to-do eighteenth- and nineteenth-century town houses.

Refronting and Rebuilding

Conscious of the competing attractions of fashionable new élite districts such as Belgravia and Holland Park, where uniform, stuccoed facades were in style, the Grosvenor Estate led the way in refronting and rebuilding Mayfair streets, grafting Italianate stuccowork, porticos, window dressings, cornices and balustrades on to buildings by means of compulsory clauses in renewed leases. This phase lasted from the 1840s until the 1870s, when it was eclipsed by the advent of Domestic Revival styles that were especially favoured by the city's *nouveau riche*. The first Duke of Westminster had as much as possible of his estate in Mayfair rebuilt in the style. The most successful and distinctive outcome was the redevelopment of Mount Street into fashionable apartment buildings with street-level shops. The status of the area was reinforced by the construction in 1896 of the Coburg Hotel as a 'home from home' for landed gentry, several of whom kept permanent suites there. Named after Prince Albert (of Saxe-Coburg), the hotel was renamed the Connaught when war broke out in 1914, to avoid any unfortunate German connotations. A few streets away, another exclusive hotel, Claridges, was rebuilt in red brick for 'the many gentlemen, noblemen, magnates and potentates, British and foreign, who wished to stay in town for a limited season'.[2]

Besides attending to the élite market, the Duke of Westminster also provided, through an enlightened self-interest, sites for limited-dividend philanthropic housing associations. Model dwellings were a good way of protecting the most lucrative parts of estates from the negative externalities of slum populations and of securing 'more efficient social segregation, with the poor removed from back streets and mews and either placed under tidy supervision in new model blocks or expelled from the estate altogether'.[3]

Edwardian London's fashion for Portland stone facades left its mark on Mayfair mostly in commercial architecture along Oxford Street and Regent Street. Elsewhere in the district the dominant architectural trend as the twentieth century unfolded was for redevelopment and infill in bulked-up neo-Georgian structures, mainly office blocks and apartment buildings. Grosvenor Square is now occupied by six-storey neo-Georgian terraces, save for the western end, where Eero Saarinen's austere and monumental

United States Embassy looms over the park, awaiting its likely conversion to an apartment building after the opening of the new embassy in Battersea in 2017.

Mayfair and Conspicuous Consumption

Mayfair's élite residential ecology and its geographic situation at the heart of the West End have made it a key location for the consumption of fashion and luxury goods since the eighteenth century. The district contains several distinctive shopping streets, each occupying a specialized niche in the retail hierarchy of the metropolis. In part, this is a legacy of the district's eighteenth-century origins, when high-quality domestic shops served local aristocratic households. More recently, it has been shaped by international tourists and the social polarization resulting from London's role as a global city.

Luxury shopping in the likes of Old and New Bond streets and North and South Audley streets dates from the district's first development as an exclusive residential area. Mount Street's luxury retailing has its roots in the first Duke of Westminster's redevelopment, but the current (sixth) duke's agents have attracted brands like Balenciaga and Marc Jacobs through selective leasing and by making parking bays big enough for chauffeur-driven limousines. Mayfair also had one of the first covered settings for luxury shopping, the Burlington Arcade, which opened in 1819, a few years before the appearance of the more famous *passages* in Paris. Arcades offered unheard-of amenities to the emerging class of bourgeois consumers in the first half of the nineteenth century. With specialized shops offering a broad range of goods and services in a contained space, along with gas lighting, warmth, shelter from rain and mud, and cafés and restaurants where shoppers could rest and observe fellow lingerers, they were magnetic in their attraction. Walter Benjamin, writing about the Parisian *passages*, saw their impact as the moment of transformation from a culture of production to one of consumption.[4] Mayfair acquired a second luxury shopping arcade, the Royal Arcade, in 1879.

The arcades of London and the *passages* of Paris were the precursors of the department stores that became central to the retail and architectural landscape of world cities during the nineteenth and early twentieth centuries. By 1910 there were several big department stores on Oxford Street, which had effectively become the High Street of the metropolis. These included Bourne and Hollingsworth (now the Plaza), D. H. Evans (now House of Fraser), Marshall and Snelgrove (now Debenhams) and Selfridges. Regent Street was redeveloped in the early 1920s and acquired its own department store, Swan and Edgar, as well as national (and, now, international) high-end chain stores. Nearby Savile Row developed into a street of exclusive men's tailors; exclusive luxury vehicle showrooms have clustered along Park Lane; and Cork Street has become the setting for galleries of contemporary art. Mayfair's retail sales constitute a very significant part of London's economy. According to the New West End Company, a Business Improvement District (BID) covering Bond Street, Oxford Street, Regent Street and twelve neighbouring streets, much of this is accounted for by overseas visitors – in particular those from the Middle East, Russia, China, Nigeria, Indonesia and the United States. The New West End BID has branded itself, depressingly, as 'London's Luxury Quarter', along with a neighbouring BID that covers adjacent streets in Piccadilly and St James's. Together they accounted for £3 billion in sales in 2013.

Royal Arcade. Opened in 1879 and running between Old Bond Street and Albemarle Street.

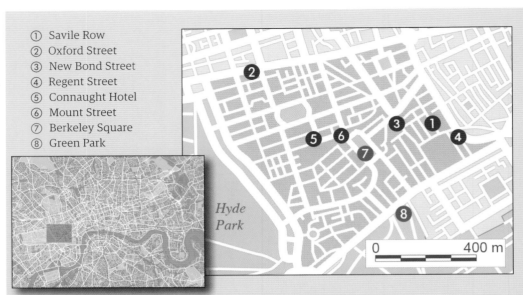

① Savile Row
② Oxford Street
③ New Bond Street
④ Regent Street
⑤ Connaught Hotel
⑥ Mount Street
⑦ Berkeley Square
⑧ Green Park

Hyde Park

0   400 m

Mayfair is one of the most clearly defined districts in London, bounded by two royal parks and four of London's most renowned streets: Oxford Street, Piccadilly, Park Lane and Regent Street. The street layout is a product of planned estate development in the eighteenth century, each of the major landowners opting for a simple rectilinear grid relieved by a principal square. Built out by 1800, the district has been continually redeveloped, its architectural personality always uncertain even though its social profile has been consistently exclusive.

❶ Savile Row

The street was laid out in the 1730s after the Earl of Burlington leased out 2 hectares (5 acres) of the land behind Burlington House in order to alleviate his financial difficulties. Initially entirely residential, it was the address of minor nobility, high-ranking military officers and physicians. Tailoring firms began to move in a century later, but it was still a good address. The architect Lewis Vulliamy lived in number 13 (on the left in the photograph) in the 1840s; and the Royal Geographical Society had its headquarters here between 1870 and 1911. The street is now lined on both sides with tailoring and outfitting shops, and its name has become an international byword for the finest men's tailoring.

❷ Oxford Street

Often referred to as London's High Street, Oxford Street was gradually colonized by retailing from the late eighteenth century, reaching a high point in the late nineteenth and early twentieth centuries when department stores like Bourne and Hollingsworth, D. H. Evans, Marshall and Snelgrove, Selfridges and Peter Robinson embodied modern progress. The stores brimmed with wave after wave of new commodities from the flood of industrial mass production and colonial exploitation. With their luxurious ambience of marble, carpets, ornaments and mannered service staff, they provided important settings for the middle class to stake its cultural identity, as well as respectable public spaces for women. By the 1970s the street had become tatty, but it has been revived somewhat by the credit-driven consumer boom that began in the 1980s.

❸ New Bond Street

The City of London Corporation developed New Bond Street on its Conduit Mead Estate during the building boom of the 1720s. High-quality domestic shops serving the wealthy households of the district evolved into exclusive luxury shopping, and Bond Street has never lost its fashionable pre-eminence as an exclusive street of jewellers, art dealers, auctioneers, couturiers and tailors.

❹ Regent Street

Regent Street has always marked one of the more significant boundaries in London's social and economic geography: between the unalloyed wealth of Mayfair and St James's to the west and the multifaceted social and economic territory of Soho to the east.

> Regent Street served a multitude of purposes. It offered a handsome speculation for London builders and enhanced the income of the Crown Estate. It provided a triumphal roadway to impress visiting royalty, and a north-south route for ordinary traffic to relieve the already notorious congestion of London's streets. It gave the idle and opulent a stage on which to display their clothes and equipages and at the same time incorporated a main line of underground sewer linking the suburban development at Regent's Park with the existing main sewer in St James's Park.[5]

The photograph shows Reginald Blomfield's grandiose rebuilding, in the 1920s, of John Nash's Quadrant.

❺ Connaught Hotel
Carlos Place

The Connaught has changed not only its name (during the First World War, when the original name, the Coburg, after Prince Albert of Saxe-Coburg, was felt to have unfortunate German connotations) but also its clientele: from 'old' money to 'new' money. Formerly associated with Britain's landed gentry, it is now popular among an international celebrity clientele. It was rebuilt in the 1890s in the image of the Grosvenor Estate, and a £70 million restoration and refurbishment in 2007 added a spa and a Japanese garden.

❻ Mount Street
Described in *The Buildings of England* as 'a paradise of pink terracotta' in the 'Franco-Flemish-Renaissance style' that the first Duke of Westminster stipulated for the rebuilding of his estate in the 1880s, Mount Street is another of Mayfair's exclusive commercial streets, with characteristically small shops and chambers above.[6] This particular terrace of houses and flats was designed for the duke by James Trant Smith and completed in 1887. The name of the street, incidentally, derives from one of the earthwork fortifications erected during the Civil War, known as Oliver's Mount.

❼ Berkeley Square

Unlike most West End squares, Berkeley Square was not conceived as a centrepiece of speculative development. Rather, it came about as a result of a restrictive covenant established in the seventeenth century to protect the northward view from Lord Berkeley's mansion. Accordingly, the north end of the square was built up only in the nineteenth century, along with the redeveloped south end, Berkeley House having long gone. After the 1920s many great eighteenth-century houses around the square were demolished for their valuable sites. The east side of the square, shown here, was rebuilt in the 1930s as Berkeley Square House, a series of offices and showrooms.

❽ Green Park

The smallest of London's eight Royal Parks, Green Park was enclosed by Charles II in 1668 and stocked with deer; it was later converted into a landscaped royal pleasure garden. It was not opened to the public until 1826, having been relandscaped by John Nash and planted with trees for the first time.

Notting Hill

Known today for its affluence and desirability, Notting Hill has gone through several cycles of physical development and social change. Until the late eighteenth century it was merely a hamlet on the old Roman road from London to Silchester. In the early nineteenth century the western fringe of the district became an instant slum, housing pottery workers making drainpipes, household bricks and tiles for the rapidly expanding metropolis. They were joined on cheap adjacent land by pig farmers who had been displaced by urban development closer to the centre of the city. It was not long, though, before the outward exodus of the capital's middle classes prompted the speculative development of the remaining countryside in the district. By the end of the nineteenth century, Notting Hill was highly polarized, its slums juxtaposed with its new bourgeois terraces: a microcosm of London itself. By the mid-twentieth century, the whole of Notting Hill had deteriorated badly and become synonymous with slum landlords and inner-city deprivation, its Victorian homes decaying, obsolescent and subdivided. But by the close of the twentieth century it had been transformed again: now trendy, with much of its physical fabric undergoing a thorough makeover. In the process, the district has acquired an extraordinary demographic mixture: rich and poor, English, Irish, Afro-Caribbean, Portuguese and Moroccan.

The Ladbroke Estate

The dominant element of the built environment of Notting Hill today is the Ladbroke Estate. Geographically and symbolically the heart of Notting Hill, it was built in fits and starts over the course of fifty years, reflecting the boom-and-bust economic cycles of the mid-nineteenth century and their associated changes in local land ownership, bankruptcies and lawsuits among the protagonists. Over the course of its development, it acquired different styles of housing, according to the aspirations of the developers and the tastes of the time. Remarkably, the overall layout of the estate retained the key features of the original design by Thomas Allason. A surveyor as well as an architect, Allason was employed by the initial landowner, James Weller Ladbroke, who sought to capitalize on the building boom of the 1820s.

Allason's design was highly original, taking advantage of the district's unusually varied topography (at least by London standards). It was focused on a large central circus, with concentric crescents and radiating streets built around garden squares - the houses arranged so that each has a small private back garden that gives access to a large communal garden square, which is private to the residents. The intention was to combine the bucolic pleasures of the countryside with the urbanity of the city. In this respect the Ladbroke Estate was to become an important influence on the English Garden City movement, which emerged at the end of the nineteenth century.

The building boom of the early 1820s soon collapsed, and Notting Hill proved to be still too far west for successful property speculation. During the lull in the housing market, the entrepreneur John Whyte leased 810 hectares (2000 acres) on the crest of the estate to build a racecourse, the Hippodrome. It opened in 1839, and from the top of the hill spectators could view races from start to finish as the horses galloped around the circular course. The district's heavy clay soil proved unsuitable for racing, however, and by the summer of 1841 Whyte had given up; he sold the racecourse to be developed into crescents and terraces. Subsequent landowners employed James Thomson as their estate architect, and he extended Allason's design for the core of the estate, alternating crescents with long straight roads. His streets

Stanley Crescent, on the Ladbroke Estate, consists of Italianate homes built in the mid-nineteenth century for upper-middle-class households escaping the congestion of the city.

St John's church. Designed by John Stevens and George Alexander as the centrepiece of the Ladbroke Estate, the church stands on the site of the grandstand of the ill-fated Hippodrome racecourse.

were broad, often lined with trees, and he carefully sited churches and large houses at focal points. Thomson favoured a Grecian treatment for his crescents and terraces, but his successor as estate architect, William Reynolds, preferred Italianate detail, pairing his three-storey buildings and facing them with stucco embellished with pilasters, architraves, balustrades and porches. They were built for prosperous middle-class households: the 1851 census lists a mixture of annuitants, lawyers, merchants, army officers, civil servants and shopkeepers. About one-third of the resident population were servants who, following rigid Victorian class observances, were not allowed to set foot in the garden squares unless accompanying their employers or their employers' children.

The southeastern part of the estate was developed in the 1850s, mostly to the designs of Thomas Allom, a founder member of the Royal Institute of British Architects and a well-known landscape artist. His designs were well suited to the increased material prosperity of the nation and the tendency towards ostentation among its growing *petite bourgeoisie*. His work resulted in theatrical and scenic compositions, with houses freely treated in the Italianate manner to meet the new ideals of grandeur and display. He is noted for making dramatic use of terrace ends, junctions and the curves in the streets, using bowed frontages, turrets and columnar screens to punctuate the streetscape.

Portobello

For a brief period, building in the district outstripped demand, leaving some properties abandoned in various stages of construction for want of funds to complete them. But with the construction in the mid-1860s of the Hammersmith and City Railway - the first of the feeder lines to be connected to the underground Metropolitan Railway - it became almost impossible to build houses fast enough. Older parts of Notting Hill were redeveloped, and empty fields were quickly platted. Even the notorious slum known simply as 'The Potteries and the Piggeries' was improved as the Metropolitan Board of Works completed a system of mains sewers, and new - although very modest - houses sprang up on former brickfields.

In the northern reaches of the district, Portobello Farm - named in honour of the capture in 1739 of Puerto Bello, a Spanish bullion-exporting port in the Gulf of Mexico, by Admiral Vernon - was developed by George Frederick Tippett, who had already built three ranges of tall terraces in the south of the farm, each backing on to shallow communal gardens in a feeble imitation of the more spacious garden squares of the Ladbroke Estate. With the opening of the Hammersmith and City line, Tippett sought to cram in as many houses on his land as he could, catering to a new clientele for whom suburban living had for the first time become possible as a result of the railway. Terraces of narrow three-storey houses, mostly with basements and only a small back yard, were the predominant form, with no pretensions to squares, crescents or communal gardens.

At the western margin of Tippett's land was Portobello Road, which had developed shops, street markets and pubs to serve the residential neighbourhoods on both sides. The rawness and bustle of the street markets had a negative effect on Tippett's early investments, however, and the tall terraces around Colville Square, Colville Gardens and Powis Square, no longer attracting middle-class families, began to be converted into flats in the 1880s. Thanks to modern travel guides and their urge to unearth 'off-the-beaten-track' places with 'character', the street market itself has gone on to become one of the main tourist attractions in London. The stalls and covered markets of the central and northern sections of Portobello Road, where fruit and vegetables, cheap clothing and household goods are sold, remain largely the province of local residents. The southern section, dominated by vendors of antiques, prints and books, relies much more on visitors and tourists.

From Rachmanism to Super-Gentrification

As the district's housing began to age, so the social composition of the inhabitants changed. Irish immigrants had moved into the Potteries and Piggeries and the Notting Dale area in the northwest of the district following the potato famine of 1845-49. As the rest of the district's housing stock became obsolescent, middle-class households moved out, large houses were subdivided into flats, and migrants and immigrants moved in. By the late 1940s Notting Hill had become established in people's minds as the epitome of a down-at-heel area of cheap lodgings.

The Rent Act of 1957, introduced by Harold Macmillan's Conservative government, preserved statutory protection against high rent increases for sitting tenants but removed rent controls once a property had become vacant. This provided lucrative opportunities for unscrupulous landlords to drive out existing tenants and replace them with new tenants willing to pay much higher rent. Britain's postwar economic boom and the arrival of tens of thousands of Commonwealth immigrants meant that there were plenty of takers. Afro-Caribbean immigrants, in particular, found few alternatives elsewhere because of racial discrimination and ineligibility for council housing.

One of the chief exponents of this situation was the notorious landlord Peter Rachman, and among his first acquisitions were Tippett's tall terraces around Powis Square. Using various forms of harassment and intimidation (unfounded threats, letting rooms to prostitutes, neglecting maintenance and so on), Rachman drove out the sitting tenants - mostly white families - and filled the vacancies with just-off-the-boat immigrants.

The process was repeated throughout the district (and, indeed, elsewhere in inner London) by Rachman and others, with the result that conditions declined rapidly while racial tension increased. Notting Hill became infamous as the site of the first race riots in Britain - and it was no coincidence that one of the very first, in 1958, took place along Talbot Road, adjacent to the Rachman properties around Powis Square.

Part of the community's response to the tension and violence was to organize a carnival. The first event, in 1964, was an entirely local affair. Now the annual Notting Hill Carnival has become symbolic of London's cosmopolitanism, attracting close to a million people when it takes place over the August Bank Holiday weekend.

Meanwhile, Notting Hill has been transformed again as a result of gentrification. 'Pioneer' gentrifiers began to move into the district in the 1970s, young professionals who understood the potential of the dilapidated housing and had the means to set about home improvement. A modest house that might have cost only £5000 in the mid-1960s would fetch £120,000 barely a decade later. As the number of gentrifiers increased, the district acquired a trendy reputation. Supercharged by enterprising estate agents, the process of gentrification quickly spread throughout the district. The house that cost £120,000 in the 1970s would now cost £1.2 million or more.

The influx of new money has meant that many Victorian houses have been brought back to prime condition, while the communal gardens of the Ladbroke Estate have been restored to resemble their original Victorian appearance. The resulting turnaround in the district's image and property values has been so dramatic that it has led to a process of super-gentrification: the first- and second-wave gentrifiers themselves are now being displaced by an élite class fraction of financial analysts, bankers and trust-fund beneficiaries with the capacity to outbid everyone else for the best properties.

Notting Hill occupies the northern portion of the London Borough of Kensington and Chelsea. Located just to the northwest of Hyde Park, it is bounded on the north by the Westway, an elevated dual carriageway built in the 1960s to ease traffic congestion into and out of the Paddington area. Another major road, the A3220 West Cross route, sets the boundary to the west, while Holland Park Avenue approximates to the southern edge of the district, merging into Kensington proper. The eastern margin of Notting Hill is less distinct, fading into the terraces of Bayswater. Mostly developed from the 1820s onwards in irregular spurts of speculative development, the district originally consisted of a dozen or so landholdings. The largest of these was the Ladbroke Estate, where the layout of the streets and the quality of the housing made for a coherent central element to the built environment. Other large estates, developed in piecemeal fashion, and with less ambitious housing, include the St Quintin Estate and Portobello Farm, in the north of the district, and the Norland Estate, in the southwest.

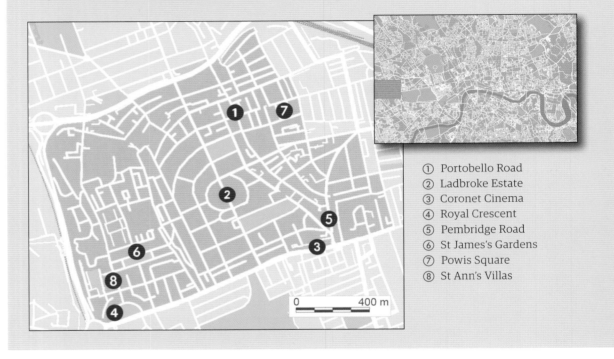

1. Portobello Road
2. Ladbroke Estate
3. Coronet Cinema
4. Royal Crescent
5. Pembridge Road
6. St James's Gardens
7. Powis Square
8. St Ann's Villas

❶ Portobello Road

Unexceptional in terms of architecture, Portobello Road became a catalyst for the gentrification of the entire district as a result of its 'authentic' grittiness and its street markets, and is now widely held to be an exemplar of London's everyday cosmopolitanism. Originally a country lane leading north from Notting Hill Gate, it was developed during the late nineteenth century, with ground-floor shops serving the residents of neighbouring estates. By the mid-twentieth century, the neighbourhood had become run-down. Antique and bric-a-brac dealers moved into this section, between Lonsdale Road and Chepstow Villas, attracted by relatively low rents. On market days the stores are supplemented by the stalls of dealers, making Portobello Road London's largest and most popular antiques market.

❷ Ladbroke Estate
Ladbroke Grove

The corner of Kensington Park Gardens and Stanley Crescent (right) and Stanley Gardens (below right) are both part of the estate developed in the 1850s by Charles Blake and designed by Thomas Allom. Besides having trained as an architect, Allom was well known as an artist. In 1853 he exhibited at the Royal Academy a picture entitled 'Stanley Crescent, Kensington Park Terrace etc. now building at Kensington Park Notting Hill for Charles Henry Blake esq from the designs and under the supervision of T. Allom' – an early example, perhaps, of the self-referential inclinations of celebrity architects.

The target market for these houses consisted of affluent upper-middle-class gentility, and Allom's imposing Italianate designs were intended to speak of social distinction. They were designed for big households: the average household size in Stanley Crescent in 1861 was 8.5, usually including two or three servants. Big houses in respectable neighbourhoods were also ideal for small private schools: there were two in Stanley Crescent and five more in Stanley Gardens. The residents included seventeen schoolmistresses and governesses.

Suburban respectability required a local church, and in a straightforward act of enlightened self-interest, the developer, Blake, provided the land: a site that was well placed to close the vista along Stanley Gardens. The church itself, St Peter's, was designed by Allom and completed in 1857. It is one of the very few Church of England churches to have been built in classical style in Victorian London.

The Ladbroke Estate steadily slipped down the social scale for the first three-quarters of the twentieth century, its big homes increasingly subdivided into flats or converted into boarding houses. Gentrification began to reverse the process in the 1970s. In 2014 unmodernized houses in Stanley Crescent were priced at £8 million or more, while single-bedroom flats on Kensington Park Gardens were priced at more than £2.5 million. In socio-economic terms, the neighbourhood is now more exclusive than when it was first occupied by the Victorian upper-middle classes.

❸ Coronet Cinema
Notting Hill Gate

A rare surviving example of a London suburban theatre and opera house, the Coronet was designed by W.G.R. Sprague, the architect of many of London's West End theatres. When it opened in 1898, it had a seating capacity of 1143. Today's more generous space standards allow seating for 333. It became a full-time cinema in 1923 and has been in operation as such continuously ever since. It survived a 1970s proposal to demolish the cinema and replace it with a retail/office building and a 1980s proposal to convert it into a McDonald's restaurant. It is now listed Grade II by English Heritage.

❹ Royal Crescent

Typical of the circuses and curved layouts that were in vogue for much of the first half of the nineteenth century, Royal Crescent consists of forty-three narrow four-storey houses with just two rooms to each floor. The layout was the work of Robert Cantwell, principal architect for the Norland Estate, and the developer of the crescent was Charles Stewart, a wealthy barrister, who put up the houses in 1846. The residents of the Crescent at the time of the 1851 census included three lawyers, two clergymen, three stockbrokers and three merchants and their respective servants, together with two private schools for girls. A dozen or so houses stood empty and remained so for several years because of a lack of people willing to live in houses that were still felt to be so far out of London.

❺ Pembridge Road

Literally around the corner from the large detached houses and grand monumental villas of the Hall-Radford Estate (one of the largest and most successful speculative developments in Victorian Notting Hill), the undistinguished terraces of Pembridge Road have become the entryway to the Notting Hill of popular imagery. Boutiques, second-hand clothes shops, souvenir shops, independent cafés and restaurants have colonized the street, taking advantage of the flow of tourists and visitors on their way from the bus stops and Tube station at Notting Hill Gate to the street market and antiques shops of Portobello Road. The colourful and edgy affect of the street contributed to the attraction of the neighbourhood for pioneer gentrifiers, whose influence has now been superseded by the super-gentrification of nearby Pembridge Square and Pembridge Gardens.

❻ St James's Gardens

St James's Square (now Gardens) was the last important part of the Norland Estate to be developed. Designed by John Barnett and built in 1847-51, it made a coherent architectural scheme, with the houses in linked pairs and the link taking the form of recessed bays containing entrances. The houses themselves were unusually spacious for the standards of the period. With frontages about 2.5 metres (8 feet) wider than those in the more conventional terraces of the district, the main rooms were attractively proportioned, and almost all of the thirty-seven houses in the square were occupied as soon as they became available. The occupants were solid middle-class households - merchants, clerks and middle-ranking military officers. In recent years most of the houses have been renovated by super-gentrifiers who have employed their own architects, interior designers and builders; house prices in the square were in the range of £5-£6 million in 2014.

❼ Powis Square

The tall terraces of Powis Square, built in the 1860s by George Frederick Tippett (who was developer, builder and architect as well as ground landlord), have experienced the full chronology of sequent occupancy that characterizes Notting Hill. The census of 1871 recorded forty-six houses with a total of 402 residents, of whom 135 were servants in households that were solidly middle-class. The arrival of the railways disturbed the social geography of the neighbourhood, however, and by the 1880s the houses had begun to be subdivided into flats. By 1922 only five of the houses in the square were listed as still in single occupancy, and by mid-century the entire square had become a slum, with many of the properties owned by the notorious Peter Rachman. Since the 1970s the square has been steadily renovated and socially upgraded through gentrification.

❽ St Ann's Villas

A stark exception to the neoclassical and stuccoed terraces of most of the district, these houses reflect a simple strategy of product differentiation on the part of a developer seeking to boost sales through novelty and distinction. The developer was Charles Stewart, the wealthy barrister responsible for Royal Crescent (see opposite). On the street leading northwards from the crescent (St Ann's Villas), Stewart began in orthodox fashion, building two short ranges of four-storey stuccoed terraces, each consisting of five houses. As in Royal Crescent, Stewart had difficulty attracting buyers because few were willing at the time (the 1840s) to live quite so far out of the city. So Stewart switched to these semi-detached villas in Tudor-Gothic and Jacobean style as he continued building northwards in the 1850s. He built six pairs of villas on each side of the street. Although of deliberately varied design, they were all executed in red and blue brick with Bath stone detailing, and they formed a unified and distinctive scheme. Unfortunately for Stewart, there was nevertheless a prolonged lack of demand for the properties, so that this experiment in the Tudor manner could be considered a failure in marketing terms. Later in the nineteenth century, the westward surge of London's middle-class population, combined with the romantic sensibilities and English Romantic aesthetic of late Victorian England, ensured the popularity of the villas. In 1969 they were listed Grade II by English Heritage.

Poplar + Isle of Dogs

For hundreds of years Poplar and the Isle of Dogs stood as sparsely settled marshland, bounded by a big, looping meander of the Thames. Then, at the beginning of the nineteenth century, the area was developed to accommodate the docks, warehouses and dock workers needed for the transoceanic shipping that sustained Britain's commercial empire. By the early 1970s the docks had become obsolete, and by 1980 they had all closed, the wharves abandoned and the warehouses derelict. Today, the Isle of Dogs is dominated by the skyscrapers and office complexes of global financial services, surrounded by the sharply contrasting landscapes of social housing.

A Working-class District

At their peak, London's Docklands employed over 30,000 labourers. On the Isle of Dogs, the West India and Millwall Docks handled bananas from the Canary Islands, sugar from the West Indies, vegetable oils, spices and tropical fruit and vegetables from Africa and Asia, grain from North America, timber from Scandinavia and wine from France and the Mediterranean. Much of the workforce initially lived off the 'island', in Poplar and in the nearby districts of Wapping, Limehouse and Stepney, but the busy docks prompted a housing boom on the island itself in the first half of the nineteenth century. Built for rent by working-class families, and severely damaged by German bombing in the Second World War, most of the housing was replaced in 1950–70 by social housing in the form of three-, four- and five-storey apartment blocks, maisonettes and terraces in what were intended to be self-contained neighbourhoods in the Modernist town-planning idiom. The Lansbury housing estate in Poplar was built as part of the 1951 Festival of Britain and included Chrisp Street Market, designed by Frederick Gibberd. Near by there emerged several 1960s landmark housing projects: the critically acclaimed but socially disastrous Robin Hood Gardens, designed by Peter and Alison Smithson; and the similarly Brutalist – but much better-quality – Balfron Tower, Carradale House and Glenkerry House towers, designed by Ernő Goldfinger.

But the economic basis of these communities was undermined as the Docklands fell into a steep decline, first as a result of competition from Rotterdam and other Continental ports, and then as a result of the introduction of containerization, which shifted London's port facilities to Tilbury, 25 kilometres (15 miles) downstream. The abandoned Docklands and marooned neighbourhoods were widely regarded as emblematic of the decline of Britain's traditional economic base, a very visible source of embarrassment to the government. At the same time, the vast amount of vacant land was readily identified by the private sector as the basis for a potentially lucrative regeneration of the island, replacing old industries with new and building upscale river-view condominiums for affluent households in place of the working-class population.

Regeneration and Social Cleansing

Following a series of plans and reports, the central government, under Prime Minister Margaret Thatcher, took some 2000 hectares (4900 acres) of land out of the hands of the local governments and Port Authority in 1981 and gave it to a specially created corporation with extensive powers: the London Docklands Development Corporation (LDDC). The regeneration of the Docklands was a deliberate attempt not simply to market this part of London to global investors but to sell the whole idea of the United Kingdom as a rejuvenated, post-industrial

Canary Wharf. The central cluster of office and apartment buildings at the heart of the regenerated area on the Isle of Dogs.

economy. The Docklands were to become the spatial expression of neoliberal enterprise culture, fostering the growth of London's advanced business services and replacing a 'redundant' - both literally and figuratively - working-class population with a middle-class one. The LDDC promptly designated the area around the West India and Millwall Docks as the Isle of Dogs Enterprise Zone, giving developers freedom from local property taxes for a ten-year period, with no development land tax and a 100 per cent capital allowance for new commercial and industrial buildings, to be offset against corporation and income taxes. Within a few years, hundreds companies had taken advantage of these tax perks to move into the Isle of Dogs.

In 1985 Canada-based Olympia & York, the world's largest property development company at the time, put together an ambitious redevelopment scheme that would provide tens of thousands of square metres of new office space. The government committed to furnish a new transportation infrastructure: a driverless light railway line - the Docklands

West India Quay.
The only original warehouses in the area to survive wartime bombing, they now contain expensive flats, restaurants, bars and the Museum of London Docklands.

Light Railway (DLR) - and a £3.5 billion extension to the Underground system. The centrepiece of the development was Canary Wharf, its flagship structure a sleek fifty-storey tower (One Canada Square) designed by the Argentine-American architect Cesar Pelli. Beneath the development was an underground shopping centre and beneath that was a multi-layered service spine for the whole development, including parking.

The first phase of the development was completed in 1991, just in time for the collapse of the global property market. It led to the bankruptcy of Olympia & York, and it took until 1997 for the development to regain momentum under a new owner

(the Canary Wharf Group). The revival of the property market on the Isle of Dogs was driven by rising demand for deep floor-plate, grade A office accommodation (which was not available in the City of London, given the conservation constraints there at the time) and boosted by the opening of the Jubilee line extension in 1999, with Norman Foster's signature-style Canary Wharf station. By 2005 the Isle of Dogs finally had the skyline profile that the Thatcher government had sought as a highly visual and symbolic manifestation of the resilience of London's role in the global economy.

The LDDC, having been widely criticized for being unaccountable and for causing social polarization and encouraging gentrification, was wound up in 1998. The subsequent incremental opportunism of developers and local government agencies has resulted in a mixture of residential, commercial, exhibition and light industrial space that is the largest single urban regeneration scheme in the world. It is, however, fragmented and polarized, with no civic spaces, no public buildings, few parks and an inadequate transport infrastructure.

The buildings are, for the most part, unremarkable. It is difficult to engage with either the architecture or the setting. Ironically, the LDDC had seen architecture and urban design as a means to establish a marketable sense of place for the Docklands. Landscaping and street furniture were deliberately designed to contrast as far as possible with the deindustrialized legacy of the district, but have served only to lend a generic sense of placelessness. The water, originally held untouchable by the LDDC, has meanwhile gradually been encroached upon by piecemeal development, and much of the remaining waterfront is now inaccessible to the public.

As development has unfolded, a broad layering has become evident in the built environment. The core of the initial development around Canary Wharf unfortunately coincided with a fashion for postmodern styling, so that - Pelli's tower excepted - the big cornerstone corporate office buildings were dressed up with the vestigial columns and pediments and overscaled entrances of pre-cast postmodern classicism. Meanwhile, smaller commercial developments on the periphery of the Canary Wharf project typically took the form of single- or two-storey lightweight structures arranged around parking courts and embellished with nautical references and bright colours. Later developments on the Canary Wharf estate, catering increasingly to international financial and publishing companies, have opted more for glassy, International Style towers. Since 2000 development has generally intensified, and in the centre of the island a 1980s suburban business park has been redeveloped into a network of private or pseudo-private 'urban villages', branded the 'Millennium Quarter'.

Polarization

The first residential developments aimed at the island's new white-collar workers gravitated to the riverfront, using stepped and angled forms to maximize the number of flats with a river view (and thereby the price premium for developers and landlords). The best sites having been taken, subsequent residential developments exploited remaining dockside sites, deploying renovated dockside cranes, ships' anchors and buoys in an attempt to restore the authenticity that had been eschewed by the LDDC's original design guidelines. Elsewhere, on land-bound sites, residential development has been in the form of high-density enclaves, mostly gated or walled. All are aimed, of course, at the upper end of the housing market. They have attracted a disproportionate number of single people and couples who have not yet had children, are not contemplating them or have had them long ago. For many of them the island is a second home: they spend their work week in central London, often socializing late with colleagues or clients before retiring to the island simply to sleep, and then resume a life elsewhere at weekends. The result is a lifelessness that contrasts dramatically with the lively bustle of the cramped public spaces around the island's office developments.

An even greater contrast, though, is with the social housing estates of Poplar and the island, whose residents remain largely excluded from the surrounding economy and whose neighbourhoods have remained largely untouched by the physical and economic regeneration. As private developers have picked off sites around Millwall Docks and in Blackwall and Cubitt Town at the south of the island, social housing built in the 1950s and 1960s has been encircled and isolated. At one time Poplar and the Isle of Dogs were famous for having the largest concentration of social housing in the United Kingdom. Today this is the most extremely polarized district in the country, with multiple pockets of households classed among the most prosperous ten per cent in the country literally interspersed among those who are among the most impoverished ten per cent, according to the Department for Communities and Local Government's index of multiple deprivation.

Millwall's waterfront apartment buildings. The sloping twenty-storey Cascades apartment building (1988) was the first private building to be completed on the Isle of Dogs as regeneration began to take shape.

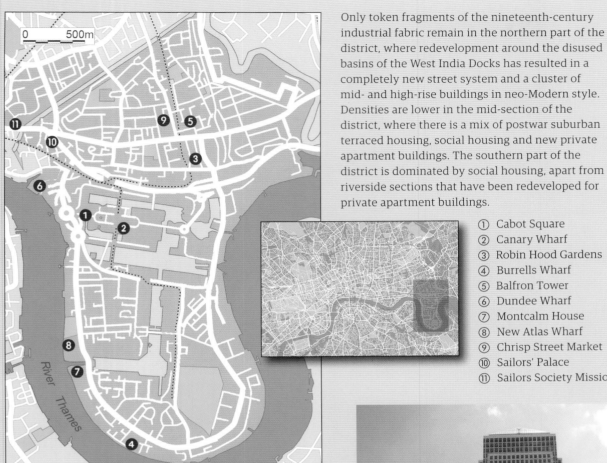

Only token fragments of the nineteenth-century industrial fabric remain in the northern part of the district, where redevelopment around the disused basins of the West India Docks has resulted in a completely new street system and a cluster of mid- and high-rise buildings in neo-Modern style. Densities are lower in the mid-section of the district, where there is a mix of postwar suburban terraced housing, social housing and new private apartment buildings. The southern part of the district is dominated by social housing, apart from riverside sections that have been redeveloped for private apartment buildings.

① Cabot Square
② Canary Wharf
③ Robin Hood Gardens
④ Burrells Wharf
⑤ Balfron Tower
⑥ Dundee Wharf
⑦ Montcalm House
⑧ New Atlas Wharf
⑨ Chrisp Street Market
⑩ Sailors' Palace
⑪ Sailors Society Mission

❶ Cabot Square

The first phase of the Isle of Dogs regeneration occupies an island of development between the north and south basins of the old West India Docks. It was an almost entirely North American creation. The Canadian developer Olympia & York hired Skidmore, Owings & Merrill (SOM) to do the master-planning, and most of the buildings were designed by American firms. The fifty-storey centrepiece, Canary Wharf Tower (One Canada Square), was designed by Cesar Pelli, who also designed the Canary Wharf DLR station, the forty-five-storey Citigroup tower (to the right of the Pelli tower in the photograph) and the first stages of the central shopping mall, Cabot Place, which runs along the axis of the development beneath the buildings. The complex is served by an underground tunnel with loading bays, thus allowing traffic-free spaces at ground level. The square is one of very few public spaces in the area, and as such it is not particularly successful: out of scale, unwelcoming, subject to Venturi-effect winds and fringed by ugly buildings.

❷ Canary Wharf

Canary Wharf's cluster of thirty-four major buildings, four shopping centres, more than 375,000 square metres (4 million square feet) of office and retail space, ten buildings of thirty to fifty storeys and about 100,000 employees is now a major business complex in its own right. Clockwise from top left: Norman Foster's Jubilee line station; 20 Bank Street, designed by SOM; South Colonnade, designed by Kohn Pedersen Fox; the Docklands Light Railway; Cabot Square; Reuters Plaza.

❸ Robin Hood Gardens
Poplar High Street

More than seventy-five per cent of residents supported the demolition of this Brutalist council-housing project when consulted by the local authority, Tower Hamlets. Designed by Alison and Peter Smithson and completed in 1972, it was sculpture posing as architecture; boxes posing as homes; revanchism posing as progressivism. In 2008 *Building Design* magazine, backed by such star architects as Zaha Hadid and Richard Rogers, ran a campaign to get the buildings listed in order to save them from destruction. English Heritage declined, noting that Robin Hood Gardens had failed as a place for human beings to live. Demolition began in 2013.

❹ Burrells Wharf
Burrells Wharf Square

Burrells Wharf is one of the earliest instances on the Isle of Dogs of the conversion of industrial buildings for middle-class residential use. Kentish Homes began to redevelop this site at the southern tip of the Isle of Dogs in the mid-1980s, well before the Docklands property boom. The Plate House, shown here, was converted into a community clubhouse as well as flats. The buildings date from the 1850s, part of the Millwall Iron works, which built steamships for the Victorian merchant navy. The SS *Great Eastern*, the largest ship in the world at the time, was built at Burrells Wharf and launched from the slipway there in 1858. The works were later given over to the production of pigments and dyes.

❺ (opposite) Balfron Tower
St Leonards Road

This is one of three housing blocks designed by Ernő Goldfinger for the LCC and built by the GLC on the Brownfield Estate in Poplar in 1965-67. It was Goldfinger's first foray into large-scale social housing, and he and his wife, Ursula, moved into Balfron for a whole two months in 1968 in order to get feedback on his design from other residents. The proximity of the area to Canary Wharf means that property values have increased dramatically since the 1980s, and since 2011 Balfron Tower has been closed for renovation by Poplar Housing and Regeneration Community Association. Architectural historians have been thrilled, but the fact that seventy per cent of the reconditioned flats are likely to be for non-social housing has led to accusations of social cleansing.

⑥ Dundee Wharf
Three Colt Street

This gated development, completed in 1997, stands on the site of one of the wharves owned by the Dundee, Perth & London Shipping Company. The company's office building stands adjacent to the entrance to the new apartment building. In the 1830s its passenger paddle steamers SS *London* and SS *Perth* carried passengers on a twice-weekly service to Dundee. The wharves also saw the departure of some of the first voluntary emigrants to Australia. The company's massive, fortress-like warehouses were cleared in 1990 to allow construction of the Limehouse Link Road, the four-lane highway that runs in a tunnel beneath the new development, linking the Docklands with the City. The crane-like attachments to the exterior of the building, which was designed by CZWG, are entirely decorative, a postmodern wink to the new Docklands.

⑦ Montcalm House
Westferry Road

Part of the Kingsbridge Estate on the western shore of the Isle of Dogs, Montcalm House was built for the LCC in the mid-1930s to house the growing workforce at Millwall Docks, just to the east. The flats were built to the LCC's new 'Type 1934, versions 3 and 4' design, which incorporated significant improvements in materials, space standards and amenities within a neo-Georgian style. It is one of few waterfront sites on this stretch of the river that has not been entirely redeveloped. In response to a Housing Green Paper in 2000 requiring all social housing to be brought to the government's 'decent homes standard' by 2010, the London Borough of Tower Hamlets transferred the estate to a charitable housing association, now operated by One Housing Group.

⑧ New Atlas Wharf
Arnhem Place

The speculative apartment blocks that have come to line the river since the regeneration of the Docklands have distinctive forms designed to maximize the number of flats with river views. New Atlas Wharf stands on part of the riverfront that played a significant role in shaping London's built environment: along this stretch of the river were patent cement and plaster works that produced the raw materials for the stucco coatings of West End terraces. Some of it was produced by burning and grinding limestone nodules from the Thames estuary, while better-quality limestone was brought by barge from the Yorkshire coast. Also on this stretch of wharfage were a terracotta works and a tar distillery, both of which contributed to the making of Victorian London. New Atlas Wharf is a gated development geared to the luxury market.

9 Chrisp Street Market
Chrisp Street

One of the first purpose-built pedestrian shopping precincts in the United Kingdom, Chrisp Street Market is part of the Lansbury Estate, a model council estate designed by Frederick Gibberd, part of the 'living architecture' element of the 1951 Festival of Britain. George Lansbury was a local social reformer who became leader of the Labour Party in 1932.

10 Sailors' Palace
Commercial Road

Like so many of the larger buildings in Poplar and the Isle of Dogs, this one has been converted into housing - this time for affordable rather than luxury units. It was funded by the philanthropist J. Passmore Edwards and erected in 1901 as the headquarters and hostel for the British and Foreign Sailors Society, catering to the religious needs of sailors. It is lavishly decorated with nautical symbols, including a ship's figurehead with a ship under each arm, cherubs blowing wind into their sails: a graphic invitation to attract sailors who would not necessarily be able to read English.

11 Sailors' Society Mission
747 Commercial Road

A very confused-looking building - part warehouse, part cathedral and part railway terminus - this was in fact a hostel for seamen. It was opened in 1924 to cater to the thousands of seamen who found themselves stranded in the Docklands between voyages. It was established as the Empire Memorial Hostel as a memorial to the 12,000 merchant seamen who died in the First World War. The Ladies' Guild of the British Sailors' Society raised the funding for the facility through voluntary contributions from around the world. When it opened in 1924 the hostel provided 205 single cabins. For decades it was full every night, but following the closure of the docks in the 1960s and 1970s, the hostel lost its clientele; it finally closed in 1979. It was sold as accommodation for the homeless, but closed in 1985 after acquiring a rather unsavoury reputation. It now provides shelter for young professionals from the City, having been converted into very expensive luxury flats in 1989.

Regent's Park + St John's Wood

This district is the origin of much of what has become familiar in modern suburbia. Regent's Park was the first step in developing the idea of a garden suburb. Its picturesque, arcadian landscape was combined with some of the most choreographed architectural facades ever to be built in the United Kingdom. Meanwhile, St John's Wood, just to the northwest of the park, was the prototype for Victorian suburbia. Its semi-detached villas were not only a radical departure from the Georgian convention of terraces and squares but also a turning point in the trend towards private domesticity and residential social segregation.

The Park

Regent's Park and its associated residential fabric are also notable as an exception to the overall process of urbanization in London: part of the city's only fling with the kind of top-down urban design that was to reshape Paris entirely a few decades later. As with Parisian urban design, it was an exercise in the representation of national greatness. It was instigated by the Prince Regent (later George IV) and carried out in the prosperous interlude after the Napoleonic Wars of the early nineteenth century.

It was the Prince Regent's self-indulgence rather than his concern for city planning that prompted the scheme. He decided to build himself a summer palace in Marylebone Park Fields (part of which later became Regent's Park) and to link it by a long processional avenue with his London palace, Carlton House. John Nash, the prince's favourite architect,

was commissioned to devise the scheme. Much of it was completed, including Park Crescent, Regent Street, Waterloo Place, Trafalgar Square and Carlton House Terrace. But the summer palace was never built, nor were the dozens of mansions in Marylebone Park Fields that were supposed to finance the rest of the project.

Marylebone Park Fields had been Crown property since 1538, when Henry VIII acquired the land and made it into a deer park. Between the late seventeenth century and the beginning of the nineteenth century, it was used as farmland, the main leases being held by a series of aristocrats and bankers who sublet the land to tenant farmers. In 1811, just as the Prince Regent was thinking about building a summer palace on part of the property, the prime minister, William Pitt the Younger, ordered a review of the use and potential of Crown Estate land as part of a new commitment to government efficiency. With London expanding westwards, Marylebone Park offered considerable potential for profitable development. An open competition for a plan to develop it as an upper-class residential enclave proved inconclusive because of the distractions of the Napoleonic Wars. But a second attempt resulted in two submissions, one of which was from John Nash, who was working at the time as senior architect of the Office of Woods and Forests. His plan was to cover the park with a pattern of streets, squares, circuses and crescents: a grandiose version of typical town-extension schemes of the period. It would have excluded the public, however, from what had previously been an accessible area. As a result, Nash was asked to revise the plan for the park, which was formally renamed the Regent's Park in 1813.

The eventual layout moved most of the housing to the edges of the park, with just a few large villas placed inside. Each of these villas was cunningly landscaped such that none could be seen from any other or from the terraces of houses overlooking the park. Although the park had a certain formality in its plan - a crescent linked to a square at the southern entrance to the park and an inner circle with

Cambridge Gate. An exception to the rule: in complete disharmony with the rest of the terraces around the Park, it was built in French style in 1875–77 and faced with Bath stone.

Cumberland Terrace. A terrace of fifty-nine houses designed by John Nash and James Thomson to give the appearance of a palace overlooking the natural landscape of Regent's Park.

the liberal use of stucco on facades and of false pediments, screens and hollow columns, following techniques pioneered by Robert Adam.

Inevitably, Nash's architecture was heavily criticized by purists for being incorrect in academic terms. But the properties sold well in the booming economic climate of the 1820s, and they were generally well received by the public. H. V. Morton, writing in 1951, wryly observed that

> I can never go to Regent's Park without thinking how brilliantly Nash ransacked the ancient world and adapted it to the requirements of the English butler. There is something exquisitely well-bred about the appearance of Regent's Park, almost as if Nash had sent Athens to Eton.[1]

Created as a garden suburb for the very rich, Regent's Park became the prototype of countless other garden estates in Britain. Its privacy and seclusion were initially absolute. There were gates at the entrances, and only 'persons well-behaved and properly dressed' were allowed to pass through on its main roads. In the 1830s, responding to the Report of the Select Committee on Public Walks (1833), the Crown opened the park to the public by stages. The motive was not simply fair-mindedness; the committee felt that one of the principal benefits would be an improvement in the character of the 'humbler classes' as they mixed, in a properly regulated open setting, with their superiors.

formal gardens - the landscaping was decidedly in the English Picturesque mode that had been made fashionable by Humphry Repton. Nash's architecture could also be called Picturesque. The Picturesque allows the traditional rules of architecture to be broken and lends itself to illusion - in this case, the illusion of grandeur. Perhaps mindful of the Prince Regent's extravagance as well as of the general sensibilities of the period, Nash strove for an ostentatious effect that would appeal to the wealthy-but-aspiring. His terraces were all neoclassical in style, craftily designed to look like a series of palatial mansions.

James Burton, who had already developed much of the eastern half of Bloomsbury, was the most active builder in the park. All the terraces were given names reflecting the various titles held by the Prince Regent and his siblings, adding to the cachet lent by the name of the park itself. Each terrace has different classical architectural references, ranging from the Corinthian pillars of Chester Terrace to the Ionic columns of Ulster Terrace. Chester, Cumberland, Gloucester and Hanover terraces all have pediments adorned with sculptured groups; and Chester Terrace also has two triumphal entry arches. These flourishes were achieved through

Decay and Restoration

Most of Regent's Park was given over to the military during both World Wars. There was considerable bomb damage to the terraces in the Second World War, and by the 1950s many of the elegant residences had deteriorated into cheap offices or been virtually abandoned. Declining rents had made maintenance increasingly unprofitable, let alone the structural repairs that were needed to buildings that were collapsing on what turned out to be insecure foundations. Several years of debate ensued. The Royal Institute of British Architects advocated partial replacement with modern buildings. Marylebone Council wanted to replace the terraces with affordable housing. The LCC insisted that the buildings be preserved as they were. The Royal Fine Art Commission favoured retention of the facades in replica. In the end, the Crown Estate restored some of the terraces, demolished some others and rebuilt them as exact replicas, while others still were partly restored and rebuilt. The economic boom of the late twentieth century meant that there was no shortage of new tenants, and the Crown Estate, recognizing the renewed fashionability of the park, commissioned six reproduction villas - imitations of imitations - for a site on the Outer Circle.

Primrose Hill

Immediately to the north of the park is another public open space, Primrose Hill. It had long been owned, along with meadowland further north, by Eton College. Early in the nineteenth century, the growth of London and the development of Regent's Park made it certain that the property would soon become valuable, and the college obtained an Act of Parliament enabling it to grant leases of land for development. Much of the land was duly built over, but the hill itself proved unattractive to speculative developers because of its steep slopes and difficult clay soil. The only interest came from the owners of the London Cemetery Company, who wanted to turn the hill into a massive cemetery, something that was in the best interests of neither Eton College nor the Crown Estate, with its nearby upmarket terraces and villas. In 1837 the Treasury stepped in and brokered a deal by which Eton College received a parcel of Crown property in Eton in return for giving up all rights to the hill. In 1842, following an Act of Parliament, Primrose Hill became a public park. With panoramic views over London Zoo and Regent's Park towards a skyline of London landmarks, the grassy park is now crossed with paths and lit with old-fashioned converted gaslights.

Villa Suburbs

St John's Wood, though late Georgian in its conception, provided the prototype for Victorian suburbia. Its detached and semi-detached Italianate villas, hidden behind high garden walls and luxuriant vegetation, offered the withdrawn seclusion and social homogeneity that its later imitators aspired to achieve.[2]

This area, to the west and northwest of Regent's Park, takes its name from its medieval owners, the knights of the Order of the Hospital of St John of Jerusalem, a fraternity of military monks. For centuries it was merely a tract of the Great Forest of Middlesex. Urban development began to appear only at the start of the nineteenth century, with the establishment of an Orphan School, the opening of Lord's cricket ground and the construction of an Army Riding School. In the 1820s, with the opening up of Abbey, Wellington and Finchley roads, building began in earnest. The largest landowner at the time was the Eyre Estate, whose trustees commissioned the architect and designer Charles Heathcote Tatham to guide its development. The best-known builder, as in Regent's Park, was James Burton. His son Decimus also contributed to St John's Wood as well as to some of the terraces and villas of Regent's Park.

Regent's Park Road. A mid-nineteenth century terrace disguised as semi-detached houses.

The construction of broad avenues of detached and semi-detached villas in substantial grounds gave St John's Wood a distinctive character and established a new model of suburban style. Privacy, the new touchstone of Victorian bourgeois values, was enhanced by brick walls 1.5-2 metres (5-6 feet) high fronting the houses along most of the principal streets. New omnibus services made it unnecessary for the residents of St John's Wood to keep carriages, and so developers were not required to include either mews quarters or shopping streets.

The result was an unprecedented degree of social segregation. The district's wealthy residents were now separated geographically from local shop-keepers and service workers, many of whom were accommodated in the cheap, high-density terraces of Portland Town, a fragment of the Portland Estate immediately to the west of Primrose Hill. Meanwhile, the Eyre Estate set the tone for development on land to the west that was owned by the Harrow School Estate. Ironically, the very success of the suburban villa mode that had made St John's Wood such a fashionable residential area also pushed land prices up so far that by mid-century developers were reverting to terrace-building. By the 1880s, with the advent of the safety elevator, escalating land prices encouraged the redevelopment of slums in Portland Town, prompting the construction of the first mansion apartment blocks in the district. By the end of the century the entire district had been built up.

From the start, St John's Wood acquired a slightly bohemian and raffish character as a result of the disproportionate number of academics, actors, architects, artists, men and women of letters, musicians, novelists and philosophers who were drawn to the new arcadian setting. In addition, a significant number of frustrated activists and intellectuals settled there after the failure of liberal revolutions across Europe in 1848 and 1849. But although cosmopolitan and fashionable, St John's Wood was not always respectable: wealth does not necessarily equate to propriety. The district's high walls and relative remoteness from central London offered the possibility of privacy for unorthodox liaisons, and St John's Wood soon acquired a reputation for tolerance in relation to mistresses ('heroines of passion and victims of propriety') and homosexuals as well as for discreet and expensive vice.

These days, St John's Wood is still fashionable and expensive, although somewhat less cosmopolitan than other districts in London and without its old reputation for loucheness. It is mentioned in tourist guidebooks only for the pedestrian crossing on Abbey Road, made famous by the cover photograph of the Beatles album of the same name.

Viceroy Court. A luxury apartment block in Moderne style, built in the late 1930s on Prince Albert Road, overlooking Regent's Park.

① Abbey Road
② Park Crescent
③ Chester Terrace
④ St Andrew's Place
⑤ Outer Circle
⑥ Regent's Park
⑦ Regent's Park Road
⑧ Primrose Hill
⑨ Carlton Hill
⑩ Islamic Centre
⑪ Blenheim Road

In terms of urban morphology, Regent's Park is connected to Marylebone and central London via the crescent of John Nash's Park Place and the continuation of his set piece of urban design that runs down Portland Place to Regent Street and Carlton House Terrace. Functionally, though, Park Place is cut off from Marylebone by the busy thoroughfare of Marylebone Road. North of the Park is Primrose Hill, bordered to the east by the locality of the same name. St John's Wood extends to the west and northwest, bounded respectively by Maida Vale and, appropriately, Boundary Road, which demarcates the City of Westminster from the London Borough of Camden.

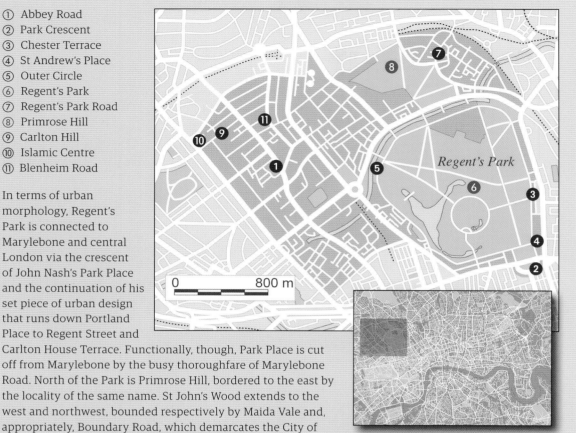

❶ Abbey Road

Significant as the first purpose-built recording studios in the world, the Abbey Road Studios (in the white building on the left) are better known for the artists who have used them - including the Beatles, whose *Abbey Road* album cover featured the band walking across the zebra crossing. The crossing, like the studios themselves, is listed Grade II by English Heritage; it has become rather a liability as local drivers become impatient at posing tourists. The studio building had been constructed as a residence in the 1830s and had been renovated as flats before being converted into a recording studio in 1931.

❷ Park Crescent

The simple elegance of the crescent's Ionic colonnades makes it the best of John Nash's urban design, although it had been intended as the southern half of a huge circus in his scheme of 1811-12. It is now orphaned from the rest of his Regent's Park terracing by the thunder of traffic on Marylebone Road. Having fallen into disrepair, it was completely rebuilt in the early 1960s to an exact copy of Nash's facade but with new interiors.

❸ Chester Terrace

The longest continuous terrace of Nash's Regent's Park plan, it was built by James Burton and completed in 1825. The whole terrace of thirty-five houses and five semi-detached houses, with its fifty-two Corinthian pillars and triumphal entry arches at either end, was intended to give the appearance of a single palace. As if this were not sufficiently grandiose, Burton placed statues on top of each of the pillars, only to have them removed at Nash's insistence.

❹ St Andrew's Place

St Andrew's Place is a cul-de-sac that, with its restored paving and Regency street furniture, has recovered some of the quiet elegance that Nash would have striven for when it was built in the 1820s.

❺ Outer Circle

The building illustrated here is the sDoric Villa, one of six private mansions commissioned by the Crown Estate for the northwestern edge of Regent's Park and built from 1987 onwards, the last being completed in 2008. The architect, Quinlan Terry, intended the six villas to be a demonstration of the range of the Classical tradition (but with interiors customized to the lifestyles of today's super-rich). Accordingly, there are Corinthian, Gothick, Veneto, Tuscan and Regency villas, as well as the Doric villa. Vulgar and ostentatious even in the context of Nash's Regency grandiosity, it is as if a row of McMansions has been transplanted from an affluent Atlanta exurb.

❻ Regent's Park

The transition from fashionable residential estate to its present appearance as a public park has been incremental. Although partially opened to the public in the 1830s, it was not until the 1850s that paths and fence lines were added. During the First World War the park was requisitioned by the Ministry of Defence, and much of it was used as a military camp and drill ground. After the war the buildings were demolished and replaced with sports fields. By that time the remaining private villas inside the park were too large and expensive to be maintained as private dwellings. The Ministry of Works began systematically to transfer properties to parkland as they became vacant. The park and its surroundings were severely damaged during the Second World War, and it took the Crown Estate Commissioners several decades to rehabilitate the park and establish its current mixture of open land, landscaped walks and attractions.

❼ Regent's Park Road

Regent's Park Road houses Primrose Hill's fashionable cluster of shops, cafés and restaurants, at the heart of a gentrified area that has evolved from what was a rather run-down and neo-bohemian neighbourhood in the 1960s. The surrounding streets of stuccoed Italianate villas had been developed in the 1860s, taking advantage of the newly opened railway service, and this commercial stretch served as the approach to the (now defunct) Primrose Hill railway station.

❽ Primrose Hill

Although only 63 metres (207 feet) in elevation, Primrose Hill provides a commanding view of London's cityscape, and the sight lines towards St Paul's Cathedral and the Palace of Westminster are officially designated strategic views that are safeguarded from inappropriate development.

9 Carlton Hill

This mid-Victorian villa was built in 1873 by W. J. Miller for a certain George Speedy. It was purchased in 1908 by George Frampton, a nationally important artist whose sculpture includes the Grade II*-listed figure of Peter Pan (1911), in Kensington Gardens, and the Grade II-listed Edith Cavell Memorial on St Martin's Place. Frampton had the villa remodelled inside and out in Arts and Crafts style, with a studio for himself and another for his wife, a painter. They were among the many better-off artists, architects, musicians and writers who were drawn to the sequestered new setting of broad streets and comfortable villas in St John's Wood.

10 Islamic Centre

Maida Vale

The Maida Vale Picture Palace opened on 27 January 1913 with a performance of a silent feature entitled *Behind the Mask,* accompanied by a cinema organ and a seven-piece orchestra. There were seats for 1500, including curtained boxes in the balcony. One of the earliest surviving works of the architect Edward Stone, it is a rare example of early picture houses. In 1949 it was converted into the Carlton Rooms Dance Hall; then in 1965 it became the Mecca Social Club bingo hall. In the 1990s it was refurbished and restored as an Islamic centre.

11 Blenheim Road

This photograph shows a small early Victorian stuccoed villa in the northern tract of St John's Wood, an area that has never fallen significantly down the social ladder. The blue plaque recognizes Charles Santley, an opera singer who lived here until his death in 1922.

Soho + Covent Garden

There is a baroque archway in Embankment Gardens that looks, at face value, like a Victorian folly. In fact it is a seventeenth-century watergate, the river entrance to York House, built for the first Duke of Buckingham in the 1620s. York House was one of a string of mansions that stood at the edge of the Thames, along the route from the City of London to the royal court at Westminster. The mansion has long disappeared, and the embankment of the Thames in the 1860s left the archway stranded 150 metres (164 yards) from the new shoreline. It serves as a reminder of how deeply layered this district has become, how much detail is embedded in its built environment, and how much it has changed.

Covent Garden and Soho occupy the former stretch of meadowland, marshes and small villages that constituted, until the seventeenth century, a 2.5-kilometre (1½-mile) gap between the commercial nucleus of the City and the institutional nucleus of Westminster. Its development was framed initially by several set-piece speculative developments and, later, by a series of late Victorian street-improvement schemes. Its social character, meanwhile, has always been shaped by a cosmopolitanism that stems from a succession of foreign immigrant groups and from the size and range of its entertainment industry.

Covent Garden and the Market

The first and most significant of the set-piece speculative developments shaped not only the growth of the district but also that of much of west-central London. Charles I granted a licence to Francis Russell, the fourth Earl of Bedford, to develop the site of the original garden of the monks of Westminster Abbey as housing 'fitt for the habitacions of Gentlemen and men of ability'. Inigo Jones, Surveyor-General of the King's Works, devised the scheme for the earl, emulating the piazzas he had seen in Italy. His plan for what became known as Covent Garden was for a paved central square with the earl's mansion, Bedford House, on the south side. A new church, St Paul's, stood on the west side, and uniform terraces of houses with arcaded fronts lined the north and east sides. Immediately beyond the piazza were Floral Street and Maiden Lane, which incorporated mews for servants and stables.

The earl, who had a reputation for financial shrewdness, insisted on a leasehold system that gave him control over the development and the eventual recovery of the property, leaving the effort and risk of building and selling to others. Developed in 1631-39, Covent Garden's combination of terraced town houses around an open area, with adjoining mews and a leasehold system of property management, became the template for two centuries of architectural taste in London.

One aspect of Covent Garden that was not widely copied was its paved piazza, which quickly lent itself to informal marketing and trading. Hoping to regularize these activities, the fifth Earl of Bedford obtained a licence in 1670 to hold a market for fruit, flowers and vegetables. It was a commercial success, but it redefined the character of the area, attracting undesirables and prompting the gentry to flee westward to newer squares and terraces. They were replaced by artists, writers, publishers and shopkeepers. In the mid-eighteenth century the market was reorganized and remodelled, but it again became congested and disorderly. Early in the nineteenth century the Bedford Estate employed Charles Fowler to build a new market house. With its Doric colonnaded fronts and central avenue of shops, it still stands in the centre of the piazza. It accommodated London's principal fruit and vegetable market until 1974, when it moved to new, purpose-built premises in Lambeth.

Rose Street. The Lamb and Flag was built as a house in 1688 but converted to a pub soon afterwards. It was once known as the Bucket of Blood because of its association with prizefighting.

Goodwin's Court. One of the few surviving rows of eighteenth-century shopfronts in London (though the shops themselves are now offices).

Filling in the Gap

The return of the royal court after the Restoration of Charles II in 1660, followed by the Great Plague of 1665 and the Great Fire of 1666, combined to make the suburban fringe between Westminster and the City very popular among the wealthy. Seeking to meet the demand, Robert Sidney, second Earl of Leicester, laid out Leicester Square in 1670, its terraces modelled on the grand houses of Pall Mall. It proved to be the second important set piece of seventeenth-century urban design. Two other squares were established in the 1670s. Golden Square, the site of a former plague pit, was one part of Christopher Wren's visionary blueprint for the redevelopment of London that was actually realized. It immediately became popular, for a while, as an ambassadorial district. Soho Square (formerly King's Square, in honour of Charles II) was the centrepiece of Richard Frith's development of Soho Fields and one of the first of London's squares to have a central garden.

In stark contrast to these squares was Seven Dials, a Baroque-inspired star pattern of seven streets laid out on St Giles' Field, open meadowland to the north of Covent Garden that had been known for centuries as the Marshland. It was a speculative development by Thomas Neale, Master of the Mint. Laid out between 1693 and 1710, Neale's design provided a larger number of houses and site frontages than development around a square, and therefore maximized rents. But Seven Dials never achieved the social cachet of the squares. The area was already in social decline as wealth and title began to move westward after 1700.

By the early eighteenth century the diversification of both the fabric and the social character of the district was well under way. The government had recognized that the exercise of any control over the growth of London had become impossible, and consequently much of the rest of the district was filled in piecemeal by various building tradesmen and financial entrepreneurs. Their legacy, for the most part, was a cramped and irregular jumble of streets, most of which were lined with houses of much more modest pretensions than those of the squares.

New social and cultural elements had also arrived in the district. Drama had been banned by the Puritans as either frivolous or seditious, but after the Restoration Charles II granted letters patent to two companies, giving them a shared monopoly of what became known as 'legitimate theatre'. One opened a theatre on Drury Lane in 1663 on the site of what is now the Theatre Royal Drury Lane. The other opened on Bow Street, on the fringe of Covent Garden. It did not take long before unlicensed, 'illegitimate' theatres opened, offering not only drama but also burlesques, extravaganzas, circuses, farces, pantomimes and performing dog shows. They tended to cluster, along with taverns, coffee houses, cock-fight pits and brothels, around Covent Garden and the Haymarket, creating spaces of plebeian immorality and political radicalism.

Immigrants represented a second new element. Greek émigrés came first, followed late in the seventeenth century by French Protestant refugees - Huguenots - many of whom were gold- or silversmiths, jewellers, glassmakers, engravers or clock- and watchmakers. As these immigrant communities established themselves, they made their mark on the built environment with the churches they established. From 1720 to 1750 there was a large influx of immigrants from some of the poorest parts of Ireland. They found work in the building and brewing industries and crowded into deteriorating seventeenth-century houses in the St Giles area, to the south of present-day New Oxford Street. It soon became known as one of London's worst 'rookeries', a place of extreme overcrowding, poverty, crime and vice in a warren of alleys and courts strung among unsanitary and dilapidated buildings. In mid-seventeenth-century St Giles, every fifth house was reckoned to be a gin shop, and many of them doubled as brothels.

The redevelopment of Regent Street early in the nineteenth century effectively established the social divide between the wealthy and aristocratic West End of Mayfair and St James's and the multi-ethnic, proletarian population of Soho and Covent Garden. While the Huguenots were eventually assimilated into the broader fabric of London, the cosmopolitanism of Covent Garden and Soho was maintained by the arrival of other French refugees as well as Germans, Italians and Swiss. The failure of liberal revolutions across Europe in 1848 and 1849 brought a diverse set of political émigrés, including Karl Marx and his family, who lived in extreme poverty for several years in Dean Street, Soho. Towards the end of the nineteenth century, large numbers of Polish and Russian Jews arrived after labour disputes had caused them to leave their initial enclave in Whitechapel.

Victorian Covent Garden and Soho, meanwhile, had become much more important as a district of entertainment. Theatres around Leicester Square provided respectable entertainment for the city's ever-expanding middle class. The sex industry also continued to thrive, catering to clients of every social class. But there was also a great variety of small-scale industry, including brewing, food-processing, metal-polishing, the manufacture of tin boxes and iron bedsteads and skilled crafts such as violin-making and cabinetmaking. All this was embedded, however, in a series of notorious slums and rookeries.

Contemporary descriptions of mid-nineteenth-century Seven Dials, for example, portray streets full of bird- and birdcage-sellers and vendors of old boots and old clothes; ragged children, pigs and poultry running loose; and the windows of decaying housing patched with rags and paper. Many of the streets in the St Giles rookery were coded dark blue ('Very poor, casual. Chronic want') on Charles Booth's poverty maps of the 1880s; several were coded black ('Lowest class. Vicious, semi-criminal').

Metropolitan Improvements

The worst of the rookeries were finally cleared around the turn of the century after the Metropolitan Board of Works and its successor, the LCC, undertook street improvements. Shaftesbury Avenue, Charing Cross Road and Kingsway were cut through the slums, displacing thousands of residents while opening up land for the construction of new apartment buildings, department stores, theatres, hotels and restaurants. Conditions in the rest of the district were improved by the works of various philanthropic institutions. Hospitals, medical dispensaries, schools, missions, working men's clubs, churches and clubs for working boys and girls popped up all over Covent Garden and Soho. Among them were the Nouvel Hôpital et Dispensaire Français on Shaftesbury Avenue, established for French-speaking immigrants; Peabody Buildings on Wild Street; and Nottingham House in Shorts Gardens, built by the Society for Improving the Conditions of the Labouring Classes. On Parker Street, formerly one of the worst slums of all, were Parker House, a lodging-house for single men and model dwellings erected by the Central London Dwellings Improvement Company.

Kingsway. Opened in 1905 and named in honour of Edward VII, Kingsway was a product of London's last great Victorian slum-clearance and road-building scheme.

Walker's Court, the centre of Soho's local economy, where cafés, bookshops and supermarkets coexist with a thriving commercial sex trade.

London's nineteenth-century transportation infrastructure - suburban trains, the Underground, omnibuses and trams - brought new audiences and clients for the district's amenities and vices. New theatres and purpose-built cinemas appeared, larger in scale and far more extravagant. The district's restaurants prospered as the new habit of eating out was boosted by the sharp decline in the number of domestic servants after the First World War. Among the luxurious new restaurants were the Café de Paris on Coventry Street, Maxim's on Wardour Street and the Floral Frascati near by on Oxford Street. New-style jazz nightclubs also appeared, including the lavish Ciro's on Orange Street, with its glass dance floor, and the Kit-Cat Club in the Haymarket, regarded in the 1920s as the most extravagant hang-out in all of Europe. In the 1920s Covent Garden and Soho were in transition from a primarily residential district to one to which people came to seek entertainment or to work in shops, theatres, restaurants, warehouses and workshops.

Denmark Street still has recording studios as well as a good concentration of shops selling music and musical instruments, especially guitars.

London's Neo-Bohemia

The decline of the Victorian manufacturing belt and the transformation of the night-time economy changed the district's economic and social character after the Second World War. Theatres, luxury restaurants and nightclubs all struggled during postwar austerity. With live theatre dead on its feet, the Tube station at Covent Garden was closed on Sundays because so few people wanted to go there. Music and the film industry, on the other hand, prospered. Leicester Square was colonized by large cinemas, while Wardour Street became the centre of the British film industry, housing the headquarters of the biggest production and distribution companies. Denmark Street became the hearth of the emergent British pop-music industry, with music publishers, music shops, rehearsal rooms and recording studios. Soho became the heart of London's jazz and R&B scene, headlined by Ronnie Scott's on Frith Street and the Marquee Club on Wardour Street.

Coffee bars - a new phenomenon - provided a magnet for youth, while writers, painters, photographers, musicians and journalists were drawn to Soho, finding it both inexpensive and conveniently close not only to publishing, film and newspaper offices but also to theatres, galleries, wine bars and drinking clubs. Soho, meanwhile, continued to provide a base for migrants and immigrants. Chinese households had begun to move into the area around Gerrard Street during the 1930s, from Limehouse in the East End, and they came in greater numbers after the war. Other postwar arrivals included Cypriots, Maltese and Vietnamese.

Meanwhile, the sex industry had become localized in the streets to the north of Piccadilly Circus and Shaftesbury Avenue. Striptease, peep shows and adult bookshops proliferated around Brewer Street in the late 1950s and early 1960s, a harbinger of the so-called permissive society. The streets behind Piccadilly Circus were notorious for male prostitutes, while Kingly Street was the equivalent pick-up spot for female prostitutes. Overall, Soho was becoming a place where people felt they could behave in ways that might be unacceptable in their own towns or neighbourhoods. But it was by no means all sleaze and licentiousness: Soho was also one of the centres of 'Swinging London' of the 1960s. Carnaby Street, formerly a side road housing low-grade garment factories, became a hub of a Mod fashion revolution and an icon of the progressive social instability of the era, along with clubs featuring fledgling rock bands.

Clean-up

All this was gradually commodified, stifling the radical and transgressive qualities of the district. Ironically, the catalyst for change was the anti-development movement. Developers and GLC planners had drafted ambitious proposals for both Covent Garden and Soho, but the prospect of wholesale demolition of large areas to make way for a Corbusian wasteland of fast-flowing traffic lanes, aerial walkways and office towers galvanized local residents. The Covent Garden Community Association was founded in 1971 and the Soho Society in 1972. Their efforts became a landmark episode of community action and conservation. The GLC's redevelopment plans were finally abandoned after the Home Secretary gave listed status to dozens of buildings in the area.

Both public policy and private investment were subsequently forced to focus on the exploitation rather than the eradication of the district's social, cultural and architectural legacy. In the 1980s Westminster Council began to promote Chinatown as a tourist attraction. A Chinese pagoda and arch were erected in Gerrard Street, and the Chinese New Year procession was officially sponsored as a key event for both tourists and the community. Chinese entrepreneurs were quick to respond: the number of Asian restaurants in Chinatown leapt from fewer than ten in the mid-1970s to more than seventy-five in 2014. Meanwhile, Charles Fowler's Market Hall and surrounding piazza were restored and redeveloped by the GLC as one of the first-ever 'festival market' settings, with tourist-orientated shops, cafés, restaurants and street performers. It soon became part of the new 'heritage' London 'in which the familiar local landscapes have been subtly reconfigured to accommodate the new imperatives of global capitalism'.[1]

Both these initiatives coincided with the growth of the 'experience economy', driven by the affluent and expanding market among London's youthful new professional classes as well as by visiting business professionals and tourists. The flourishing night-time scene of clubs, discos, bars, pubs, restaurants and theatres has been facilitated by the regulation of the sex industry and by a relaxed attitude on the part of Westminster Council to public entertainment licensing.

St Giles High Street. Once part of the infamous St Giles Rookery, the street is now dominated by this cheap-looking mixed-use development, Central St Giles, designed by Renzo Piano.

The small factories and workshops that were characteristic of the district have continued to move out and have been replaced by design studios, media services and information and technology firms attracted by relatively low rents. The formerly edgy area around Seven Dials and Neal's Yard has been colonized by trendy shops and promoted as 'Covent Garden's Hidden Village'; while the merchants of formerly avant-garde Carnaby Street have joined with those in neighbouring streets in branding themselves as 'Carnaby, a Style Village'. Old Compton Street, formerly associated with Soho sleaze, has developed into a commercial area for gay men as entrepreneurs have successfully exploited the high income of some gay households. Altogether, Covent Garden and Soho remain the heart of the city's entertainment district but recast in response to the expectations of international tourists and the preferences of contemporary consumers.

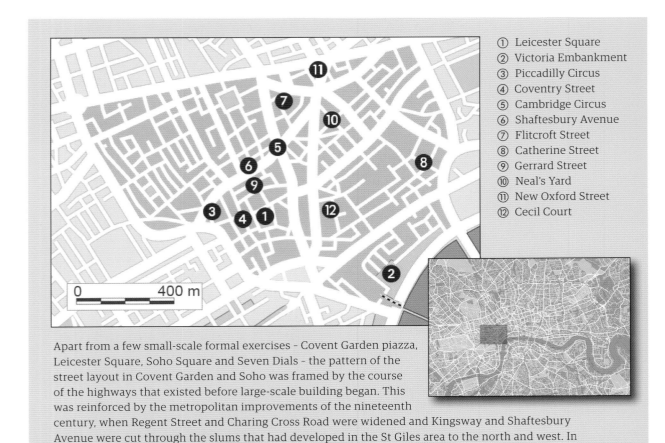

① Leicester Square
② Victoria Embankment
③ Piccadilly Circus
④ Coventry Street
⑤ Cambridge Circus
⑥ Shaftesbury Avenue
⑦ Flitcroft Street
⑧ Catherine Street
⑨ Gerrard Street
⑩ Neal's Yard
⑪ New Oxford Street
⑫ Cecil Court

Apart from a few small-scale formal exercises - Covent Garden piazza, Leicester Square, Soho Square and Seven Dials - the pattern of the street layout in Covent Garden and Soho was framed by the course of the highways that existed before large-scale building began. This was reinforced by the metropolitan improvements of the nineteenth century, when Regent Street and Charing Cross Road were widened and Kingsway and Shaftesbury Avenue were cut through the slums that had developed in the St Giles area to the north and west. In between these planned elements and major streets, it was the pattern of ancient field boundaries and landholdings that shaped the street layout as the district was rapidly developed in small increments, uncontrolled either by the Crown or by the landlords of great landed estates.

❶ Leicester Square

Leicester Square, laid out in 1670, is one of the early West End squares and was for a long time quite fashionable. By the late eighteenth century it was no longer so, and by the 1850s theatres had begun to replace the houses around the square. By the late nineteenth century Leicester Square had become the heart of London's entertainment quarter. Cinemas have replaced the theatres, but the square is still very much part of Theatreland. Dewynters, a theatrical marketing and public-relations company that also produces theatre programmes and souvenir brochures, still operates from the square. By day, the square is busy with ticket booths and restaurants; by night it has a vibrant ambience - except when invaded by hordes of provincial sports fans.

❷ Victoria Embankment

The public gardens along the embankment were a bonus feature of the great engineering project of the Metropolitan Board of Works in the 1860s under the direction of its chief engineer, Joseph Bazalgette. The project not only provided a state-of-the-art water and sewage system, a new road and a route for the Underground Metropolitan line, but also improved river navigation by speeding the flow of the Thames. Above ground, the embankment was laid out spaciously, in the style of a Parisian *quai*. The mansions that had originally stood along the riverside found themselves 150 metres (164 yards) or more from the new shoreline. This baroque archway in Victoria Embankment Gardens was a watergate built in 1626 as the riverside entrance to the Duke of Buckingham's York House. It still bears the Buckingham family coat of arms.

❸ Piccadilly Circus

John Nash's Regent Street project required a major road junction with the long-standing shopping street of Piccadilly. Later in the nineteenth century, when Shaftesbury Avenue was created, the junction became even more important. In the mid-twentieth century it became notorious for prostitution, but it has been cleaned up and is now a busy meeting place and a tourist attraction in its own right. It is surrounded by several major attractions, including several large shops, the Shaftesbury Memorial fountain with its winged statue of Eros, and big neon signs mounted on the corner building on the northern side.

Theatreland

The social and cultural shifts associated with the Industrial Revolution were reflected in new spaces of consumption as well as a new social geography. Theatregoing, newly fashionable among the city's expanded middle and upper-middle classes, had long been focused on venues in Covent Garden and Soho. The slum clearances and road improvements of the late nineteenth century provided an ideal setting for purpose-built new theatres. By 1911 there were six of them on Shaftesbury Avenue alone: the Apollo, the Lyric, the Hicks (now the Gielgud), the Royal English Opera House (now the Palace), the Queen's and the Shaftesbury. The theatre boom that continued until the outbreak of the First World War in 1914 also saw the opening near by of the Aldwych, the Ambassadors (now the New Ambassadors), the Coliseum, the Duke of York's, Her Majesty's, the London Palladium, the New Theatre (now the Noel Coward), the Peacock, the Savoy, the Waldorf (now the Novello) and Wyndhams. Three architects dominated the design of theatres during this great building boom: W.G.R. Sprague, Thomas Verity and Bertie Crewe. Their preferred styles were ornate, mixtures of the Italian Renaissance, the Baroque and French classicism.

Another theatre boom, sparked by the cultural energy of the Roaring Twenties, added still more theatres, including the Arts Theatre, the Apollo Victoria, the Cambridge, the Duchess, the Phoenix, the Piccadilly and the Prince Edward. The Windmill Theatre opened in a converted cinema on Great Windmill Street and became notorious for staging nude *tableaux vivants*. It famously never closed during the Second World War, despite the Luftwaffe's bombing raids. But after the war live theatre - including live revues and vaudeville - was unpopular, displaced by cinemagoing and television. Theatres began to be

4 **Coventry Street**. The Art Deco structure of the Prince of Wales Theatre, built in 1937 and designed by Robert Cromie, replaced an earlier (1884) structure.

demolished to make way for the grand schemes of the postwar property boom.

It was not until the wave of economic and cultural globalization that began in the early 1980s that live theatre once again became popular, driven largely by the international popularity of musical shows. Most of the forty or so theatres in the district were rather cramped and lacking in amenities, the result of confined sites and, in many cases, the protected status of the buildings. Their shortcomings, however, did not hinder the popularity of spectacular big-production musicals like *Cats*, *Chicago*, *Les Misérables*, *The Lion King*, *Mama Mia!* and *The Phantom of the Opera*. The box-office success of these shows has been tied closely to the increasing importance

Leicester Square. The centre of London's night-time economy.

of London as a tourist destination. Yet while blockbuster musicals have become emblematic of Theatreland, as it is now branded by Westminster City Council, the night-time economy of the district still relies heavily on 'legitimate' theatre, on the dozen or so cinemas that between them have about 6500 seats, and on the dense array of bars, pubs, supper clubs and restaurants that cater not only to the pre- and post-performance crowds but also to visitors who are drawn to the buzz of the district and who come to eat, drink and stroll.

Other important elements in the ecology of Theatreland include the various professional and institutional elements that contribute to the forces that bind the district. London's oldest theatrical costumier (whose trade now involves supplying cosmetics and teaching make-up skills to the district's transvestites) is Charles Fox, on Tavistock Street. The famous Elms Lester scenery painting rooms are on Flitcroft Street. The Society of London Theatre, a trade association that represents the producers, theatre-owners and managers of theatres in central London, is in Rose Street, a little alley between Floral Street and Garrick Street in Covent Garden. The headquarters of Equity, the actors' union, is in St Martin's Lane, while *The Stage*, the newspaper for the performing-arts industry, is published from the Bedford Street location of the Club for Acts and Actors. The Garrick, just off Leicester Square, is a private members' club orientated to Theatreland, with an important theatrical library that includes many manuscripts and documents and a comprehensive collection of theatrical paintings and drawings. In Leicester Square is Dewynters, a theatrical marketing and public-relations company that also produces programmes and souvenir brochures. The alleyway of antiquarian bookshops in Cecil Court includes Drummond's, which specializes in books about actors and the theatre, along with posters, postcards, manuscripts and theatre memorabilia.

6 **Shaftesbury Avenue** is widely regarded as the heart of Theatreland, with six theatres and three cinemas.

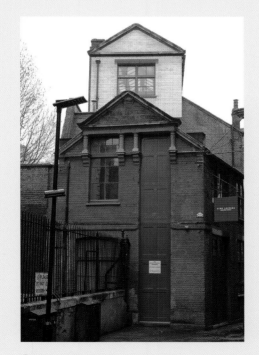

7 **Flitcroft Street**. Elms Lester Painting Rooms, the West End's last surviving painters of theatrical scenery. Note the outsize 'taking in' door.

5 **Cambridge Circus**. The Palace Theatre, designed by Thomas Collcutt in 1891, was intended to be the home of English grand opera. Its 1400-seat capacity has made it a profitable venue for the blockbuster musicals for which Theatreland has become famous.

⑧ Catherine Street

The original offices of *The Builder* were housed in Number 4 Catherine Street. The first issue of the magazine was in December 1842, and over the course of the second half of the nineteenth century it became very influential. It helped not only to shape the profession of architecture and influence the thinking of the city's master builders, but also to shape Victorian aesthetics and recast the image of London among influentials. George Godwin, an early editor, was an advocate of the professionalization of architecture and a promoter of the distinction between the craft of builders (who, he asserted, should aim to meet physical needs) and the liberal art of architects (who should seek to satisfy the desire for beauty).

⑨ Gerrard Street

Part of a seventeenth-century Nicholas Barbon scheme, Gerrard Street was the home in the 1760s of Joshua Reynolds and Samuel Johnson's Literary Club, whose members included Edmund Burke, Adam Smith and James Boswell. While there are a few remaining buildings from the seventeenth and eighteenth centuries, the street's social and cultural composition has become an important element of the district's cosmopolitanism. By the early twentieth century the street was known for its Italian restaurants, and in the 1930s the Italian community was joined by a few Chinese businesses. After the Second World War, the low rents in the run-down street attracted many more Chinese, and Gerrard Street became the centre of London's Chinatown, with Chinese restaurants, bakeries, supermarkets, hairdressers, tailors and accountants. The concentration of ethnic businesses provided an emotional focal point for Chinese families from across the metropolis: a place to buy a Chinese newspaper and experience solidarity, a sense of identity and a feeling of belonging. The street's restaurants steadily drew more and more tourists, and in the 1980s Westminster Council began to promote Chinatown as part of its economic development strategy.

⑩ Neal's Yard

Tucked away off an alley leading from the pedestrianized Neal Street is a small yard that was part of the supporting economy of the Covent Garden fruit and vegetable market, with store-rooms, a wheelwright and a packing-case manufacturer. The yard took on an entirely new aspect after the market closed in 1974, largely through the entrepreneurship of Nicholas Saunders, a leader in the campaign to save Covent Garden from comprehensive redevelopment. He bought an old ware-house in the yard and opened a wholefood shop and, later, a dairy, a café and an apothecary specializing in alternative remedies. The yard was also the headquarters of the Monty Python comedy team for a while, before becoming a chic little hub of organic health and natural-remedy shops and cafés.

⑪ New Oxford Street

This shop, with its surviving nineteenth-century plate-glass shop-front, is in one of the houses built when New Oxford Street was driven through St Giles in the 1840s. James Smith & Sons moved here in 1857, by which time New Oxford Street had become a very fashion-able shopping street. The firm made and sold umbrellas, sword-sticks, riding crops, whips, Malacca canes and shooting sticks. Until the 1920s a cane was an essential part of the well-dressed male's equipment. Umbrellas and walking sticks, some of which are still made in the shop's basement, are now the biggest sellers.

⑫ Cecil Court

Laid out in the late seventeenth century and linking Charing Cross Road and St Martin's Lane, Cecil Court was realigned and rebuilt in the late 1880s. Among the first tenants of the new buildings were early film distributors and publishers of trade journals for the emerging British film industry. They were joined early in the twentieth century by booksellers and publishers. The shopfronts have not been altered for more than a century, and Cecil Court is now a specialized alleyway of antiquarian books, maps and prints and related printed material including stamps and banknotes.

South Bank + Bankside

Long thought of as parts of Lambeth and Southwark respectively, the South Bank and Bankside have recently developed into a distinctive district as a result of the regeneration of the southern bank of the Thames. The western stretch of the district, between the Hungerford Bridge and Blackfriars Bridge, is generally referred to as the South Bank; the stretch from Blackfriars Bridge to Shad Thames, just east of Tower Bridge, has become branded as Bankside.

Early Development

A bridgehead location at the approach to London from Portsmouth and the Southeast, Bankside was a place of some importance from medieval times. Several ecclesiastical dignitaries from the south of England acquired or built town houses near London Bridge, probably because it was easy to get to the City across the bridge and to Westminster by water. The approaches to the bridge were dominated by inns and taverns, partly because travellers arriving after dusk would find the Bridge Gate closed. For centuries the river was a physical barrier, and in fact until very recently it remained a socio-cultural boundary. South of the river, being beyond the jurisdiction of the City and comparatively undeveloped, tended to be a place of refuge for the dispossessed and outcast; for unlicensed artisans and traders; for noxious activities like lime-burning, tanning and brewing; and for theatres and lowbrow entertainments like bear-baiting, bull-baiting and cock-fighting. The district also had a particular reputation for its tolerance of brothels (or 'stews', as they were known), many of them in holdings owned by successive bishops of Winchester.

Industrial Development

As London's trade expanded, Bankside began to be taken over by wharves and warehousing. A series of 'legal quays' were established in the late sixteenth century, and their presence in turn attracted a variety of industries, including brewing, leather-working, sawmills and the manufacture of tarpaulin, soap, glass and pottery. With the construction of new river crossings - Blackfriars Bridge (1769), Vauxhall Bridge (1816), Waterloo Bridge (1817), Southwark Bridge (1819) and the Hungerford Suspension Bridge (1845) - the area became an integral part of the metropolis. The bridgehead character of the district persisted until the 1860s, when railway crossings over the Thames were constructed on the new Cannon Street Bridge, and the Hungerford and Blackfriars bridges rebuilt. By that time, London Bridge station had been established next to Tooley Street, its approach tracks resting on a continuous viaduct 6 kilometres (3¾ miles) long, with 878 arches. When London Bridge was linked with Cannon Street station and with Charing Cross station (via the Hungerford Bridge), railway tracks established both a physical and a psychological barrier between the riverside district and the rest of Lambeth and Southwark.

The growth of overseas trade that followed Britain's colonial and imperial expansion recast the entire district as docklands. The Industrial Revolution added new industries and working-class housing. Transoceanic steamships were too large for Bankside's old quays, and the river frontage was redeveloped during the nineteenth century. Massive warehouses dominated, along with the processing plant of industries with large quantities of noxious effluent to discharge into the Thames. The concentration of towering warehouses along Tooley Street was such that Bankside was often referred to as 'London's Larder'. The warehouses, in turn, attracted food-processing industries, including many well-known

City Hall, headquarters of the Greater London Authority, was designed by Norman Foster and opened in 2002; Tower Bridge (1886–94) is behind.

brands such as Sarson's vinegar, Crosse & Blackwell chutneys, Pearce Duff custard, Hartley's jams, Peek Frean biscuits, Oxo stock cubes and Spillers pet food.

Victorian industry brought Victorian slums. The Metropolitan Board of Works, under Joseph Bazalgette, dealt with the slums by driving roads through them. In the early 1860s the construction of Southwark Street eliminated about 400 houses in connecting Blackfriars Road and the terminus of the South Eastern Railway at London Bridge. It was the first street in London where a special duct for water, gas and telegraph utilities was provided under the road. The street was quickly lined with commercial buildings in the Italianate Romanesque and Gothic styles that were fashionable at the time, featuring much elaboration of detail in brick, stone, terracotta and tile. Today it is one of the most extensive stretches of that period still remaining in London.

Redevelopment

By the end of the nineteenth century, the ugly industrial character of the townscape along the south bank of the Thames had become a problem: an unfitting vista for the heart of an imperial capital. This persisted until well into the twentieth century. Patrick Abercrombie and John Forshaw, in their *County of London Plan* (1943), envisaged a 'Great Cultural Centre' that would replace the dispiriting panorama of the South Bank. Among the sites left vacant by wartime bombing was an extensive area next to the Hungerford Bridge. This area became the site of the Festival of Britain in 1951. Most of the Festival consisted of temporary pavilions, but the Royal Festival Hall was a permanent legacy, the kernel of Abercrombie's Great Cultural Centre. In the 1960s the National Theatre,

Hay's Galleria. Formerly an enclosed dock – Hay's Wharf – surrounded by warehouses, it was converted into shops and office accommodation in the 1980s.

Hayward Gallery and Queen Elizabeth Hall complex was added. The Modernist concrete Brutalism of the entire ensemble was unloved by the London public, and, together with the adjacent monolith of the Shell Centre office building (1953–63), it prompted a widespread reaction against modern architecture. For the most part, though, the postwar South Bank and Bankside retained the sights, sounds and smells of old-fashioned industry. New activities included the manufacture of office furniture, packaging and confectionery, while modern social housing began to replace Victorian terraces and tenements. The most striking addition to the Surrey side of the river was Bankside Power Station (1952), designed by Giles Gilbert Scott: a new oil-fired plant that replaced a nineteenth-century coal-fired facility.

Meanwhile, deindustrialization hit the area hard, resulting in depopulation, social deprivation and dereliction. Dockside industries moved downstream, and warehouses were demolished. Bankside Power Station ceased operations in 1981 as a result of increased oil prices and stood semi-derelict, a symbol of the district's plight. The GLC's response was to re-zone the riverside for office and hotel development. This promptly resulted in a series of undistinguished speculative buildings in muted postmodern style. Local planners' strategies for the district focused on the prospect of large-scale office development schemes, hoping to exploit the commuter hinterlands of Waterloo and London Bridge railway stations. Their plans were vigorously opposed by the local community. The 'Coin Street Campaign' eventually halted office development schemes in favour of affordable housing and the improvement of public spaces.

Regeneration

The neoliberal regime introduced by the Thatcher governments of the 1980s introduced public-private partnerships as agents of neighbourhood change. The energy behind the Coin Street campaign was channelled into a new organization, Coin Street

Coin Street Family and Community Centre. The focal point of the social enterprise and development trust that has transformed a largely derelict 5-hectare (12-acre) site into a thriving mixed-use neighbourhood.

Community Builders, which partnered with the London Borough of Lambeth, the London Borough of Southwark and other groups to purchase a largely derelict 5-hectare (12-acre) site and transform it into a mixed-use neighbourhood by creating new co-operative homes, an indoor swimming pool and leisure centre, shops, galleries, restaurants, cafés, a park and a riverside walkway, and by providing childcare and enterprise support programmes.

It has been the broader impact of neoliberal reform, however, that has underpinned the regeneration of the South Bank and Bankside. The deregulation of the financial sector and the consequent surge in London's world-city functions, together with the economic boom of the 1980s and 1990s and the growth of international tourism, have combined to reposition the South Bank and Bankside as part of central London rather than south London. This shift has meant the regeneration of the district as a tourist, entertainment and office district, and much of what has taken place has been design-orientated and architecturally led.

The first phase of this regeneration took place along Shad Thames, just east of Tower Bridge, where developers had seeded converted warehouse space in Butler's Wharf with artists and young professionals as a means of raising the cultural image of the area. During the property boom of the 1980s, the developers promptly evicted their neo-bohemian tenants

and re-redeveloped Butler's Wharf into luxury flats. Warehouse buildings on Tea Trade Wharf, Cinnamon Wharf and St Saviour's Wharf were also converted into luxury loft apartments; galleries and upscale restaurants were opened at street level; and the entrepreneur Terence Conran opened the Design Museum next door. Shad Thames suddenly became trendy. Public investment had helped to make it more accessible through the Queen's Walk, a riverside trail developed for the Queen's Silver Jubilee in 1977.

Designed to link tourist landmarks, the Jubilee Walkway already gave access to the tourist attraction of HMS Belfast, and from the late 1980s public policy was to turn the riverside into a series of signature buildings: a 'string of pearls'. A reconstruction of Shakespeare's Globe Theatre opened on Bankside in 1997. But the pivotal element of the strategy was the transformation, with the help of government Lottery funding, of the derelict Bankside Power Station into the Tate Gallery of Modern Art. Opened in 2000, Tate Modern soon became one of London's biggest tourist attractions. Its success was greatly assisted by the construction of the Millennium Footbridge, linking the Tate Modern with St Paul's Cathedral and the continuation of the Jubilee Walkway into central London. The decade following the opening of Tate Modern saw the realization of the 'string of pearls', albeit of varied function and quality. Meanwhile, a new City Hall, designed by Norman Foster, had opened on Bankside, followed by a complex of office buildings, 'More London', the name signalling the district's integration with the financial sector in the City. On the other side of London Bridge station stands the centrepiece of the district's regeneration, the Shard: a ninety-five-storey tower (the tallest in Europe) containing premium office space, a hotel and luxury residences.

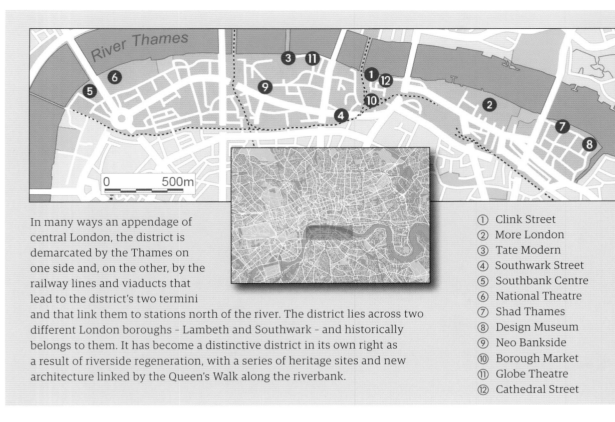

In many ways an appendage of central London, the district is demarcated by the Thames on one side and, on the other, by the railway lines and viaducts that lead to the district's two termini and that link them to stations north of the river. The district lies across two different London boroughs - Lambeth and Southwark - and historically belongs to them. It has become a distinctive district in its own right as a result of riverside regeneration, with a series of heritage sites and new architecture linked by the Queen's Walk along the riverbank.

① Clink Street
② More London
③ Tate Modern
④ Southwark Street
⑤ Southbank Centre
⑥ National Theatre
⑦ Shad Thames
⑧ Design Museum
⑨ Neo Bankside
⑩ Borough Market
⑪ Globe Theatre
⑫ Cathedral Street

❶ Clink Street

On the left of the photograph are the remains of the Great Hall of Winchester House, the town residence of the bishops of Winchester from the twelfth to the seventeenth century, surrounded by the gaunt riverside warehouses of Clink Street. The street takes its name from the former prison next door to Winchester House. Clink Prison was owned by the bishop of Winchester and was in use from the twelfth century until 1780, when it was burnt down by the Gordon rioters. Because of its notoriety, the Clink became a synonym for all prisons. In 1485 Henry VII ordered the bishops to imprison in the Clink any priest found guilty of adultery, incest or fornication. Later, Queen Mary I - 'Bloody Mary' - sent Protestants to the Clink for torture or starvation. Her half-sister and successor, Queen Elizabeth I, continued to use the Clink for religious persecution, but this time it was mainly Catholics who were on the receiving end.

❷ More London
More London Place

The central stretch of Bankside has been regenerated to become, effectively, a south-of-the-river exclave of the City, with a total workforce estimated to be in excess of 15,000. The office buildings, known as More London Place and More London Riverside, are occupied mainly by financial services and advanced business services firms. More London was designed by Foster & Partners, and, like most new corporate office developments, it meets contemporary planning expectations in providing public access, public space and mixed uses at ground-floor level. The complex has shops, restaurants, a hotel, a children's theatre and public spaces with water features and sculptures. The focal point of the development is City Hall (2002), housing the chamber for the London Assembly and the offices of the mayor and staff of the Greater London Authority. In signature Foster style, it has a striking curvilinear form and claims to be sustainable and non-polluting. It somehow looks dated already. On the other hand, the rest of the buildings are unexceptional, lending an overwhelming corporate ambience to the area, something that is reinforced by the fact that the shops and offices are all branches of major national or international chains.

3 Tate Modern (left and opposite)

Bankside

Tate Gallery of Modern Art (normally referred to simply as Tate Modern) has been a major factor in the cultural repositioning and economic regeneration of Bankside. Housed in a disused power station, the galleries and refurbished turbine hall were designed by the Swiss architectural practice of Herzog & de Meuron. The oil-fired power station had originally been designed by Giles Gilbert Scott and opened in 1952. The quadrupling of oil prices by the OPEC cartel in the 1970s rendered it uneconomic, and it was eventually closed in 1981. Thirteen years later the derelict building was acquired by Tate, and with the help of funding from the Millennium Commission, Tate Modern opened in 2000. The London Millennium Footbridge opened a month later, giving access across the river to St Paul's Cathedral. The combination was instantly popular.

4 Southwark Street

About 400 houses were pulled down in 1857 to form a new street between the West End of London and the terminus of the South Eastern Railway at London Bridge. Completed in 1864, it was the first of the major improvements undertaken by the Metropolitan Board of Works. During the following decade it was lined with large commercial buildings in the Italianate Romanesque and Gothic styles that were fashionable at the time.

❺ Southbank Centre

Belvedere Road

The Southbank Centre is Europe's largest arts complex. Abercrombie and Forshaw's wartime *County of London Plan* envisaged a 'Great Cultural Centre' on the South Bank, and that began to be realized with the opening of the Royal Festival Hall during the Festival of Britain in 1951. A product of the LCC's Architect's Department, it was lauded by the architectural press, but the public did not warm to it. The Queen Elizabeth Hall was added in 1967 to the complex that now goes under the brand name of the Southbank Centre, with the Hayward Gallery in 1968 and the National Theatre (below) completing the ensemble of concrete Brutalism in 1976. Now part of the 'string of pearls' of cultural amenities amid gentrifying neighbourhoods, the Southbank Centre was for many years a local anachronism, synonymous with highbrow arts in the midst of severe socio-economic deprivation. It has not worn well, although the constantly renewed street art that decorates the undercroft of the Centre, where skateboarders have established a small but widely known skatepark, provides some welcome colour.

❻ National Theatre

South Bank

The Royal National Theatre complex, containing three separate theatres, was designed by Denys Lasdun and opened in 1976. The design follows the deck concept that unites the whole Southbank Centre, with a pyramidal arrangement of concrete decks punctuated by lift towers and ventilation shafts. The satirical magazine *Private Eye* alluded to it as the 'National Car Park'. The Prince of Wales described it more ponderously as 'a clever way of building a nuclear power station in the middle of London without anyone objecting'. But in the 1990s it was cleaned up, and the road that separated the theatre from the river was removed, creating a new public space, Theatre Square, for outdoor performances. This coincided with the overall regeneration of the South Bank and Bankside, and the National Theatre with its bookshop and café now fits more comfortably along the Jubilee Walkway.

❼ Shad Thames

Most of the warehouses along Shad Thames were built in the 1880s and 1890s, adjacent to the deep section of the river known as the Pool of London and along the 300-metre-long (328 yards) tidal inlet (at one time the mouth of the River Neckinger) of St Saviour's Dock. The warehouses here were highly specialized, handling tea, coffee, grains and spices, and together they comprised the largest warehouse complex on the river. Rendered obsolescent by bigger ships and new freight-handling technology, the last of the warehouses closed in 1972, leaving the streets of the area as the most visually dramatic of London's Victorian industrial heritage. Property developers were quick to spot the potential of the distinctive setting and the dramatic river views afforded by the buildings. By the late 1980s the makeover was complete, with loft-style apartments, boutiques and fancy restaurants catering not only to incoming households but also to tourists.

❽ Design Museum
Shad Thames

Part of Shad Thames and integral to the social and cultural repositioning of the area, the museum was opened in 1989 in a former banana warehouse that was remodelled by Terence Conran in the style of 1930s Modernism. It was the first museum in the world to focus on the exhibition of mass-produced items. It features modern industrial and fashion design, graphics, architecture and multimedia. The collections trace the history of design developments from the origin of mass production to contemporary works. Complete with a trendy café with river views, the museum attracts an estimated 200,000 visitors annually.

❾ Neo Bankside
Sumner Street

The ultra-exclusive complex of four residential pavilions comprising Neo Bankside is unintentionally symbolic of both the neoliberal political economy of 'global' London and of the hollowness of the rhetoric of superstar architects. In stark contrast to the approach of nearby Coin Street Community Builders (locally orientated and socially responsible), Neo Bankside, its apartments priced at between £2.5 and £5.5 million, is aimed at City bonus-day millionaires and the internationally wealthy (the sales website has both Russian and Chinese versions). A partnership between the developers Native Land and the development arm of the Grosvenor Estate, Neo Bankside was designed by Rogers Stirk Harbour + Partners. The firm's principal, Richard Rogers, a Pritzker Architecture Prize Laureate, has often said the right things about urban development, especially in his roles as Chair of the Labour government's Urban Task Force and as Chief Adviser on architecture and urbanism to the former mayor of London, Ken Livingstone. The Neo Bankside project, though, makes a mockery of such rhetoric.

Dwarfed by Neo Bankside and in stark contrast to the ethos it projects are Hopton's Almshouses, funded with money left by the merchant Charles Hopton. Built in the 1740s, they have been protected since 1950 by their Grade II* English Heritage listing. The trusteeship of the homes was taken over in 2011 by Southwark-based United St Saviour's Charity, which rents the homes to people over the age of sixty on low incomes and with little capital who have lived in Southwark for at least three years prior to application.

⑩ Borough Market
Southwark Street

One of the oldest of London's produce markets, Borough Market has been repeatedly rebuilt and updated. Most of the current market structure dates from the 1890s and 1930s, but the most recent addition (in 2003) is the relocated mid-nineteenth-century portico of Covent Garden's Floral Hall (above, right). There are enough surviving Victorian industrial and commercial fragments and streetscapes around the market to make the area popular with television and film producers, but the regeneration of Bankside has spilled over to the market area, and residential development, shops, restaurants, galleries and bars have replaced most of the local industry. The market itself, meanwhile, has been rebranded by its Trustees as 'London's Larder' - the popular Victorian name for the cluster of warehouses along Tooley Street and Shad Thames.

⑪ Globe Theatre
Bankside

The reconstructed Globe Theatre opened in 1997. Although it has become a feature of regenerated Bankside, it was not planned or supported by the Borough of Southwark - understandably, since although great pains were taken to ensure that the reconstruction of the theatre was accurate, it lends a distinctively kitschy element to the area.

⑫ Cathedral Street

Another element in the commercialization and festivalization of Bankside, this replica of Francis Drake's *Golden Hinde* is berthed in the ancient landing-place of St Mary Overie Dock. The replica is a fully working ship that has sailed more than 225,000 kilometres (139,800 miles), including retracing much of Drake's around-the-world route in 1979-80.

Spitalfields

A traditionally working-class area on the fringe of London's business and financial precinct, Spitalfields has been home to successive waves of migrants and immigrants. For some time now it has been in the process of being reconstructed both physically and socially. Developers, aided by government agencies, have made major investments in commercial property throughout the western edge of the district that is adjacent to the Broadgate office complex in the City. Residential gentrification has seen affluent households move into Spitalfields' restored town houses and terraces, while commercial gentrification has seen design-, media- and fashion-related firms move into its old industrial spaces. In the eastern half of Spitalfields, the built environment remains relatively unchanged, but its residential character has been transformed by the consolidation of the Bangladeshi community, Spitalfields' most recent immigrant group.

Spitalfields takes its name from a contraction of 'hospital fields', the area surrounding an Augustinian priory and its hospital - the New Hospital of St Mary Without Bishopsgate - which was founded in 1197 on the site of a former Roman cemetery. Part of the hospital's fourteenth-century charnel house, where the bones of victims of the Black Death were placed, can be seen beneath the pavement at Bishops Square, off Bishopsgate. The district's geographic situation - just beyond the City boundary - has subjected it to constant social and material change. For a long time, though, Spitalfields was marginal to the City: a natural location for dirty trades such as leather-working and brick manufacture. Brick Lane, running through the heart of Spitalfields, was the route along which carts carried bricks from the kilns of Spitalfields to Whitechapel, Shoreditch and beyond.

As London grew, Spitalfields came increasingly within the orbit of City life. The Great Fire had left many homeless Londoners to camp out on open ground in Spitalfields, and it did not take long for enterprising builders to transform the area from open fields and nursery gardens into streets of poorly built houses for the accommodation of displaced workers. In 1682 Charles II granted a license at Spitalfields for a market to facilitate London's trade in 'flesh, fowl and roots'.

Ethnic Succession

Late in the seventeenth century, French Protestant refugees - Huguenots - came to Spitalfields after they had been driven out of France by the Catholic king Louis XIV. Many of them were silk-weavers and merchants. In the early eighteenth century a decline in the Irish linen industry led to the arrival of Irish weavers to take up work in the textile trades. Sustained by a continuous supply of semi- and unskilled immigrant labour, Spitalfields became an important centre for weaving, tailoring and the clothing industry. 'Weaver Town' thrived and became world-famous for its fancy silk and brocade. By 1750 there were approximately 500 master weavers in Spitalfields, with an estimated 15,000 looms at work and an additional 50,000 local residents dependent on the trade.

The Huguenots built a new church (*La Neuve Eglise*) in the heart of Spitalfields in 1743, while Huguenot master weavers built some of London's first brick town houses. Their street facades were generally imposing even where the interiors were unpretentious. More humble weavers' dwellings were clustered around the Tenter Ground - the place where woven cloth was washed and then hooked to frames called tenters to dry. This, incidentally, is the origin of the expression 'to be on tenterhooks'.

Brick Lane. The southern half of Brick Lane, with its curry shops and Bangladeshi businesses, has been branded the heart of 'Banglatown'.

Brick Lane Jamme Masjid at the junction of Brick Lane and Fournier Street. It was originally built by Huguenots as *La Neuve Eglise* in 1743.

Victorian Poverty

Over time, the Huguenots began to disappear as a distinct Spitalfields community, mainly as a result of marrying into the indigenous population. The Huguenot chapel closed in 1819 and was taken over by a Methodist congregation. Meanwhile, Spitalfields became increasingly impoverished as the silk industry declined. That decline proved terminal after a free-trade agreement was established between Britain and France in 1860. It allowed the import of less-expensive French silks of superior design and quality, and plunged many Spitalfields weavers into ruin. When Commercial Street was cut through the district in the 1840s, the shockingly pauperized and vicious character of the area was starkly revealed to polite society. Most of nineteenth-century Spitalfields was in fact the archetype of Victorian urban poverty: the rookeries described by Charles Dickens and later mapped and catalogued by Charles Booth.

The district's distress and its consequently cheap accommodation drew in substantial numbers of destitute Yiddish-speaking Russian and East European Jews who came to London to escape the pogroms that followed the assassination in 1881 of Tsar Alexander II of Russia. Some found employment in the sweatshops of the garment manufacture and tailoring trade; others eked out a living through small craft enterprises making shoes, slippers, caps and cheap cabinetry. Brick Lane became the heart of the *shtetl*, with a local economy distinctive for its bagel shops and tailors' workshops. Jews took over the houses built by their Huguenot predecessors and adapted the back gardens for workshop production, and in 1898 they took over the old Huguenot chapel, which became the Spitalfields Great Synagogue, with an adjoining Talmud school. Meanwhile, the worst slum areas in Spitalfields had acquired additional notoriety from their association with the victims of Jack the Ripper in the 1880s. This hastened the rebuilding of the rookeries with large blocks of tenements under the Artisans Dwellings Act of 1875, and prompted those in authority to attempt to pacify the district with improved streets, schools, police stations, workhouses, chapels and a new market hall.

By the first decades of the twentieth century, Spitalfields had indeed become relatively pacified as well as economically more stable. Many of the more prosperous Jewish households began to move out to suburban districts, while a new population of immigrants – this time merchant sailors and ex-soldiers from the region of Sylhet in East Bengal – began to filter into the district, many of them after jumping ship in the Docklands. After the Second World War the Sylheti community provided a safe haven for migrants from Bengal who were drawn to the opportunities afforded by Britain's postwar economic boom. The arrival of wives and dependants from Bangladesh during the 1980s and 1990s led to the development of Brick Lane as a distinctive ethnic high street and to the dedication of its old chapel/synagogue as the community mosque for the Bangladeshi population, which had come to constitute more than half of the district's inhabitants.

Regeneration and Reinvention

The consolidation of the Bangladeshi community in Spitalfields coincided with the 'entrepreneurial turn' of British urban policy of the late 1980s. In central London, this translated into a 'Cityside' strategy: extending the financial district of the City on to cheaper land, promoting the construction of offices and shops through subsidy, providing regulatory relief to property-development firms and encouraging the diversification of the local economy, especially leisure and tourism.

In Spitalfields, the prime site for this strategy was Spitalfields Market, at the western end of the district and close to Liverpool Street railway station and the City's Broadgate complex. The market had been relocated to Leyton, 6 kilometres (3.7 miles) to the northeast, in 1991, leaving its 1880s iron and glass hall empty and in danger of demolition. After a heated local campaign, a compromise was reached that allowed part of the old market square to be retained for stalls selling food, clothing and crafts. The eventual design, by Foster + Partners, involved the demolition of two-thirds of the historic market buildings to make room for several high-rise office buildings and a landscaped 'public' space – Bishops Square – with an outdoor performance area and water feature. The regeneration project also involved a general tidying-up of the facades and remaining interior spaces of the old market to accommodate boutiques, cafés and upscale chain restaurants as well as the retained market space, now named 'Crispin Square' and covered by a glazed canopy that connects it to the new office buildings.

The Cityside strategy and the Bishops Square development coincided with the expansion of the financial district of the City of London during the economic booms of the 1980s and 1990s. Inevitably, this led to the gentrification of the western fringe of Spitalfields, where the restored Huguenot town houses in Spitalfields Conservation Areas were especially attractive to the moneyed class. The redevelopment of the old Truman's Brewery on Brick Lane into design studios, bars, nightclubs, cafés, galleries, speciality retailers and event space in the 1990s shifted the gentrification frontier eastwards to the Bangladeshi community. Meanwhile, the area was also discovered by design-, media- and fashion-related firms. The Milanese fashion school Istituto Marangoni, for example, has taken advantage not only of inexpensive property but also of the opportunity to exploit a unique address, moving into an abandoned shopping arcade on Fashion Street, just across from a newly opened office of the architect Rafael Viñoly.

The proximity of Spitalfields to City offices and tourist destinations has also prompted community groups and local government agencies to exploit the district's gritty character, its street markets and its curry shops. Through a combination of urban design interventions, branding and invented traditions, it has simultaneously been exoticized and made accessible, safe and visually appealing to visitors. Edgy but safe, the transitional dynamism of Spitalfields is increasingly driven by a lunchtime and night-time experience economy catering to students and young white-collar workers. Much of Spitalfields thus functions as a backdrop and context for entertainment and consumption.

This, in turn, has stimulated the politicization of the Bengali community and the reclamation by Bangladeshi entrepreneurs of the idea of 'Banglatown' (originally a pejorative term used by white youth)

Wilkes Street. Badly damaged in the Blitz and subsequently long neglected, this street of early Georgian houses has been repaired, rebuilt and gentrified.

as a distinctive cultural and commercial sub-area. It has allowed the Bangladeshi community not only to profit from the district's new visitor economy but also to resist displacement by gentrification. Meanwhile, the existence of remaining tracts of underdeveloped property has left Spitalfields poised for a further phase of transition, with developers envisaging a further series of high-rise, mixed-use regeneration schemes, while community groups and established gentrifiers campaign to 'Save Spitalfields'.

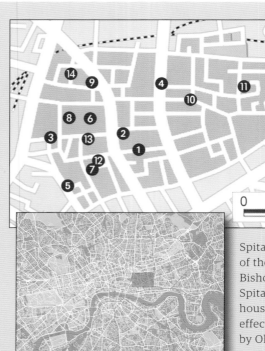

① Fashion Street
② Christ Church
③ Brushfield Street
④ Brick Lane
⑤ Petticoat Lane Market
⑥ Spitalfields Market
⑦ Brune Street
⑧ Bishops Square
⑨ Commercial Street
⑩ Hanbury Street
⑪ Deal Street
⑫ Jewish Soup Kitchen
⑬ Brushfield Street
⑭ Elder Street

0   300 m

Spitalfields is located immediately to the northeast of the City of London, the formal boundary following Bishopsgate and Middlesex Street. To the east, Spitalfields merges imperceptibly with the social housing estates of Mile End, while to the north it is effectively bounded by railway lines and to the south by Old Montague Street. The irregular street pattern was established in the seventeenth century, but only fragments of the original fabric survive. In fact, many of the present buildings are the third or fourth to be erected on sites first developed in the late seventeenth century. As a result of the piecemeal development of the district for successive iterations of low-income populations, there were none of the squares so typical of much of London, and no calculated vistas. (The present vista of Hawksmoor's Christ Church is a result of the recent redevelopment of Spitalfields Market.)

❶ Fashion Street

With the transformation of Spitalfields from inner-city dereliction to residential and commercial gentrification, the name of the street took on new value. It has attracted, among others, the FM Model Agency and an office of the star architect Rafael Viñoly. The London branch of the prestigious Milanese fashion school, Istituto Marangoni and the British School of Fashion, an outpost of Glasgow Caledonian University, both occupy the unusual Moorish-style buildings shown here. They were built in 1905 as a market arcade by entrepreneurs Abraham and Woolf Davis, but the venture was unsuccessful. The arcade was converted to industrial use in 1909 and had been derelict for several decades before the street address became irresistible to fashion- and design-related tenants.

❷ Christ Church
Commercial Street

Christ Church was designed for the Anglican Church as a prominent statement in an area noted for its nonconformity. In 1711 Parliament had passed an Act for Building Fifty New Churches across London: part of a Tory strategy to maintain the Church of England as an arm of the state. The Act allocated money from the Coal Tax to the Commission for Building Fifty New Churches, and the Commission's design guidelines laid stress on imposing exteriors and impressive entrances for the new churches. Only twelve churches were ever built under the Act - Christ Church was one of them. The architect was Nicholas Hawksmoor, Christopher Wren's senior assistant at the Office of Works. Hawksmoor designed five of the other churches built under the Act and shared in the design of two more. His design for Christ Church, in his hallmark Anglicized Baroque style, was approved in 1714, and the church was consecrated in 1729. It is widely considered to be Hawksmoor's best work. In white Portland stone and with a 69-metre (226-foot) spire, it would have thoroughly dominated eighteenth-century Spitalfields. It was extensively - and clumsily - altered in the nineteenth century, and by the mid-twentieth century its condition had deteriorated so far that it had to be closed (in 1958). Restored to Hawksmoor's original design, it reopened in 2004 as a place of worship, a concert hall and a theatre.

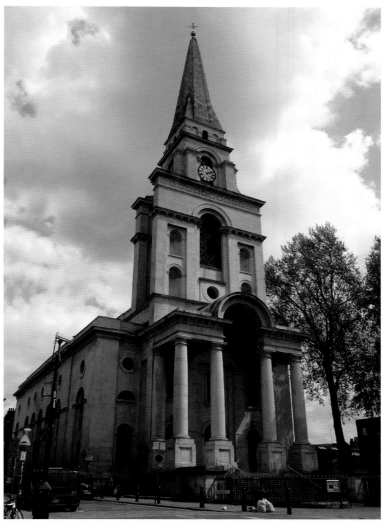

❸ Brushfield Street

London's organic growth has resulted in few examples of vistas such as this, looking east along Brushfield Street from Bishopsgate. It took a major conservation battle to secure the preservation of market offices on the north side of the street, while the western section of the south side is part of the Middlesex Street Conservation Area. But the eastern section, including the auction hall of the London Fruit and Wool Exchange (1929; inset), is scheduled for demolition and development. The Art Deco-style Fruit and Wool Exchange has a significant place in local history, having sheltered up to 2500 people at a time in its basement during the Blitz. The decision to approve its demolition and redevelopment was made by London Mayor Boris Johnson after the proposal had twice been rejected unanimously by Tower Hamlets Council.

Brick Lane

Brick Lane has become internationally known as the heart of one of London's most distinctive ethnic communities and – more specifically – as a street of curry shops and balti houses. There is little remaining evidence of Brick Lane's previous iteration as the high street of Spitalfields' Jewish community: just a couple of bagel shops selling salt-beef sandwiches. Jewish households began to move out of Brick Lane in the 1950s, leaving behind inexpensive rented accommodation and a garment industry eager for cheap, hard-working labour. Their place was taken by immigrants from south Asia, and in particular from the Sylhet region of what was to become Bangladesh. Chain migration, with families from Sylhet moving into Spitalfields by word-of-mouth contact with friends and relatives already settled there, gradually displaced the Jewish population. By the 1970s Brick Lane had become notorious as the front line of defence of the diasporic Bangladeshi community against racist violence orchestrated by the National Front and the British National Party.

Today, more than half of the population of Spitalfields is of Bangladeshi origin, and Brick Lane has become a tourist stop and night-time entertainment strip rather than a site of racial tension. It is often cited as an exemplar of London's cosmopolitanism. Locals shop in sari fabric stores and Bengali minimarkets and attend employment agencies and barber shops; outsiders frequent the balti houses, bagel shops, internet cafés and indie clothing and record shops.

Branded as Banglatown, Brick Lane has been promoted to tourists as well as City employees and business visitors. Ornamental gateway arches in the style of those in Chinatown have been introduced, along with new signage and new, brighter streetlamps, custom-designed to incorporate 'Asian' motifs. Guidebook and media coverage, together with notoriety stemming from the popularity of Monica Ali's novel *Brick Lane* (2003) and its film adaptation (2007), have brought international tourists into the heart of what had hitherto been a vibrant but relatively unknown area.

The Bangladeshi community itself has been able to secure public funding for mosques, madrassas and Islamic community organizations by leveraging its sheer weight of numbers in local elections. In this way, Bangladeshis and other local Muslims have been able to resist their domestication into post-imperial London and assert their own control over local space. The leadership of the Brick Lane community has nevertheless become involved in alliances with state and private funding organizations. Among their first successes was funding for new 'invented traditions' – a Brick Lane Bengali New Year Festival (*Boishakhi Mela*) and a fortnight-long Brick Lane Curry Festival. Ties with Bangladesh, and Sylhet in particular, remain strong. Sylhet's weekly paper, the *Sylheter Dak*, has an office in London. The Sylhet region, meanwhile, has been changed by its association with the Brick Lane community. Sylhet itself is now one of the most prosperous towns in Bangladesh, with new shopping centres and other building projects funded by 'Londoni' money.

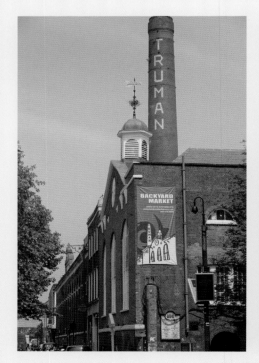

❹ **Brick Lane landmarks**: the Truman Brewery (left) and the Jamme Masjid (right).

The Markets

Spitalfields is renowned for its markets, and in recent years they have become a significant element of the district's cosmopolitanism. Colourful and vibrant, with a slightly anarchic atmosphere, they have been crucial to the local visitor economy. They have also been an important ingredient of the district's counter-cultural appeal to young gentrifiers.

Spitalfields Market is by far the largest and most important in economic terms, but the district's street markets are key to its distinctive character. The best-known is Petticoat Lane Market on Middlesex Street. It became a market for old-clothes dealers in the sixteenth century, after they had been evicted first from London Bridge and then from Cornhill. A century later it was colonized by Huguenot immigrants trading in textiles and clothing. By the late nineteenth century it had become one of the great sights of London, dominated by Jewish rag-trade merchants. Today the Jewish traders have been largely replaced by Bengalis, and the flavour of the market has changed: it is now rather dreary, dominated by stalls selling very cheap clothing.

Old Spitalfields. The last remaining portion of the market of 1887, renovated in 2003 with an interior covered market square for stalls selling food, crafts and clothing.

Less than 500 metres (550 yards) away is Brick Lane, which has been an important market street since the eighteenth century, when Essex farmers sold their produce there. In more recent times it was notorious as a place where stolen bicycles were traded, but it is now best known for its trendy food stalls and its indie music and fashion scene. The heart of its Sunday market is in the old Truman Brewery, where there are stalls selling vintage clothing and accessories, vintage records and clothes by aspiring new designers, as well as food stalls selling everything from Belgian waffles to Chinese dumplings and stir-fries, Japanese takoyaki and okonomiyaki, and Venezuelan arepa. All this spills out into Brick Lane itself, and beyond to Sclater Street and Cheshire Street, just to the north in Bethnal Green, where the stalls sell clothes, furniture, books, electrical goods, tools and collectibles as well as food. A little further to the north again is Columbia Road, in Bethnal Green, where the Sunday market specializes in plants, shrubs, cut flowers and trees.

⑤ Petticoat Lane Market. Prudish Victorians renamed Petticoat Lane itself Middlesex Street in the 1830s to avoid referring to underwear.

⑥ Spitalfields Market. An arcade of shops connects the old market square with the Bishops Square development.

❼ (opposite) Brune Street

Carter House and Brune House are part of the LCC's Holland Estate, a slum-clearance project built in neo-Georgian style in 1927–36 and now managed as social housing by Eastend Homes. At the end of the street is the thirty-three-storey Nido Spitalfields, purpose-built private student accommodation. Property companies have found such projects attractive because there is strong demand for high-quality student accommodation among London's many foreign students, while planning and regulatory systems make fewer demands on student housing than on other types.

❽ Bishops Square

This is a classic example of the new form of 'public' space in London: privately owned and controlled, a product of the 'planning gain' extracted from developers in return for permission to demolish and rebuild. The surrounding development, designed by Foster + Partners, accommodates 3700 square metres (39,800 square feet) of retail space and 72,000 square metres (775,000 square feet) of offices, and is effectively an extension of the financial quarter of the City. *The Buildings of England* is unforgiving: 'The baleful effect of this cannot be overemphasized and marks the continued, and doubtless irresistible, empire building of the City of London in place of the domestic and social needs of the East End.'[1]

❾ Commercial Street

Commercial Street was cut through the area in the 1840s and 1850s to provide access from the docks to north and west London. It was soon lined with warehouses and workshops, and the Peabody Trust acquired this site on the corner of Commercial Street and Folgate Street for the first of its model housing developments, completed in 1864. It was designed for the Trust by Henry Darbishire, who had used similar Gothic styling for philanthropist Angela Burdett-Coutts's Columbia Square in Bethnal Green (see page 44). The Trust went on to build more than 19,000 dwellings in London by 1890, pioneering such unheard-of amenities as separate laundry rooms and interior courtyards for children to play. This first project is very different in appearance from Darbishire's subsequent Peabody projects, with their standard layout, plain styling in yellow brick and absence of ground-floor shops. It was converted in 1999 into flats for sale.

⑩ Hanbury Street

Hanbury Street has become a popular place for street art. The crane on the gable end is by the Belgian artist Roa, whose murals of animals and birds have appeared elsewhere in the city as well as in other cities in Europe. Other well-known muralists to have been featured on Hanbury Street are Alex Face, Mau Mau, Guy Denning and DALeast. The street gained notoriety as the site of the second of the Ripper murders: the body of Annie Chapman was found in the back yard of number 29 (now replaced by brewery buildings) on 8 September 1888.

⑪ Deal Street

Victoria Cottages, part of Mile End New Town, were built in 1865 for the Metropolitan Association for Improving the Dwellings of the Industrious Classes. The Cottages were intended for families who could not afford the higher rents of the Association's tenement dwellings. It was an early experiment in creating an urban estate with housing more typical of country districts, and the Association was criticized at the time for using its land for housing of such a low density.

⑫ Jewish Soup Kitchen
Brune Street

The Soup Kitchen for the Jewish Poor was founded in 1854 to help Jews fleeing from pogroms, who were arriving in London with no money and no immediate prospect of employment. Its charge was to supply soup, bread and meat twice a week during the winter to impoverished members of the Jewish community. It was originally located in Leman Street before moving to Black Horse Yard, Aldgate, then to Fashion Street and finally to these purpose-built premises on Brune Street (called Butler Street at the time) in 1903. Rationing during the Second World War put an end to the kitchen, but families on the charity's books continued to receive an allocation of bread and groceries three times a week. As many as 1500 people were served in this way each week in the 1950s, before the district's Jewish population began to disperse. The building was finally vacated by the organization in 1991, and in 1997 it was converted to luxury flats.

⑬ Brushfield Street

The four-storey Georgian town houses opposite Spitalfields Market on Brushfield Street had become seriously dilapidated by the late twentieth century. But the regeneration of the market in 2003–2005 made investment in the properties worthwhile and brought a more affluent clientele to the street. Previous occupants of the ground-floor shops in the town houses include furriers, bootmakers, drapers, bookbinders, milliners and an orange-importer. The two shops shown here - Gold's and Verde's - have both been restored to evoke on old-fashioned ambience geared to nostalgia for small, independent shops. Both cater to an increasingly wealthy local workforce and resident population as well as to tourists, and both offer 'foodie'-orientated menus.

⑭ Elder Street

This street of early Georgian houses - they date from the 1720s and 1730s - played an important part in the modern evolution of the district. Under threat of demolition and redevelopment in the 1970s, several buildings were occupied by protesters. After the developer had given up, houses were repaired and resold, thereby seeding the gentrification of the street and of nearby Folgate Street and Fleur De Lis Street. The Spitalfields Housing Trust helped to restore many of the properties, such that the area now has a distinctive character that has become closely associated with the entire district. While the fronts are often embellished with handsome doorcases, the interiors are plain. Most of the houses were originally only one room deep, with each upper floor consisting of a single L-shaped room with windows front and back.

Wapping + Limehouse

The Wapping shoreline was rapidly lined with quays, warehouses and alehouses when settlers drained the marshland and built river defences in the early fourteenth century. With the expansion of the British Empire and the development of transoceanic trade, the entire district came to be dominated by maritime industries. An enclosed basin, London Dock, was created in the centre of Wapping by the great engineer Thomas Telford in 1801-1805. A few years later the docks were enlarged, with Tobacco Dock serving Alexander's New Tobacco Warehouse complex and Shadwell Basin extending the facility east and providing a third opening to the Thames.

At the same time the former Regent's Canal Dock at the southern end of Limehouse Cut was deepened and enlarged to form Limehouse Basin. This allowed ships to unload their cargo on to canal barges for onward passage along the Regent's Canal and the national inland canal network. At the other end of Wapping, close to the Tower of London, the Hospital of St Katharine and its fourteenth-century church were demolished and thousands of people were forcibly removed from their homes - most without compensation - to make way for the construction of the St Katharine Dock (1825-28). The excavated soil and gravel from the dock basin was transported by barge to the Duke of Westminster's estate and used to raise the marshy land above flood level, providing the foundations for development in Pimlico and Belgravia (see page 35).

Dockland Industry and Immigrants

The docks were private ventures and, by nature of their business, had to be well secured. Dock walls were constructed along the northern boundary of the surrounding warehouses, creating a distinctive 'island' atmosphere and identity. As the riverfront became increasingly industrial, the prosperous merchants and shipbuilders who had homes as well as businesses in Wapping moved away. Their legacy to the district is a picturesque stretch of early Georgian houses on Narrow Street. Most of the river frontage along Wapping High Street and Wapping Wall was redeveloped with a new industrial architecture of large warehouses and wharves designed to take cargo directly from barges or small ships moored alongside.

In between were some notable survivors from the pre-industrial phase of the Docklands, including a few of the more than thirty pubs on Wapping High Street (like the Prospect of Whitby and the Town of Ramsgate, both dating at least from the 1520s and each with a claim to be London's oldest surviving pub), and a few narrow passages giving access to the river. One of these passages was Execution Dock (near the present-day Captain Kidd pub), which gave access beyond the low-tide mark of the river. The tidal reaches of the Thames were technically the jurisdiction of the Admiralty, which until 1830 administered capital punishment for piracy, acts of mutiny that resulted in death, and murder on the High Seas. Culprits were hanged at Execution Dock and their corpses left to be covered by three successive high tides. Near by was Wapping Old Stairs, next to the Town of Ramsgate pub. Convicts were chained up in the pub cellar before being taken down the Old Stairs to be put on to transport ships bound for Australia.

Wapping filled with a broad spectrum of shipping-related enterprises such as ropemakers, sailmakers and mastmakers as well as shipbuilders and chandlers, engineers and warehouse-owners. Sailors and stevedores arrived from all over Britain and much of the rest of the world looking for work.

Cinnabar Wharf.
A radical conversion of nineteenth-century warehouse buildings.

The construction of the docks, warehouses and workshops effectively squeezed Wapping's resident population into the remaining eighteenth-century streets, which soon deteriorated into teeming slums. Nineteenth-century Wapping was notorious for its poverty, disease and violence. The district also became notable for London's first Chinatown, developed in the Limehouse area by Chinese sailors, stewards, cooks and carpenters who arrived on ships that brought tea from China in the late nineteenth century. For several decades Limehouse was the subject of sensational journalism and spawned a literary sub-genre that played on a series of anxieties: the contamination of the city by a vector of disease ('Yellow Peril'); the corruption of West End society by opium dealers; the fear of 'white slavery'; and, of course, simple racism.

In fact, Chinatown was never more than a few streets of shops and boarding houses, and even these streets were never at any time exclusively Chinese. Chinese boarding houses and shops existed side by side with British working-class families, pubs and shops, just like the cafés, pubs, boarding houses and dance halls that specialized in serving Wapping's other nationalities: Germans, Greeks, Italians, Maltese, Spanish and Swedes, among others. The numbers of Chinese in Limehouse began to fall away in the 1920s as Soho became the preferred area for Chinese migrants. After Wapping was badly bombed in the Blitz, the only evidence left of the Limehouse Chinatown was a few street names - Canton, Mandarin, Pekin, Ming and Nankin streets.

By the 1930s it was the turn of another East End minority - the Jewish population - to be the focus of racism. This came to a head in Wapping in 1936 when Oswald Mosley led 3000 followers of the British Union of Fascists on a highly publicized march towards the Jewish heartland of the East End with an escort of around 6000 police. They were met by anti-fascists, estimated to be well in excess of 100,000 in number, including Jewish, Irish, socialist and communist groups, who set up barricades and halted the marchers. A Diego Rivera-style mural on Cable Street, started in 1979 by Dave Binnington and later completed by Ray Walker, Paul Butler and Desmond Rochfort, commemorates this 'Battle of Cable Street'.

Slum Clearance

Wapping's poor and insufficient housing stock presented a classic dilemma to architects and policymakers in the 1920s and 1930s. Although the LCC's principal strategy was to alleviate inner-city slum problems by building social housing estates in various parts of outer London, Wapping's population depended heavily on casual employment in the Docklands, and was sustained socially by networks that tied them to the district. But there was very little land suitable for new housing estates in Wapping.

This pointed to a strategy of multi-storey apartment buildings, the approach favoured by Modernist architects, housing reformers, gas and electricity suppliers, the construction industries and Conservative politicians. The local council - Stepney Borough Council - was, however, controlled by Labour and strongly opposed to the 'multi-storey barracks' of evangelical Modernism. Their preferred solution was streets of two-storey cottages with gardens, an ideal supported both by the Garden City Movement and by the conclusions of the Tudor Walters Report of 1918.[1] In the end, space constraints led to compromise, exemplified in Riverside Mansions, designed by Culpin and Bowers, architects best known for their advocacy of low-rise Garden City housing. Their solution was a block of six-storey maisonettes - 'self-contained cottages' - stacked in three tiers with the top floor disguised in the roof and the mass of the building broken up with different surface treatments.

Renewal and Regeneration

Before long, the Luftwaffe had created a great deal more buildable space, while the exigencies of postwar recovery left little scope for architectural refinement of either Modernist or Garden City variety. The postwar priority for the Docklands was the designation of

Clearance Areas, the widening of arterial streets and the construction of social housing estates. Whole streets disappeared under new layouts of four- and five-storey deck-access apartment blocks.

This postwar urban-renewal programme had assumed a continuation of Dockland employment, but it became clear by the early 1960s that containerization, competition from other ports and shifts in patterns of trade had doomed Wapping's obsolescent wharves and basins. The docks were closed to shipping in 1968. The London Docks were crudely filled in, and Wapping Pier Head, originally the main entrance from the river, was made into a garden, joining the two handsome late-Georgian terraces of dock officials' houses that had previously flanked the entrance lock. St Katharine Dock, conveniently adjacent to the tourist icons of the Tower of London and Tower Bridge, was redeveloped commercially, an early example of planned mixed development. Of the surviving architecture around St Katharine Dock only the Dockmaster's House (1828), one warehouse (the Ivory House, 1856–60) and some of the marine infrastructure were preserved, to lend character and authenticity to a combination of disappointingly routine new luxury apartment and office blocks, an ersatz nineteenth-century inn and a criminally ugly sixteen-storey hotel.

In the 1980s Shadwell Basin and Limehouse Basin were similarly redeveloped into marinas surrounded by undistinguished private apartment blocks, while much of the London Dock site was taken over by the vast printing works of News International (known locally as 'Fortress Wapping' because of its forbidding appearance and tight security). The adjacent Tobacco Warehouse was reopened in 1990 as a shopping centre at a development cost of £47 million, designed by the Terry Farrell Partnership in a quixotic attempt to create a Disneyfied, postmodern, East End version of Covent Garden. Within five years it stood abandoned and the development company was in administration. In 2003 it was placed on the Buildings at Risk Register by English Heritage.

It remains deserted, apart from occasional use as a film location. In 2005 News International moved its operations out of London, leaving its Wapping complex empty. The property was bought in 2012 by St George, part of the Berkeley Group, for conversion into shops and luxury flats.

The London Docklands Development Corporation (LDDC) was involved with the planning and execution of several of these faltering redevelopment projects. The centrepiece of the LDDC strategy, the regeneration of the Isle of Dogs, also had an impact on Wapping through the construction of the Limehouse Link, which connects Canary Wharf and the Isle of Dogs to the City of London via Wapping, and in the process it knocked out some of the postwar social housing on the St Vincent Estate. Social housing, however, was never a priority of the LDDC. Rather, the aim was to attract middle-class households to the district and, in so doing, to foster social mixing. The LDDC's master planning and site preparation in Wapping, as elsewhere in the Docklands, have effectively subsidized private capital and ensured the production of housing for gentrification, both through conversions (of warehouses and social housing) and through newly built luxury flats.

Wapping's cultural capital – its historic marine and industrial character – has been commodified and niche-marketed by developers. 'Urban living' for the upper-middle classes has been packaged and sold to households that are wealthier than traditional or pioneer gentrifiers but have less time to invest in sweat equity. River views, reserved for the wealthiest new residents, provide a premium for developers. The riverside has been opened up, with pathways provided by developers as 'planning gain' in return for permission to build luxury flats. But the planning authorities have failed to encourage mixed uses, with the result that much of Wapping now has a rather lifeless landscape of tidied-up industrial buildings and mid-rise apartment complexes.

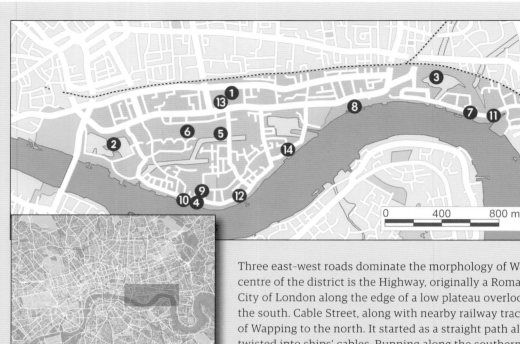

① Cable Street Mural
② St Katharine Dock
③ Limehouse Basin
④ Oliver's Wharf and
   Wapping Old Stairs
⑤ Tobacco Dock
⑥ Fortress Wapping
⑦ Narrow Street
⑧ Thames Path
⑨ St John's Old School
⑩ Wapping Pier Head
⑪ Dunbar Wharf
⑫ Wapping High Street
⑬ St George-in-the-East
⑭ Wapping Wall

Three east-west roads dominate the morphology of Wapping. Running through the centre of the district is the Highway, originally a Roman road running east from the City of London along the edge of a low plateau overlooking low-lying tidal marshes to the south. Cable Street, along with nearby railway tracks, is the unofficial boundary of Wapping to the north. It started as a straight path along which hemp ropes were twisted into ships' cables. Running along the southern shoreline is Wapping High Street, the axis of commercial maritime activity that first developed in the thirteenth century.

❶ Cable Street Mural

(detail)

The mural commemorates the Battle of Cable Street in 1936, when a march by Oswald Mosley and members of his British Union of Fascists, aimed at intimidating Cable Street's Jewish population, was turned back from the East End by an overwhelming number of local residents and sympathizers. Started in 1976 by the artist Dave Binnington on the west wall of St George's Town Hall, the present mural is the work of a number of local artists, who finally finished it in 1993 after far-right activists had vandalized it several times.

❷ St Katharine Dock

The St Katharine Dock Company, a consortium of ship-owners and City merchants, commissioned the great Victorian engineer Thomas Telford to design its complex of dock basins and warehouses on the site of the medieval Hospital of St Katharine, just east of the Tower of London. Opened in 1828, the dock was at the heart of Britain's global trading network, specializing in wool and luxury goods such as ivory, feathers, exotic shells, marble, wine and spices. There was no provision for railway access, however, and by the mid-nineteenth century, steamships were too large for the dock basins. Badly bombed during the Blitz, St Katharine Dock was closed in 1969 and became the first of London's docks to undergo redevelopment. Its luxury flats, marina facilities, cafés and shops provided a blueprint for subsequent Docklands redevelopment projects downstream.

❸ Limehouse Basin

Originally known as Regent's Canal Dock, the basin was opened in 1820 to allow cargo to be transferred from ships and river barges to canal barges, and vice versa. The basin was connected to the river by three locks, one for ships and two for barges, and it specialized in bulky cargo like timber, coal and coke. Like St Katharine Dock, its use declined with the growth of the railways and because the facilities were too small for larger steam-powered ships. The railway viaduct along the north of the basin is one of the oldest in the world, designed by Robert Stephenson and G. P. Bidder for the London and Blackwall railway, which opened in 1840. It is now used by the Docklands Light Railway, and the nearby Limehouse station is a major asset for the property companies that have shoehorned apartment buildings on to the disused wharves of the basin.

❹ Oliver's Wharf and Wapping Old Stairs

Wapping High Street

Oliver's Wharf was the first warehouse in Wapping to be converted into flats, in the mid-1970s, and the first to have apartments reconverted, in the 1990s. It had opened in 1870 as a general warehouse, but specialized in handling tea. Next door is the sixteenth-century Town of Ramsgate pub, where convicts were chained in the cellar before being taken down the Old Stairs to be put on to transport ships bound for Australia.

❺ Tobacco Dock

Porters Walk

Of all the sites left derelict after Tobacco Dock closed its doors to seaborne trade in 1969, the handsome brick vaults at Alexander's Tobacco Warehouse seemed to have the most potential for an interesting regeneration project. But the festival marketplace designed by the Terry Farrell Partnership turned out to be an expensive failure: now totally empty and eerily quiet, rented out only for the occasional corporate event. Tobacco Dock was built in 1811-13 to designs by John Rennie and used to store tobacco, wine and, upstairs, animal skins and furs. It is now owned by a Kuwaiti investment company and awaits a second redevelopment, perhaps as a conference venue.

❻ Fortress Wapping

Pennington Street

Established as part of Rupert Murdoch's strategy of breaking free of the restrictive practices and unions in the Fleet Street publishing industry, 'Fortress Wapping' was built and clandestinely equipped in the early 1980s and activated when several thousand newspaper workers went on strike in 1986. It was built on the site of the old North Stack warehouses of the Western Dock. After just twenty years News International closed its operations in Wapping. The new owner has secured planning approval for a redevelopment with 1800 new homes, 20,000 square metres (215,275 square feet) of commercial space and a twenty-five-storey centrepiece tower.

❼ Narrow Street

Just south of Limehouse Basin is the apex of a bend in the Thames that made for a natural landfall with deep water. Wharves were developed here as early as the fourteenth century. Narrow Street runs parallel to the river for 600 metres (656 yards), hemmed in by the river to the south and the now-drained Wapping Marsh to the north. There are a few survivals of the riverside dwellings typical of the street's heyday, including the early Georgian terrace shown here, which dates from 1718. The shuttered lower floors were formerly shops or stores. The street provided a setting for several of Charles Dickens's books, most especially *Dombey and Son*. It is still one of the most attractive streets in London, and was one of the first to be gentrified, in the 1950s.

❽ Thames Path

The Thames Path is a National Trail running 290 kilometres (180 miles) along the banks of the river. Starting at the Thames Flood Barrier at Woolwich, it ends at Kemble in Gloucestershire. The redevelopment of parts of the Wapping waterfront has opened up large stretches of public access with a new infrastructure of promenades and pathways, as here, near Jardine Street. Free Trade Wharf, the ziggurat-style red-brick apartment building in the distance in this photograph, was one of the key projects in the London Docklands Development Corporation's Limehouse Area Development Strategy. It was built in the 1980s on the site of warehouses owned by the East India Company.

❾ St John's Old School

Scandrett Street

Before the Elementary Education Act of 1870 introduced compulsory, free, state education, formal education for city children was provided mainly by charity schools. St John's Old School is a rare surviving example of one of them. Funded by private subscription, such schools taught reading, writing and arithmetic, and the girls were also taught needlework and domestic skills. St John's was founded in 1695 and rebuilt in 1756. There were separate entrances for boys and girls, and internally the building was segregated down the middle, with twin staircases and separate classrooms for boys and girls. In niches over the double front doors are Coade stone figures of children in traditional blue Charity School uniform. The building ceased to be used as a school in the mid-twentieth century, and by the 1960s was a gutted shell. It was restored in the 1990s and converted into four self-contained houses.

⑩ Wapping Pier Head
Wapping High Street

Wapping Pier Head was originally the main entrance from the Thames into London Dock. Two stone piers, lined with handsome late Georgian terraces of houses for officials of the London Dock Company, led to an entrance lock to Wapping Basin, which in turn led to London Dock. After the docks were closed in 1969, the lock was filled in and made into a garden, and the terraces were renovated as single blocks of flats.

⑪ Dunbar Wharf
Narrow Street

Located on Limekiln Dock, an ancient inlet where lime kilns produced quick-lime for building mortar, Dunbar Wharf was founded by Duncan Dunbar, a Scottish brewer and wine merchant, in 1796. His son ran a fleet of merchant ships from 1826 to 1862, some of which left from Dunbar Wharf, taking emigrants to Australia and North America.

⑫ Wapping High Street
Wapping High Street, once the narrow, bustling centre of life and commerce in the district, is now a dreary canyon of converted warehouses, the old corner shops and some of the pubs now occupied, tellingly, by the offices of estate agents. It was first established in the 1570s when workshops and warehouses spread along this stretch of the river. At one time the street had as many as thirty-six pubs along its 1.5-kilometre (1-mile) length, scattered among marine trades such as rope, timber, sails, barrels, weapons and charts. The surviving buildings along the street date mostly from the nineteenth century, with some contemporary infilling on Second World War bomb sites. One of the warehouses on this stretch, King Henry's Wharf (c. 1880), was used for the storage of coffee, cocoa and sugar, and was the last of Wapping's working warehouses. Along with the adjacent Phoenix Wharf (c. 1840), it is now subject to a redevelopment proposal for luxury flats. Borough planners have failed to encourage mixed uses in such proposals, with the result that Wapping's High Street has a rather sad and lifeless atmosphere.

⓭ St George-in-the-East
Cannon Street Road

In the wake of the Acts of Settlement designed to ensure the Protestant succession when Queen Anne came to the throne in 1702 and the return of a Tory government in 1710, the New Churches Act of 1711 established a Commission to build fifty new churches in populous districts of London. The agenda was to build imposing edifices towering over the homes of the working classes as an assertion of the national religion; that was needed especially in the East End, it was believed, where immigration was taking hold and there were many dissenters. St George-in-the-East, an 'architectural meteorite' in Portland stone, was one of the six churches designed by Nicholas Hawksmoor, who had worked as Christopher Wren's domestic clerk.[2]

Hawksmoor was self-educated and had never travelled, but he was fascinated by ancient and classical architecture, and had gained a vast knowledge from books and drawings. The Fifty New Churches Act allowed him the resources to exercise his knowledge and realize his dreams. In St George-in-the-East he deployed a combination of classical and ancient motifs, including six circular Roman sacrificial altars on top of the church tower. The project ran far over budget, as did the other churches built under the Act of 1711, and the scheme came to an end after only twelve had been built.

The church was hit by a bomb during the Blitz, and the original interior was destroyed by the resulting fire. A new interior was reconsecrated in 1964. One of the first priorities of the London Docklands Development Corporation in 1982 was to clean the sooty exterior, apparently after Michael Heseltine, then Secretary of State for the Environment, had singled it out for attention - a faint echo, perhaps, of the Act of 1711.

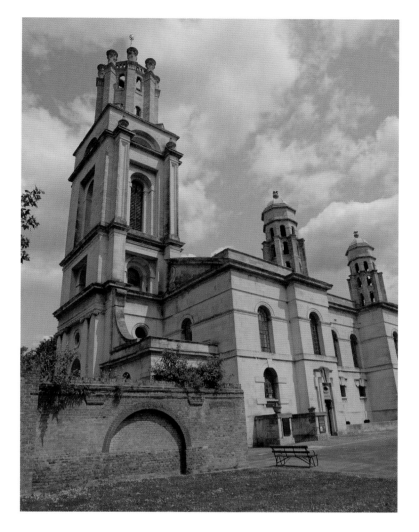

⓮ Wapping Wall

Wapping's river walls were originally built to protect the inland marshes from the tidal flow of the Thames. Wapping Wall is now characterized by a continuous 'wall' of substantial nineteenth-century warehouses: Pelican Wharf (1886–87), Metropolitan Wharf (1862–70), New Crane Wharf (1873–85) and Great Jubilee Wharf (c. 1865 and 1890). Like most of industrial Wapping, the buildings have been 'sensitively restored' by developers - converted to luxury flats and office studios, in other words. The industrial architecture and associated equipment of wall cranes, loading bays, riveted girders, pumps and so on lend character to a corridor otherwise sanitized and purged of vitality.

Westminster + St James's

Westminster was the second nucleus of London's development: the institutional core that emerged 3 kilometres (2 miles) upstream of the commercial and municipal core in the City. Crammed with institutional buildings, Westminster is the public face of the national and imperial capital. The iconography of the Houses of Parliament, Westminster Abbey, Trafalgar Square and the edifices of state bureaucracy along Whitehall, the embankment and Victoria Street provide the setting for much of London's routine pageantry as well as for the country's legislature and executive and their senior bureaucracy. Intimately bound up with Westminster's royal palaces and national institutions is the rectilinear network of broad streets, handsome town houses and élite clubs of St James's.

The Minster and the Court

At the heart of the district is Westminster Abbey - the 'West Minster' itself, of course. Its origins are obscured by legend, but we know that it was rebuilt in the eleventh century by Edward the Confessor, who also established London's first royal palace, next to the Abbey. The medieval settlement grew up along approach roads from the north and west. After the Norman invasion in 1066, William the Conqueror chose to be crowned at Westminster and establish his court there. William agreed to respect the liberties of the merchant City, but he also put it under the guard of two fortresses: Baynard's Castle (long disappeared) near Blackfriars, and the White Tower, now at the core of the Tower of London complex. His successor, William II, built a royal banqueting hall near the Abbey: Westminster Hall, arguably the finest surviving medieval hall in Europe. Between the thirteenth and the nineteenth centuries, it served as the centre of royal justice and administration.

Westminster grew rapidly as the court and institutional buildings of the early Norman monarchs drew clerical élites, lawyers, advocates, clerks and royal officials, and they in turn attracted all sorts of suppliers and lower-grade service workers. Unlike the crowded City, Westminster had plenty of space for growth, although the prime sites along the riverside were soon filled with the mansions and palaces of wealthy nobility. A network of commercial and residential streets developed during the late medieval period, forming a distinctive suburb around the institutional core. The adjacent royal parks, now such an important feature of west London, were established in the first half of the sixteenth century, effectively limiting the westward expansion of the district. At the same time, Westminster itself changed significantly, as a great deal of power and property passed out of the hands of the Church after the Reformation (1538-41).

Classical Ensemble

Subsequent building styles also changed, with classical and Renaissance forms becoming dominant. The most important surviving example is the Banqueting House, designed by Inigo Jones and built on Whitehall in 1619-25 for James I, who intended to use it for festivities and ceremonial occasions (happily unaware that his son Charles I would step from one of its windows to the scaffold). The Restoration of Charles II in 1660 reinforced Renaissance sensibilities and attracted a still greater flow of people coming to visit or to stay for 'the season'. St James's Square was laid out immediately after the Restoration to create a public space 'for the conveniency of the Nobility and Gentry who were to attend upon His Majestie's Person, and in Parliament'. It was enclosed by Act of Parliament in 1725, and the landscape gardener Charles Bridgeman was employed to create a circular

Statue of Richard I. Modelled by Baron Carlo Marochetti in 1856 and displayed on the Old Palace Yard fronting the House of Lords.

Westminster Abbey and the Sanctuary. The Sanctuary office building (right) was completed in 1854 to designs by George Gilbert Scott.

basin of water in the middle, designed to help with the tackling of fires. The building boom that followed the Restoration saw St James's built over, together with most of the land to the south of St James's Park. The principal format was terraces of large town houses with a strong classical flavour. High-end retailing began to emerge along Piccadilly, including Fortnum & Mason's grocery shop, now a very upmarket department store catering to the district's élite residents. Gentlemen's clubs and bachelor chambers began to appear in St James's later in the eighteenth century. The clubs were upscale versions of the coffee houses, chocolate houses, taverns and gambling dens of the City.

Several important buildings, meanwhile, were added to the ensemble at the heart of Westminster, including a new Treasury building on Whitehall (1733-37) and the Horse Guards barracks complex (1750-59) on the site of Henry VIII's old tiltyard, with frontage on Whitehall and a parade ground facing Buckingham House (now Buckingham Palace). Both were designed by William Kent, London's leading architect of the time and an ardent advocate of Palladian style. Meanwhile, Robert Walpole, effectively Britain's first prime minister, had a couple of rather ordinary late seventeenth-century terraced houses transformed into what was to become another icon of Westminster: Number 10 Downing Street.

Horse Guards. Built during the 1750s on the site of Henry VIII's old tiltyard to a design by William Kent.

Imperial Architecture and the Battle of the Styles

Britain's ascendance as a global industrial and imperial power in the nineteenth century required a steady programme of clearance and rebuilding around Westminster's core buildings and institutions. Trafalgar Square was formed in the 1820s by moving the Royal Mews and demolishing a mass of old buildings in front of the church of St Martin-in-the-Fields. What is now Canada House was built for the Royal College of Physicians on the western flank of the square, followed in the 1830s by the National Gallery on the north. Nelson's Column was added in 1843, the most prominent of the statuary that gradually came to populate the precinct. The square itself, meanwhile, became a symbolic site of Britain's evolving national identity.

In 1834 a fire destroyed the old Houses of Parliament, creating the opportunity to build a suitably magnificent replacement. The competition for the new design stipulated home-grown 'Gothic or Elizabethan' and was won by Charles Barry, assisted by A.W.N. Pugin. The Palace of Westminster, as it is properly called, was completed in the 1860s, and its silhouette is now iconic, not just of Westminster but also of London and indeed the United Kingdom.

By this time London - and Westminster in particular - was the capital of an expanding worldwide empire and of a radically changing domestic scene that required increasing state involvement in various aspects of the economy and public health. In order to cope, new government departments were created and existing ones greatly expanded and reorganized. This resulted in the need for new office space, which, in turn, raised the vexed question of the appropriate architectural style for government buildings.

A competition in 1857 to design the Foreign Office (eventually won by George Gilbert Scott) had sparked a fierce public debate about whether the Gothic or classical architectural style was to be preferred. Although the Gothic character of the new Palace of Westminster was popular, the debate, known as the 'Battle of the Styles', was won by the adherents of classical form. The Foreign and Commonwealth Office (Pevsner: 'Neo-Renaissance') and the India Office ('inventive') were completed in 1873; the new Colonial and Home Offices in 1875 ('opulent without being showy'); new Treasury offices ('Neo-Baroque') and a whole complex of buildings that included the Cabinet and War offices ('Italianate') were constructed in 1900-15.

The Treasury. Built as Privy Council and Cabinet Offices (1824–26) by John Soane; remodelled and altered as the Treasury (1844–47) by Charles Barry.

The nineteenth century also saw a second wave of élite clubs in and around St James's. They served the increasing number of gentlemen, civil servants and professionals working in and around Westminster. Not so different in external appearance from the classical architecture of the mansions and institutional buildings of the district, they were places where gentlemen members could relax and network, hold informal meetings, read the newspapers, eat meals and spend evenings playing cards or reading. Whereas the earlier clubs in St James's had catered to the gentry, the clubs founded in the nineteenth century were more specialized, reflecting the changing social, economic and political divisions of Victorian London. Some examples are: the Athenaeum (for men of intellectual influence and achievement as well as wealth and title), the Carlton (founded by Tories in 1832 after their hammering at the General Election that year), the Oxford and Cambridge, the Travellers', the Reform (founded in 1836 by supporters of the electoral Reform Act of 1832) and the United Service Club. For those not in town frequently enough to warrant club membership, the opulent Ritz Hotel came to the rescue; it was built in 1906 on Piccadilly to resemble a stylish Parisian block of flats.

The Embankment

Meanwhile, Westminster, like much of the rest of the capital, was subject to a series of metropolitan improvements. The construction of a new Westminster Bridge and its approaches (1862) removed some badly deteriorated housing and created several broad new streets. The area immediately to the north of the approach road was completely razed to build the new government buildings. Immediately to the south, Parliament Square was enlarged, to make a better setting for Parliament and the Abbey. A few hundred metres to the southwest, the Westminster Improvement Commissioners had already driven through a slum known as 'The Devil's Acre' to create Victoria Street.

Victoria Tower Gardens. Laid out in 1879 after the embankment of the Thames, and enlarged in 1914 to their present extent.

Victoria Embankment. Mature London plane trees line the embankment, with raised seating to provide unobstructed views of the river.

By far the most significant of the Victorian improvements in Westminster, however, was the embankment of the river. The project had been recommended by a Royal Commission in 1844 in order to prevent flooding and to increase the flushing effect of the river by narrowing it. Parliament was finally prompted to act after the 'Great Stink' of 1858, when an unusually hot summer coincided with the Thames being overloaded with raw sewage. Improving the sewage system was the responsibility of the newly formed Metropolitan Board of Works and its Chief Engineer, Joseph Bazalgette.

The Board was also responsible for street improvement, and Bazalgette came up with a bold plan that merged a series of major infrastructural improvements into one continuous linear project that was a marvel of Victorian engineering. The plan was approved in 1860, and by 1870 the first 2 kilometres (1¼ miles) of the Victoria Embankment, between Westminster and Blackfriars, had been completed, dramatically changing the city's relationship to the river. The embankment narrowed the river and reclaimed more than 1500 hectares (3700 acres) of land for new buildings, public gardens and a riverside boulevard furnished with distinctive benches, lamp posts and decorative mooring rings. Beneath were massive sewer, gas and water pipes, electricity conduits and a tunnel for the new Metropolitan District Railway. In the 1880s the wharves and jetties to the south of the Palace of Westminster were removed, and the embankment was extended southwards, creating Millbank and Victoria Tower Gardens.

'An Irredeemable Horror'

Institutional buildings and widened streets did not leave a great deal of space in Westminster for speculative development, but one such project was a controversial landmark with broad implications both for London's building codes and for metropolitan lifestyles. Queen Anne's Mansions, between Victoria Street and St James's Park, was London's first high-rise apartment building and an innovative marketing experiment. Its unprecedented range of amenities – hot and cold water laid on at all hours, speaking-tubes, an impressive coffee room with newspapers, a billiard room, a smoking room and a laundry – was geared to 'bachelors of means'. The experiment was commercially successful, and the developer, Henry Alexander Hankey, gradually extended the original ten-storey, 35-metre-high (115 foot) building of 1875, achieving by stealth (and an ability to work at and beyond the margins of legality) an unprecedentedly tall structure that by 1888 stood at twelve storeys.

Pevsner called it 'an irredeemable horror', and *The Builder* described the mansions as 'monster blocks of dwellings' and 'Babel-like structures'. Out of scale, Queen Anne's Mansions prompted the newly formed London County Council to sponsor the LCC (General Powers) Act of 1890, which limited the height of new construction on established streets to 27 metres (90 feet) plus two floors in set-back roof space. Four years later the London Building Act 1894 reduced this to 24 metres (80 feet) plus two storeys, a restriction that effectively remained in force until after the Second World War. Queen Anne's Mansions was converted into office space for the Admiralty in 1940 and eventually replaced in the 1970s by the gruesome cast-stone monumentality of Basil Spence's Home Office (Bradley and Pevsner: 'mulishly proportioned').

① Portcullis House and Victoria Tower
② Foreign and Commonwealth Office
③ Ministry of Defence
④ Former New Scotland Yard
⑤ St James's Palace
⑥ Admiralty Arch
⑦ Banqueting House
⑧ Ministry of Justice
⑨ Millbank Tower
⑩ Jewel Tower
⑪ Westminster Fire Station
⑫ Barton Street
⑬ Jermyn Street
⑭ Fortnum & Mason
⑮ Clubland
⑯ St James's Park
⑰ Queen Anne's Gate
⑱ Tate Britain
⑲ The Albert
⑳ Chelsea College of Art and Design
㉑ Carlton House Terrace
㉒ Caxton Hall
㉓ Page Street
㉔ Millbank Estate

Trafalgar Square marks the northern extremity of Westminster, along with Northumberland Avenue, created in the late nineteenth century on land reclaimed from the Thames after the construction of the Victoria Embankment. The northern spine of Westminster is formed by Whitehall and Parliament Street, the linear core of government buildings. The buildings on the western side of Whitehall and Parliament Street are hemmed in by St James's Park. The park and the Thames give the precinct its strongly defined linear character. To the north of the park is St James's, a rectilinear network of broad streets enhanced by John Nash as part of his Regency-era plan for the West End. To the south of the park, Westminster extends as far as Vauxhall Bridge Road, constructed early in the nineteenth century through what were still fields and gardens, to link the new Vauxhall Bridge with Belgravia and Mayfair.

❶ **Portcullis House and Victoria Tower** (above)
Canon Row
Victoria Tower (background) houses the Parliamentary Archives; Portcullis House, opened in 2001, houses offices and facilities for Members of Parliament.

❷ Foreign and Commonwealth Office

King Charles Street

The decisive expression of victory in the 'Battle of the Styles', George Gilbert Scott's neo-Renaissance design became the template for late Victorian institutional buildings in London: 'Whitehall Baroque'. The other contending style, Gothic, had been Scott's original preference. The massive complex, set around a 1.6-hectare (4-acre) courtyard, was originally constructed for four government departments - the Home, Colonial, Foreign and India offices - and was finally completed in 1873. Gradually, as its workload has grown, the Foreign Office has come to occupy the whole of the complex. Scheduled for demolition in the 1960s, the building was reprieved by being listed Grade I in 1970, not least because of its sumptuous interiors. A £100 million restoration process was begun in 1984 and completed in 1997.

❸ Ministry of Defence

Horse Guards Avenue

A significant break from Late Victorian 'Whitehall Baroque' that would not have looked out of place in Mussolini's Rome or Hitler's Berlin, the Ministry of Defence was designed by Vincent Harris in 1913-15. Construction eventually began in 1939 but was interrupted by the Second World War, and the complex was finally completed in 1959. The interiors were modernized by HOK for the Ministry in 2001-2004, saving the building from conversion into a hotel, or worse. The Horse Guards Avenue entrance, shown here, is flanked by sculptures by Charles Wheeler representing Earth and Water. Fire and Air were intended for the Richmond Terrace entrance on the south side of the complex, but were disallowed by the Treasury. The building stands on the site of a privy garden laid out in 1545 as part of Henry VIII's residence.

❹ Former New Scotland Yard

Victoria Embankment

The old headquarters of the Metropolitan Police was designed by Richard Norman Shaw and completed in 1890 on land created by the embankment of the Thames (and originally allocated for a National Opera House). The granite facings of the first two storeys were quarried by prisoners on Dartmoor. The floors above feature the bright-red brick and Portland stone detailing that Shaw and others had made popular in Knightsbridge, Kensington and Chelsea in the 1870s and 1880s. The building was converted for use as parliamentary offices in the 1970s when the Met moved to the newest New Scotland Yard, on Broadway, 600 metres (656 yards) to the southwest. The original headquarters were in Great Scotland Yard, off the northern end of Whitehall, from 1829 until 1890.

⑤ St James's Palace

Marlborough Road

Henry VIII commissioned the palace in 1531. It was built on the site of a former leper hospital for women that had been named in honour of St James. It became the principal royal residence in 1702 when Whitehall Palace had been destroyed by fire in 1698 and Queen Anne moved to St James's. It is still the official residence of the sovereign, even though Buckingham Palace became the actual chief residence after the accession of Queen Victoria in 1837. Large sections of St James's Palace had been destroyed by fire in 1809. Much survives of the red-brick building erected by Henry VIII, including the gatehouse in this photograph, currently serving as the offices of Princes William and Harry.

⑥ Admiralty Arch

The Mall

Admiralty Arch was part of a master plan by the architect Aston Webb to turn the Mall into a royal boulevard. It serves as both a triumphal arch (commissioned by King Edward VII, who dedicated the structure to his mother, Queen Victoria) and a barrier between the congestion of Trafalgar Square and the more stately atmosphere of the Mall. Originally used as the offices and residences for the Sea Lords, it has been sold off by the Cabinet Office and is now being converted into a five-star hotel, including 'royal' and 'presidential' apartments.

⑦ Banqueting House

Whitehall

With the Banqueting House, completed in 1625, the architect Inigo Jones introduced a new style of architecture to England, based on the Renaissance ideals of Andrea Palladio. For two decades it was used for state banquets, receptions of ambassadors and masques; but the fun stopped during the English Civil War and subsequent revolution. Following the Restoration, the Banqueting House was again used for royal functions, but this began to decline in the eighteenth century. The facade was originally built in three different types of stone, but was replaced with Portland stone in the nineteenth century. The building is managed by Historic Royal Palaces and open to the public.

8 Ministry of Justice
Petty France

Overbearing and monumental, this Brutalist office building stands on the site of another much-derided landmark, the 'irredeemable horror' (Pevsner) of the Victorian-era Queen Anne's Mansions. Originally built as a speculative office development for prospective government use, it was duly occupied by the Home Office after construction was completed in 1976. The architect was Basil Spence, with Fitzroy Robinson & Partners. By 2004 it was held to be cramped and obsolescent, and the Home Office moved out. After a £130 million refurbishment, it became home to the Ministry of Justice in 2008, the new tenants and the Brutalist design of the building combining to lend an Orwellian affect to the street (which was known for its cluster of French wool merchants' houses in the fifteenth century).

9 Millbank Tower
Millbank

Shortly after the Second World War, planning policy recognized riverside sites as suitable locations for the tall buildings that were expected to spring up in London. Other settings that were seen as appropriate were the edges of green space (no doubt inspired by Le Corbusier's *Ville Radieuse* and images of Central Park in New York) and as focal points at major road intersections. Millbank Tower (built as the Vickers Tower for the Legal and General Assurance Society, in conjunction with the British engineering firm, the Vickers Group) was one of the first to appear. Completed in 1963, it was London's tallest building until it was overtaken in 1965 by the Post Office tower (see page 63), which itself was surpassed by Centre Point (see page 57) the following year. The tower's thirty-one storeys are set on a two-storey podium that parallels the Thames and brings the tower neatly into the riverside townscape. It has remained a landmark on the London skyline but has not - yet - been joined by other towers. It has always been occupied by various public bodies, not-for-profit organizations and international agencies, along with commercial tenants. The Labour Party rented space in the base of the tower between 1995 and 2002, and ran its successful General Election campaign of 1997 from there. Millbank subsequently became synonymous with ruthless New Labour control-freakery and political spin.

10 Jewel Tower
Abingdon Street

The three-storey tower was built by King Edward III in the 1360s on land appropriated from Westminster Abbey, at the edge of the privy garden at the southwest corner of the original Palace of Westminster. The building served as a secure storeroom for the king's private collection of jewels, gold and silver, protected by high walls and a moat. The architect-builder was Henry Yevele, the master mason credited with popularizing the Perpendicular Gothic style. In the Tudor period the Jewel Tower became a general storehouse. Henry VIII left the palace after a fire broke out in 1512. The Jewel Tower is one of four surviving sections of the medieval palace, the others being Westminster Hall, the cloisters and chapter house of St Stephen's and the chapel of St Mary Undercroft. From 1621 the tower was used to store official documents from the House of Lords.

11 Westminster Fire Station
Greycoat Place

In 1866 the Metropolitan Fire Brigade was founded as part of the Metropolitan Board of Works. It was the first publicly funded authority in Britain charged with saving lives and protecting buildings from fire. In 1889 the fire brigade passed to the newly formed LCC, and the Fire Brigade Branch of the LCC's Architect's Department set about designing distinctive and commanding district fire stations. This one, with flats above, was opened in 1906. It was closed in 2014 and put on sale to the highest bidder as a part of the London Fire and Emergency Planning Authority's cost-cutting plan.

12 Barton Street

The quiet streets immediately to the south of Westminster Abbey were developed early in the eighteenth century and have always been popular with senior Westminster figures. Barton Street and its immediate eastern continuation in Cowley Street were built speculatively in the mid-1720s by Barton Booth, a wealthy actor whose principal residence was in Cowley, Middlesex. They are exceptionally well preserved: Bradley and Pevsner rate them as 'amongst the most perfect Early Georgian Streets in Westminster'.[1]

Trafalgar Square

Conceived as part of John Nash's grand design for Regency London, Trafalgar Square was reconceived as an imperial space in the nineteenth century, when it simultaneously became a national site of political demonstration and protest. As the country's collective imagination has intertwined with history, it has since become an iconic setting of immense symbolic significance, a place where the representative and the everyday have combined and evolved to express and shape conceptions of national identity.

The square was effectively carved out as an enlarged road junction early in the nineteenth century, part of Nash's plan to link Regent's Circus, Portland Place and Regent Street to Pall Mall. The New Streets Commission endorsed the idea of a formal square in 1825, and the following year Nash produced the first of many plans for it. In the end, no particular plan was followed. Like London itself, Trafalgar Square evolved piece by piece. Among the buildings cleared to make space for the square was the old Royal Mews, which had been rebuilt in 1732 to in neoclassical style by William Kent. Its contemporary, the church of St Martin-in-the-Fields, has survived to become a key element of the ensemble that makes up the square today.

Trafalgar Square was heavily freighted with symbolic meaning from the start. Named after the decisive naval victory at the Battle of Trafalgar in 1805, and with Nelson's Column at its centre, it already featured the equestrian statue of the absolutist monarch Charles I. A more democratic element was introduced in the 1830s with the construction of the National Gallery. As the 'Nation's Mantelpiece', dependent on parliamentary funding, it has been regularly implicated in debates about education, social values and national heritage.

Trafalgar Square (northeast corner). The statue of George IV with St Martin-in-the-Fields behind.

The present layout of the square derives from designs by Charles Barry in the 1840s. He was responsible for the north terrace fronting the National Gallery, for the siting of four plinths for statuary (one in each corner of the square), and for the two fountain basins that were intended not only for decoration but also to hinder too large a crowd from gathering. From the 1860s the tenor of the square was influenced by the development of new state buildings in Whitehall. This was a time when national identity was closely bound up with the fact of empire, and in many of the major cities of nineteenth-century Europe the signs of empire were prominently displayed in the built environment. In this context, London appeared a poor second to Paris and the capitals of other lesser powers.

Nevertheless, of course, London does have its imperial iconography, not least within Trafalgar Square. Two of Barry's four plinths are occupied by statues of army generals, both of whom were prominently involved in British imperial activity in south Asia. A third plinth carries echoes of Roman imperial statuary with its equestrian por-

trayal of George IV in Roman dress. A statue of a third imperial general, Charles George Gordon, was erected in 1888 on a pedestal between the two fountains. Gordon was an imperial hero who had died at the siege of Khartoum in 1885. The statue was moved to the embankment after the Second World War. Meanwhile, the southwest corner of the square had been restructured with the addition of Admiralty Arch as part of the national monument to Queen Victoria. This provided a processional opening and a new vista to the Mall and to Buckingham Palace. The busts of three Royal Navy admirals - Jellicoe, Beatty and Cunningham - had also been added to the square, and the High Commissions of two of Britain's Dominions - Canada and South Africa - had established themselves in ponderous neoclassical buildings facing the square.

The busy traffic in the roads surrounding the square has always provided a sharp counterpoint to its monuments, institutional architecture and imperial iconography, as has the heavy everyday stream of pedestrians in and around the square. Together, they convey

The National Gallery, on the north side of the square. The fountains were designed by Edwin Lutyens in the 1930s as memorials to David Beatty and John Jellicoe, admirals of the Royal Navy.

an altogether different affect, one of a central space in constant motion, a site of restless commerce and frenetic activity, symbolic of London's centrality in the world economy.

The square's prominence as the 'heart of empire' and its everyday accessibility to both workers and visitors have also made it an important site for political protest and, therefore, a site of challenge and resistance, a place of contested meanings. Significant demonstrations have been held in the square in support of female suffrage, labour movements and nuclear disarmament, and against fascism and unemployment.

On the other hand, the square has also been the focal point of national celebrations, both planned and spontaneous: for example VE Day and VJ Day at the end of the Second World War, New Year celebrations and the celebration of national sporting victories. Recent programming of events in the square has emphasized Britain's – and especially London's – cosmopolitanism, celebrating Chinese New Year, Saint Patrick's Day, Diwali and Vaisakhi, for example. It is also now routinely used for pop-cultural and educational events, all of which, given the square's symbolic importance, contribute to the evolving discourse on national identity.

Meanwhile, the built environment of the square itself has continued to be implicated

Trafalgar Square looking west from St Martin-in-the-Fields. The equestrian statue to the right of Nelson's Column is of Charles I, created in 1633 by the French sculptor Hubert Le Sueur.

in that same discourse. The Prince of Wales famously intervened in 1984, describing a scheme for an extension to the National Gallery as a 'monstrous carbuncle on the face of a much-loved and elegant friend'. Under Mayor Ken Livingstone in the 2000s, the square was remodelled as part of the city's 'World Squares for All' programme. The north side of the square was pedestrianized, and a central staircase was constructed linking the National Gallery directly to the square. From 1999 to 2001 the Royal Society of Arts sponsored the exhibition of contemporary art on the square's fourth plinth, which had been vacant since the 1840s. Since 2005 the Greater London Authority has taken over the project, and most of the sculptures and installations have deliberately provoked discussions of identity, tolerance, diversity, history and modernity.

Nelson's Column commemorates the victory of Admiral Horatio Lord Nelson over the French fleet at the Battle of Trafalgar, on 21 October 1805. It was completed in 1843, and the statue of Nelson is by Edward Hodges. The four huge lions at the base of the column were added later, in 1868, sculpted by Edwin Landseer.

⑬ Jermyn Street

One of London's élite, specialized shopping streets, Jermyn Street was laid out in the 1660s and 1680s on Crown land that had been granted to an influential courtier, Henry Jermyn, Earl of St Albans. By the early nineteenth century, the street was known for a series of upmarket hotels; only one of these, the Cavendish, remains. Most of the rest of the street was redeveloped, piecemeal, in the late nineteenth and early twentieth century, when it became known for its fashionable men's shops, especially shirtmakers like T. M. Lewin & Sons and Turnbull & Asser, and boot and shoe retailers like Foster & Son and Crockett & Jones. Scattered among them is a variety of other specialized stores that cater to a wealthy and mainly male clientele: tailors, barbers and perfumers, a hatter, and provision merchants like Paxton & Whitfield and Wiltons, who are able to supply such essentials as bespoke picnic baskets.

⑭ Fortnum & Mason
Piccadilly

Possibly the most smugly snooty of London's emporia, the shop was founded in Piccadilly in 1707 when the small-shopkeeper Hugh Mason went into business with Charles Fortnum. Fortnum had been a footman to Queen Anne and had been allowed to keep half-used candles, which he then sold. He invested the profits in the new enterprise, but also brought with him an acute sense of the needs and wants of the upper echelons of the court. The shop prospered by stocking exotic luxury goods, a strategy that was greatly strengthened by the firm's close association with the British East India Company. Fortnum & Mason gained a reputation for having fancy and exotic foodstuffs that could not be obtained elsewhere. In the 1790s the shop even operated its own postal service, bringing foot traffic through its doors from among the gentry of the district.

Thriving on the affluence and consumer culture of upper-middle-class Victorians, the shop developed a new and distinctive speciality: ready-to-eat luxury foods. Customized wooden boxes containing honey, dried fruits, spices and preserves were shipped to the soldiers - officer class, of course - at various imperial fronts. Meanwhile, ready-prepared hampers of expensive treats were sold to racegoers, shooting parties and guests at Cowes Week, Henley Regatta and the like. The shop even had a department dedicated to expeditions, preparing the necessities of the good life for Britain's explorers and adventurers. It was completely rebuilt in the 1920s, when the company took the opportunity to add new, non-food departments. The baroque-looking clock above the main entrance dates from 1964. On the hour, the figures of Mr Fortnum and Mr Mason emerge to bow to each other. The clock bells are from the Whitechapel Bell Foundry, a world away in the East End.

⑮ Clubland

St James's Street and Pall Mall

The cluster of gentlemen's clubs and professional clubs in and around St James's is a unique and distinctive element in the social geography of the metropolis. For more than 200 years the clubs have dominated the character of the area, reinforced the values and attitudes of their members, policed certain aspects of their comportment (and tolerated others), and propagated and maintained key networks of social and political power. White's Club is the oldest, its members (men only, still) being drawn from the start from the country's richest and most distinguished families. It was founded in 1693 and moved to purpose-built premises on St James's Street (above, left) in 1778, where it became the unofficial headquarters of the Tory Party. By then, other clubs were appearing in St James's, including Brooks's, founded in 1764 with new premises on St James's Street (above, right) that opened in 1778. Brooks's was dominated by Whig politicians and influentials. Like several other clubs, it had a reputation for heavy gambling among its wealthy and aristocratic members. Other early clubs include the Athenaeum (left, middle), Boodle's and the Travellers Club. Over the course of the nineteenth century many more clubs were established in St James's, most of them catering not so much to old and titled money as to subsets of the new Victorian élite. Among them were the Carlton, Conservative, Constitutional, East India, Eccentric, Devonshire, Oxford and Cambridge, Pratts and Reform clubs. The Royal Automobile Club was established in 1897 and moved to its grand club rooms on Pall Mall (left) in 1911.

16 St James's Park

St James's Park is the oldest Royal Park in London, on land acquired by Henry VIII as yet another deer park. He put a fence around it and built St James's Palace. James I kept a menagerie in the park, as well as aviaries of exotic birds along what is now Birdcage Walk. Fifty years later, Charles II had the park redesigned, with lawns and French-style geometric flower beds. The centrepiece was a canal, lined with trees. During the eighteenth century, Horse Guards Parade (which can be seen to the rear of the photograph at the left) was created by filling in one end of the canal. It is still officially part of St James's Park. In the 1820s the park received another makeover, this time to the naturalistic designs of John Nash, commissioned by George IV. The canal became a curving lake, winding paths replaced formal avenues, and shrubberies took over from formal flower beds.

17 Queen Anne's Gate

The part of Queen Anne's Gate pictured here was originally built as part of a close called Queen Square. Its terraced town houses were built in the early eighteenth century. As such they are technically pre-Georgian, precursors of London's classic pattern-book Georgian terraces and squares. They are distinctive for their carved keystones and intricately carved wooden door-hoods – features that disappeared in later terraces. Close to St James's Park and Whitehall, the street has been home to a series of notables, including Lord Palmerston, Lord North, Jeremy Bentham, John Stuart Mill and Admiral of the Fleet Lord Fisher.

⑱ Tate Britain
Millbank

In 1889 Henry Tate, an industrialist who had made his fortune as a sugar refiner, offered his collection of British art to the nation. With insufficient space for it in the National Gallery, a new National Gallery of British Art, under the directorship of the National Gallery, was built to house not only Tate's gift but also the works of British artists from various other collections. Sidney R. J. Smith was chosen as the architect for the new gallery. His neo-Renaissance design is the core building of a gallery complex that has seen seven major extensions since it was opened in 1897. In 1955 the gallery became wholly independent from the National Gallery, and since the opening of Tate Modern on Bankside in 2000, the Millbank gallery has become Tate Britain.

⑲ The Albert
Victoria Street

A Victorian landmark surrounded by the glass-and-steel high-rise buildings of Victoria Street, the Albert is a well-preserved late Victorian tower pub. The Beer Act of 1830 had liberalized the regulations governing the sale of beer in order to promote competition among brewers. An early nineteenth-century surge in the consumption of spirits - and a consequent increase in public drunkenness - was believed to have been a result of the very poor quality of available beers. This in turn was held to be because of the near-monopoly of a handful of major brewers, who owned the pubs and controlled what they sold. Liberalizing the sale of beer did result in a significant increase in beer consumption at the expense of spirits, and competition among pubs and breweries also resulted in significant investment in the comfort and style of the pubs themselves. Many, like the Albert - built for Joseph Wood's Artillery Brewery in Victoria Street in the mid-1860s and named after the Prince Consort (who had died in 1861) - were built or remodelled gin-palace style, with etched-glass windows; ornate ceilings, mouldings and mirrors; and gilding.

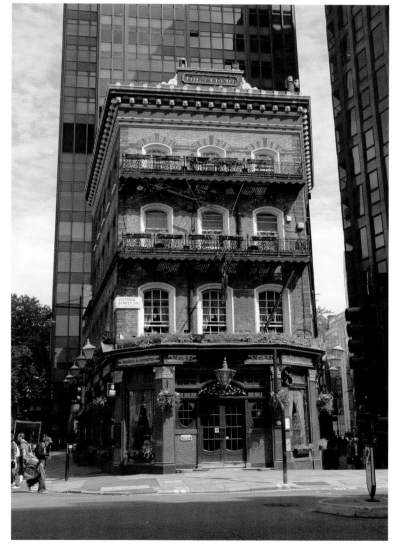

⑳ Chelsea College of Art and Design
John Islip Street

Part of the University of the Arts London, the college occupies the former Royal Army Medical College, next to Tate Britain. The North Block, shown here, dates from about 1898. The Army Medical College provided postgraduate training in military surgery, army pathology, and military as well as general medicine until 2005, when teaching moved to Portsmouth. The buildings were designed by J.H.T. Wood and Wilfred Ainslie and stand on part of the site of the notorious Millbank Penitentiary (1821-90), based on the social reformer Jeremy Bentham's concept of constant and general inspection in a 'Panopticon'.

㉑ Carlton House Terrace

After George IV moved into Buckingham Palace and demolished his former residence, Carlton House, he had John Nash design an exclusive terrace of town houses on the site, overlooking the Mall. Clad in stucco in classical style, with a Corinthian-columned facade surmounted by an elaborate frieze and pediment, the houses are enormous. So large, in fact, that by the twentieth century the size and cost of upkeep as family residences had become prohibitive. For several years the Nazi swastika flew above numbers 7-9 Carlton House Terrace, which was leased by the German Embassy. Other occupants along the terrace have included the British Red Cross, the National Portrait Gallery and a casino. But in 2006, when the Crown listed part of the terrace for sale, the homes were seen once more as suitable for residences: this time for the global super-rich. The buyers were the Hinduja family, who paid £58 million for four interconnected town houses totalling 6225 square metres (67,000 square feet). After the family had spent a similar amount on renovations, the property was estimated by *Forbes* magazine in 2013 to be worth more than £275 million.

㉒ Caxton Hall
Caxton Street

Opened in 1883, Caxton Hall originally served as Westminster Town Hall. The hall's first notable role was as a meeting place for the suffragettes. In 1907-14 the Women's Social and Political Union held a 'Women's Parliament' in Caxton Hall before every parliamentary session. During the Second World War the hall was used by the Ministry of Information as a secure venue for Churchill to hold press conferences. But Caxton Hall is best known for its function as the register office for Belgravia and much of Mayfair, and so was constantly in the news as celebrities were married there. It was redeveloped in 2006, the facade and former register office at the front of the building converted into luxury flats, the former central tower converted into a three-storey, open-plan penthouse apartment, and the meeting rooms at the rear demolished to make room for a new office building.

㉓ Page Street

Built on a slum-clearance site in the early 1930s, Westminster City Council's Grosvenor Estate is strikingly different from anything else in the district. The architect was, improbably, Edwin Lutyens, best known for the design of houses for wealthy clients. Lutyens had been working as the consulting architect for nearby Grosvenor House, and the second Duke of Westminster leased the land to Westminster City Council for 999 years for the peppercorn rent of one shilling with the condition that Lutyens should be the architect for a redevelopment of 'dwellings for the working classes ... and no other purpose'. In the 1980s the Conservative-controlled Westminster City Council - London's flagship Thatcherite borough - shamelessly argued that the term 'working class' had become meaningless and that the stipulation should be overturned, allowing them to sell the leaseholds of the flats to anyone. The sixth duke disagreed, maintaining that the properties should remain available as low-rent accommodation. The council took the case to court, and lost.

㉔ Millbank Estate
Erasmus Street

One of the high points of social housing provision in London, the Millbank Estate was an attempt to apply the same aspirations of good and pleasing design to social housing as to fashionable private-sector flats. When the Millbank Penitentiary was closed in 1890, a Royal Commission recommended that a large portion of its site be set aside for housing. This land was acquired in 1896 by the LCC, which commissioned an estate for 4430 people, in principle mainly those displaced by the redevelopment of the Clare Market area in Holborn, a dilapidated warren of sixteenth-century streets and alleys. The LCC's Architect's Department had a permanent staff of eight dedicated to the Housing of the Working Classes, following the Act of 1890 that empowered local authorities not only to demolish the worst slums but also to build and manage new accommodation. Designed by R. Minton Taylor and completed by 1902, the Millbank Estate represented a significant advance on the LCC's first housing scheme, the Boundary Street Estate in Bethnal Green (see page 48), as none of the new tenements in Millbank had to share toilets and sculleries. It was also rather less institutional-looking, its Arts and Crafts and Domestic Revival influences more in line with the middle-class mansion apartment buildings that had appeared throughout west London in the 1880s and 1890s. The estate has been well maintained, but Westminster Council has been one of the keenest advocates of Margaret Thatcher's right-to-buy policy, and by 2014 more than half of the 561 flats in the estate were privately owned.

Whitechapel

London's rapidly increasing population began to spread beyond the City walls in the later Middle Ages. To the east, the first settlement developed along the ancient Roman road to Colchester, past the thirteenth-century church of St Mary Matfelon, known as the *alba capella* or the white chapel. The nascent suburb took the form of a string of coaching inns and taverns and a jumble of houses and workshops for trades, such as metalwork, that were considered a nuisance or a hazard in the City. Beyond the jurisdiction of the City's guilds and livery companies, early Whitechapel also attracted opportunists who were keen to exploit the absence of regulation and control over the quality of their products. This prompted an early example of land-use policy, when Elizabeth I issued a proclamation in 1580 banning the building of all new houses and tenements within 3 miles (4.8 kilometres) of the City gates. With no detailed legal codes or personnel to back it up, the proclamation was duly ignored, and by the mid-seventeenth century Whitechapel was firmly established as part of the metropolis.

The Jewish East End

The seventeenth century brought a mix of industry, including silk-weaving, sugar-refining and brewing, while Sephardic Jewish immigrants from Spain and Portugal arrived in 1656 to form the nucleus of a community that would later become known as 'the Jewish East End'. Because of its rapid growth (and, for the Establishment, the worrisome number of dissenters, nonconformists and Jews among the

population), Whitechapel was allocated two of the new Anglican churches funded through the New Churches Act of 1711. Other building was, for the most part, haphazard and cramped. As cottages and workshops aged, they were razed and replaced in equally haphazard and cramped style. The only large landowner in the district was the London (now Royal London) Hospital, whose trustees began to allow the speculative development of 'improved' plain red-brick tenements on their estate after 1790.

Over the course of the nineteenth century, Whitechapel's population became progressively more overcrowded and impoverished. The arrival of thousands of Ashkenazi Jewish refugees from eastern Europe made Whitechapel one of the most densely occupied districts in London. Silk-weavers fell on hard times as a result of foreign competition, and the silk industry degenerated into the manufacture of cheap clothing, which in turn spun off a local specialization in the wholesale side of the second-hand clothing trade. Other prominent Whitechapel industries included bootmaking, cigar manufacture, brewing and sugar-refining. By the mid-nineteenth century Whitechapel was a dense mixture of decaying cottages, poorly built tenements and cramped courts and alleys. A few older parts had been cleared - Commercial Street was cut through in the 1840s to provide access from the docks to north and west London - but for the most part Whitechapel was an impenetrable slum: *terra incognita* as far as the rest of London was concerned.

Glimpses of the poverty, disease, crime and dereliction of Whitechapel were provided by writers such as Dickens and Henry Mayhew and by Gustave Doré, an illustrator, and its hopelessness was portrayed in a widely circulated poem, 'The City of Dreadful Night', by James Thomson. But such glimpses only generated fear and loathing: the general view of the East End in Victorian London was singularly unsympathetic, the poor blamed for their own circumstances and typically represented as a degraded race apart. The Methodist preacher William Booth and his wife, Catherine, launched the 'Christian Mission to the

Whitechapel Road.
Lined with shops and market stalls selling everything from Indian snacks to Nigerian fabrics, Whitechapel Road serves as the high street for the East End's multi-ethnic community.

Nelson Street. A nineteenth-century terrace that was in the heart of the Jewish area.

Heathen of our Own Country' in Whitechapel in 1865, and thirteen years later it became the Salvation Army. In fact, of course, Whitechapel's working-class communities did have a robust moral system – albeit with mores that were significantly different from those of the Victorian middle classes. The pious superiority of polite society turned to apprehension and hysteria in 1888 with the serial murder of prostitutes ascribed to the unidentified killer known as Jack the Ripper. Thanks to the sensationalism of Victorian newspapers and the appetite of modern television audiences for murder mysteries, Whitechapel has become synonymous with 'Ripper murders' and their backdrop of damp, foggy streets and alleys.

Progressive Reform

Meanwhile, Whitechapel had been the focus of many of the progressive reform movements of the nineteenth century. The Association for Promoting Cleanliness Amongst the Poor, founded in 1844, set about establishing bath and laundry houses in the East End and opened its first model baths

Eastern Dispensary. Built on Leman Street in the 1850s using voluntary contributions, this was one of the first attempts to provide medical treatment to the poor of the area. It is now a gastropub.

in 1847 in Goulston Square. The Peabody Trust built model housing in Whitechapel that represented the first tangible results of the 1875 Artisans' and Labourers' Dwellings Act, which allowed for the compulsory purchase of areas of slum dwellings in order to clear and then rebuild them. Other limited-dividend philanthropic companies active in Whitechapel included Lord Rothschild's Four Per Cent Industrial Dwellings Company, the Improved Industrial Dwellings Company and the Metropolitan Association for Improving the Dwellings of the Industrious Classes. The single most influential of the Victorian reformers in Whitechapel was Samuel Barnett, Vicar of St Jude. Conscious of the failure of most limited-dividend housing (always allocated to 'steady, thrifty and socially ambitious working men') to trigger an upward-filtering effect for poorer households, he founded the East End Dwellings Company in 1884 with the intention of housing the really poor.

That same year, Barnett and his wife, Henrietta, founded Toynbee Hall, the first university settlement house of the British settlement movement. Named in honour of their friend and fellow reformer Arnold Toynbee, it was designed in Vicarage Gothic style by Elijah Hoole, the architect of many of Octavia Hill's philanthropic housing schemes in London. The idea of the university settlement was to create a place for future leaders to live and work in the East End, bringing them face to face with poverty while undertaking voluntary work, offering free legal advice and organizing extension classes. The men and women who spent time at Toynbee Hall included many of those who were to lay the foundations of social reform that culminated in the establishment of the British Welfare State. Not least among these were William Beveridge, author of the seminal *Report on Social Insurance and Allied Services* (the 'Beveridge Report', 1942), and Clement Atlee, prime minister 1945–51.

The Barnetts were also instrumental in establishing a public library in Whitechapel. The social purposes of the 1890 Public Libraries Act fitted with

Wool House. One of several large wool warehouses on Back Church Lane, initially converted to offices, now redeveloped as flats.

Whitechapel Road as one of the Borough of Tower Hamlets' new generation of public libraries.

Gritty Authenticity

Whitechapel was significantly affected by bomb damage in the Second World War, and because of its place within the spatial planning of Greater London, it was designated for commercial and industrial use rather than housing. As a result it was spared the wholesale redevelopment that took place further east in the 1950s and 1960s. A good deal of the district's older fabric therefore remains, albeit repurposed in various ways. Whitechapel certainly has its share of cheap-looking commercial space, characterless neo-Georgian style shopping parades and medium-rise social housing blocks. But it has also retained, in places, a gritty authenticity from its nineteenth-century brickwork, alleyways and courtyards.

In the 1960s and 1970s the district's surviving older fabric was progressively vacated by Jewish households (moving up the socio-economic ladder and out to more distant suburban settings).

Darul Ummah Community Centre, incorporates the Jamiatul Ummah Muslim boys' secondary school in a former London Board School built in the 1870s.

They were replaced by south Asian immigrants, mainly of Bangladeshi origin. At the same time, the authenticity of Whitechapel's built environment, coupled with its relatively inexpensive property, made parts of the district a target for young gentrifier households. More recently, Whitechapel's proximity to the booming business-service sector in both the City and Canary Wharf has resulted in a certain amount of commercial overspill, mostly in rather ostentatious built form, as if making up for the absence of a City or Canary Wharf address.

the overall aims of philanthropic reform, but they saw the Whitechapel Library as something more - as a community centre and a nerve centre for radicalism and experiment: a 'University of the Ghetto'. The Whitechapel Library opened in 1892, and, like several other libraries in east London, it was part-funded by the philanthropist J. Passmore Edwards. He also financed the Whitechapel Art Gallery, built next door to the library in 1901 in an Art Nouveau style that was all the more striking for its East End setting. The gallery was an attempt to establish an art institution of national standing in the East End with a programme devoted mainly to exhibitions of modern art. It took over the neighbouring library space in 2003, while new library space in the progressive tradition of the original - the Whitechapel Ideas Store, designed by David Adjaye - was opened in 2005 further along the

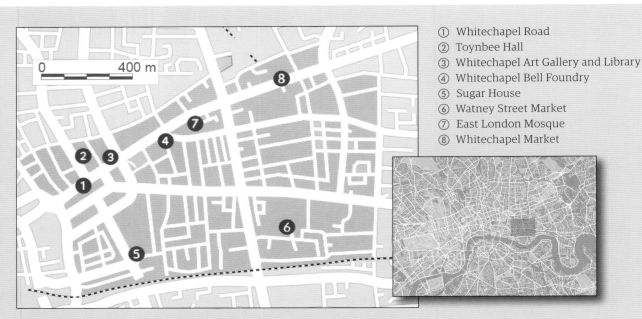

① Whitechapel Road
② Toynbee Hall
③ Whitechapel Art Gallery and Library
④ Whitechapel Bell Foundry
⑤ Sugar House
⑥ Watney Street Market
⑦ East London Mosque
⑧ Whitechapel Market

Whitechapel has its own identity as part of the East End, but its precise boundaries are far from clear. To the west, it abuts the ancient boundary of the City, while to the south it is limited by the railway lines leading to Fenchurch Street and Tower Gateway stations. To the east, Whitechapel shades into the streets of anonymous social housing estates of Stepney. To the north, just beyond Whitechapel Road, the district merges into Spitalfields. The layout and morphology of the district is mostly a product of piecemeal speculative development, which has left a legacy of short, rectilinear streets, many of which are now lined with medium-rise developments of social housing. The only significant parcel of land to have been under single ownership was the London Hospital Estate in the north of the district, where late eighteenth-century cottages were cleared for the hospital itself, only for subsequent development to be rather disjointed.

❶ Whitechapel Road

Slowly developed along an ancient highway into the City before becoming an East End high street in the nineteenth century, Whitechapel Road is now on the threshold of large-scale redevelopment. The approaches to Aldgate at the western end of the road have already been reshaped with office and apartment towers, and planning permission has been granted for much more. The twenty-storey building on the left of this photograph, Aldgate Tower, and the twenty-one-storey building on the right, One Commercial Street, were both completed in 2014.

❷ Toynbee Hall

Commercial Street

Toynbee Hall was founded in 1884 by Samuel Barnett, a Church of England curate, and his wife, Henrietta. Their radical vision was to bring privileged young graduates to live and work as volunteers in London's East End, bringing them face to face with poverty. Toynbee Hall enabled them to establish a new form of community work, free from the institutional constraints and conservatism of the Church. Whitechapel is still one of the most disadvantaged districts in the entire United Kingdom, and, while the university settlement concept has not survived, Toynbee Hall continues to provide free support and advice for people struggling with debt, benefits, welfare and legal problems.

❸ Whitechapel Art Gallery and Library

Whitechapel High Street

Whitechapel Library, on the right in the photograph, was another of Samuel Barnett's projects. Like many other Victorian reformers he saw libraries as havens and librarians as missionaries spreading the light of knowledge. It opened in 1892, having been funded in large part by J. Passmore Edwards, publisher of, among other things, the weekly *Building News*. The Whitechapel library was the first of three that he helped to establish in the East End. He also financed the Whitechapel Art Gallery, next door, one of Henrietta Barnett's projects. It opened in 1901 in a distinctive Arts and Crafts building designed by Charles Harrison Townsend. Samuel Barnett was the first chair of the Board of Trustees. The opening exhibition, which included work by the Pre-Raphaelites, Constable, Hogarth and Rubens, attracted more than 200,000 visitors. The gallery has now expanded into the library building, the space having been vacated after Tower Hamlets opened a new library 750 metres (820 yards) to the east on Whitechapel Road.

❹ Whitechapel Bell Foundry
Whitechapel Road

This anonymous-looking building houses the workshops of a singular enterprise: one that has been in continuous business since 1570, making only one product - bells of various sizes - apart from a spell during the Second World War when production shifted to casting aluminium submarine parts for the Admiralty. The foundry moved to its present site in 1738. Among the famous bells produced here are the Liberty Bell (1752) and Big Ben (1858).

❺ Sugar House
Leman Street

Once the centre of operations for supply chains of affordable goods for the United Kingdom's working-class families, the former headquarters of the Co-operative Wholesale Society (CWS) found itself co-opted to accommodate the spillover of office boys from the City in 2008 when it was converted into luxury flats and penthouse apartments. It was built in the 1880s as a sugar warehouse and office complex for the CWS on a site next to the now-demolished Midlands Railway goods depot. There had been a number of small sugar refineries in Whitechapel since the eighteenth century, when the growing popularity of coffee and tea generated a demand for 'improved' sugar. Raw sugar came from West Indies plantations as part of the triangular trade that took slaves from West Africa to the plantations and brought sugar, rum and timber to England. The building still carries the CWS logo, a wheatsheaf symbol of co-operation (on the basis that one stalk cannot stand alone) with the words 'Labor and wait.' The American spelling of labour was used deliberately, to express solidarity with those fighting slavery in America.

6 Watney Street Market

At one time more famous than Petticoat Lane, the market in Watney Street has been reduced to a small and rather drab collection of stalls located in the pedestrian precinct that occupies the space between rows of GLC deck-access housing. It stands on the site of an early Victorian street, Devonshire Street, that was notorious as one of the most impoverished and socially degraded in the metropolis. Rebuilt as Watney Street, it had become a thriving commercial strip of more than 100 shops by the early twentieth century, with hundreds more street stalls. After the Second World War, the market began to decline, while many of the buildings had become obsolescent. In 1965 plans for new council housing were approved. It took several years to complete the rebuilding and, meanwhile, customers drifted away and stallholders left. There are now only a couple of dozen stalls, selling fruit and vegetables, cheap clothing and gadgets.

7 East London Mosque
Whitechapel Road

The East London Mosque is London's oldest. It moved to the present site in purpose-built structures in 1985. The adjacent London Muslim Centre opened in June 2004, and a nine-storey addition devoted to spaces and facilities for women, the Maryam Centre, opened in 2013. Disappointingly, it has been the focus of controversy. The mosque has been criticized for encouraging the enforcement of 'Islamic norms' and for hosting homophobic speakers. In 2014 it was the focus of intimidating street tactics by a so-called Christian Patrol, part of a far-right group, apparently in response to reports of groups of young men attempting to create 'Muslim zones' by stopping people in the neighbourhood who they believed were not conforming to Islamic law.

8 Whitechapel Market
Whitechapel Road

This stretch of Whitechapel Road near the Royal Hospital has accommodated a street market for more than 200 years. As the character of the district has changed, so has that of the market. Stallholders as well as customers are now mainly from Whitechapel's Bangladeshi community, and market staples include exotic fruits, vegetables and spices, silk saris and Bollywood DVDs, as well as electrical and household goods. The shops along this north side of the street are effectively part of the market. Many have the beaten-up appearance of market stalls; but above street level many buildings retain their original features. Some of them have already been restored as the neighbourhood around the Tube station has begun to pick up in anticipation of the Crossrail connection (2018-19) that will make it only thirty-nine minutes from Heathrow Airport and three minutes from Canary Wharf.

Notes

A City of Districts

1. Tung, A. M., *Preserving the World's Great Cities: The Destruction and Renewal of the Historic Metropolis*. New York: Clarkson Potter, 2001, p. 282.
2. Olsen, D. J., *The City as a Work of Art*. London: Yale University Press, 1986, p. 27.
3. Low, S., Jr.,*The Charities of London, Comprehending the Benevolent, Educational, and Religious Institutions, their Origin and Design, Progress, and Present Position*. London: Sampson Low, 1862.
4. Sutcliffe, A., *London: An Architectural History*. London: Yale University Press, 2006, p. 178.
5. Hatherley, O., *A New Kind of Bleak: Journeys through Urban Britain*. London: Verso, 2012, p. xxvi.
6. *Ibid.*, p. 347.
7. *New London Quarterly*, 19, 2014 <newlondonquarterly.com>.

Bayswater and Paddington

1. English Heritage Grade I buildings are considered to be 'of exceptional interest, sometimes considered to be internationally important'; Grade II* buildings 'are particularly important buildings of more than special interest'; and Grade II buildings – 92 per cent of all listed buildings – 'are nationally important and of special interest'.

Bethnal Green

1. Cherry, B., O'Brien, C., and N. Pevsner, *The Buildings of England. London 5: East*. New Haven, CT: Yale University Press, 2005, p. 548.

Borough and Southwark

1. Quoted in Tames, R., *Southwark Past*. London: Historical Publications, 2001, p. 122.
2. Booth, C., *Life and Labour of the People in London: Inner South London*. London: Macmillan, 1902, p. 8.

Camden

1. Godfrey, W. H., and W. McB. Marcham (eds), 'Camden Town', *Survey of London: Volume 24: The Parish of St Pancras, Part 4: King's Cross Neighbourhood*, 1952, p. 134. <british-history.ac.uk/report.aspx?compid=65574> Date accessed: 25 May 2014.
2. Sutcliffe, A., *London: An Architectural History*. London: Yale University Press, 2006, p. 106.

The City

1. Hatherley, O., *A New Kind of Bleak: Journeys through Urban Britain*. London: Verso, 2012, p. 341.

Clerkenwell

1. Temple, P. (ed.), *Survey of London, Volume 46: South and East Clerkenwell*. London: Yale University Press, 2008, p. 21.
2. *Ibid.*, p. 6.

Greenwich

1. <whc.unesco.org/en/list/795> Date accessed: 25 July 2014.
2. Jennings, C., *Greenwich*. London: Abacus, 2001, p. 128.

Holborn

1. From the preamble to the Act of 1735, quoted in Riley, W. E., and L. Gomme (eds), *Survey of London: Volume 3: St Giles-in-the-Fields, Part 1: Lincoln's Inn Fields*, 1912, p. 22.

Lambeth

1. Renier, H., *Lambeth Past*. London: Historical Publications, 2006, p. 63.
2. Charles Booth Notebooks B365 [June 1899], p. 45. Quoted in Barratt, N., *Greater London*. London: Random House, 2012, p. 247.
3. Cherry, B., and N. Pevsner, *The Buildings of England. London 2: South*. London: Yale University Press, 2002, p. 329; Renier, *op. cit.*, p. 155.

Marylebone

1. Malcolm, J. P., *Anecdotes of the Manners and Customs of London during the Eighteenth Century; Including the Charities, Depravities, Dresses, and Amusements of the City of London during that Period; with a Review of the State of Society in 1807. To which is added a Sketch of the Domestic and Ecclesiastical Architecture, and of the various Improvements in the Metropolis, illustrated by fifty Engravings*, (1808; another edition 1810).
2. Baynham, S., *Revitalisation of Marylebone High Street* <hdwe.co.uk/en/the-estate/development/the-revitalisation-of-marylebone-high-street-by-simon-baynham.cfm> Date accessed: 25 May 2014.
3. Cherry, B., and N. Pevsner, *The Buildings of England. London 3: North West*. London: Yale University Press, 2002, p. 650.

Mayfair

1. Summerson, J., *Georgian London*. London: Yale University Press, 2003 (first published 1945), p. 95.
2. F.H.W. Sheppard, et al., 'The Development of the Estate 1720–1785: Introduction', in *Survey of London: Volume 39: The Grosvenor Estate in Mayfair, Part 1 (General History)* (1977), p. 6. <british-history.ac.uk/report.aspx?compid=41821> Date accessed: 25 May 2014.
3. Olsen, D. J., *The Growth of Victorian London*. New York: Holmes & Meier 1976, p. 145.
4. Benjamin, W., *The Arcades Project*, trans. H. Eiland and K. McLaughlin. Cambridge, MA: Harvard University Press, 1999.
5. Olsen, D. J., *The City as a Work of Art: London, Paris, Vienna*. New Haven, CT: Yale University Press, 1986, p. 19.
6. Bradley, S., and N. Pevsner, *The Buildings of England. London 6: Westminster*. London: Yale University Press, 2003, p. 540.

Regent's Park and St John's Wood

1. Morton, H. V., *In Search of London*. London: Methuen, 1951, p. 362.
2. Olsen, D. J., 'Victorian London: Specialization, Segregation, and Privacy', *Victorian Studies*, 17 (3), 1974, pp. 272–73.

Soho and Covent Garden
1. Kerr, J., 'Introduction', in Kerr, J., and A. Gibson (eds), *London from Punk to Blair* (revised 2nd edition). London: Reaktion, 2012, p. 31.

Spitalfields

1. Cherry, B., O'Brien, C., and N. Pevsner, *The Buildings of England. London 5: East*. New Haven, CT: Yale University Press, 2005, p. 408.

Wapping and Limehouse

1. *Report of the Special Committee on Housing 1918*. London: HMSO, 1919
2. W. Palin,'Wonders and Blunders', *The Guardian*, 31 August 2003. <theguardian.com/artanddesign/2003/sep/01/architecture.wondersandblunders>. Date accessed: 25 May 2014.

Westminster and St James's

1. Bradley, S., and N. Pevsner, *The Buildings of England. London 6: Westminster*. New Haven, CT: Yale University Press, 2003, p. 699.

Further Reading

General

Ackroyd, P., *London: The Biography*. London: Chatto & Windus, 2000
Allinson, K., *London's Contemporary Architecture*. Oxford: Architectural Press, 2009
Barratt, N., *Greater London: The Story of the Suburbs*. London: Random House, 2012
Birch, E., and D. Gardner, 'The Seven-Percent Solution: A Review of Philanthropic Housing, 1870–1910', *Journal of Urban History*, 7, 1981, pp. 403–38
Black, J., *London: A History*. Lancaster: Carnegie, 2009
Bold, J. A., and T. Hinchcliffe, *Discovering London's Buildings*. London: Frances Lincoln, 2009
Bradley, S., and N. Pevsner, *The Buildings of England. London 1: The City of London*. London: Yale University Press, 2002
——, and N. Pevsner, *The Buildings of England. London 6: Westminster*. London: Yale University Press, 2003
Campkin, B., *Remaking London. Decline and Regeneration in Urban Culture*. London: I. B. Tauris, 2013
Cherry, B., and N. Pevsner, *The Buildings of England. London 2: South*. London: Yale University Press, 2002
——, and N. Pevsner, *The Buildings of England. London 3: North West*. London: Yale University Press, 1991
——, and N. Pevsner, *The Buildings of England. London 4: North*. London: Yale University Press, 1998
——, O'Brien, C., and N. Pevsner, *The Buildings of England. London 5: East*. London: Yale University Press, 2005
Davies, G., and J. Reynolds, *Five Hundred Buildings of London*. New York: Black Dog and Leventhal, 2006
Dennis, R., 'The Geography of Victorian Values: Philanthropic Housing in London, 1840–1900', *Journal of Historical Geography*, 15 (1), 1989, pp. 40–54
——, '"Babylonian Flats" in Victorian and Edwardian London', *London Journal*, 33 (3), 2008, pp. 233–47
Eade, J., *Placing London: From Imperial Capital to Global City*. Oxford: Berghahn, 2000
Farrell, T., *Shaping London*. Chichester: Wiley, 2010
Hamnett, C., *Unequal City: London in the Global Arena*. London: Routledge, 2003
——, 'Gentrification and the Middle-class Remaking of Inner London, 1961–2001', *Urban Studies*, 40 (12), 2003, pp. 2401–26
Haywood, R., 'Railways, Urban Form and Town Planning in London: 1900–1947', *Planning Perspectives*, 12, 1997, pp. 37–69
Hebbert, M., *London: More by Fortune than Design*. Chichester: Wiley, 1998
Hollis, L., *The Phoenix: The Men Who Made Modern London*. London: Phoenix, 2008
——, *The Stones of London: A History in Twelve Buildings*. London: Phoenix, 2011
Imrie, R., et al. (eds), *Regenerating London: Governance, Sustainability and Community in a Global City*. London: Routledge, 2009
Inwood, S., *Historic London*. London: Macmillan, 2008
Jenkins, S., *Landlords to London: The Story of a Capital and its Growth*. London: Book Club Associates, 1975
Jones, E., and Woodward, C., *A Guide to the Architecture of London* (5th edition). London: Phoenix, 2013
Kerr, J., and A. Gibson (eds), *London From Punk to Blair* (revised 2nd edition). London: Reaktion, 2012
Kynaston, D., *The City of London*. 4 volumes. London: Pimlico, 1995–2005
Lawrence, H. W., 'The Greening of the Squares of London: Transformation of Urban Landscapes and Ideals', *Annals of the Association of American Geographers*, 83 (1), 1993, pp. 90–118
Longstaffe-Gowan, T., *The London Square*. London: Yale University Press, 2012.
McKean, C., and T. Jestico, *Guide to Modern Buildings in London 1965–75*. London: Warehouse Publishing, 1976
Marriott, J., *Beyond the Tower: A History of East London*. London: Yale University Press, 2011
Marshall, G., *London's Industrial Heritage*. London: The History Press, 2013
Moran, J., 'Early Cultures of Gentrification in London, 1955–1980', *Journal of Urban History*, 34 (1), 2007, pp. 101–21
Morton, H. V., *In Search of London* (1951). London: Da Capo, 2002
Newland, P., *The Cultural Construction of London's East End*. Amsterdam: Rodopi, 2008
Olsen, D. J., 'Victorian London: Specialization, Segregation, and Privacy', *Victorian Studies*, 17 (3), 1974, pp. 265–78

——, *Town Planning in London: The Eighteenth and Nineteenth Centuries*. London: Yale University Press, 1982
——, *The City as a Work of Art: London, Paris, Vienna*. London: Yale University Press, 1986
Pepper, S., and P. Richmond, 'Upward or Outward? Politics, Planning and Council Flats, 1919–1939', *Journal of Architecture*, 13 (1), pp. 53–90
Porter, R., *London: A Social History*. Cambridge, MA: Harvard University Press, 1995
Powell, G., *Square London: A Social History of the Iconic London Square*. Kibworth, Leicestershire: Matador, 2012
Powell, K., *21st Century London: The New Architecture*. London: Merrell, 2011
Ross, C., and J. Clark, *London: The Illustrated History*. London: Penguin, 2008
Rycroft, S., 'The Geographies of Swinging London', *Journal of Historical Geography*, 28 (4), 2002, pp. 566–88
Saint, A. (ed.), *London Suburbs*. London: Merrell Holberton, 1999
Schwartz, L. D., 'Social Class and Social Geography: The Middle Classes in London at the End of the Eighteenth Century', *Social History*, 7 (2), 1982, pp. 167–85
Summerson, J., *Georgian London*. Edited by H. Colvin. London: Yale University Press, 2003 (first published 1945)
Sutcliffe, A., *London: An Architectural History*. London: Yale University Press, 2006
Weinreb, B., et al., *The London Encyclopaedia*. London: Macmillan, 2008
White, J., *London in the Eighteenth Century*. London: Vintage Books, 2013
——, *London in the Nineteenth Century*. London: Vintage Books, 2008
——, *London in the Twentieth Century*. London: Vintage Books, 2008
Worsley, G., 'Inigo Jones and the Origins of the London Mews', *Architectural History*, 44, 2001, pp. 88–95

Bayswater and Paddington

Elrington, C. R. (ed.), *A History of the County of Middlesex: Volume 9: Hampstead, Paddington*. <british-history.ac.uk/report.aspx?compid=22666> Date accessed: 8 July 2013
Raco, M., and S. Henderson, 'Flagship Regeneration in a Global City: The Remaking of Paddington Basin', *Urban Policy and Research*, 27 (3), 2009, pp. 301–14

Belgravia and Pimlico

Walford, E., 'The Western Suburbs: Belgravia', *Old and New London: Volume 5* (1878), pp. 1–14. <british-history.ac.uk/report.aspx?compid=45218> Date accessed: 8 July 2013

Bloomsbury and Fitzrovia

Ashton, R., *Victorian Bloomsbury*. London: Yale University Press, 2012
Edwards, B., 'Tottenham Court Road: The Changing Fortunes of London's Furniture Street 1850–1950', *London Journal*, 36 (2), 2011, pp. 140–60
Hodgkinson, P., 'The Eclipse of the Brunswick', *Architectural Review*, 221, 2007, pp. 40–41
Murray, N., *Real Bloomsbury*. Bridgend: Seren, 2010
Woodford, F. P. (ed.), *Streets of Bloomsbury and Fitzrovia*. London: Camden History Society, 1997

Borough and Southwark

Godley, R. J., *Southwark: A History of Bankside, Bermondsey and 'The Borough'*. London: Southwark Heritage Association, 1996
Tames, R., *Southwark Past*. London: Historical Publications, 2001

Camden

Camden History Society, *Streets of Camden Town*. London: CHS Publications, 2003
Pepper, S., 'Ossulston Street: Early LCC Experiments in High-Rise Housing, 1925–29', *London Journal*, 7 (1), 1981, pp. 45–64
Richardson, J., *Camden Town and Primrose Hill Past*. London: Historical Publications, 2002
Wates, N., *The Battle for Tolmers Square*. London: Routledge, 1976.
Woodford, P. (ed.), *From Primrose Hill to Euston Road*. London: Camden History Society, 1995

Chelsea

Denny, B., *Chelsea Past*. London: Historical Publications, 1996
Walker, A., and P. Jackson, *Kensington and Chelsea: A Social and Architectural History*. London: John Murray, 1987

The City

Forshaw, A., *New City: Contemporary Architecture in the City of London*. London: Merrell, 2013
Hatherley, O., *A New Kind of Bleak: Journeys Through Urban Britain*. London: Verso, 2012
Hebbert, M., and E. McKellar, 'Tall Buildings in the London Landscape', *London Journal*, 33, 2008, pp. 199–200
Kenyon, N. (ed.), *The City of London: Architectural Tradition and Innovation in the Square Mile*. London: Thames & Hudson, 2011
Kynaston, D., *The City of London* (4 vols). London: Pimlico, 1995–2005

Clerkenwell

Ainsworth, A., *Clerkenwell: Change and Renewal*. London: Oblique Image, 2010
Tames, R., *Clerkenwell and Finsbury Past*. London: Historical Publications, 1999
Temple, P. (ed.), *Survey of London: Volume 46: South and East Clerkenwell*. London: Yale University Press, 2008
—— (ed.), *Survey of London: Volume 47: Northern Clerkenwell and Pentonville*. London: Yale University Press, 2008

Greenwich

Aslet, C., *Greenwich Millennium*. London: Fourth Estate, 1999
Bold, J. A., 'The Later History of Greenwich: A River Landscape and Architectural Statement', in Doran, S., and R. J. Blyth (eds), *Royal River: Power, Pageantry and the Thames*. London: Scala Books, 2012, pp. 114–20
Jennings, C., *Greenwich*. London: Abacus, 2001
Platts, B., *A History of Greenwich*. Newton Abbot, Devon: David and Charles, 1973
Smith, M., 'A Critical Evaluation of the Global Accolade: The Significance of World Heritage Site Status for Maritime Greenwich', *International Journal of Heritage Studies*, 8 (2), 2002, pp.137–51

Hoxton and Shoreditch

Bullman, J., Hegarty, N., and B. Hill, 'The Safe Area: Arnold Circus', in J. Bullman, et al., *London: The Secret History of Our Streets*. London: BBC Books, 2012, pp. 189–236
Harris, A., 'Art and Gentrification: Pursuing the Urban Pastoral in Hoxton, London', *Transactions of the Institute of British Geographers*, 37 (2), 2012, pp. 226–41
Tames, R., *East End Past*. London: Historical Publications, 2004

Islington

Bullman, J., Hegarty, N., and B. Hill, 'The Thoroughfare: Caledonian Road', in J. Bullman, et al., *London: The Secret History of Our Streets*. London: BBC Books, 2012, pp. 139–88
Butler, T., and L. Lees, 'Super-Gentrification in Barnsbury, London: Globalization and Gentrifying Global Elites at the Neighbourhood Level', *Transactions of the Institute of British Geographers*, New Series, 31 (4), 2006, pp. 467–87
Roberts, S., *Story of Islington*. London: Robert Hale, 1975
Shields, P., *Essential Islington*. London: Sutton, 2000
Temple, P. (ed.), *Survey of London. Volume 47: Northern Clerkenwell and Pentonville*. London: Yale University Press, 2008
Zwart, P., *Islington: A History and Guide*. London: Sidgwick and Jackson, 1973

Kensington

Sheppard, F.H.W. (ed.), *Survey of London: Volume 37: Northern Kensington*, 1973. <british-history.ac.uk/source.aspx?pubid=363> Date accessed: 8 July 2013

—— (ed.), *Survey of London: Volume 38: South Kensington Museums Area*, 1975. <british-history.ac.uk/source.aspx?pubid=364> Date accessed: 8 July 2013
—— (ed.), *Survey of London: Volume 42: Kensington Square to Earl's Court Area*, 1986. <british-history.ac.uk/source.aspx?pubid=366> Date accessed: 8 July 2013
Walker, A., and P. Jackson, *Kensington and Chelsea: A Social and Architectural History*. London: John Murray, 1987

Knightsbridge

Girling, B., *Belgravia and Knightsbridge Through Time*. London: Amberley Publishing, 2013
Greenacombe, J., *Survey of London: Volume 45: Knightsbridge*. London: Athlone Press, 2000

Lambeth

Renier, H., *Lambeth Past*. London: Historical Publications, 2006

Marylebone

Mackenzie, G., *Marylebone: Great City North of Oxford Street*. London: Macmillan, 1972
Wolstenholme, G., 'A Harley Street Address', *Journal of the Royal Society of Medicine*, 92, 1999, pp. 435–48

Mayfair

Girling, B., *Mayfair Through Time*. Stroud, Gloucestershire: Amberley Publishing, 2012
Sheppard, F.H.W., et al., *Survey of London: Volume 39: The Grosvenor Estate in Mayfair, Part 1 (General History)*. London: Athlone Press, 1977

Notting Hill

Bullman, J., Hegarty, N., and B. Hill, 'A Street of One's Own: Portland Road', in J. Bullman, et al., *London: The Secret History of our Streets*. London: BBC Books, 2012, pp. 237–90
Moore, D., *Notting Hill*. London: Frances Lincoln, 2007
Sheppard, F.H.W. (ed.), *Survey of London: Volume 37: Northern Kensington*, 1973, pp. 276–97. <british-history.ac.uk/source.aspx?pubid=363> Date accessed: 8 July 2013

Poplar and Isle of Dogs

Butler, T., 'Reurbanizing London Docklands: Gentrification, Suburbanization or New Urbanism?', *International Journal of Urban and Regional Research*, 31 (4), 2007, pp. 759–81
Carmona, M., 'The Isle of Dogs: Four Development Waves, Five Planning Models, Twelve Plans, Thirty-five Years, and a Renaissance … of Sorts', *Progress in Planning*, 71, 2009, pp. 87–151
Cox, A., *Docklands in the Making: The Redevelopment of Isle of Dogs, 1981–1995*. London: Athlone Press, 1996

Regent's Park and St John's Wood

Richardson, J., *Camden Town and Primrose Hill Past*. London: Historical Publications, 2002
Saunders, A., *Regent's Park: A Study of the Development of the Area from 1086 to the Present Day*. New York: Augustus Kelley, 1969
Sheppard, M., *Regent's Park and Primrose Hill*. London: Frances Lincoln, 2010
Summerson, J., 'The Beginnings of Regent's Park', *Architectural History*, 20, 1977, pp. 56–62, 90–99
Tames, R., *St John's Wood and Maida Vale Past*. London: Historical Publications, 1998
Woodford, P. (ed.), *From Primrose Hill to Euston Road*. London: Camden History Society, 1995

Soho and Covent Garden

Camden History Society, *Streets of St Giles. A Survey of Streets, Buildings and Former Residents in a Part of Camden*. London: Camden History Society, 2000

Sheppard, F.H.W. (ed.), 'General Introduction', in *Survey of London: Volumes 33 and 34: St Anne Soho*, 1966, pp. 1–19. <british-history. ac.uk/report.aspx?compid=41022> Date accessed: 8 July 2013

—— (ed.), 'General Introduction', in *Survey of London: Volume 36: Covent Garden*, 1970, pp. 1–18. <british-history.ac.uk/report. aspx?compid=46080> Date accessed: 8 July 2013

Tames, R., and S. Tames, *Covent Garden & Soho*. London: Historical Publications, 2009

Walkowitz, J., 'The Emergence of Cosmopolitan Soho', in Bridge, G., and S. Watson (eds), *The New Blackwell Companion to the City*. London: Blackwell, 2011, pp. 419–29

South Bank and Bankside

Baeten, G., 'From Community Planning to Partnership Planning. Urban Regeneration and Shifting Power Geometries on the South Bank, London', *GeoJournal*, 51, 2000, pp. 293–300

Boast, M., *The Story of Bankside*. London Borough of Southwark Neighbourhood Histories No. 8, 1985

Brandon, D., and A. Brooke, *Bankside*. Stroud, Gloucestershire: Amberley Publishing, 2011

Godley, R. J., *Southwark: A History of Bankside, Bermondsey and 'The Borough'*. London: Southwark Heritage Association, 1996

Newman, P., and I. Smith, 'Cultural Production, Place and Politics on the South Bank of the Thames', *International Journal of Urban and Regional Research*, 24 (1), 2000, pp. 9–24

Teedon, P., 'Designing a Place Called Bankside: On Defining an Unknown Space in London', *European Planning Studies*, 9 (4), 2001, pp. 459–81

Spitalfields

City of London Corporation, *Revitalising the City Fringe: Inner City Action with a World City Focus*. London: City Corporation, 1996

Lichtenstein, R., *On Brick Lane*. London: Hamish Hamilton, 2007

Shaw, S., 'Marketing Ethnoscapes as Spaces of Consumption: "Banglatown – London's Curry Capital"', *Journal of Town & City Management*, 1 (4), 2011, pp. 381–95

Sheppard, F.H.W. (ed.), *Survey of London: Volume 27: Spitalfields and Mile End New Town*, 1957. <british-history.ac.uk/source. aspx?pubid=361> Date accessed: 8 July 2013

Wapping and Limehouse

Borden, I., 'Limehouse Link: The Architectural and Cultural History of a Monumental Road Tunnel in London's Docklands', *Journal of Architecture*, 16 (5), 2011, pp. 589–613

Pepper, S., and P. Richmond, 'Stepney and the Politics of High-Rise Housing: Limehouse Fields to John Scurr House, 1925–1937', *London Journal*, 34 (1), 2009, pp. 33–54

Seed, J., 'Limehouse Blues: Looking for Chinatown in the London Docks, 1900–40', *History Workshop Journal*, 62, 2006, pp. 58–85

Smith, A., 'Gentrification and the Spatial Constitution of the State: The Restructuring of London's Docklands', *Antipode*, 21 (3), 1989, pp. 232–60

Westminster and St James's

Sawyer, S., 'Delusions of Grandeur: Reflections on the Intersection of Architecture and History at the Palace of Westminster, 1789–1834', *Transactions of the Royal Historical Society*, 13, 2003, pp. 237–50

Shepherd, R., *Westminster: A Biography: From Earliest Times to the Present*. London: Bloomsbury Academic, 2012

Whitechapel

Marriott, J., *Beyond the Tower: A History of East London*. London: Yale University Press, 2011

Tames, R., *East End Past*. London: Historical Publications, 2004

Index